B-29
"Superfortress"

Co-produced by Mark A. Thompson,
Independent Publishing Consultant
for Turner Publishing Company

Author: Philip St. John, Ph.D.
Book Design: Elizabeth Dennis

Library of Congress Catalog
Card No. : 94-60016

ISBN: 978-1-68162-202-6

Limited Edition

*Cover art courtesy of artist Fred N. Takasumi
and provided by the Boeing Company Archives.*

CONTENTS

Acknowledgements

It is with great pleasure that we introduce to you this publication on the B-29 "Superfortress", in commemoration of the 50th Anniversary of World War II.

We especially want to thank the many individuals who were responsible for making this book possible, particularly the men who took the time to submit photographs and historical material.

We owe our deepest gratitude to all of you for fighting the wars that could have changed our way of life permanently. With this being the 50th Anniversary of World War II, we felt that this was the perfect time to record and document the unique and interesting story of the B-29.

Turner Publishing Company leads the way in military history book publishing, and we hope that all who were involved with the "Superfortress" enjoy our newest title that chronicles the history of the gallant plane—the B-29.

Dave Turner, *President*   **Mark A. Thompson**, *Associate Publisher*

THE HISTORY OF THE B-29

"SUPERFORTRESS"

B-29 planes fly in formation on way from Guam to Japan. (Courtesy of Robert Le Mon)

The World at War

World War II lasted six years and a day, from 1 September 1939 when German tanks and bombers attacked across Poland's western border to begin the war in Europe, to 2 September 1945 when representatives of the Japanese government signed an Allied surrender document on board the battleship *U.S.S. Missouri* in Tokyo Bay to end the war in the Pacific. It was a war based on a hunger for territory and power and riches by Italy in Africa, Germany in Europe and Japan in Asia. A human disaster of incomparable proportions resulted. Some have placed the total military and civilian deaths in all war theaters over the war years at 50 million.

World War II was a global conflict by any definition, and for the first time in warfare the airplane became a significant - often decisive - weapon in the hands of the strategic planners. While the heavy bombers of the American 8th and 15th Air Forces and Britain's R.A.F. were systematically decimating Germany's industrial capabilities in Europe, another air war half way around the world in the Pacific and Far East was being waged; in this theater of war Japan replaced Germany as the Allies' antagonist. And this was a different war in many respects. The long, drudging missions, the flak, and the deadly enemy fighters were the air crews' lot in both wars; but the geography, sheer distances, and profusion of targets in the Pacific challenged the imagination. The 3.8 million square miles of Europe was comprehensible to Allied Air Force planners, for virtually the entire area was within range of heavy bombers (the B-17, B-24, and Lancaster) from bases in England and Italy. In contrast, the Pacific Ocean and its islands, more than 64 million square miles in area, in addition to the vast Far East mainland of Burma, Thailand, Malaya, and China, required a whole new approach to waging a successful war on the ground, at sea and in the air. Since the subject of this story, the B-29 Superfortress, flew in combat only in the Far East, most of our attention will directed to the war in that theater.

In September of 1931, Japanese soldiers in southern Manchuria were involved in a clash with Chinese troops. Japan used this minor incident as an excuse to occupy all of Manchuria, subduing the region by early the following year and establishing the puppet state of Manchukuo. The League of Nations condemned Japan for its aggression but took no action and did not even impose sanctions.

From 7 July 1937 when Japan invaded China (again using a minor clash with Chinese troops near Peking) to the middle of 1941, the Japanese Empire expanded unchecked to subjugate the peoples along the entire coast of China south to include most of French Indochina. Japan had millions of men under arms, massive naval and air power, and hundreds of bases to launch and nourish these mighty forces. By contrast, the Allies - the U.S., Britain and China in this area and at this time - were out-manned and out-gunned in every category. For three years following the China invasion, isolationist America took no action to curb Japanese expansion.

The Japanese prime minister hoped that the United States would accept Japan's expansionist actions in the Far East, but finally, in September of 1940 after the Japanese had occupied Hanoi, the United States imposed an embargo on its exports of scrap iron and steel to Japan, materials which the Empire sorely needed. Japan joined the Axis powers in Europe on this month. By this time Germany had overrun all of western Europe, and England entered its darkest days, fighting for its life against the German Luftwaffe. In July of 1941 President Roosevelt froze all Japanese assets in the United States and with this action virtually all U.S.-Japanese trade ended, including the stopping of vital oil imports to Japan. The Japanese government lost no time in preparing its preemptive response.

The Bombs of December

On 7 December 1941 aircraft from a Japanese carrier task force attacked the U.S. Naval base at Pearl Harbor, Hawaii; the U.S. had most of its Pacific fleet moored in the port at this time. The Japanese attack fleet was 28 surface ships strong and included six carriers, two battleships, three cruisers and nine destroyers plus eight oilers and at least three escorting submarines. The 350 Japanese carrier planes that mauled Pearl Harbor in two waves sank or damaged 21 ships, three of them (all battleships) destroyed, and the Army Air Force and Navy lost 169 planes and another 130 severely damaged — almost all on the ground. The three battleships (one, the *Utah*, had been converted to a target ship) were beyond salvage and five more were badly damaged; three light cruisers, three destroyers and several smaller vessels were sunk or sustained severe damage. The eighteen damaged ships, even those sunk, were eventually repaired and returned to duty, some within a few weeks, but the American Pacific forces had been dealt a nearly fatal blow on this Sunday morning.

Although surprise was total, the attack was not perfect. Concentrating on large surface ships and airfields, the Japanese strike force ignored the base's oil storage tanks, repair shops and the submarine base, oversights which they would later regret. And perhaps fortunately for the U.S. there were no American aircraft carriers at Pearl Harbor at the time of the attack. The Japanese carrier pilots pleaded for a third attack wave but they were overruled by the fleet commander, Vice Admiral Nagumo, and the carrier force turned back toward Japan. The final count of American casualties was 2,403 dead and 1,178 wounded. The Japanese lost 29 planes (six of them to two P-40 fighter pilots) and 64 air crewmen. (By war's end, the U.S. Navy would sink all the carriers, battleships and cruisers of this attack fleet).

By this attack the Imperial government of Japan had hoped — some even assumed — that America would sue for peace and leave them a free hand in the Far East. The assumption was curious at best and would eventually become a fatal one for them. There were, in fact, dissenting voices among military leaders in Tokyo, and from Japan's Prime Minister and the Emperor himself, but they were unheard. The Pearl Harbor strike was only one of many Japanese attacks throughout the Far East. Almost immediately following the strike on Hawaii, Japanese naval, air and ground forces attacked Wake Island, Guam, British Malaya, Singapore, the Dutch East Indies, Burma, Thailand, and the Philippines. Undefended Guam fell on 10 December, but the tiny garrison on Wake Island held off Japanese amphibious assaults until the 23rd. The United States formally declared war on Japan on 8 December, and on Germany and Italy on 11 December 1941. By the spring of 1942 the Japanese brought under their control vast areas in east central China, Burma, Thailand (Siam), the Malay Peninsula, all of the Netherlands East Indies, Sumatra, Java, Celebes, Borneo, the Philippines, some western and eastern areas of New Guinea (plus northern coastal pockets), and the Gilbert and Solomon Islands. Before the war with the U. S. began, they were already occupying the Marshall and Caroline Islands, the Marianas (except Guam), and the Palau Islands.

Early in February of 1942 the U.S. Navy had recovered sufficiently from the Pearl Harbor disaster to conduct hit and run carrier plane raids on Japanese-held islands in the Marshalls and Gilberts. On 18 April Lt. Col. **James H. Doolittle** led a small strike force of 16 B-25 Mitchells from the carrier *Hornet* to bomb Tokyo, Yokohama, Kobe and Nagoya. They completed the mission but 15 of the planes ran out of fuel and crashed in China. The remaining plane with its 5-man crew landed safely in Siberia. Sixty-seven of the 75 men that crashed in China (including Doolittle) were led to safety by the Chinese army and underground fighters. Of the remaining 8, one died when his parachute failed to open and seven were captured. Two of those captured were executed, one died in prison and four were imprisoned for the remainder of the war. The raid was a big morale boost to Americans back home, but it showed up a desperate need for a long-range bomber that could reach the enemy homeland from a land base. America would build this bomber but it would be over two years before it could be used to strike Japan again.

Between 4 and 8 May 1942 a Navy task force commanded by Adm. **Frank J. Fletcher** hunted down and mauled a Japanese fleet in the Coral Sea south of the eastern tip of New Guinea, ending Japanese expansion southward toward Australia. The combatants each lost a fleet carrier and each had other carriers severely damaged (the *Yorktown*, CV-5, limped to Hawaii for repairs). Then a month later, between 4 and 6 June, Fletcher and Adm. **Raymond A. Spruance** intercepted a large Japanese fleet, commanded by Admiral Yamamoto, of over 100 surface ships protected by 600 carrier planes and submarines heading for Midway Island, about 1,100 miles northwest of Hawaii. The Japanese had hoped to lure the remains of the American fleet from Hawaii and with its larger force finish off the U.S. Navy in the Pacific. The American Navy, never a service to turn down an invitation to fight, put to sea from Hawaii and the battle did not go as the enemy had planned. American Navy fighters, dive bombers and torpedo bombers were launched from three carriers (*Yorktown*, *Hornet*, and *Enterprise*) and found the enemy fleet. The *Yorktown*, still only partly functional from its Coral Sea battle damage, was sunk by a Japanese submarine after being gutted by bombs and aerial torpedoes; the U. S. also lost a destroyer. But Navy pilots sent four enemy fleet carriers to the bottom and 322 aircraft (280 sinking with their carriers), in addition to sinking a heavy cruiser, the whole resulting in 3500 enemy dead, a blow from which the enemy naval air arm never fully recovered. Admiral Yamamoto, commanding the enemy task force, withdrew toward Japan. The cost to the U.S. Navy in aircraft and men was not cheap: 307 lives and 100 carrier-based and 38 Midway-based airplanes were lost (many of the Grumman F4F Wildcat fighters running out of fuel and crashing into the sea), but Japanese expansion eastward had finally been stopped and now the rollback westward of the Empire could begin. The U.S. Marines would start it two months after this sea battle, on Guadalcanal in the Solomon Islands.

The Need for a Very Heavy Bomber

Because of the vast area involved, the war in the Pacific saw the employment of several U.S. Air Forces and their support groups. Although capable of striking virtually all Japanese installations in the Pacific (and many on the Asian mainland) none was able to reach the Japanese home islands. The 11th Air Force was charged with security of the North Pacific, and was based on the Aleutian Islands, Alaska. The 10th and 14th Air Forces were in the Far East, the 10th operating out of Bengal province in India, and the 14th based in China. The 5th and 13th Air Forces flew together much of the time in the Southwest Pacific. Their path took them through the Solomon and Admiralty Islands, the Bismarck Archipelago, along the north coast of New Guinea, the Philippines, and finally Okinawa. The 7th Air Force's hunting grounds were north of the 5th's and 13th's, its path westward taking it along the Gilbert, Marshall, and Caroline Islands, Palau, the Mariana Islands and Okinawa. A dozen Navy squadrons flew their land-based heavy bombers along with the 5th, 7th, and 13th Air Forces, complementing one another, in the south and central Pacific. The Navy also flew their Wildcat fighters and Dauntless dive bombers from land bases in support of the Marines' amphibious assaults. Most of these Air Forces were woefully under strength; the 11th, 7th, 10th and 14th were composed of a single bomb group each, the 13th had two groups, and the 5th was rich with four groups (although one of them was flying out of a base near Darwin, Australia).

The heavy bomber flown by these Air Forces and by Navy crews throughout most of the Pacific war was the B-24 Liberator (PB4Y-1 was the Navy version) with help from B-17D and E's early in the war. At war's inception, the B-17 was the only heavy bomber available in any number to beleaguered American forces in the Pacific and their crews did what they could to slow the Japanese onslaught (a flight of twelve B-17s reached Hawaii from California *during* the Japanese attack on 7 December 1941). **Sgt. Douglas Logan** — later commissioned a Lieutenant — was a waist gunner in a B-17D (later a tail gunner in the newer E model) and was in the Philippines on 7 December 1941. In 14 months of combat **Logan** was awarded many decorations for his gunnery — eight zeros shot down, confirmed, and five probables. Most of the available B-24s were doing ferry duty across the North Atlantic although there were some of the early export versions (called the LB-30) plying the Pacific. The Liberator was really America's only choice of heavy bomber in the Pacific theater of war (before the arrival of the B-29s) due to its considerable range of operation. But even the mighty Liberator was not up to the final task of taking the war to the Japanese homeland. In all fairness, the Lib could carry enough fuel for a long round trip to Tokyo from bases in China or the Mariana Islands, but not with a significant bomb load (if any at all) on board to make the trip worthwhile. This job would be that of a new airplane, flying in a new Air Force: the B-29 Superfortress, and all of the nearly 4,000 that were built and that would see combat would be assigned to two Bomber Commands in the new 20th Air Force. That airplane is, in part, what this story is about. The other part is many stories — the stories of the men who flew them.

Origin and Evolution of the B-29

The U.S. War Department issued specifications and a request for data for a "Hemisphere Defense Weapon" — a bomber — which was received by various aircraft companies on 5 February 1940.

nearly two years before America would be propelled into World War II. This foresight for a need for a very long-range bomber stands as an enduring credit to the War Department planners of the time, and even at this early date it was almost too late. The new bomber would be a replacement for the B-17 Flying Fortress (which at that time was nearly 5 years old) and presumably also for the B-24 Liberator which had made its first flight only one month before these specifications were issued. The new bomber must be able to carry a 2,000 pound bomb load 5,333 miles and heavier loads over shorter distances. Speeds were to approach 400 (!) miles per hour in level flight, faster than any production fighter of the day. Douglas Aircraft submitted its bid in the form of the XB-19, a very large but under-powered airplane for its huge size (212-foot wingspan), which first flew on 27 June 1941. Only one was built and Douglas withdrew from the competition. Lockheed Aircraft had entered the competition but also withdrew. Consolidated-Vultee Aircraft's entry was the excellent B-32 Dominator, of which 115 were built but only about 20 seeing active duty late in the war, flying out of Okinawa.

Boeing in Seattle, Washington, offered its Model 341, which later (when the Army changed its specifications) evolved into the Model 345 and which the Army would designate the XB-29. Submitted to the Army Air Corps in May of 1940, the design claimed to meet the War Department's revised requirements for a bomber that could carry 10,000 pounds of bombs 4,000 miles at an altitude of 30,000 feet and at speeds above 250 miles per hour. The new bomber was quickly called the Superfortress, the logical successor to Boeing's B-17 Flying Fortress which, due to its exploits in the war in Europe, was soon to become the most widely known and celebrated 4-engine bomber in the short history of air

warfare. The Army Air Corps awarded a contract to Boeing in September, 1940 for the first XB-29.

Boeing's Model 345 would undergo a number of changes on the drafting table (and after test flights) before a production design was achieved. Even then, hundreds of modifications would be necessary on the finished product. The B-29 in its final configuration would be the largest production airplane flying at that time and without question would be the most complex machine ever devised by man. This was to be the airplane that would take the war to Japan and the instrument (although not foreseen at the time) that would deliver to the enemy the final death blow and force an end to the war.

By World War II standards the B-29 was huge; its wing span was 25 feet longer than the post-war, six-jet B-47 (which would replace the B-29 in 1955) and only 44 feet shorter than the behemoth eight-engine B-52 intercontinental jet bomber whose first flight was in 1952. A comparison of dimen-

sions and performance with America's two workhorse heavy bombers of World War II, the B-17 Flying Fortress and the B-24 Liberator, is instructive (*see tables below*).

From receipt of the War Department's specifications to the first flight of the XB-29, over $2^1/_2$ years passed. Boeing's ace test pilot and Director of Aerodynamics and Research, **Edmund T. "Eddie" Allen**, first flew the XB-29 on 21 September 1942. (The Air Corps — now the Army *Air Force*, since June of 1941 — had already ordered 764 B-29s before this first one ever flew). Eddie Allen had learned to fly in 1917 when he was 21 years old, and he was probably the most experienced test pilot in the country at this time. This first model (41-002) had Curtiss electric three-bladed propellers and Eddie Allen reported after this flight that the plane felt to him somewhat under powered, but handled well. A more disturbing observation was that the big 2,200 horsepower Wright engines (-13 model engines powered the XBs) were running hotter than expected. Disaster almost struck

Comparative Dimensions

Aircraft:	B-29A	B-17G	B-24J
Span:	141'3"	103'9.5"	110'0"
Length:	99'0"	74'4"	66'4"
Height:	27'9"	19'1"	17'11"
Weight, max. (lbs.):	133,500	55,000	65,000
Engines (4):	Wright R-3350	Wright R-1820	P&W R-1830
Horsepower, each:	2,200	1,200	1,200

Comparative Performance

Aircraft:	B-29A	B-17G	B-24J
Maximum speed (mph):	365	300	303
Cruising speed (mph):	220	170	175
*Normal range (miles):	4,100	1,850	2,100
Normal bomb load (lbs.):	12,000	4,000	4,000
†Service Ceiling (feet):	31,850	35,000	28,000
Normal crew number:	11	10	10

* Range varies with quantity of fuel on board (limited by weight of internal bomb load), and engine throttle, mixture and propeller pitch settings which affect fuel consumption. Much heavier bomb loads (within permissible gross take-off weight) could be carried by all aircraft over short distances. The B-29, for example, could carry 20,000 pounds of bombs on shorter (or long range but low altitude) missions.

† Service ceiling is the highest altitude at which a climb rate of 100 ft. per minute is achievable.

on 30 December on the initial flight of XB-29 #2 (41-003) when two engines caught fire and a third was about to fail before the big plane was landed safely. The Wright engine people and Boeing's designers went to work on the heat problem. It is interesting to note that there were almost no changes in the original airframe design once construction began. Flight tests showed that no changes were necessary; the over all design was near perfect. All the major problems were with the engines. This second XB-29 (with two of its engines and other parts cannibalized from B-29 #1) was on its ninth flight on 18 February 1943 when, with Eddie Allen at its controls, the No. 1 engine caught fire forcing Allen to turn back toward Boeing Field. The time was 12:09 in the afternoon. The cockpit crew quickly extinguished the fire and feathered the propeller. Unseen, the fire still raged inside the left wing and the intense heat quickly caused structural damage to the forward wing spar and external pieces of the wing blew off. Barely three miles from touchdown Allen lost control and the huge plane crashed into a building. The time was 26 minutes after noon. Allen and all 10 men of his crew were killed (three had jumped but too low for their parachutes to open) in addition to 20 civilians on the ground. The wrecked plane and the bodies of the three that had jumped showed evidence that the fire had penetrated to the interior crew compartments before the crash took 31 lives. Only five months after its initial flight, it was not an auspicious beginning for Boeing's big bomber but now there was no turning back. There were already Air Force orders for 1600 B-29s on Boeing's books. The #1 XB-29 continued to fly as a test plane although it was grounded until the following August, and was so used throughout the war with Boeing's ace test pilot **Robert M. Robbins** at the controls for nearly 500 of its total of 576 flight hours. This historic plane, aptly dubbed *The Flying Guinea Pig* — the first B-29 to fly— was finally scrapped after five years and eight months of invaluable service, in May of 1948. (**Robbins** was the pilot on the initial flight of the six-jet Boeing B-47 in 1947).

By June of 1943 a third Superfort was flying (41-18335) and soon 14 others rolled from Boeing's Wichita, Kansas assembly lines and began undergoing service tests by the Air Force (as the YB-29). The engine induction system fire problems were gradually brought under control. Modifications to the airframe and engines were aimed primarily at cooling the hot running engines and stopping every possible fuel leak. Drains and vents were added in critical areas, wing tank filler pipes were relocated, fire bulkheads were added, changes were made in the exhaust collector rings and cowl flaps, and oil distribution to the valves and re-tooling of the valve stem guides of the big 18-cylinder Wright engines. For the most part, catastrophic engine fires stopped but overheating and the potential for fire never ceased to be a problem.

The first three XBs were manufactured at Boeing's Seattle plant and the next 14 YBs at its Wichita plant. The YB-29's per unit cost was just over 1.4 million dollars; production models would eventually sell for $639,000. The YB service test aircraft (now with the Wright model -21 engines installed) were just that: they were used by the Air Force as test beds, trainers and mock-ups for every conceivable idea. A few were turned over to newly forming Bomb Groups as trainers; one was towed back and forth over airfield ramps and runways to see if the concrete would buckle under the 65-ton weight of the bomber; one had Allison liquid-cooled engines installed; one was tested with 20 (!) .50 caliber machine guns mounted instead of the planned 10 to 12; another YB was fitted with manned (instead of remotely-controlled) gun turrets. Most of these test modifications never went into production.

The three-bladed Curtiss electric propellers of the XBs and YBs were replaced in production models by geared-down, slower turning, 16-feet, 7-inch diameter Hamilton four-bladed props making the big engines more efficient in the thin air of high altitudes. Propeller speed was slightly over one-third engine crankshaft speed so that at full take-off engine revolutions the big propellers were turning at less than 1,000 revolutions per minute. The original Sperry gun-aiming system was replaced with a computer-controlled General Electric remote gun system. With most of the major early design problems solved the B-29 was beginning to look combat-worthy and Boeing swung into mass production. But a myriad of less major problems continued to plague the design. The first Superfort from Boeing's Wichita production facility (42-6205) came off the line on 7 October 1943; the Wright model -23 engines were on these production aircraft. When these lines shut down the Wichita plant had turned out 1,630 B-29s.

One of the Superforts built at Wichita was actually paid for by the men and women that worked at the Wichita plant and they presented it to the Air Force as their contribution to the war effort. These proud men and women named their gift the *Eddie Allen* after Boeing's famous test pilot who, as mentioned above, met his untimely death in a test flight of B-29 #2 in February of 1943. We will have more to say of the *Eddie Allen* later.

To increase production, a Bell Aircraft Company plant at Marietta, Georgia, and a Glenn L. Martin Aircraft Company plant at Omaha, Nebraska were contracted to also manufacture the B-29. Bell's first completed airplane rolled off the line on 30 December 1943, and Martin's first production aircraft five months later on 31 May 1944. Boeing also started up a production line in Renton, Washington, near Boeing Field, to mass-produce the B-29A. The first plane from this plant rolled out on 1 January 1944, two days after Bell's first plane at Marietta, Georgia.

Airframe

The B-29 was an engineering marvel (more than 1.4 million engineering man-hours and 8,000 engineering drawings went into its development) and in fact design and engineering and constant modifications continued right through the crash-program of production of the aircraft. There was no luxury of time in the development and production of the Superfortress; the big bombers were needed urgently in the Pacific war. This was the first aircraft with double main wheels and a double, steerable nose wheel, all retractable. (The 56-inch diameter main landing gear wheels, incidentally, were interchangeable with those used on later model B-17 and B-24 aircraft; the tires were rated to sustain at least 100 landings).

It was the first bomber to be built with pressurized crew compartments: a forward compartment was pressurized back to the forward bomb bay bulkhead and housed bombardier (in the glass nose), the pilot, copilot, navigator (behind the pilot), flight engineer (facing aft behind the copilot), a radio operator (behind the flight engineer) and in B-29B models a radar operator; the first five crew members noted were usually commissioned officers. The navigator was supplied with an astrodome - for celestial navigation purposes - located just aft of the top forward turret.

9

This forward compartment was connected to an aft pressurized crew compartment, located behind the aft bomb bay, via a 33-foot long, 34-inch diameter tube or tunnel, circular in cross section. The aft compartment housed a left and right gunner, an upper gunner at a central fire control (CFC) station, and in B-29 and B-29A models, the radar operator. The tail gunner had his own pressurized compartment and was separated from the aft compartment by a non-pressurized fuselage section. The fuselage itself was circular in cross section. Airframe structural metal, internal and external, was aluminum alloy and the external "skin" was flush-riveted to reduce drag. An air pressure equivalent to that at 8,000 feet (supplied by the engine superchargers) could be maintained to an altitude of 30,000 feet. (Air Force procedures required depressurization and use of oxygen masks by the crew on entering a combat zone if above 10,000 feet).

The wing shape of the Superfortress was designed specifically for this aircraft (Boeing's 117 airfoil) to have high lift and low drag. This was achieved by a relatively high aspect ratio (wing span divided by wing chord at the root) of 11.5; this aspect ratio however resulted in a wing loading of 69 pounds per square foot of wing area, a heavy loading which constantly worried Air Force procurement officials. In fact, some Superforts flew in combat grossly overloaded (more than 136,000 pounds gross weight at take-off) to near 80 pounds per square foot of wing loading! The wing was a single unit, tip to tip, mounted to the fuselage in the Wichita, Marietta and Omaha built aircraft. Wing dihedral angle was a relatively shallow 4.5 degrees from the horizontal. Deicing equipment was initially installed on the leading edges of all flight surfaces but was later removed as a combat hazard. To reduce landing speeds the B-29 was designed with very large Fowler-type wing flaps which increased wing area about 19% when fully extended. In B-29A models build by Boeing at its Renton plant, the left and right wing panels were mounted to an integrally formed center wing section.

Ailerons, elevators and rudder were fabric covered. Self-sealing fuel tanks were built into each wing between double spars. Each compartmented wing tank held 4,100 gallons of gasoline. Each engine was fed by direct tank-to-engine fuel lines incorporating the usual engine-driven pumps, boost pumps, fuel filters, fuel transfer valves and lines (to shift fuel between tanks) and shut-off valves. Two auxiliary fuel tanks could be mounted in each bomb bay. Each tank held 640 gallons of gasoline. The flight engineer controlled all fuel transfer and shut-off operations from his station in the forward crew compartment.

Except for the primary flight controls which were cable-operated without mechanical boost of any kind, and some alternating current-driven electronic instruments, all equipment was operated by 28-volt D. C. electric motors — some 150 of them on board. This included the landing gear and doors, cowl flaps (controlled by the flight engineer), gun turrets and wing flaps and secondary flight control surfaces. The major non-electrical exceptions were the hydraulically-operated brakes (and hydraulically-operated propeller feathering) and pneumatically-opened bomb bay doors. A two-cylinder direct current auxiliary power generating unit (located in the unpressurized aft fuselage section) provided emergency electrical power and power for engine starting. This auxiliary unit was shut down after the engines were started and running; operation of this unit was the responsibility of the tail gunner. The aircraft also included an electric stove and oven for heating meals.

Armament

The gun aiming system was all remote, except for the tail gunner's two machine guns and his 20 millimeter cannon, when the latter was carried. In the B-29 and the B-29A models there were four fuselage turrets, two on top (one forward and one aft) and two on the underside (again one forward and one aft). The forward top turret mounted four .50 caliber guns and the other three turrets two such guns. In most combat-ready models, each gun was supplied with 500 rounds of ammunition. The tail gunner's cannon had available 110 rounds of 20 millimeter ammunition and was loaded by a hand-wound spring. The cannon was deleted in later models. All turrets tracked their targets (azimuth and elevation) via electric motors. The gunners never touched these guns; they were aimed and fired remotely via an analog computer from the gunner's stations. The bombardier had primary control over the top and bottom forward turrets. The gun commander (Central Fire Control gunner, CFC), sighting from a bubble on top in the aft pressurized compartment, had primary control of the top aft turret and secondary control of the top forward turret; the two side gunners on the CFC's left and right shared primary control of the lower rear turret and secondary control of the lower forward turret. The computer calculated turret tracking speed and direction and accounted for bullet trajectory when the gunners aimed at a fast moving target, say an enemy fighter, with their remote sighting mechanism.

There were two bomb bays with quick-acting bomb bay doors that could snap open in less than one second via a pneumatic actuator triggered by the bomb sight (although it took several seconds to close them). Earlier B-29 production models were equipped with slower-opening, electrically-actuated doors. Up to 80 shackles could be accommodated on the bomb bay racks for an equal number of 100-pound bombs. Maximum internal bomb load was with forty 500-pound bombs (20,000 pounds) which could be carried on short missions or on relatively longer missions but at lower altitudes which conserves fuel. Shackles were available also for carrying four 4,000 pound "block buster" bombs.

Engines

The B-29 was powered by four Wright Cyclone R-3350 double-bank, 18-cylinder, air-cooled radial engines, each with two exhaust-driven General Electric turbo-superchargers capable of maintaining sea level horsepower at very high altitudes (exceeding 30,000 feet). Take-off horsepower was 2200 at 47.5 inches of mercury manifold pressure. The crankcase housing that mounted the eighteen cylinders was made of magnesium. These engines required 100-octane fuel. Various improved models of this basic engine (fuel injection, changes in the cylinder and cylinder head cooling fins and oil supply) were installed on various production models of the B-29. The B-29A built by Boeing at its Renton, Washington plant, was powered by the model -57 variant of the Wright engine. As already noted, the early engines were subject to catastrophic induction (air/fuel intake) system fires; this problem was, for the most part, eventually overcome but overheating continued to plague the production models. Propellers in production models were by Hamilton, four-bladed, hydraulically actuated variable pitch and featherable. Reduction gears in the forward crankcase section rotated the propeller shaft at slightly less than one-third crankshaft speed.

Electronics

In addition to the complete range of standard radio communications gear (command and liaison radios and interphone equipment) various Superforts also carried other electronic navigation and communications equipment including a marker beacon, radio compass, a blind landing system, a radar altimeter (SCR-718) and an IFF (Identification Friend or Foe, SCR-729) radio. The B-29 and B-29A carried the AN/APQ-13 airborne radar system used for both navigation and bombing. The position of its 30-inch radar antenna is visible as a covering, retractable dome on the underside of the aircraft between the two bomb bays (this dome was carefully painted out on almost all photographs of the Superfortress during the war years). The APQ-13 displayed a 360-degree screen picture. A different kind of radar, the AN/APQ-7, was fitted to the underside of B-29B models produced by Bell Aircraft. This "Eagle" radar system was more sensitive than the APQ-13 radar and displayed a more detailed (60-degree sector) screen picture. The APQ-7 Eagle antenna was an 18-foot oscillating airfoil mounted transversely to the aircraft's long axis at the same position as the APQ-13 dome (this wing antenna was also deleted from war-time photographs). The Eagle radar system could be coupled to the optical Norden bombsight, allowing the bombardier and the radar operator to cooperate on a bomb run.

Production

Production numbers of various models by the three different manufacturers of the B-29, are recorded on chart to the right. The total number manufactured - including the original 3 XBs at Seattle - was 3,965. The "A" and "B" models indicate major engine and/or equipment modifications.

At full production, some 60 different plants across the United States were turning out various sub-assemblies and shipping these to the four major construction sites. Engine nacelles, for example, came from the Fisher Body plant of General Motors, in Cleveland and gun turrets from Emerson Electric in St. Louis. Other airframe subcontractors included Cessna Aircraft (Wichita), Chrysler (Detroit), McDonnell (St. Louis), Republic Aviation

(Farmingdale) and Goodyear (Akron). Design, testing and production was done with such haste that it was inevitable that numerous flaws and problems in the construction should appear. These first production airplanes could fly but they would be death traps in combat: ignition problems, breaking exhaust valves, sky-high cylinder head temperatures, constant oil leaks at various places in the engines - especially around the critical superchargers, fuel cell leaks, and so on. By the closing months of 1943 the first 175 aircraft manufactured had to have nearly ten thousand faults corrected. The situation was not helped by severe shortages of some parts and assemblies (gun turrets, for example) and a general lack of skilled workers.

Production statistics

1. **Boeing-Seattle: XB-29-BO, [3]**
   #1 First flight on 21 Sep. 1942
   #2 first flight on 30 Dec. 1942
   #3 first flight on 16 June 1943
2. **Boeing-Wichita: YB-29-BW, [14]**
   First delivery on 7 Oct. 1943*
3. **Boeing-Wichita: B-29-BW, [1,630]**
4. **Bell-Marietta: B-29-BA, [357]**
   First delivery on 30 Dec. 1943
5. **Martin-Omaha: B-29-MO, [53]**
   First delivery 31 May 1944
6. **Boeing-Renton: B-29A-BN, [1,119]**
   First delivery on 1 Jan. 1944. Boeing-Renton manufactured last B-29A on 28 May 1946
7. **Bell-Marietta: B-29B-BA, [311]**
   Remote gun turrets deleted. With four-bladed Curtiss electric propellers plus many radio, radar and other armament modifications

[Production numbers in brackets]
*All with three-bladed Curtiss electric propellers. One of these (41-36954, "Spirit of Lincoln") became the XB-39 test plane with 4 Allison V-3420-11 engines [2600 h.p. ea., 24 cylinders, liquid cooled].

Total **XB-29** =	3	[by Boeing-Seattle]
Total **YB-29** =	14	[by Boeing-Wichita]
Total **B-29** =	2,518	[by Boeing-Wichita, Bell, Martin]
Total **B-29A** =	1,119	[by Boeing-Renton]
Total **B-29B** =	311	[by Bell]
TOTAL =	3,965	

The XXth Bomber Command and Training

The first production planes were slated for Gen. **Kenneth B. Wolfe's** 58th Bombardment Wing which had been activated on 1 June 1943, the first B-29 unit of the (not yet organized) XXth Bomber Command scheduled for combat. First headquarters of the new 58th Wing was at Marietta, Georgia, near the Bell plant. It would be the XXth Bomber Command's only Wing. The XXth Bomber Command was formed at Smoky Hill Army Air Field near Salina, Kansas (80 miles north of Wichita) in November 1943 and Gen.

Wolfe would be assigned to command it also. (They would go to bases in India and later central China; this was as close as we could get to Japan at this stage of the war). The result of all the production problems was that special modification centers were set up to put these defects right. These centers were set up in Alabama, Colorado, Georgia, Oklahoma, Nebraska and Texas. Some began to call the B-29 a "dog." It was not; Boeing, Bell, Martin and the Air Force were simply compressing the usual several years of development and testing and modification — then more testing and modification — into a few months. They had no choice. As has been said by others, the B-29 was being invented as it was being built.

During September of 1943 the 58th Bomb Wing moved its headquarters to Salina, Kansas. Training bases were established at Pratt, Walker, Smoky Hill and Great Bend, all in central Kansas. Their equipment at these bases initially consisted of one B-29 per squadron so most of the training was done in other bombers, primarily B-17s and B-26s. As 1943 raced on, more Superforts began to arrive at the Kansas training fields from the modification centers and still not one of them was operational. The crews at Salina worked around the clock to get these "modified" Superforts ready for combat. It was a losing battle; there were often no parts on hand to complete the job. By the beginning of 1944 there was not a single B-29 at the 58th's fields that any crew would dare to fly into a combat zone. Major production changes — not just post-production modifications — were required in the electrical system, radar, propellers, remote gun fire control, in the engines (again), tires and on and on. The 58th was scheduled by the Air Force to leave for India on 10 March 1944; by 9 March not one B-29 was ready.

General **H. H. Arnold**, Air Force chief, soon to take over command of all B-29 strategic operations, flew to Salina from his Washington offices. He was furious at the delays and started issuing orders to his staff aimed at getting all the Superforts assigned to the 58th Wing ready for battle in India by 15 April. That meant that the first B-29s had to leave Kansas for a trip half way around the world in two weeks. Maj. Gen. **B. E. Meyers** was the point man in this "Battle of Kansas"; he and his staff called every errant B-29 parts supplier and subcontractor in the country and ordered them to load waiting Air Transport Com-

mand planes with all the parts required to complete modification of the Superforts waiting at the training fields in Kansas. They were to work around the clock to make and ship these parts. He wanted no excuses or explanations or paperwork. Just the parts — and now.

Winter in Kansas is sometimes brutal. Most of the work had to be done outside for there were few hangers available to park the B-29s under cover. Almost immediately the parts started arriving at Salina in what seemed like a never-ending stream of transport planes, day and night. Mechanics worked around the clock in heavy, high-altitude flying clothes in an attempt to keep warm against the bitter cold and sleet of the Kansas plains as they replaced literally hundreds of parts and made dozens of modifications on the big bombers. Gen. Arnold had set the deadline for these airplanes to be in India by 15 April and no one gave a thought that any forgiveness was built into that date. The ground maintenance crews were already on their way to India, having left the States in February. The 58th Bomb Wing's ground crews were split into two groups; half went to India via the Pacific and Australia, and the other half to India via the Atlantic, the Mediterranean and the Suez Canal. The Pacific crew arrived in India nearly a month before the Atlantic crews arrived.

As an interesting aside to this gargantuan undertaking, a decision had already been made to use the B-29s only in the war in the Far East. It was firmly believed that the war in Europe would be over by the end of 1944 (it lasted five months into 1945), and there would not be enough Superforts ready to fly by that time to make any significant difference in that war. The need was in the Far East. But a decision was also made to show off the B-29 in the European theater — by flying one to England for a tour — in the hope that Germany might just be intimidated enough by this monster to lose some of its fighting zeal, or at least divert some of its manpower and energies in concocting some defense against it. D-Day, the invasion of the continent, was already scheduled for sometime in June 1944. And a Superfort in Europe would be a cover for the mass flights to India now scheduled for arrival there in April.

So, in the middle of March of 1944 a single combat-ready B-29 named *Hobo Queen* (#963) with a spare engine in the bomb bays, took off from Salina for Miami. Col. **Frank Cook** commanded this plane.

He left Miami at night and headed eastward over the ocean, then turned northeast toward Newfoundland. From Newfoundland Cook guided the big bomber toward England and within the hour of landing a German reconnaissance plane had pictures of the first (and only) B-29 to be flown to Europe. No. 963 made a low-security tour of English bases, showing off its might to everyone interested. Its tour lasted two weeks and then it left for India. It was hoped that the Germans would at least be a little concerned about B-29s flying in Europe.

The 58th Wing Goes to War

On 26 March the first of the XXth Bomber Command's B-29s, #663, left Salina for India, Col. **Leo "Jake" Harman** at the controls, fully armed except for a bomb load, and ready to join the fight. The "Battle of Kansas" had been won. Nine or ten Superforts per day would leave Kansas until the XXth Bomber Command was at least 150 planes strong in India. In the Command's sole 58th Wing were now four Bombardment Groups: the 40th (at Pratt), 444th (at Great Bend), 462nd (at Walker) and the 468th (at Smoky Hill). All crews had trained in Kansas, but so far their experience in controlling this big airplane had been meager, some crews with less than 20 hours in the air in B-29s. Most aircraft commanders had no more than 50 to 75 hours in B-29s. And the engines were still running hot. The airplane was still undergoing development, even on its way to war. Yet to come was the four-gun top forward turret, the astrodome, the pneumatically operated bomb bay doors, and numerous engine modifications that eventually would allow them to run cool — or at least, cooler.

Another cover story had been released for this flight. This one said that the long range bomber had not performed as expected (close to true) and it was being modified as a transport (also soon to be true) and was being sent to India on a test flight to deliver supplies over the "Hump" (the Himalayas) to hard pressed Allied forces in China. (The Air Transport Command had been flying the route since April of 1942 from Assam, India, a distance of about 600 miles to the China bases, bulling their way through some of the world's worst weather. The Japanese armies in

China had cut the Burma Road in April of 1942 and it had been unusable since that time. By the beginning of 1943 the Command was delivering 3,200 tons a month of ammunition, fuel, medicines and other kinds of supplies to beleaguered forces in China). The long runways already being built in India and China were for this 'transport' plane; so the Japanese were not to worry or take precautions that a new bombing weapon was about to be unleashed on them. It is unlikely that many among the enemy believed this story.

Following Harman from Salina were several more Superforts. They turned northeast and set a course for the air base at Gander, Newfoundland Island, on the shores of 35-mile long Gander Lake, 2500 miles away. One Fort had mechanical trouble and landed at the Air Force base at Presque Isle, Maine; all the rest made it to Gander, non-stop, averaging eleven hours for the trip. A fierce north Atlantic gale then bore down on the island. Harman beat it out before it hit, but the other Forts were snowbound for the next two days. When the storm abated the crews of the Superforts at Gander scrambled into their planes and took off on the next leg — 3,000 miles across the Atlantic to Marrakech, French Morocco, in West Africa. From numbing cold to blistering heat, the crews were learning new things about their airplane they didn't have time to learn in their accelerated training program. With favorable westerlies, all the planes made it safely to Marrakech, a city of some quarter million French and (mostly) Arabs, in about 10 hours.

Harman stayed in Marrakech only long enough to refuel and check his airplane, then he was off on the next 2,400-mile leg to Cairo. But now bad things began to happen to the Superforts. Engine overheating and power loss again. One Superfort had lost so much power that it couldn't get up enough speed to get off the ground and it crashed and burned off the end of the runway. Quick action by ground personnel and the 11- man air crew themselves saved everyone on board. The remaining Superforts took off and headed for the Atlas Mountains, struggling with reduced power to get enough altitude to clear the 14,000-foot range east of Marrakech. All this was friendly territory now; the Germans had been cleared from North Africa less than a year ago, Sicily had fallen, and the Allies were pushing the Germans back up the Italian boot.

By the time the little armada of bombers made it to Cairo, all of them were in trouble. Engines needed changing, instruments needed calibration and endless checklist items had to be looked after. Civilian technicians and mechanics were flown in from the States. These airplanes were not ready to fight yet. All this took nearly a week for some of them. Finally Harman said he was leaving and everyone rushed to finish their work to keep up with him. Then they were off on the third leg of their trip, 2,400 miles across Saudi Arabia, the Persian Gulf and the southern tip of Iran to Karachi, on the west coast of India. At the Karachi field the temperatures on the ground were over 110 degrees and engine temperatures soared into the red almost immediately after start up. Red hot cylinder heads began to melt and crack even before the monstrous engines could be shut down. Two more Superforts were lost to engine problems at Karachi, one disappearing into the ocean on take-off. The crews became sullen. Some were beginning to hate this airplane.

The planes were serviced and babied again at Karachi and finally the crews were ready for the final 1,500-mile westward flight to Bengal Province in northeast India, and their new homes. Harman was out front again. General Kenneth B. Wolfe, Commander of the XXth Bomber Command was at the field at Chakulia about 150 miles west of Calcutta, when radio men there picked up Harman's radio message announcing his position and ETA (estimated time of arrival). Harman touched down at Chakulia about noon, on 2 April 1944, a Sunday. It had been seven days from Salina. The rest staggered in from Karachi, more B-29s left the States and by the middle of the month there were 32 Superforts at Chakulia. But there were other planes grounded from Kansas to Karachi with (mostly) engine troubles. By the end of the month the ferrying resumed and by the end of the first week in May there were 130 B-29s in India at several fields all west and north of Calcutta. Most of these names are no longer on modern maps of the area; the new fields were located at Kharagpur, (110 miles west and a little south of Calcutta, home of the 468th Bomb Group), and at Chakulia (40th Bomb Group), Dudhkundi (444th Bomb Group — they were originally at Charra), and Piardoba (462nd Bomb Group), all these within a few hours by road or rail west and northwest of Calcutta. These fields eventually were to become major B-29 bases while a fifth at Kalaikunda was to be an auxiliary supply base. Calcutta was the major port of entry for ship-borne supplies for the planes of the XXth Bomber Command — their bombs, ammunition, fuel, oil, and spare parts. As noted above, by 8 May there were 130 Superforts in India. Eventually more than 250 Superforts would make the trans-Africa flight to India.

The following is quoted from a history of the 40th Bombardment Group by Capt. **F. G. Wood, Jr.**:

"May...was a month of intense activity...and searing, disabling heat. The highest...temperature was 113°F, and the average was 94°F ....under deep shade conditions. Temperature on the runway ....was 130°F., and higher inside the planes. ....During the day metal became too hot to touch ....maintenance could only be done at night and early morning hours.

"During May [1944] an average of 61:37 man hours per day of maintenance were performed on each airplane. On 13 May the average percentage of hours aircraft were out of commission was 34%, but on 24 May the percentage was 50%. This could, in part at least, be attributed to the fact that an increasing number of planes were awaiting parts."

"An epidemic of front collector ring failures constituted the major engineering problem during May, resulting in many cylinder and a few engine changes. The trouble was that the metal would crack and burn through at the ball socket joint next to the cylinder. If this condition were not discovered in its early stages the burning continued until there was a complete severance. Then the hot exhaust gases passed back over the cylinder heads, burning them through. With no new collector rings available it was a battle with welding rod and torch to keep as many of the damaged ones as serviceable as possible."

The buck stopped at General Wolfe's desk in this Superfort operation, and it was an enormous operation. The B-29 was to be used not only to strike targets in Burma and Malaya, but also in Japanese-occupied China, in Manchuria, and — the reason for the B-29 in the first place — the Japanese home islands. Wolfe had arrived in India in January and set about developing airfields and runways in northeast India and in central China, the latter as advanced bases for long range B-29 strikes against Japan and the south China coast. These advanced bases would be in the vicinity (within 50 miles) of Chengtu, (now Chengdu) China and would have to be supplied — fuel, bombs, ammunition, everything — from the Bengal bases, over 1200 miles away. The plan was code-named TWILIGHT. Beginning in January 1944, four 8,500-foot runways were built in the Chengtu area by (according to some records) an estimated 430,000 Chinese laborers; this was rock crushing by hand and pulling big rollers by human power. The laborers were paid about 25 cents per day, up to 40 cents to their work bosses. Generalissimo Chiang Kai-shek charged the U.S. some 200 million dollars (in gold, no paper money, thank you) for this work. Wolfe was tireless. He flew back and forth across the dangerous "Hump" route, enlisting the aid of Generals **Joseph W. Stilwell**, Commander of U. S. ground troops in the China-Burma-India theater (CBI), and **Claire L. Chennault**, former Commander of the famed American Volunteer Group — the "Flying Tigers" — and now Commander of the 14th Air Force in China. Wolfe visited every base in India and China, setting up the logistical nightmare of transporting B-29 supplies and key personnel into China. He pleaded, cajoled, ordered and prayed; it seemed at times he was doing all this single-handed. But Stilwell loaned him a construction battalion (the 382nd), pulled off building the Ledo Road in northern Burma, and building of the long runways needed (at Kharagpur) went into high speed. (The north-south Ledo Road was to join the Burma Road to China, the latter having been cut by the Japanese two years before; the Ledo Road was 470 miles long and was completed in January of 1945). The 853rd Engineer Aviation Battalion arrived in February and it was sent to Chakulia for the back-breaking work of extending a short fighter strip there. It was still winter in Bengal but at 23 degrees north of the Equator, the noon-day temperatures were usually in the mid-90s.

When the first B-29 landed on 2 April, these two bases were nearing completion and Gen. Wolfe knew he was going to make it. Except for Wolfe and a few of his top aides, no one had ever seen a B-29; most of Claire Chennault's fighter and bomber crews in central China had never even heard of it. Two days later on 4 April the 20th Air Force was organized in Washington, but its organization was kept a secret. It would be announced later in June. On 19 April the XXth Bomber Command and its sole 58th Bombardment Wing, (Wolfe commanded both) was assigned to the 20th Air Force. The 20th was born as a global Air Force, not to be assigned to any particular theater of war commander but capable of flying and fighting anywhere in the world. Gen. Arnold was in total command of this new Air Force and all major decisions would emanate from his office. The bombers of the 20th Air Force would be of only one kind — the B-29.

The XXth Bomber Command was far from the first American bombing unit to operate against the Japanese in this area. General **Davidson's** 10th Air Force had been operating out of Bengal Province since the spring of 1942, at one time down to one squadron in one group. The bomber flown by the 10th was the B-24 Liberator, and through the last half of 1942, all of 1943, 1944 and 1945 to war's end in August this workhorse airplane pounded enemy targets within their considerable range all over southeast Asia. On a good day the 10th could put up 60 or 70 B-24s for a strike — with fighter cover. Claire Chennault's B-24s and B-25s and fighters of the 14th Air Force, operating close to enemy lines in China, did the same. As noted before, the 14th had to be supplied with the tools of war by the gallant crews of the Air Transport Command, flying the Hump (the Himalayas) from bases in Assam, India. These were frustrating years for the bomber crews as they were for America's strategic planners because there were a lot of critically important enemy targets they could not reach, and the Japanese home islands were well beyond their range from any Allied land base. The two Air Forces often took a terrible beating (one mission over Rangoon in December of 1943 drew up 60 enemy fighters and six Liberators and 60 men went down over the target). But they fought on. When the first Superforts arrived in India in April of 1944, the B-24 crews were awed. This was the biggest airplane any of them had ever seen. All knew at a glance that this was the giant that finally could take the war to Japan.

There followed several weeks of rigorous training for the B-29 crews, most flying done in the late afternoon to avoid the engine-destroying mid-day heat. But even then the engines were still overheating and refused to generate their rated power. There weren't enough spare engines on hand to change many of them; some engines underwent major alterations on a daily basis. And construction of the other B-29 fields was going too slowly. Construction of the advanced bases in China 1200 miles away was proceeding fairly on schedule, but supplying them with even the bare necessities of life from the Bengal bases was becoming a serious and burdensome task. Everything had to be flown in to the Chengtu fields over the Himalayas, and flying the "Hump" was as dangerous a run as going into combat. Twenty thousand-foot peaks lined the north edge of the Hump corridor, often hidden in thick clouds, and the enemy-held Burmese jungle stretched southward on the other side. Enemy fighters often challenged the passage of the supply transports. A post-war report noted that more than 600 Air Transport Command aircraft were lost on this Hump run from all causes, crashing into mountain and jungle, from icing and mechanical problems to enemy fighters. But the horrendous weather conditions caused most of the problems. These aircraft took 1,000 crewmen to their deaths.

The transports were Curtiss C-46s, Douglas C-47s Consolidated C-87s (the transport version of the B-24 Liberator), and from April 1944, stripped-down B-29s. It was a toss-up whether flying the Hump or the Aleutian Islands was the Air Force's worst duty. Wolfe had ordered in some 19 C-87s but it was soon obvious that these would not be enough to get the China supply job done. Time was running out. If the war was to be carried to Japan the China bases had to get operational, so Wolfe ordered his B-29s to start flying the Hump route with war supplies to the staging bases in China. The B-29s would have to supply themselves — the Air Transport Command was already stretched thin. Once there was a sufficient stockpile of bombs and fuel at the Chengtu bases, a mission would be flown to a Japanese target, the planes would return to the China bases and then back to the relative safety of their India bases. One mission from India to Japan and return would take four days. The number of planes that could be readied for a mission from Chengtu was very variable; sometimes only few or a couple of dozen to 40, 60 or 80. On one occasion on 14 October of 1944, over 103 planes struck an aircraft factory at Okayama, Japan from the China bases. The logistics turned out to be almost impossible. It was estimated that to send one Wing of B-29s (about 130 planes for the 58th Wing) to a target in Japan from the China bases — just one mission — would require 700,000 gallons of gasoline. Each

Sgt. E. Bernstein in the tent area . 45th Sq. at Chakulia, India in May 1944.
(Courtesy of C. Gordon Brough)

Modern shower facilities at Dudkhundi, India in 1944. (Courtesy of Glen Ralston)

B-29 would have to make *at least* seven trips over the Hump to the China bases carrying extra fuel in its bomb bays, to supply *itself* with enough gasoline for *one* mission to an enemy target. Finally on the next trip the B-29's bays were full of bombs. They would gas up at Chengtu and take off on the mission. It wasn't going to work for very long. Eventually the XXth Bomber Command had to turn to the Air Transport Command for help as it sandwiched its supply runs in between bombing missions from India and China.

The first B-29s flew the Hump into China on 24 April 1944 with "Blondie" **Saunders**, the 58th Wing's Commander, leading the pack, and they landed at Kwanghan, the first field to be completed. Kwanghan would be the China base for the 444th Bomb Group. Three others, one about 10 miles east of Pengshan (A-7, the 468th's base, 40 miles south of Chengtu), one near Kiunglai (462nd's base) and another near Hsinching (A-1, the 40th's base) were almost finished. These planes carried experienced Air Transport Command "safety" pilots on board. Two days later

another Superfort of the 444th Bomb Group piloted by Maj. **Charles Hansen** was attacked by six enemy fighters. Side gunner **Walter Gilonske** was hit. Seconds later tail gunner **Harold Lanhan** smoked an incoming fighter and it dove into the undercast. The big plane received several hits but sustained little damage. That was fortunate for it was ferrying 1,900 gallons of gasoline in its bomb bays.

All through April and May the newly arriving crews went through training: bombing (radar and visual), gunnery, formation flying for the pilots, navigation. And always the mechanics worked feverishly on the balky engines. The air and ground crews were finally getting familiar with their big plane. And the supply runs over the hated Hump continued and one by one, B-29s were lost on the Hump run; fighters, engine failures, icing. Sometimes the crews escaped their burning planes and sometimes they made it back safely through the jungles of Burma or foothills of the Himalayas. But the XXth never really conquered the Himalayan Mountains.

Charles Gordon Brough was a Staff Sergeant in the 40th Bomb Group, an electrical specialist on B-29s, and with a good mechanical background on the B-29 airframe and engines as well. He arrived at Chakulia with the 45th Squadron in April of 1944. Every day he would go out to the line to work on his squadron's planes, readying them for the Hump run or (later) repairing battle damage. He kept a diary which allows us to re-live those days:

"Work on the line continued under terrible conditions of heat and humidity. Rain every day, until our shoes and equipment stank of mildew and clothes hung in the tent began to turn green. At long last some prefab sheds were put up by the Engineering Corps and we finally had a place to store spare parts and test modules which we needed to keep dry at all times.

". . . Arising early, before the day's heat began, even in the rainy season, we would crawl out of sweat-soaked cots, check shoes for scorpions, shower in tepid water if any was available in the tank truck, slip on shorts, shoes, and cut off shirt — later to be discarded — grab a

quick breakfast, use the slit trench if absolutely necessary, catch a ride to the "line", and work in the heat until planes became too hot to touch, usually 1100 hours. A run to the "area" for lunch, then off-duty because of heat until 1500 when it would be time to go to work again.

"...In India, one learned that "Mess" was aptly named. The food was consistently below poor. Early on, through May and June, food was stored in an earthen pit into which was lowered ice brought from Calcutta and whatever meat had been obtained. Noon meals consisted of stewed water buffalo or similar, okra, canned peaches, and a bread of sorts. Cooked under an open mess tent, meals were served into the men's mess kits by the K.P.'s. Walking across the open field from mess tent to dining tent, one had to be careful of the hawks which only too often would dive into a man's kit, rising triumphantly with a piece of meat in its claws! Sometimes the claws caught a hand instead.

". . . There were improvements in time. The mess tents gave way to a cement floored bamboo structure with stuccoed walls and thatched roof. Food was "improved" by a rank-smelling powdered milk and an imitation butter which refused to soften below the consistency of heavy grease and never quite reached an acceptable taste level. Army coffee, ever notorious, reached new lows with local water. In time, also came the Red Cross, with a large, new building. . ."

The Bombing Begins

From Calcutta, Bangkok is southeast across the Bay of Bengal and the Andaman Sea, 950 miles as the crow (and B-29) flies. On 4 June 1944 100 crews — 1100 men — were briefed by operations officers on the XXth Bomber Command's first target — the shipyards and the Makasan rail complex at Bangkok, Siam (now Thailand). Finally the Superfortress was about to do what its four and one-half years and its three billion dollars of design and construction was all aimed at: bombing the enemy. The rail center at Bangkok supplied all the Japanese forces fighting in Burma, and it was to be the primary target. It would be a training mission, a crew and airplane shakedown mission in a way; the mission was not overly long, much of it was over water and so not over enemy occupied land, and the rail yards themselves were fairly easily identified through a bomb sight. The 58th's four Group leaders, Cols. **Leonard "Jake" Harman** (40th), **Alva Harvey** (444th), Ri-

chard Carmichael (462nd), and **Howard Englar** (468th), briefed their respective squadron commanders and crews on the details — the course, weather, rendezvous point, initial point to begin the bomb run, armament carried, secondary targets, routes back, emergency fields, and so forth. This was to be a daylight, precision bombing mission, per direct order of General Arnold in Washington. Arnold also prohibited Gen. Wolfe from accompanying the mission.

100 Superforts were scheduled to take off from Chakulia, Dudhkundi and Piardoba around dawn on 5 June, 1944. Each carried 10,000 pounds of high explosive and incendiary bombs, 6,800 gallons of fuel, and 11 men. One had engine problems and never took off; another crashed and exploded on takeoff when an engine failed, killing 10 of its crew. On the way to Bangkok one airplane after another developed various mechanical problems until 18 of the Superforts had turned back toward Calcutta. Eighty left. Formations broke as visibility decreased over the Bay of Bengal and many just struck off on their own toward the target. As they approached the rendezvous point south of the target three more planes had to turn back with mechanical troubles as the rest climbed to altitudes between 17,000 and 25,000 feet. Seventy-seven left. Col. Jake Harman was leading the attack. The target was completely obscured by clouds so the bombardiers quickly switched from visual to radar bombing, got a good radar echo on a bridge near the target, and opened their bomb bay doors. The 77-ship armada dropped their bombs making runs on the target from different directions and at different altitudes. The attackers were over the target for more than an hour and a half, in waves of small groups. A few enemy fighters came up to take a look and Superfort gunners damaged three of them. Flak was at all levels but mostly wide of the mark. The 77 beat it for home and most of them made it. One crashed near Kunming, China, killing one crewman, and another north of Calcutta; its crew survived. Two others ditched in the Bay of Bengal, and four crewmen died in the splashdowns. 73 of the 77 planes that bombed Bangkok made it safely back to their own or to one of the other bases. But five B-29s had been destroyed on this mission (at $639,000 each), 15 men had lost their lives (no price could be put on them) — and later reconnaissance photos showed that the target was virtually untouched. This was

going to be a long war. But soon news arrived that the Allies had landed in France. D-Day at Normandy, France, 6 June in Europe. At least something was going right.

While the crews of the Bangkok mission were wondering what went wrong, Gen. Arnold was already planning the next strike — on Japan; he ordered a 70-plane mission to the Yawata iron works at the far north end of the southern Japanese home island of Kyushu. Wolfe looked at the maps. This one obviously would have to be staged from the Chengtu bases; these bases were 1200 miles from Calcutta and from Chengtu the nearest Japanese home island of Kyushu was another 1500 miles of land and sea — almost all under enemy control. The stockpiles of bombs and fuel at the four fields were sufficient for a 75-plane mission to Japan — with bomb bay tanks. The date was set for 15 June 1944 and it was no coincidence that the U. S. Marines would storm the beaches of Saipan in the Mariana Islands on this day. Bombed up and with tanks full, the crews were anxious to get going to Japan — the first raid on the Japanese home islands since the Doolittle B-25 strike more than two years ago.

The heavily loaded Superforts started their China-base take-offs late in the afternoon. This was to be night bombing, and eight "pathfinder" bombers took off a few minutes ahead of the main armada to mark the target with fire bombs. One plane crashed and burned before it could even get airborne; the crew by some miracle walked away from the burning, exploding wreckage. In all, 68 Superforts carrying 750 men lumbered off their runways and headed east. Four planes returned to their bases almost immediately with various mechanical problems; 64 still airborne. It was a long, boring, seven hours to the Yawata Imperial Iron and Steel Works. Then a few minutes of sheer terror as 48 of the 64 Superforts rained bombs on the primary target. Searchlights lit up the planes as the bomb bay doors opened. Then flak bursts began creeping up to the bombers' altitude. There were few fighters protecting Yawata on this raid; the enemy pilots did not like night fighting, perhaps because of a lack of effective on-board radar. The remaining 16 B-29s either bombed their secondary target or so-called "targets of opportunity" or jettisoned their bombs for various reasons. Seven B-29s did not return from this raid, a much too high loss rate of 11%. Back in the States, the newspapers reported that the

Steel and Iron Works had been destroyed. The psychological boost to the forces fighting in China was tremendous, and the despair in Japan was of an equal magnitude. Some of the enemy saw it (correctly) as the beginning of the end. An observer on one of the Superforts, Col. **Alan Clark**, made a more careful analysis of the raid:

"The results of the mission were poor. Of the bombs dropped on the Yawata area, only a very small proportion came within the target area, and some were as far as 20 miles away . . ."

The primary reason for the poor results was the use of radar to bomb the target. The bombardiers and radar operators simply didn't have enough experience with this new weapon. A crash training program was instituted and results improved. The raid had nearly depleted the fuel stores at the Chengtu bases and not all the B-29s could take off for India the next day. Following the Yawata raid the existence of the 2-month-old 20th Air Force was announced. Wolfe's XXth Bomber Command had earlier (in April) been assigned to the 20th Air Force. (The XXth Bomber Command was actually formed four and a half months before the 20th Air Force existed). In August of 1944 a second Bomber Command and a second Wing were assigned to the 20th Air Force: these were the XXIst Bomber Command (organized the preceding March) and the 73rd Bombardment Wing. General **Haywood S. "Possum" Hansell, Jr.**, was assigned to the command of the XXIst Bomber Command. Arnold also appointed Hansell his Chief of Staff for the 20th Air Force; Arnold had to spread some of the responsibility. Hansell would take his Command to Saipan in October.

The number of sorties (a sortie is one airplane on one mission) varied through the summer and fall months of 1944 as mechanical problems continued and were overcome and the air crews gained more experience: 145 sorties in June; 87 in July (only three missions); 142 in August; 199 in September. (A year from this time the Superforts of the XXIst Bomber Command would be flying over 5,000 sorties a month from the Marianas). In between raids the XXth Bomber Command's 58th Wing continued ferrying fuel and bombs over the Hump to Chengtu. Sasebo on Kyushu, Hankow, China, and the Showa Steel Works in Manchuria, 1300 miles from Chengtu, were hit in July. Bombing results were

getting better. In August the XXth Bomber Command was able to mount three more missions, two from the China bases. Two of these three went to Japan — one to Nagasaki on the 10th, and the other to Yawata again, on the 20th.

But the third mission deserves special attention. It originated from Ceylon (now Sri Lanka) off the east coast of India to bomb Palembang and mine the Moesi River, both at the far eastern end of Sumatra. The Palembang mission was planned for the 10th to coincide with the Nagasaki mission — to show the enemy that we were capable of this diversity. The double mission was code-named "Operation Boomerang." But more importantly, the Japanese were believed to be deriving at least 75% of their high-octane gasoline from the Sumatra refineries (and over 20% of her oil) and to put these plants out of operation would be a serious blow to the enemy's war effort. Mining the river would hopefully interfere with tanker movements to and from the ports. It would be the longest bombing mission of the war: more than 3800 miles round trip, over 18 hours in the air, and they would bomb at night. About half the Wing flew to Ceylon, and the other half to China, to bomb Nagasaki.

The following remarks are by Rear Admiral **Kenneth L. Veth**, USN, on his being honored by the 58th Bomb Wing Association on July 29, 1978. Then Lt. Cmdr. Veth was an observer on the Palembang mission flying in one of the mine-laying planes:

MISSION: PALEMBANG
10 AUGUST 1944

"In Washington, there was a desire to impress the Japanese with U. S. strike capabilities by conducting simultaneous bombing missions against Nagasaki, Japan and Palembang, Sumatra. This double-strike effort was called "Operation Boomerang." The refinery at Palembang supplied about 1/4 of the Japanese fuel oil and 3/4 of their aviation gasoline. It was obviously important to the Japanese and a worthwhile target for us. Because Sumatra was in Adm. Mountbatten's S. E. Asia Theatre, his concurrence for the mission was needed and requested. He gave it, but he expressed the hope that a portion of the effort could be diverted to mining the Moesi River, going up to Palembang. This was the channel through which oil shipments were made. After considerable discussion and debate on the Air Staff in Washington, Gen. Arnold, over-ruling some of his own

senior staff members, made what then seemed to be a rather crucial decision to include the mining. Brig. Gen. Saunders agreed and designated the 462nd Bomb Group to do the job.

"Going to Palembang was not going to be easy for any of the B-29s. It was a long mission, in fact, the longest non-stop one conducted during the war — 3, 800 miles round trip. Gen. Arnold and others were rather apprehensive about the number of planes that could complete the long round trip. In order to minimize the distance, it was planned to stage through the British R.A.F.-operated China Bay Airfield near Trincomallee on the east coast of Ceylon. Still it was 3, 800 miles and because all possible gasoline had to be loaded, there would only be room for two 1, 000 lb. mines or bombs to be carried in a bomb bay of normal capacity of twenty - 1, 000 lb. bombs. Preparations in the rather hot, humid climate of Ceylon proceeded. Much of the British Fleet in that theatre was deployed to the east of Ceylon to pick up what was expected to be a significant number of B-29s Which might have to ditch on the return trip due to lack of fuel.

"I suspect the story of each individual plane that made the trip would be an interesting one. Some 56 B-29's took off from China Bay, 14 of them from the 462nd Bomb Group, scheduled to mine; the remaining from the 40th, 444th and 468th, scheduled to bomb the refinery. Rumor had it that the British had patrols near the airfield to keep elephants from wandering in the path of the A/C taking off. For reasons I never quite understood, some or maybe all the A/C had to take off downwind. The plane in which I had the privilege of riding . . . was piloted by Col. Richard H. Carmichael. A Major Collander was co-pilot and Major Ed Perry, navigator. The 10 mph downwind push didn't make the take-off easy. Neither did the fact we couldn't initially get the nose wheel up. We skimmed over wave tops for ever so long and I began to think that maybe I was going to get some sea-duty after all. Finally, the nose wheel came up, we gained a little altitude and prospects seemed to improve. About that time, a crew member suggested putting on a life jacket, as there was a fire forward in the plane. Fortunately, it turned out to be a false alarm, and what had actually happened was that some rough air had caused some gasoline to splash out so that the gas fumes were very strong and a fire was possible, but not actual.

"The rest of the trip to Palembang was probably routine for most airmen but exciting enough for a passenger. In climbing over the 10,000 ft. mountains to get over Sumatra, the sky was filled with

A damaged B-29 after experiencing a belly landing. (Courtesy of Bob Boles)

The aftermath of a belly landing of the B-29 "Nipp on Ese". (Courtesy of Clem Heddleson)

enough lightning and thunder to make one think it was the Fourth of July. A seat in the tunnel over the bomb bays with head in the astrodome gave one a good view of this electric display. Navigation was perfect throughout. The Pilot and Navigator found the mouth of the Moesi River with no difficulty, and proceeded to fly up it some 35 miles at 500 ft. altitude. As we approached the drop point, a tanker was sighted in the middle of the River. The temptation of firing on it was great and Col. Carmichael ordered it strafed. The ship returned some small-caliber fire, as did some small arms along the river bank. This was probably the first and last instance of a B-29 strafing a ship during the war. There probably were not many instances of B-29's operating over enemy territory at an altitude of 500 ft. either. Seven other planes from the 462nd Group dropped two mines each along the river channel for a total of 16 mines. About the same time as the mines were being dropped, Col. Carmichael's plane was picked up in a searchlight beam. A sharp bank to the left soon avoided that exposure. About that same time the bombing planes started to drop bombs on the refinery at Palembang (about 5 miles away). These bombs along with searchlights and some anti-aircraft fire provided some spectacular fireworks for the rest of us cruising at our low altitude.

"The return trip was without incident, except, again there was considerable thunder and lightning going over the Sumatra mountains; and it was the first time some of us ever saw St. Elmo's fire running down the leading edge of the wings and off the wing tip. After the return landing at China Bay, the pilot and engineer confided that for a period before and after the mining, they had been forced to shift to a rich carburetor mixture which would have cut our fuel to where we would be about 500 miles short on the return leg. Fortunately, it cleared up and that, combined with a tail wind both going and returning, permitted us to return with an hour's reserve fuel.

"The entire operation, both bombing and mining, was a success in all respects. But the results which really impressed the planners back in Washington was the highly classified intelligence they received about the closure of the Moesi River Channel to all shipping for over a month. A total of 3 enemy ships were sunk and 2 more damaged. This produced a serious interruption in Japanese fuel supplies. These very favorable results from a relatively small effort were a very influential factor in making the decision to use B-29s to mine the mainland of Japan, the "Operation Starvation"..."

"As I said, considering the purpose for which the B-29 was originally built, it was a tribute to Gen. Arnold that he saw the potential and agreed to the mine-laying. In the beginning, persons like Gen. Saunders, commanding the 58th Bomb Wing, his staff, plus Cols. Carmichael and Kalberer of the 462nd were all open-minded and receptive to this possible secondary mission of the B-29s. Later, Gen. LeMay arrived on the scene and was in Command when all 58th Bomb Wing groups got involved in another long bombing and mining mission to Singapore—an effort which had great impact on Japan's military strength in that area, and an operation which received a "well done" message from Adm. King. . . "

Fifty-six B-29s got airborne for this mission (almost half of the total strength of the 58th Wing). The first of these arrived over Palembang at midnight of the 10th. Twelve of these never dropped their bombs due to a variety of reasons (engine problems, bomb rack malfunction, inability to locate the target) but of the remainder, 31 hit the primary target (some bombing by radar) and three hit a secondary target. Eight other planes as noted in Adm. Veth's statement above, mined the river. Dodging flak and fighters, 55 got back to Ceylon safely and one had to ditch short of the base; one crewman died in the ditching. The overall results of the bombing were fair but far from expectations; the refineries were still operating if perhaps not at 100% capacity. Mining the river however did slow down the shipping for several weeks. The Superforts were back at their Calcutta bases by 12 August.

Early in July Gen. Wolfe was reassigned to Washington. His immense knowledge about strategic bombing was needed badly there. General "Blondie" Saunders assumed command of the XXth Bomber Command and the 58th Wing until a tragic accident in a B-25 ended his career. Maj. General **Curtis E. LeMay** took over command of the XXth at the end of August, fresh from the command of the 3rd Bombardment Division in the 8th Air Force in England. LeMay was young, tough and experienced. He had flown combat in B-17s over Germany and he knew how to do it and he knew the problems. He soon started rigorous training programs for everyone. He revamped the maintenance system for the Superforts and reduced significantly the turn around time when battle damaged planes returned from a mission. LeMay was a fighting man's fighting man.

There were two missions in September, both against the steel works at Anshan, Manchuria. This was the second and third raids to Anshan; the first had been in late July when more than 70 Superforts hit the steel works. The stockpiles at Chengtu allowed four days of raids in October of 1944 (seven missions totaling 258 sorties), three to Formosa (Taiwan) and the rest to Kyushu.

A raid from A-1, one of the forward Chengtu bases on 26 September to a primary target, Anshan, is of some interest. Not because of Anshan particularly, but because of events of one B-29 at the secondary target of Dairen. Dairen (now Dalian) is 150 miles southwest of Anshan, at the tip of a peninsula that juts out from near North Korea. The following narrative is by **Robert L. Hall** Central Fire Control gunner on the Dairen plane, and is taken from issue #27 (May 1989) of the 40th Bomb Group Association's publication "Memories." (**John Topolski** was the radar operator on this mission. He would be involved in a hair-raising mission to Singapore some five months later):

Harry M. Changnon, 40th Bomb Group, sets the stage:

"The primary target for this mission was the coke ovens at Anshan, Manchuria. Secondary target was the harbor facilities at Dairen, Manchuria. Target of last resort was the railroad yards at Sinsiang, China. Twenty-seven planes staged from Chakulia together with a photo-recon B-29. Twenty-two planes were airborne for the mission from Hsinching on the 26th of September. Four aborted on the ground. Bob Haley, in #407, aborted 400 miles out. Fifteen planes were in formation at the Initial Point. Weather from the IP to the target was 10/10 undercast. Numerous cloud layers existed to 24,000 ft., making formation flying to the target extremely difficult and hazardous. Bombs from one aircraft were accidentally salvoed short of the target which caused the bombardiers of two other planes to drop their bombs prematurely. The 40th dropped 162 500-pound General Purpose bombs on Anshan. One aircraft was unable to drop its bombs due to a rack malfunction and its crew later manually released the bombs one at a time while returning to Hsinching. All aircraft landed safely at A-1. Average flying time was 12:20 for the 2,800 mile trip. Shortly after interrogation, a three ball alert caused everyone to head for the trenches. Twin engine Jap bombers overhead sounded like a cluster of washing machines."

Recollections of Robert L. Hall, Central Fire Control Gunner:

"I remember the mission against Anshan when we (meaning William A. Hunter's crew) bombed the alternate target at Dairen. That mission was one of the things that helped to make Frank McKinney something of a legend as a bombardier. There was quite a lot of cloud cover as we flew across China. The formation managed to assemble, and our crew was at the extreme left side of the formation, in the high element.

"As the formation flew on its briefed course towards the target at Anshan there was some discussion on intercom about the bad weather—lots of clouds up ahead. After a while the formation entered the clouds, and immediately Hunter, following SOP, banked sharply to the left and flew a timed period before returning to our briefed course. We could not see anything at that point. Eventually we broke into the clear again, but there were still lots of clouds around, and we could not see the other planes from the formation anywhere. We searched for a while without success. The orders were to approach the primary target only in formation, and to hit the secondary target if we were not in formation. So Hunter, sounding annoyed and disappointed, asked our navigator, Leonard Jellis, for a heading to the secondary target, which was a big, square warehouse-like building on the waterfront at Dairen. As we neared it, it appeared that we would have to bomb by radar because there were still lots of clouds, about 8/10ths, I believe. We opened bomb-bay doors and started in on radar, but I believe that the radar operator was having trouble getting clear indications of the target location.

"Suddenly, Frank McKinney, the bombardier, announced on intercom that he had the target in sight and would take the run. As he started to sight on the target, however, the very cold air at our high altitude, together with all the cloud moisture, apparently caused the glass panel in front of his bombsight to frost over completely before he could finish the bomb run. Thinking fast, Frank leaned over to look around the bombsight at the target, made some quick judgments of angles, and when the target's position looked about right to him, he salvoed the bombs and called "bombs away." We stayed on course long enough for the side gunners to see the bombs strike the target building directly. I do not remember if we got bomb-strike pictures. Without even using the bombsight, Frank got a "shack." (The building destroyed was the eight-story main office building of the Anshan Steel Company in the heart of Dairen's business district, and no other building was hit).

"It was about six weeks later that Frank McKinney got another "shack" at Singapore, managing to place all three of his bombs right on the control shack and sliding steel caisson of the dry dock there. I remember hearing at the time that Hunter had recommended McKinney for a decoration for his high-altitude precision bombing at Singapore. The rumor was that the high brass said that one success was not proof of anything, and that Hunter came back with some comment like, 'Well, of course he hit the bull's eye from high altitude at Dairen, too, but there he didn't use the bombsight.' "

October 1944 saw the arrival at Isley Field on Saipan of General Hansell, the XXIst Bomber Command's chief, flying in *Joltin Josie*. The dust had hardly settled from the fierce battle to take Saipan from the defending Japanese, when construction gangs started building runways for B-29s. By 10 August both Tinian Island and Guam would be in U. S. hands and before October ended (it was the 28th), fourteen B-29s flew a combat mission from Saipan — a shakedown mission to enemy submarine pens on Dublon Island in the Truk group, a short run of 650 miles southeast of Saipan. October also saw the U. S. Navy destroy much of what remained of its Japanese counterpart in the Battle of Leyte Gulf. And in October General MacArthur made good on his promise of over two years ago: he returned in force, landing on Leyte in the Philippines. October was a big month for the Allies in the Pacific.

General Emmett "Rosey" O'Donnell brought his 73rd Bombardment Wing to Saipan in October of 1944 and on 24 November the first Superfort mission to Japan flew from the Marianas. The Japanese immediately sent bombers to the Mariana Islands from Iwo Jima, 700 miles to the north. This volcanic island was now the only land base available to them from which they could reach the Marianas. A Christmas day raid on Saipan broke through Isley Field's flak screen and destroyed eleven Superforts and damaged forty-three others. This infuriated Hansell and he sent his B-29s to knock out the airfields on Iwo Jima. A week later the Marianas were no longer a target for the enemy air force for there was no enemy air force left on Iwo Jima. Several more raids on Iwo kept its airfields inoperative through the next two months until the Marines assaulted the island on 19 February 1945.

The following paragraph was written by Philip A. Crowl and appeared in "Campaign in the Marianas", Office of the Chief of Military History, Chapter XXI:

"Even before the bombs began to drop, many Japanese were aware that the loss of the Marianas, and especially of Saipan, was a crucial, if not the decisive, turning point in the war. The most immediate repercussion was the fall of Premier Tojo and his entire cabinet. Japanese leaders were aware of the tremendous potentialities of the B-29 (although not of the atomic bomb), and they fully realized that with the loss of the Marianas those potentialities could be quickly brought to bear against Japan. Prince Naruhiko Higashikuni, Commander in Chief of Home Defense Headquarters stated:

"The war was lost when the Marianas were taken away from Japan and when we heard the B-29s were coming out . . . We had nothing in Japan that we could use against such a weapon. From the point of view of the Home Defense Command we felt that the war was lost and said so. If the B-29s could come over Japan, there was nothing that could be done."

. . . According to Premier Kantaro Suzuki: "It seemed . . . unavoidable that in the long run Japan would be almost destroyed by air attack so that merely on the basis of the B-29s alone I was convinced that Japan should sue for peace."

In October of 1944 one squadron of each of the 58th Wing's four bomb groups was disbanded (the 395th, 679th, 771st and 795th), so each group now was composed of three squadrons. For the next three months the XXth continued its Hump runs to supply its China staging bases with fuel and bombs. They were able to get off three or four missions per month to Japan or occupied China targets. In between these long range missions the XXth would hit targets in Bangkok, Saigon and Singapore, staging from their home bases around Calcutta. 314 sorties in November (four missions from Chengtu); 285 sorties in December (six Chengtu missions); 436 sorties in January (eight Chengtu missions).

Charles G Brough's diary describes what it was like to fly the Hump to the China bases:

"The date: November 18, 1944; [Time: 0700; Plane #275, Snafuper Bomber]. The weather: visibility unlimited. The silver plane climbed four thousand feet on the warm, humid, heavy

The crew of the B-29 "Indiana" of the 9th Bomb Group, 313th Wing in Tinian. (Courtesy of Margaret Ellis)

air, taking a heading of of 55° magnetic which would take them slightly north of Calcutta's restricted flight zone. Suddenly, they smelled the unmistakable odor of 100 octane gasoline. We caught the odor as word came on the intercom to douse all cigarettes and unneeded electrical equipment. We needed no second word from the A/C [aircraft commander]. The Flight Engineer [Leonard Koenig] and crewmen had shut down all possible, and the ship went on manual. Koenig made a check of the gas tanks in the bomb bay. The front bomb bay held two, 640 gallon rubberized tanks of the highly explosive 100 octane. Everyone stood ready, parachutes secured, as the hills swept below. If a spark were to occur in the wrong place, no parachute, we thought, would help us! In what seemed an eternity, Koenig reported he had found a hose line leak which he had been able to stop. At the time, we were carrying three bomb bay tanks and 12 HE's [high explosive

bombs]. As someone wryly remarked, "This makes one hell of a flying bomb.
"We gradually relaxed once again and after a long wait were able to light a cigarette and have a cup of coffee heated by the electrical stove on board. Below, the Indo-Ganges swept by. The Captain noted that they were just north of Calcutta at about 10,000 feet. Calcutta was a place to avoid. The British had the reputation, as protectors of the restricted space over the city, of shooting first and asking questions afterwards, an entirely undeserved reputation which had probably been started when a British Beaufighter had shot down a B-29 which had strayed over the forbidden zone. The -29 crew bailed out safely enough, but the navigator, it was rumored, had died by drowning in the river. The report was that the IFF, or radio, or something in the -29 had not been working correctly. At any rate, the Brits would include, in their base trophy room, among the red sun emblems of Jap planes shot down, the unmistakable emblem of a B-29!

"With safety belt tightened, I could still lean forward, seeing in the hazy distance the confluence of the Bhagiraibi and Jalang Rivers which form the Hooghly River above Calcutta, that turbid waterway which washes the ghats of that city and winds its way to the Indian Ocean, thick with the pollution of the dead and the excrement of the living. On we flew, over Barrackpore and the flat, colorless plains of eastern India. I had the feeling that a giant relief map was passing below me.
"Past Barrackpore we passed over the confluence of one of the greatest rivers of all, the Brahmaputra and the Ganges. Looking southward, the city of Chandpur could just be seen at the edge of this great body of water. The giant Superfort droned smoothly over Imphal and the 13,000 foot Naga Hills, over the western demarcation of the deepest penetration the Japs made into Burma. Continuing, #275 flew on over the Burma-Assam border, the Chindwin River near

Layshi, and on over the northern end of the Kabaw Valley where I snapped a picture of Lake Indagwyi which was set in the base of rising peaks of the Kumon Range.

"The Pilot held to a course passing over the Irrawaddy, the China-Burma frontier north of Myitkyna, and over the Saiyang Pass through the 13,000- to 18,000-foot Hengduan Shan Range above Pichiang. For a brief time the Burma Road exposed its scars through the green carpet of jungle south of the plane. The air, colder now, tested the ability of the -29 to provide comfort as we cruised at 30,000 feet.

"So far, except for the gasoline leak, the trip had been uneventful. The Central Fire Control section, which included the "Radar Room" — in all, an area about 90 square feet — was kept automatically pressurized to an equivalent altitude of 8,000 feet by the excess air put out by the superchargers, as was the Pilot's compartment and that of the rear gunner. We were able to heat K-rations brought with us by means of the electric oven, and this, with hot coffee, provided a satisfactory lunch.

"A cigarette and final cup of coffee raised everyone's spirits. A few jokes were passed, then each of us studied the air above and below. Guns were cleared, the orange tracers sailing out and down as each set was tested, then the tail bounced a bit as a few rounds of 20 mm were fired into the mountain off to one side. I then gave my attention to the landscape below, always fascinating.

"... I studied the villages seen from the plane — one in particular named Weisi (Wexi). It was near here that Long [Sgt. O. B., electrical technician] had noted a collection of huts surrounded by a wall, a small plateau atop a precipitous peak, and had, with the aid of the Bausch & Lomb 7 X 50 M1 binoculars kept as standard equipment on the plane, watched a fur clad native armed with a crossbow look upward at the warplane, either in fear or anger.

"Lichiang came in sight as we crossed the Yangtze River. The Pilot requested a heading from the Navigator, then banked gently northeast past the 18,000-foot snow-covered peak lying below and north of their course. The left gunner spoke of this as a landmark on the China flights.

"Shortly, now on a heading for Hsinching, the four engine bomber crossed the Yunnan-Schezwan border into Lo-Lo country, where the natives had developed a virulent dislike for strangers - in particular the English and, by association, Americans. These people occupied the lowlands, so crews had been briefed to head for the hills if forced down here. I placed my trust in the flight crew to get us over this stretch!

"Over Muli now, the left gunner pointed down towards Hsichang to the south where #326, Jay Woodruff's plane, had been forced to land, sometime back in June of '44. With the aid of the 7 X 50s, I could make out the plane even through ground haze.

"Crossing the Yalung River, #275 flew on, continuing northeast over the yellow and green terraced hills found in this area. Passing over these, we came to the flatlands and the Min River, on a heading for Hsinching airfield, the forward base designated A-1.

"At 1600 hours, the plane touched down, tires protesting and smoking as the Commander applied brakes after backing off the throttles, and brought the big Superfort to a stop. Revving engine #4 and turning, Cowden [Pilot] rolled the plane to its assigned location and braked."

General LeMay commanded the XXth Bomber Command based at Kharagpur until 20 January 1945 when he relieved General Hansell and assumed command of the XXIst Bomber Command in the Marianas. The new commander of the XXth was Brig. Gen. **Roger Ramey** who had been Hansell's

"The Natural" being loading with bombs. (Courtesy of Robert LeMon)

The crew of "The Natural" (l. to r.) Standing: Endicott, Axthelm, Kolton, Roach, Walz, and LeMon. Kneeling: Pierce, Jones, Kazimer, Robinson, and Calder. (Courtesy of Robert LeMon)

chief of staff in the Marianas. A week after Gen. LeMay officially left the XXth Bomber Command for the Marianas, the XXth closed down its Chengtu operations. The last mission from Chengtu was an eight-plane raid on targets in southeast China on 17 January 1945. These operations from Chengtu, 1200 miles from the supply bases in India, seemed like a drudge to the B-29 crews. True, flying from the China bases was the only way they could hit targets in Japan — up to late November of 1944 when missions began originating from Saipan — but flying the Hump with their own supplies took a lot of men and machines and time just in a trucking operation. And occasionally men and machines were lost. These missions to Japan and Manchuria and Formosa — only a few a month could be supported — did not do great damage to the Empire. Some damage to be sure, but not a great deal compared to what was in store. But what these China-based operations did do was at least two-fold: first, it made it clear to the enemy that his home islands were no longer an unreachable sanctuary, and second, the missions made each B-29 and its crew an integrated, highly trained fighting machine. Most of the serious "bugs" had been worked out of the big bomber during the summer and fall of 1944; pilots and flight engineers learned precisely what their big plane could and could not do on a mission (they were constantly being surprised at what it could do), gunners and bombardiers and radar men became expert and deadly at their trade and navigators sharpened their skills to pin-point precision. By the end of 1944, the B-29 had vindicated itself; in experienced hands, it had become the Air Force's deadliest weapon. As it was soon to turn out, it was only the beginning. So with the Mariana fields in operation, and missions from there able to reach Japan, the China bases were closed down.

But the XXth Bomber Command with its single 58th Wing kept on slugging it out with the Japanese in February and March of 1945, hitting targets from their bases around Calcutta. In February the XXth flew more sorties (460) than in any month since they had arrived in India ten months before. Maybe it was a celebration for not having to fly the despicable Hump route any more; more likely, there were just more planes available from the now ended Chengtu-based missions. On 1 February a small armada of Superforts flew a long 3500-mile round trip from the Calcutta bases to

Crew from the 830th Bomb Squadron. (Courtesy of Milton Sprouse)

Singapore to hit a floating dry dock. **Denny Pidhany**, the 58th Bomb Wing Association's Recording and Historical Secretary, noted this mission in a meeting of the Wing members at which a painting depicting this mission was dedicated to Admiral Lord **Louis Mountbatten** who was Commander of the Southeast Asia Command (SEAC) at this time:

"During the time from November, 1944 to March 26, 1945, the missions run were for two masters. One was the Commander of the Southeast Asia Command (SEAC), and the other was the United States Joint Chiefs of Staff (JCS). Those for SEAC were places such as Bangkok, Rangoon, Kuala Lumpur, etc., and those for the JCS were Singapore and Saigon. Some 12 missions were run for SEAC and 15 for the JCS. The SEAC missions hit railroad yards, round houses, ammunition dumps, bridges, etc. The JCS missions were the bombing of dry docks and mine laying of the channels. . . .

"In November, 1944, the 20th Bomber Command/58th Bomb Wing began a series of missions against Singapore. At that time, the historian of the 25th Bomb Squadron had these words to say: 'On the heels of the Rangoon Mission, came orders for the 20th to strike the main dry dock installation at the Singapore Naval Base. This was to be in conjunction with and follow up to the great naval battle which is taking place off Formosa and in

the waters around the Philippines. After careful consideration, the mission looked impossible. It was thought that the B-29s could fly the 4100 miles, but only without a bomb load. However, a wire from General Marshall himself settled the question . . .'

"The Singapore missions were long hauls from the bases in the Calcutta area to the Naval Base in the 'Straits (between Malaya and Singapore). Further, the naval shipboard anti-aircraft fire was the most accurate and deadly that the Wing encountered in its tour of service.

"Along with the bombing of the graving or land-locked dry docks, some very effective mine laying of the Straits was accomplished. . . . As the Japanese mined the area each side of the safe passage slot eastward, we then mined their safe passage slot. This was some very good work. On the Singapore missions we lost a number of crews, a group commander, plus some severely damaged aircraft.

". . . The floating dry dock was considered of primary naval significance in that it could service a battleship. The dry dock was 855 feet long and 172 feet wide.

"From an altitude of 19,000 feet, some eleven flights totalling 88 aircraft, passed northeast over the dry dock. As the aircraft passed over, it was observed that a ship, a 10,000-ton tanker called Shirectoko, was in the floating dry dock. The first wave of aircraft came from the 25th Bomb Squadron. The lead bombardier, Lt. Joseph D. McCraw, dropped his

bombs on the ship in the floating dry dock. This wave of four aircraft achieved what is for the most part, a dream of bombing experts. A few minutes after the first wave passed over the target, the aircraft in the rear position piloted by **Richards** was shot down and lost. No record has ever come of the crew. One aircraft in the later flights was heavily damaged, and did return to base, but never to fly again. The floating dry dock was put out of commission for good. In 1951 or 1952, it was raised and cut up for scrap metal.

"The missions run for Admiral **Mountbatten** *were most successful. These were in support of the coming return of General* **William J. Slim's** *Fourteenth Army to Burma and the Malay peninsula. He was appreciative of our work. During one of his visits, he spent time with Group Commander Col.* **James V. Edmundson**, *and these words come to light:*

" 'Before we departed Kharagpur for Tinian, Lord Louis Mountbatten came up to visit Kharagpur and spent a morning with us. He talked in the briefing room. Later, I had a private conversation with him. Also, he called in selected crew members, commanders, staff members and crew chiefs to have a chat in a private audience in the back yard. He talked to them one at a time. Lord Louis Mountbatten told me, 'You know, you embarrassed me when you sunk the floating dry dock. I had assured topside that it was safe to let you bang away because we knew you'd never hit [it]; and further, it was out in such a place that you wouldn't hurt anything around it.' He said, 'The first time I turned you loose on it, you sunk it, and I got called on the fire for letting you destroy crown property.' He concluded, 'You put me on the spot when you did that, but I was awfully proud of you.'

" 'He was a great guy, as you know. Those who were touched by him have never forgotten him.' "

But it was not all sweetness and light. The following narrative is by **James Lyons**, pilot of B-29 #804, and was printed in Issue #21 (May 1988) of the 40th Bomb Group Association's publication "Memories." Narratives of other surviving crew members are the same in all essential details.

MISSION: SINGAPORE 26 FEBRUARY 1945

"Memories" Editor's Introduction:

"Returning from a photo mission to Singapore on 26 February, 1945, the crew of plane #804 was forced to bail out after being attacked by a Japanese fighter.

In an extremely rare instance, a British submarine participated in the rescue. The submarine, HMS SEADOG, survived the war. Portions of the log of the SEADOG are used in telling the story of the rescue in which nine of the 12 crew members were brought to safety. [A British PBY rescued several of the crew].

Members of the crew were: Pilot. - **James Lyons**; Co-Pilot - **Mills Bale**; Navigator - **Nathan Teplick**; Bombardier - **William Kintis** (KIA); Flight Engineer - **Frank W. Thorp**; Radio Operator - **Joseph M. Dimock**; Radar Counter Measures- **Vernon Lester**; Radar Operator - **John Topolski**; Central Fire Gunner - **J. M. Moffit** (KIA); Right Gunner - **Anthony P. Peleckis**; Left Gunner - **Louis L. Sandrick**; Tail Gunner - **J. J. Carney** (KIA).

Lyons, Bale, Thorp, Peleckis and **Sandrick** were rescued by the British PBY. **Teplick, Lester, Dimock** and **Topolski** were rescued by the British submarine and transferred to a second PBY. **Kintis, Moffit and Carney** were never found after jumping.

Memories of **Jim Lyons**, Pilot of #804

"Our crew was a last minute replacement for Joe Williams' crew. We flew their plane which had the cameras installed. I was having a most successful night at poker when I received word to report to Operations. The flight to the target and the photo mission itself was uneventful...beautiful weather, no enemy action, and according to the person running the cameras, excellent pictures.

*"On the return flight, I changed seats with Bale and relaxed in the co-pilot' seat. An hour or so later we saw a fighter (later identified as a Jack) approaching us from one o'clock high. **Bale** turned to take him head on, and our forward guns opened up. The fighter was untouched, and to this date I believe those guns were out of sync. On his first pass we received a shell in the nose that started a hydraulic fire and turned **Bill Kintis** (bombardier) into a human torch and knocked out #2 engine. While **Bale** and the engineer were feathering the engine, **Joe Dimock** and I put out the cockpit fire with the extinguisher, dousing **Kintis** in the process. Actually **Dimock** shouldn't have been flying as he still had a bullet wound in his arm, received in a previous accident when ammunition exploded on a nearby plane. My hands were burned while I was attempting to pull **Bill Kintis** out of the flames, but I did not realize this until sometime later.*

*"During this time, the Jack made two or three more passes, and in so doing, set our [rear] bomb bay tank on fire. For some unknown reason, he then broke off the attack and flew away. When the gunners informed us of the fire in the bomb bay, **Bale** went back to assist [**Topolski**] and I took over the controls. **Teplick** and **Dimock** managed to get the bomb bay doors open, but the bomb bay tank would not release. The gunners stood in the open bomb bay and chopped at the shackles with an axe. It finally came loose, but in falling, struck the doors so that they would not completely close. This negated any thought of ditching at that time.*

"I was able to maintain a reasonable altitude and speed, but the cockpit was an utter shambles . . . maps burned, etc. At this point, the other -29 caught up to us and gave us an accurate position and course home. I thought that, with any luck at all, we would make it home, but two hours or so later, conditions changed radically. We had thrown everything we could overboard and were maintaining altitude when I noticed a small spot on the leading edge of the wing adjacent to the feathered #2 engine. I glanced at it from time to time and suddenly realized it was getting larger and there had to be fire in the wing.

*"We made preparations to bail out, including rigging a line to **Bill's** chute. We hoped we could drop him and land close enough to keep him afloat. He was badly burned and had never regained consciousness, but we couldn't bear to leave him behind. We stayed in the air about another hour, gradually losing altitude and constantly monitoring the wing. Now we were at about two thousand feet and the fire could be seen. During that hour, **Bale** had taken over the flying because I had finally become aware of the condition of my hands. When I tried to release the wheel I left skin behind. We opened the doors and two of us dropped Bill out and tried to go with him, but his chute opened almost immediately and we never saw him again. I am sure it was no coincidence that we never saw **Carney** and **Moffit** again as they wore chest-type chutes and could not break free of them.*

"Parachuting into the sea is tricky. I found it very difficult to judge my height from the surface of the sea. This is critical as you have to drop out of the chute, otherwise the chute can envelop you and pull you under.

"We had nearly waited too long, as the plane blew up before I hit the water [Others reported the left wing breaking off]. I dropped free of my chute much too

high and went quite deep. I pulled the cords of my Mae West, only to find there were no cylinders. When I finally surfaced, I managed to partially inflate the vest manually, kick off my shoes, and discard everything on my person (including my wallet, thick with over 3000 rupees from the poker game).

"I soon found that it is much easier to stay afloat in sea water than in the old swimming pool. Luckily, four of us landed within shouting distance of each other and eventually managed to get together. We tied ourselves together and for the next twenty-five or so hours, the boys would take turns holding me up out of the water so I could inflate my Mae West."

(A framed clipping from a British news paper hangs over the desk of **Jim Lyons** today. It picks up the story).

"Signals were picked up at the Strategic Air Force HQ of Eastern Command that the B-29 was on fire and as soon as the crew was known to have bailed out, R.A.F. and U.S.A.A.F. rescue aircraft were on their way to the last recorded position—300 miles away.

"Five of the men were located at daybreak of the second day of the search by captain of the first Catalina F/O E. A. Lickorish. He spotted a yellow object, circled 50 feet above the waves and discovered it was an injured flyer [**Topolski**, later picked up by the British submarine]. Within an hour he [E. A. Lickorish] found and picked up five other survivors [**Bales**, **Lyons**, **Thorpe**, **Sandrick** and **Peleckis**] and flew them to Calcutta.

"The other four men [**Lester**, **Teplick**, **Dimock** and **Topolski**] were picked up first by a submarine and then transferred to another [British] Catalina captained by F/Lt. C.R. Bradford, which was just finishing the third day of the search when it had a message from the submarine. One of these men [**Topolski**] had been in the water 36 hours."

(The way in which we obtained this clipping, says **Jim Lyons**, is a story in itself. My father-in-law's family and the pilot of our rescue plane lived in the same township in England. They recognized my name in the clipping and mailed it to my wife.)

Louis L. Sandrick remembers:

"We had an extra gas tank in the bomb bay full of gas. So the bomb bay doors were opened to drop the tank. Before I could notify the pilot that the tank was only half way out, they closed the doors. The doors then got bent. The doors were opened again and I was told by the pilot to take the fire axe and go out on the cat walk and free the tank. One of the shackles did not open, so I gave it a good whack with the axe and out went the tank. I was shaking in my shoes because I was afraid and worried about falling out of the plane. I did not have on my parachute."

Anthony P. Peleckis remembers:

"With each passing minute, we were getting closer to home and I began to feel that somehow, some way, we were going to make it. And then the order to bail out came over the phones. I couldn't believe it. everyone hesitated, no one wanted to be the first one out. Again the order to bail out came and I guess reality set in and so out we went. As it turned out, we got out none too soon, because while I was still coming down, our plane banked right and blew up."

John Topolski remembers:

"One of the PBY search planes flew around the area looking one way and then banking to look the other and trying to see directly below the plane. It seemed like the plane was within 50 feet of me. I waved and tried to signal to them, but they didn't see me and eventually flew away. The desperateness of being alone in the water can't be described. You search in vain for something — anything — to hold on to, even a pencil or a twig but there is nothing."

Mills Bales remembers the shark attack while floating (with a defective life vest):

"The first shark came in and went between my legs. He hit me so hard it nearly up-ended me and my legs flew apart . . . It wasn't long 'till he was back again. I had taken off my shoes as soon as I hit the water, but kept my socks on. The second time he snapped my left foot . . . He came by once more on the surface about four inches from my right elbow. I hit him a swat and that was the last I saw of him. The rest stalked me for several hours, roaming about 50 feet away. . ."

John Topolski (first on right) along with other airmen pulled from the ocean. (Courtesy of John Topolski)

The submarine was the *H.M.S. Seadog* captained by Lt. E. A. Hobson; Lt Hobson kept a very detailed record of his part in this rescue, a small part of which reads as follows:

"At 1548 on 27th February, 3 American airmen [Lester, Teplick and Dimock] were picked up from a raft, and as 5 had already been rescued by a CATALINA, this left 4 still unaccounted for. H.M.S. SEADOG commenced an up-wind search, since the 4 remaining airmen were known to have only 'Mae Wests'. At 1850, one more airman was picked up [Topolski], and a circling B-29 so informed. . . . He was utterly exhausted and clearly would not have lasted another night. Search continued throughout the night with no success. At 1116 on the 28th February, a CATALINA landed by request, and the 4 airmen were transferred to her. At 1830 on 28th February, search was abandoned and H.M.S. SEADOG was ordered to resume patrol off PORT BLAIR."

In March, the last month of the XXth Bomber Command's India operations, the number of sorties dropped to 371. During these two final months the Superfort crews hit targets at Bangkok, Singapore, Saigon, Rangoon, Kuala Lumpur and numerous other exotic sounding places. Eleven missions in February and eleven more in March. The final day of the XXth's war came on 29 March when two missions were sent out to Malayan targets. At this time the U. S. Navy had gained virtually uncontested control of the seas guarding the southern and eastern approaches to Japan and was in effect strangling the Empire. It was able to range over the expanse of the South China Sea from Saigon to Tokyo Bay, striking virtually any target it chose with its carrier-borne Hellcats, Helldivers and Avengers and with the big rifles of its capital ships. But the Navy, with all its incomparable firepower, could not eliminate the Empire's home war effort or its war industry. This required the delivery of many thousands of tons of high explosives and only the 20th Air Force had that capability.

The XXth Bomber Command had done its job; it had been the first to take the Superfortress into battle. Now the combat-ex-perienced crews of the XXth Bomber Command were needed in the Marianas. The air crews flew to the Marianas via China and the Philippines where the 58th Wing was incorporated into the XXIst Bomber Command (at West Field, just north of Tinian Town); the ground crews went by boat via Australia — it took them a month. They would become fully operational in the Marianas by early May. By this time several B-29 fields on Saipan, Tinian and Guam were operational. On Guam, North Field near Ritidian Point and Northwest Field inland of Pati Point, were in full operation by the beginning of the summer of 1945.

The XXIst Bomber Command
Target: Japan

General LeMay, now in command of the XXIst Bomber Command, set up his headquarters on Guam. Guam had been a possession of the United States before the war; the Japanese had conquered the little garrison there on 10 December 1941. The Marines assaulted the island on 21 July 1944 and in three weeks of bitter fighting had brought it back under the U. S. flag. Saipan and Tinian had already been secured by this time. By the time LeMay relieved Hansell in the Marianas, the Superforts had made about 20 missions to Japan (over 800 sorties) and the air crews were racking up a lot of experience. They were long trips, most about 15 hours in the air.

Tinian was to be especially valuable as a Superfort base. Approximately 10 miles by 5 miles, the island is fairly flat compared to Saipan and Guam so was a good site for long runways. The 2nd and 4th Marine Divisions assaulted the island on 24 July 1944 and in 9 days killed virtually every one of the 9,000 enemy defenders on the island with 1,900 Marine casualties. North Field, on the site of the original Japanese runways near Marpi Point, was the first field on the island to become operational in February of 1945. West Field, near Tinian Town, became operational in March 1945. The 313th Wing flew the first B-29 mission from Tinian on 10 February 1945. The 58th Wing (from India) flew its first mission to Japan from Tinian on 5 May 1945. North Field would consist of four parallel runways, running east and west, each 8,500 feet long and 200 feet wide.

Early on, the Command was hard-pressed to launch many more than 70 air-craft on a mission, usually far fewer, and new B-29s and their crews weren't being delivered as fast as had been expected. But, by the end of February there were about 350

Lt. James M. Ellis of 9th Bomb Group, 313th Bomb Wing sitting atop a large bomb. (Courtesy of James Ellis)

Superforts in the Marianas and the sorties per mission started to grow. LeMay's first month commanding the XXIst Bomber Command was not all roses. He got off about 16 missions to Japan by the end of February and lost 45 B-29s and many of their crews in the process. At least a dozen of these just disappeared into the Pacific and were never heard from again. And almost as bad, reconnaissance photos showed that most of the targets aimed at were still standing and in full operation although some 5,000 tons of high explosives had been aimed at them. Much of the trouble was due to the abominable weather over Japan. In clear weather and with the precision Norden bombsight, a bombardier could place a bomb within a few hundred yards of his aiming point from five miles high. Almost never were the targets in plain, unobscured view, so radar bombing was resorted to and the bombardiers and radar men were not yet that good at it. LeMay was frustrated at what to do. Single planes, large formations, day, night, high altitude, medium altitude — nothing was working.

On 4 March 179 planes reached Tokyo with high explosives in the bomb bays. The results were again disappointing. LeMay took a 5-day respite from almost daily Superfort launches from the Marianas, and decided it was time to make a drastic change in tactics. The residential areas of Tokyo, and of most other Japanese cities, were essentially built of wood. Back in the States experiments had already been completed on developing super-hot incendiary bombs that would start mock-up villages burning, and burning so fiercely that the fire fighters were overwhelmed. It was a napalm-type bomb of jellied gasoline.

LeMay decided to try incendiaries on Tokyo; the raid would be a big one— 334 B-29s would be launched. The take-off date was set for the early evening of 9 March 1945 and the bombers would be over Tokyo from just after midnight on the 10th. On this mission would be Gen. **Emmett O'Donnell's** 73rd Wing from Saipan, Gen. **John Davies'** 313th Wing from Tinian and Gen. **Thomas Power's** newly arrived 314th Wing from Guam. On orders from LeMay, Gen. Power would lead this mission. Also there would be no gunners or machine gun ammunition carried on this raid. Pathfinder Superforts, each with over 180 blindingly bright magnesium bombs, took off a few minutes early before the first of the 73rd Wing's planes;

A crewman of the 93rd Squadron, 19th Bomb Group works on the engine of a B-29 on the North Field in Guam. (Courtesy of James McFalls)

Tire change on a B-29 of the 93rd Squadron, 19th Bomb Group in Guam. (Courtesy of James McFalls)

A stack of 100lb. bombs prior to being loaded in a B-29. (Courtesy of James McFalls)

Ground crew of 93rd Squadron, 19th Bomb Group on Guam. (l. to r.) Hodge, Sees, Rankin, McFalls (pointing), and Karger. (Courtesy of James McFalls)

"Ole Boomerang" of the 458th Squadron, 330th Bomb Group in Guam. (l. to r.) Standing: Leaf, Scribner, Ormand, Hodge, and Wamboldt. Kneeling: McLeod, Vesely, Sellers, Seibee, Keister, and Schulich. (Courtesy of Curtis McLeod)

they would light up the targets as aiming points for bombardiers in the planes to follow. This attack, in addition to the sole use of fire bombs as ordnance, would be different; the formations would come in under the weather at between 5,000 and 8,000 feet. Because they didn't need all the extra fuel to climb to the usual 25,000 or 30,000 feet (the usual bomb bay tanks were not carried on this mission), extra bomb weight could be carried in the bays. Most of the big Superforts this night carried about 16,000 pounds of incendiaries. LeMay had built up a stockpile of incendiaries in the Marianas that would allow five such fire bomb raids, each raid bringing up to 2,400

tons of bombs to the target. Later, as more Superforts arrived, each mission from the Marianas would be carrying 3,000 tons of high explosives and incendiaries to targets in Japan.

Many of the planes that were launched had to abort for various mechanical reasons such that fewer than 300 finally reached Japan. The results of this first incendiary bomb raid were devastating. The 8 tons of fire bombs dropped by each Superfort set fire to a rectangular area about 500 feet wide and a half mile long. These burning rectangles then coalesced, fanned by 40-knot winds. Nearly 16 square miles of Tokyo were consumed in a gigan-

tic wind-spread conflagration started by over 2,400 tons of incendiaries. 78,000 of its citizens perished, many suffocating from a lack of atmospheric oxygen which was consumed by the fires, and 267,000 buildings burned to ashes. At least a million citizens were made homeless. The flak was inaccurate at these low altitudes and the night fighters were flown by inexperienced pilots, all the Empire had left. The B-29s were over Tokyo for nearly three hours that night. The thousands of tons of high explosives delivered in past raids had not caused such total decimation. The mission lost 14 Superforts but even with these losses the mission was extraordinarily successful.

In quick succession, the XXIst Bomber Command launched the next four incendiary raids: 11 March, 285 planes, Nagoya (only one loss in a take-off ditching; 2 square miles destroyed); 13 March, 274 planes, Osaka (8 square miles destroyed); 16 March, 331 planes, Kobe (3 square miles destroyed); 18 March, 290 planes, Nagoya again (another 3.5 square miles destroyed). In 10 days of operations, the Command had launched over 1500 sorties from their island bases, the loss rate had been low (21 aircraft lost — 1.4% of those launched — for all five missions, with 156 casualties), a significant number of the enemy's urban areas and war industries had been destroyed (33 square miles), and enemy morale plummeted as that of LeMay's air crews soared. The XXIst finally ran out of incendiaries and returned to carrying high explosives to Japan.

Now, for the last mission of the *Eddie Allen*. It will be recalled that this plane had been built and paid for by the men and women at Boeing's Wichita assembly plant. It had gone to India with the 40th Bomb Group and got its baptism of battle flying out of its base at Chakulia. It flew the Hump to China and hit just about every target within range of the 58th Bomb Wing's planes. In April of 1945 the *Eddie Allen* was flown to Tinian and joined the XXIst Bomber Command to continue its war from the Mariana Islands. The *Eddie Allen* had become something of a legend and was scheduled to be returned to the United States after its 25th mission. The *Eddie Allen* completed 24 missions and then gave up the ghost. This is the story of the last mission of the *Eddie Allen* written by its Commander, Col. **Eino E. Jenstrom**, USAF (Ret.). The story was published in AIR FORCE magazine, August 1980.

MISSION: TOKYO
23 MAY 1945

"The briefing was at 11:00 a.m., May 23, 1945. The target: Tokyo. A total of 550 B-29s fully loaded with incendiary bombs was to enforce the harsh realities of war on the Japanese. The Superforts were to be led by the Pathfinders, XXIst Bomber Command's elite crews, going in at low level to mark the target. The rest would follow at 9,000 to 11,000 feet. The aircraft of the 58th Bomb Wing began their takeoffs from West Field on Tinian Island shortly after 4:00 in the afternoon. The Eddie Allen would be in the main stream at 9,000 feet.

"Big **John Mahli**, crew chief and master of Hardstand 11, the built-up coral and asphalt island home of the Eddie Allen, met the truck delivering the eleven-man combat crew to 'his' airplane.

"Big John was all business. 'We're all set. Write-ups cleared. Number three is the high-time engine: the others are in the second hundred hours. Radar and radio check out. Gas tanks topped off. Forty clusters loaded. Full load of ammo.'

"Bombardier Lt. **Fred Billingsley** disappeared in the bomb bay to check each cluster of incendiaries. Flight engineer Sgt. **Olan Garret** climbed on the wing to inspect the fuel and oil quantities. Radar operator Flight Officer **Walter Kraus** clambered into the aft compartment to preflight the radar set. The gunners checked ammunition and remote sight operation of the turrets studding the aircraft above and below. Nothing was left to chance. The margin for error was nil.

"The crew watched the clock. With more than a hundred airplanes moving into the air from Tinian's two parallel runways, everything and everyone had to act with precision. Start engines, taxi, and takeoff were scheduled to the minute. A slip-up meant moving to the end of the bomber stream. Nobody wanted to be last. A thirty-minute planned fuel reserve for fifteen and a half hours of flight was a meager margin.

"The Eddie Allen shuddered at the end of the runway as I applied full power: the Superfort strained and inched forward on the fully set brakes. Copilot Lt. **Lou Bicknese** counted off the last ten seconds. Brake release. We felt the forward surge. Airspeed up — nose up — airborne with a swirl of coral dust from the end of the short runway, and we skimmed a scant 200 feet over the Marine encampment on the ridge line a mile away. Then the dip down to a few hundred feet over the water to raise the wing flaps and gain airspeed for the climb. The Eddie Allen was on its way!

"Now came the long haul into the night, cruising smoothly, skirting the tops of the broken cloud deck over the peaceful Western Pacific. After Iwo Jima, the bright moon and navigational stars were obscured by a thin high overcast, forecasting the approach to the persistent band of storm clouds lying across our course to the east of Japan and parallel to the coastline. Finally we emerged from the front into the lighter blackness.

"Tokyo! Light from the fires in the city shone on the overcast clouds and was reflected back on the black waters of Tokyo Bay. The net effect revealed the totality of the city to bombardiers, matching the daylight target photos taken earlier in the week.

"We could see a stream of planes over the southern end of Tokyo Bay and alongside Mount Fuji to the initial point, a town thirty miles southwest of Tokyo lighted by the Pathfinders. Some of the planes were caught in the crossed beams of searchlights, absorbing punishment from antiaircraft fire, but holding their steady inexorable course onward to the target.

"Suddenly left gunner Cpl. **Vic Braeunig** shouted a warning. There was no time to act. All that we saw was the dark hulk of another bomber passing a few feet below the Eddie Allen. Taut nerves drew tighter as we pressed on.

"Nearing the initial point, the airplane ahead was caught by searchlights. Flak focused on it as it turned toward the target, weaving to escape the lights. The Eddie Allen was no more than 500 yards behind. Off to the right another plane, paralleling our course, was pinned to the cloud ceiling by the lights.

"Successive lines of searchlight and flak batteries picked up the B-29 in front and swung past us to spear the airplane behind. Ahead and to the left, a plane exploded — the victim of flak or enemy fighters. The pieces fell for a very long time. There were no parachutes. Another B-29, wavering in the lights, turned from the target area eastward to the sea, trailing a plume of white smoke from one wing.

"Tokyo was now partially shrouded by an enormous column of smoke as the fire storm grew with each additional load of bombs. We learned later that the ground wind feeding air to the fire storm was said to have approached a hundred miles an hour.

"Our aiming point was the edge of the fire storm. Bombardier **Billingsley** had the target in his bombsight, the bomb run was on. Airspeed, altitude, and heading became critical. The Eddie Allen was committed for the next three minutes to steady, unwavering flight.

"Then lights hit the plane with what seemed physical force. Contrasts in the cockpit were remarkable — shadows appeared to be made of solid substance while the rest was brighter than day. Then the flak began — to the left and slightly to the rear.

"**Billingsley** leaned forward to look below and threw himself back with a shout: "Wow!" Slowing visibly in its upward flight, an antiaircraft shell passed a foot in front of the nose of the Eddie Allen, exploding harmlessly a hundred feet above and behind.

"Eddie Allen" of the 45th Bomb Squadron, 40th Bomb Group. (Courtesy of C. Gordon Brough)

"Bombs away! Bomb bay doors closed!" **Billingsley** shouted.

"Almost simultaneously, the Eddie Allen was slammed hard. The left wing was thrown upward. Tail gunner Cpl. **Jim Taliaferro** cried, "We're hit!" Then he was silent.

"The top gunner, Sgt. **Dan Thorne**, called over the intercom: "Tail gunner, tail gunner, this is CFC [Central Fire Control]. Come in! Come in!"

"**Taliaferro** came back, 'I'm O.K. We're hit! Can't see much.'

"Another round of flak lifted the Eddie Allen with great force. The plane slid to the right, diving, turning seaward, accelerating faster and faster. The airspeed needle approached the red line. Any faster and structural failure might occur. The searchlights still held the plane tightly, but flak fell further behind. The plane slowed, leveled off, and headed east. The Eddie Allen entered the welcome darkness of the weather front.

"It was time for me to take stock of the battle damage. I went into the front bomb bay. Hydraulic fluid dripped from broken lines and cables hung loose. The rear bomb bay told the same story. Miraculously, the radar equipment between was unscathed.

"In the aft gunners compartment, the crew stuffed cushions into holes in the fuselage. Unbelievably, none of the men had been wounded by penetrating shrapnel. Right gunner Cpl. **Bob Mautner** had the narrowest escape; a piece of shrapnel had buried itself in his seat.

"A gaping hole a yard in diameter had been blasted in the elevator, not six feet from the tail gunner. It looked bad, but until landing the pressures on this control surface would be minimal. It would probably hold.

"Navigator Flight Officer **Frank Moch**, waiting at the front end of the crew tunnel, announced calmly, 'Captain, the leading edge of the left wing outboard of number two is red hot.'

"I looked from the astrodome to the left wing. There was a long, dull red line, a foot behind the true leading edge, a glow feathered back toward the rear of the wing. A thin wisp of white smoke peeled back from the number one engine.

"Left gunner **Braeunig** reported, 'Smoke from number one engine increasing — more sparks than before.'

"Decision: 'Feather number one.'

"The propeller ground to a position of attention, blades turned into the slipstream.

" 'How's the smoke?' copilot **Lou Bicknese** asked.

" 'Appears to be thinning, fewer sparks,' **Braeunig** reported.

" 'Request permission to transfer fuel from number one fuel cells,' came from flight engineer **Garrett**.

" 'Roger! Start pumping,' I replied.

" 'Smoke real thin now, hardly any sparks,' **Braeunig** announced.

"A short time later the flight engineer reported that only 800 gallons had been transferred from the outer fuel cells of the left wing — 800 when it should have been 1,100. Our reserve fuel was gone. We would have to stop at Iwo Jima, the halfway mark between Tokyo and Tinian. Besides refueling, there would be repairs to be made. It would be days before the Eddie Allen would be back at Hardstand 11 and under the care of crew chief **Mahli.**

"Fifty miles from Iwo, radio operator Sgt. **Ralph Desch** called for clearance to land, reported battle damage and requested weather.

" 'Iwo weather zero zero. Expected to remain for the next six hours. Crashed aircraft on the runway. Iwo closed to all air traffic. Enter orbit area Charlie. Stand by,' came the reply.

"Six hours! Six hours? It would take less time than that to reach Tinian, yet according to the fuel gauges, flight log, and charts, the fuel reserve for four-engine flight was lost. Reaching Tinian on three engines did not seem possible. The Eddie Allen would have to ditch on the open sea. The question was, Where? Here at fog-shrouded Iwo or as near as possible to sunny Tinian? It had to be Tinian.

"We radioed for an escort. At least a sea search would not be necessary. Moments later a nearby B-29 answered navigator **Moch's** marking flare from the Very pistol, and the Eddy Allen had an escort.

"Now was time for the most extraordinary precision in flying, navigation, and engine power management. Throttling back to settings below the demands of the maximum range charts and flying as smoothly as possible, we headed for Tinian and home. We took every opportunity to penetrate the occasional tall clouds, to feel the life-giving turbulence within them that lifted us fifty feet — one hundred feet — once as much as 300, and to slide gently downward to the next cloud, and the next.

"It seemed impossible. The fuel gauges sank steadily, but slower than the charts specified. Altitude lost was fought for and surrendered grudgingly. The Eddy Allen passed the point where ditching at sea had been predicted. Suddenly there was Tinian Island, the air crowded with B-29s landing in a steady stream!

" 'West Tower, Victor One Nine. Emergency landing. Battle damage. Minimum fuel. Flare marks position.'

"The single red flare arched skyward. The approaches were emptied of airplanes. The runway was cleared for the Eddy Allen. Wheels down. Elevator reaction sluggish, but firm. Flaps down half way. Little difference in reaction noted. We were going down.

"The Eddy Allen settled smoothly on the runway. The nose gear took its share of the weight as the airspeed fell. The right wing settled to rest, but the left wing hung drooping like that of a winged mallard!

"Taxiing slowly, the Eddy Allen rolled to a stop on Hardstand 11. Mission number twenty-four was over.

"The Eddy Allen had been mortally wounded and there'd never be a mission number twenty-five.

"A hole in the lower surface of the sagging left wing near the root of number one engine was large enough for head and shoulders. The entire internal wing structure was visible. Dividing walls between the fuel cells were burned away. The Eddy Allen had taken a dud round of antiaircraft fire, but the friction of that hot shell had started the fuel burning in the cells. We had transferred fuel from this burning tank. Less than fifty gallons of fuel remained in the other tanks. We had flown sixteen hours on fuel for fifteen and a half. Incredible!

"The path of the dud was still clearly visible in the upper part of the wing, but the dud itself was gone. The main wing spar checked out later at one-half its specified hardness.

"Repair was out of the question, but so was destruction. The name, the indomitable spirit of Eddie Allen, was a thing to be preserved. And it was! The Eddie Allen, stripped of nonessentials, was moved to our training area. There, beside newly constructed Quonset huts, it became a classroom for practicing emergency procedures until the war ended some three months later.

"What happened to the plane? I don't know, but I do know eleven men owed their lives to some force — some spirit — that averted the midair collision, shielded the crew from flying shrapnel, caused the round that hit the wing to be a dud, put out the fire, held the weakened wing together, and kept the engines turning long after their fuel should have been gone.

"Eddie Allen once told his staff, 'Remember, it is not enough that these planes fight the enemy. They must endure; they must bring their crews home.' The B-29 that bore his name had met that ultimate test."

By the late spring of 1945, the Japanese Empire was in tatters but the enemy refused to acknowledge defeat (or did not

Daylight formation of B-29s in 1945. (Courtesy of Glen Ralston)

Bombs away by B-29s over Japan in 1945. (Courtesy of Glen Ralston)

recognize it). Except for a few enemy bases in the Pacific that had been by-passed and neutralized and so effectively out of the war, the Japanese had been driven from the Solomons, the Marshalls and the Gilberts, the Carolines, the Marianas and all of New Guinea. The Philippines had been invaded at Leyte by troops of Gen. Walter Kreuger's Sixth Army on 20 October 1944, Manila was liberated by 3 March 1945 and most of the rest of the Philippines secured by June 1945. On 19 February the Fourth and Fifth Marine divisions (part of the Third Marine Division was called in later) stormed ashore on Iwo Jima, half way between the Marianas and Japan, and secured the strategic island in four weeks of the most brutal fighting of the entire war. The tiny (5 miles by 3 miles) island would be of immense value to the

XXIst Bomber Command, even before it was finally cleared of the enemy defenders. In March, when the fighting on Iwo Jima was barely over, the 20th Air Force would station its 7th Fighter Command there whose aircraft (P-51s) had sufficient range to escort the Superforts all the way to Tokyo. General **"Mickey" Moore** commanded the 7th Fighter Command. By the time Iwo fell to the Marines the U. S. Navy was sweeping clean all sea approaches to Japan and by the spring of 1945, the Empire's life lines to its overseas supplies — oil, iron and aluminum — had been cut. By war's end, only a few months away now, Japan's merchant fleet would be reduced to a fraction of its war-time peak tonnage and would be nearly useless. The once vast Empire was now reduced to a besieged, strangled, starving few islands.

In reference to the role played by Iwo Jima in the bombing efforts of the B-29s from the Marianas, the following is excerpted from LeMay and Yenne's excellent book "Superfortress" (pp. 128-9):

*"The first B-29 to be saved because of Iwo Jima landed there not two weeks after the Marines had taken the airfield. The runway was yet to be widened, there were no facilities to support a B-29, and the island was still under constant fire from Japanese positions when a Superfort piloted by Lieutenant **Raymond Malo** came away from a mission over Japan badly shot up and with a malfunctioning fuel system. The transfer switch that should have given the plane access to its reserve tanks was shot out and there was only one alternative to ditching at sea—Iwo Jima. [The actual date of this event is hard to*

The B-29 "The Spearhead" was named as a tribute to all who fought for the island of Iwo Jima. (Courtesy of Dave Rogan)

come by but it appears to have occurred on the 4 March mission to Tokyo. Lt. **Malo** was in the 1st Bomb Squadron, 9th Bomb Group, 313th Wing on Tinian; he was lost on another mission a couple of weeks later. Auth.]

"The B-29s had yet to be cleared for landings on Iwo's barely functional runway, but **Malo** and his crew decided to take the chance. **Malo** managed to contact the jury-rigged entity that constituted the Iwo Jima control tower, and explained their desperate situation. 'Okay Monster,' the air traffic controller replied in reference to the huge plane's call sign. 'You can land. Runway 4000 feet [the B-29s were used to 8500 feet]. Under mortar fire . . . steel craters on the left. Come on in. Good luck.'

"**Malo** would need that luck. He would be landing a damaged plane on a crude half-length runway that was under

heavy mortar fire. The plane hit the runway hard, brakes and tire rubber steaming black smoke from the heat of friction, but it stopped. Safely.

"Four hours later, the mortars had been silenced, and the big plane took off again for Tinian with its tanks full. **Malo's** Monster *was the first of 2400 Superfortresses that would live to fight another day, thanks to the invaluable field on Iwo Jima. Eventually the runway was lengthened, widened, and even paved. The Marines paid a heavy price for Iwo, but their sacrifice saved the lives of thousands of U.S.A.A.F. crewmen."*

This event was remembered from another viewpoint, that of **Frank Gardner**, who was a member of a Marine Air Support Control Unit on the ground at Iwo. This Unit identified targets for air strikes by carrier planes. **Gardner** remembers the day that the first B-29 landed on the island:

"One late afternoon early in the first week of March, 1945, after we had completed our work of directing air strikes, a distress call came over our radio. One of the Army's B-29s was flying south over the Pacific Ocean, short on fuel because of damage from enemy antiaircraft fire over Japan. It would not be able to reach its base and would have to splash down in the ocean unless Motoyama Airfield Number One on Iwo Jima was ready to accept an emergency landing.

"We responded by radio to the crippled bomber that the newly captured airstrip was still being repaired by the Navy but an emergency landing could be attempted. We suggested that the aircraft circle offshore south of the island to use up fuel to make the landing attempt less hazardous, and to come in under cover of darkness, thereby not provoking enemy artillery fire, which was still capable of hitting the airfield from its entrenched positions on the higher ground north of our front line.

"At nightfall, with the airfield in complete darkness and the aircraft flying without lights, we used radar and radio communications to 'talk' the bomber down to a near perfect landing. At the northern end of the runway, it collided with an embankment of black volcanic ash, inflicting minor damage to one of its propellers."

The taking of Iwo Jima spurred a sort of love affair between the 20th Air Force and the U. S. Marines, such that a new B-29 was named in honor of the 5th Marine Division, the "Spearhead" Division, that assaulted Iwo Jima, along with the 4th Marine Division. Maj. **Dave Rogan** remembers the event:

"By this time, our B-29 Man-O-War had been shot up and patched up after 17 missions and we were due for a new aircraft. General Rockey, commander to the Fifth Marine Division, requested of General Davies, commander of the 313th Bombardment Wing, that a B-29 be named for the Fifth Marine Division. Our crew was selected and the crew was proud to have a new ship named Spearhead.

"The brass of the Fifth Marine Division and the 9th Bombardment Group got together and had a dedication ceremony on Tinian August 17, 1945. About 100 Marines took part, including their band. The flight crew of the Spearhead also took part in the ceremony. All in all, it was fun, and since our crew led manly of the missions, the Spearhead was an appropriate name.

"..... our two waist gunners were twins (**Burton** and **Langdon Dyer**) and, as far as I know, were the only twins ever to fly combat missions together."

The final great land battle for American troops began on Okinawa on 1 April 1945 and lasted until 21 June. Between these dates (on 9 May) Germany had surrendered and the war in Europe was over. Now massive amounts of supplies, equipment and men were released from that theater of war and were on their way to the Pacific, including Gen. Jimmy Doolittle's 8th Air Force from England and later 12th Air Force air support units from Italy.

The XXIst Bomber Command was enlisted to help out in the invasion of Okinawa as it had helped on numerous missions to Iwo Jima in preparation for the invasion of that island. Okinawa was Japanese soil (a prefecture) and it was heavily defended. While the Iwo campaign was still raging, the U. S. Navy was sending its carrier planes to Okinawa, hitting airfields and anything else that might give our invading troops troubles. They were able to deliver between 100 and 200 tons of high explosives per day on Okinawa, a very considerable quantity of ordnance for carrier-based sorties. The B-29s started flying missions to Okinawa in the middle of April and continued them until the middle of May (with as many missions to Japan as could be fitted in). The Superforts delivered 2,500 to 3,000 tons of ordnance per day on Okinawa. Airfields were the prime targets when the weather was good (bombardiers had to actually see an airfield with the Norden bombsight in order to hit it), otherwise radar was used to bomb strategic targets on the island through an undercast. Over Okinawa, the skies rarely cleared in the spring and the air crews got a lot of radar bombing experience.

The Japanese introduced a new weapon in 1945 which they used to its potential during the battle for Okinawa. This was the kamikaze or "Divine Wind" suicide air attacks. Desperately seeking a way to avoid defeat, Japan began to employ suicide as an officially sanctioned weapon. Young pilots who joined the kamikazes, were trained to crash their bomb-laden planes into Allied ships. There were many volunteers. The kamikaze pilots were first seen at Leyte Gulf in October 1944. At Okinawa they made 1,500 individual attacks on Allied ships. Altogether, they sank 34 naval craft (none larger than a destroyer), and damaged 358 others, many severely. Despite these deadly assaults, the kamikazes had little affect on the pursuit of the war and no affect on its final outcome.

On 12 April 1945 President Franklin D. Roosevelt, exhausted from years of stress and overwork, died at Warm Springs, Georgia. Vice President Harry Truman assumed the Presidency of the United States.

This day of 12 April had additional importance for the crew of the B-29 *City of Los Angeles* in the 52nd Bomb Squadron, 29th Bomb Group of the 314th Wing flying out of Guam's North Field. Maj. **George A. "Tony" Simeral** was the Aircraft Commander on this mission to the Empire, and his radio operator was S/Sgt. **Henry E. "Red" Erwin**. On this mission **Erwin** was to perform an act of incredible heroism that would earn for him the Congressional Medal of Honor, the only Medal of Honor to be awarded to a member of the 20th Air Force. The following is taken from Edward F. Murphy's excellent book "Heroes of World War II."

MISSION: TOKYO
12 APRIL 1945

The City of Los Angeles *was the lead B-29 for the 52nd Bombardment Squadron's attack on Koriyama, Japan, on April 12, 1945. As the lead plane it would give the signal at the Initial Point — the start of the bomb run — for the other B-29s to join in a tight formation. The signal was a white phosphorus bomb dropped from a release pipe in the B-29's belly.*

Aboard the City of Los Angeles, *S.Sgt.* **Henry E. Erwin**, *the radio operator, had the responsibility for launching the signal bomb. Encased in a steel canister*

approximately thirty inches long and four inches in diameter, the smoke bomb weighed about twenty pounds. Equipped with a six-second delayed-action fuse, once free of its release pipe the bomb would fall for about three hundred feet before igniting. It would burn at several thousand degrees Fahrenheit for about five minutes before going out.

Many of the B-29's crew felt the release pipe was too close to the ship's bomb bay for comfort. The City of Los Angeles *carried more than three tons of incendiary bombs in its main bay that day. If the signal bomb should somehow reach the incendiaries the resulting explosion would obliterate the* City of Los Angeles *and any planes unfortunate enough to be near it.*

Erwin *had enlisted in the Army Air Force for flight training on July 27, 1942, at age twenty-one in his hometown of Bessemer, Alabama. Midway through Aviation Cadet training he washed out. Because he'd shown skill with the radio, the Army sent him to radio school for further training. By April 1945 he was the senior radioman on the* City of Los Angeles. *He had ten missions under his belt. Fifteen more and he could go home.*

Erwin *relaxed as the pilot, Capt.* **Anthony Simeral**, *leveled the B-29 at altitude for the run to Koriyama. The furthest target yet for the Marianas-based bombers, Koriyama lay northeast of Tokyo. Because it hosted a complex of important chemical factories, Koriyama would be well defended by Japanese fighters and antiaircraft guns.*

The flight was uneventful until they neared the Japanese coast. Then enemy fighters tore into the B-29 echelons, weaving in and out of the formation at speeds exceeding four hundred miles per hour. Soon the black clouds of exploding antiaircraft shells dotted the sky.

Captain **Simeral** *maintained his position. Experience had taught him that evasive action offered no real protection against the enemy fighters. Besides, he had to fly straight and level to the IP.*

Erwin *prepared the signal bomb. He held it over the release pipe. His finger found the triggering mechanism.* **Simeral** *spoke over Erwin's headphones, "Now, Sergeant Erwin." Erwin let the silver cylinder slide through his hands.*

What happened next was a one-in-a-million unpredictable fluke. The signal bomb failed to clear the gate at the bottom of the release tube. Then it ignited. The blast blew the bomb back up the tube, full into **Erwin's** *face. As he recoiled backwards, his nose melting*

off his face, the white-hot missile fell on the floor of the plane. It lay only feet from the incendiaries.

The other crewmen froze. Thick clouds of white smoke spewed forth from the burning bomb. At any minute it could ignite the firebombs.

Erwin, *despite the pain engulfing his face, crawled toward the bomb. Through eyes nearly closed from white blisters he could just make out the blur of the superhot bomb. As he reached it the* City of Los Angeles *suddenly lurched downward. The billowing smoke had filled the cockpit.* **Simeral** *and his copilot, Lt.* **Roy Stables**, *choking on the smoke, were having a hard time controlling the plane. The heavy bomber dove toward the earth.*

In the bomb bay **Erwin** *reached for the bomb. His fingers rolled the missile toward him. He scooped up the blazing projectile, rose to his feet, and started toward the cockpit. Behind him, the other crewmen watched in frozen horror as* **Erwin**, *a mass of flames from the waist up, moved toward the copilot's window.*

Erwin *staggered forward, his once-wavy hair now singed off. His nylon life jacket melted into his skin. Flames burst forth from his trousers and shoes. The smell of roasting flesh filled the plane. The pall of smoke completely filled the narrow corridor.* **Erwin** *moved solely by instinct.*

A few feet short of the cockpit **Erwin** *found the navigator's collapsible table blocking his way. Incredibly, he tucked the white-hot projectile under his arm, fumbled for the table's latch with his free hand, found it, and folded the table out of the way.*

Stables *stood in shock as the flaming apparition stumbled into the cockpit.* **Simeral** *still fought to control the plane. The smoke blocked his view of the instruments and out the window. Behind him,* **Erwin** *screamed, "Open the window! Open the window!"*

Stables *lurched for the side window. As soon as he had it open* **Erwin** *lobbed the bomb through it, then collapsed in flames on the floor of the bomber.* **Stables** *and another crewman sprayed* **Erwin** *with fire extinguishers until all the flames on his body were out. The once-handsome youth moaned quietly at first, then deep shrieks of pain escaped his burnt throat. His fifteen-second journey through hell had ended, but his real ordeal was only beginning.*

Once the smoke cleared the cockpit, **Simeral** *pulled the B-29 out of a dive just three hundred feet above the hills of Japan. Then, while* **Stables** *adminis-*

Lt. Eugene J. Voss looking out the window of the 314th Wing B-29 showing records of the 19th, 29th, 39th and 330th Bomb groups. The flags are missions made by each Bomb Group under the 314th Bomb Wing of the 20th AAF. (Courtesy of Eugene Voss)

tered morphine to ease **Erwin's** horrible pain, **Simeral** set a course for the emergency strip on Iwo Jima.

Crash wagons met the *City of Los Angeles* as she ended her roll-out on Iwo's main strip. They rushed **Erwin** to the hospital. For the next several days doctors frantically worked on him. Nearly every inch of his body from the waist up was covered with third-degree burns. He received whole blood transfusions, injections against infection, internal surgery, and the first of hundreds of skin grafts. Though conscious throughout most of the ordeal, **Erwin** hovered on the brink of death. Few of the doctors expected him to live.

Because of the very real danger that **Erwin** would not survive his extensive burns the officers of his squadron prepared a Medal of Honor recommendation the very night of his deed. At 5:00 A.M. the next morning they hand-carried the documents to the headquarters of the Twentieth Air Force on Guam. Gen. **Curtis LeMay** was awakened. He read and signed the recommendation. The recommendation was flashed to Washington. Two days later word came back: Approved.

Erwin, in the meantime, had been flown from Iwo Jima to the more complete medical facilities on Guam. It was there, while he lay swathed in bandages from head to toe, that the Medal of Honor was pinned to his bandages on April 18, 1945. The award was one of the quickest on record. Because of the haste behind the ceremony, a Medal of Honor on display at Army headquarters in Honolulu had been specially flown to Guam. General **LeMay**, who made the presentation, said to **Erwin**, "Your effort to save the lives of your fellow airmen is the most extraordinary kind of heroism I know."

Erwin answered simply, "Thank you, sir."

From Guam **Erwin** was flown to the burn unit at the Army's Valley Forge hospital outside Philadelphia. There he began the painful daily debridement baths necessary to wash away dead skin and commenced therapy and more skin grafts.

Miraculously, **Erwin** survived his severe burns. He was discharged from the hospital on October 8, 1947. At home again in Alabama **Erwin** went to work for the Veterans Administration. He also married and raised a family.

The *City of Los Angeles* was nearly lost again on a June mission to Kobe. **"Tony" Simeral** was at its controls again: The following is taken, in part, from the AIR FORCE magazine, January 1994, and was written by John L. Frisbee:

MISSION: KOBE, JAPAN
5 JUNE 1945

On the morning of June 5, 1945, B-29s of the 52nd Bomb Squadron, 29th Bomb Group, lifted off the runway at North Field, Guam, for the long flight to Japan, their target the industrial city of Kobe. Leading the squadron was Maj. George A. "Tony" Simeral, one of the most experienced aircraft commanders in the 314th Wing. In 1942 and 1943, he had flown thirty combat missions in the Mediterranean as a B-24 commander. Then came a year as a B-24 instructor — duty he considered dull and almost as dangerous as combat. He volunteered for B-29s and was assigned to the 29th, which arrived at Guam in February 1945 with Major Simeral as commander of a lead crew.

(Prior to June 5, **Simeral** had flown twelve B-29 missions. He was the pilot of

City of Los Angeles on April 12, when his radio operator, Medal of Honor recipient S/Sgt. **Henry "Red" Erwin**, saved the crew by carrying a burning phosphorus bomb to the flight deck and throwing it out the copilot's window).

When the B-29s arrived at the assembly point for their Kobe strike, enemy fighters attacked. As City of Los Angeles began the twelve-minute bomb run heavy guns defending the target opened fire. The deputy leader was shot down, and Major **Simeral's** aircraft took flak hits on the number four engine, ripping a three-foot hole in the outer wing panel through which 800 gallons of fuel began siphoning away.

With the Superfortress's wing and engine sheathed in flames and only two minutes from release point, Major **Simeral** had two alternatives. He could drop out of formation and concentrate the crew's attention on controlling or putting out the fire. The formation would then be without a lead bombardier, on whose release all other bombardiers dropped their bombs. It would be too late for the other bombardiers to bomb accurately. The mission would fail.

Major **Simeral** instead chose to keep power on the burning engine, increasing the danger of explosion, and lead the squadron to the release point. His bombardier, Lt. **Bill Loesch**, made the necessary final adjustments and put the squadron's bombs on target. Mission accomplished. Now **Tony Simeral's** mission was to save his crew.

He shut down the burning engine and was forced to drop out of formation. Twelve enemy fighters immediately attacked the lone and damaged bomber. Lieutenant **Loesch** and the waist and tail gunners, Cpls. **Herb Schnipper, Vern Widmayer**, and **Ken Young**, shot down three fighters and damaged several others, driving them off. Near land's end, the fire was extinguished. Then a second wave of fighters closed in. The situation rapidly deteriorated from perilous to critical. Sgt. **Howard Stubstad's** upper forward and aft turrets were out of ammunition, but from the now-distant formation a B-29, piloted by Lt. **Leo Nathans**, dropped back in time to drive off the fighters.

Without enough fuel to return to Guam and with undetermined damage to the right wing, a dead engine, and two turrets out of ammunition, Major **Simeral** told navigator Capt. **P. I. Youngkin** to set course for Iwo Jima. Flight engineer Sgt. **Vern Schiller** calculated that with precise cruise control, fuel for the 700-mile flight was marginally adequate. **Simeral** was informed that there were enemy fighters in the vicinity of Iwo. If they made it, they would have to rely on friendly antiaircraft artillery and fighters to protect the nearly defenseless bomber.

Three hours later, Iwo came into view as their fuel gauges hovered near zero. However, the crew's relief was short-lived A damaged B-29 ahead of City of Los Angeles crashed on the runway, closing it down. With what little fuel remained, Major **Simeral** had to attempt a landing on a short fighter strip, which they would have to share with a fuel-starved P-51. To add to the tension, the strip could not be seen from the flight deck of a B-29 until the last moment because of terrain.

Once the strip came in sight, there was another unhappy surprise. The left wing flaps extended fully, but those on the right wing went down only part way. The B-29 started to roll. Unable to raise the flaps, **Simeral** and his copilot, Lt. **Roy Stables**, used their combined strength to level the bomber and spike it on the runway.

Airmen of 5th Squadron, 9th Bomb Group, 313th Wing. (l. to r.) Standing: Howes, Carpi, Scheaffer, Frick, and Bates. Kneeling: Watson, Merhood, Mika, Simard, Lafflin, and Williamson. (Courtesy of Leonard Carpi)

Another duty assumed by the Superforts of the 20th Air Force was a concerted mine laying effort in Japanese home waters. For this job, Gen. **Davies'** 313th Wing based on Tinian was chosen; the usual mine-laying mission was made up of from 25 to 30 planes. The first mission was on 27 March followed by another on the 30th; four more missions were launched in April, ten in May, eleven in June and twelve in July. By wars end, the 313th had flown over 1500 mine laying sorties. Mines were sown at harbor approaches and entrances on the Japan and Korea coasts but most of the effort went into mining of the Shimonoseki Strait, a narrow waterway running between the main home islands of Honshu and Kyushu. This channel was the main passage for ships from Korea and north China ports to the eastern ports of the Japanese home islands. The 313th mined the Strait almost constantly to the end of the war and virtually shut down shipping through this waterway. Before the mine laying began the Japanese were sending over a half million tons of shipping through the waterway each month. At war's end the monthly shipping tonnage had been reduced to about 5,000 — with the help of about 8,800 tons of mines. Since much of this cargo was food from the Asian mainland, the 313th was slowly starving the Empire's home population.

With Okinawa firmly in Allied hands by the end of June, 1945, the strategic planners began looking at the details of the final invasion of the Japanese home islands — Kyushu (Operation Olympic) and Honshu near Tokyo (Operation Coronet). Elements of the 8th, 12th and 15th Air Forces with their B-17s and B-24s and B-25s were to be flown to Okinawa from their European bases. With the 5th, 7th, 13th and 20th Air Forces in the Pacific, the 10th and 14th Air Forces on the Asian mainland and the 11th Air Force in the Aleutians, there easily could have been *ten thousand* heavy and very heavy bombers available for the invasion of Kyushu, scheduled for November, 1945 and Honshu in 1946.

The "She Wolf" was a cartoon in the base newspaper at Walker AAB, Kansas. The cartoonist gave permission to Crew K-5 to use the name. The plane was renamed the "City of Duluth" before the war ended, and toured that city in celebration after the war. (Courtesy of William Grossmiller)

The crew of the B-29 "Miss You". (Courtesy of F. McDowell)

Following the Okinawa missions the XXIst Bombing Command returned to the business it was best at doing: the strategic bombing of the Japanese home islands. From the middle of May forward, The Command could launch from 400 to 500 planes per mission — or more — whenever the target required that number. By July there were more than 1,000 B-29s based in the Marianas, those of the 58th Wing of the XXth Bomber Command having arrived by air and ship to West Field on Tinian from India during April and May. On 1 August,

836 Superforts were launched to four Japanese cities, the largest B-29 mission of the Pacific war. As the stockpile of incendiaries was replenished, the fire bomb raids were resumed: 633 incendiary sorties in April; 2,994 sorties in May; 3,191 sorties in June; and 4,862 sorties in July. The 25 May incendiary raid on Tokyo by more than 400 planes was devastating: twenty-two square miles were burned out and now half the city of Tokyo had been destroyed. The Empire was not only starving, it was being burned to the ground.

Several types of incendiary bombs were used on these fire raids. The M-50 was a four-pound magnesium bomb that had a time-delay fuse on it; it could burn through steel, and water had no effect on the burning. The M-69 was set to burst at about 2,000 feet altitude and discharge 38 smaller incendiary munitions of about six pounds each that were spread over a wide area. Other incendiaries were designated M-47, a 100-pound napalm bomb, against which water was useless, used most often by the pathfinder airplanes; the 20-pound TE-4, and the huge 500-pound M-17 and M-76. Other types of incendiaries used less often bore the designations E-28, E-36 and E-46 clusters, all fusible to be discharged at 2,000 to 2,500 feet. The use of these types varied with the nature of the target; M-69s were most effective against wooden structures, and the M-50s against steel and concrete buildings and steel bridges. On most raids mixtures of these were used along with some conventional high explosives.

Another excerpt from LeMay's and Yenne's book "Superfortress" gives the flavor of the decisions that were made on a daily basis during these Superfort operations from the Marianas. Quoting LeMay:

"I had a directive which was never changed and was approved by the Joint Chiefs, a list of targets ranked by priority. When we were ready to run a mission, we would get the airplanes loaded with fuel and bombs, and the crews would be briefed and prepared. If the weather was good we'd hit a precision target that had a high priority on the target list. If the weather wasn't good I would pick a target out of what was left of the good incendiary targets. We always assigned secondary targets in case the bombers didn't have a chance at the primary because of the weather, but I don't remember what they were. Usually if the weather was bad over the primary target it was bad over the secondary target too, in which case the B-29s would scatter their bombs all over the place by radar. They didn't do very well from high altitude with radar. We would hit one of the areas that had a low priority on the target list and burn down a dozen targets in addition to the whole damn town. By June 1945, however, we were hitting the high-priority industrial areas just as fast as we could, bombing both at night (low-flying incendiary missions) and in the daytime (high-alti-tude precision bombing). When the war ended, our score was more than sixty-five cities completely burned down.

"At night we couldn't hit precision targets that were high on the target list, such as airplane plants, because we couldn't see them. These were the targets that we had to see in order to bomb accurately. At night or in bad weather, though, we could hit a big industrial area, or a section of a city that we could identify. At night we could identify a city without identifying anything in it. We would then try to get our best radar operators in there first to put down some incendiaries. That would get a fire started that would show up the target and orient the rest of the bombers as they came in. We could get an area, like the south side of a city for instance, or the whole town when we had enough airplanes. We wouldn't hit an oil refinery or a shipyard during the night until the 315th arrived in June with the AN/APQ-7 Eagle radar. From that point, we could bomb as many as four precision targets nightly."

To illustrate the rapid build-up of forces in the Marinas the arrival dates of the various Wings on the islands is of interest (a Wing at this time could contain up to 200 aircraft). Gen. Hansell, first Commander of the XXIst Bomber Command, flew in the 73rd Wing's first B-29 to Saipan's Isley Field on 12 October 1944; by December two long runways were operational on Saipan and space was constructed for 60 B-29s. Gen. **O'Donnell** commanded the 73rd. The second Wing to arrive in the Marianas was Gen. **Davies'** 313th on 27 December 1944; the 313th was stationed at North Field on Tinian and one of its groups would do most of the mine laying in Japanese waters later in the spring of 1945. Gen. **Thomas Power's** 314th Wing arrived at North Field, Guam, in January of 1945 in time for the first large incendiary bomb raid on Tokyo on 9 March. And Gen. **Frank Armstrong's** 315th Wing arrived at Northwest Field, Guam, in April of 1945; the 315th's Superforts (B-29Bs) were equipped with the new high-resolution AN/APQ-7 Eagle radar. These planes in addition were devoid of gun turrets except for the the tail turret (which was equipped with an additional protective radar). As noted before, Gen. **Roger Ramey's** 58th Wing arrived from India in April of 1945, closing down operations of the XXth Bomber Command there. It joined the 313th on Tinian. Additionally, the 3rd Reconnaissance Squadron with their F-13s (the photo-recon variant of

the B-29) was based on Guam with the 314th and 315th. The men of the 3rd Recon Squadron earned their pay every day with their often highly dangerous photo missions over Japan, keeping LeMay appraised of the progress of the bombing. So, with the arrival of the 315th Wing in June of 1945, there were five B-29 Wings and a Recon Squadron based in the Marianas with over a thousand Superforts available to the mission planners; a maximum effort by all five Wings (20 Bomb Groups) could launch more than 800 planes to Japan on a single mission. Very soon, 1,000-plane Superfort raids over Japan would have been commonplace, but the war didn't last that long. Arriving on Tinian in June, about the same time that the 315th Wing arrived on Guam, were the Superforts of Col. **Paul W. Tibbet's** 509th Composite Group (Nuclear). The XXIst Bomber Command had grown into a force capable of unimaginable destruction.

As noted above, following the Okinawa missions, the months of June, July and August 1945 saw an increase in the intensity of the Superfort raids on Japan from the Mariana bases. American B-24 Liberators and fighters — P-51s and P-47s — began to range over Japan from their new Okinawa bases. Now the Empire was being decimated day and night with high explosives and incendiary bombs, and its waters were strewn with mines. Twenty-four missions in June, thirty-one in July and nineteen in August, and then the enemy had had enough and sued for peace. Targets during these months numbered every conceivable kind of military installation. During the Okinawa missions the major targets were airfields on Kyushu Island, airfields that were the source of the hated kamikaze flights. From June the targets were all on the Japanese home islands: urban and industrial areas of the major cities, aircraft and engine factories, arsenals, oil refineries, petroleum storage depots, rail yards and other transportation targets. And throughout this rain of both high explosives and incendiary bombs, Superforts of the 313th Wing continued to mine numerous ports, harbors and waterways throughout Japan and Korea; enemy shipping into and out of their home ports was now virtually shut down. The list of cities struck by the XXIst Bomber Command looked like a gazetteer in a Japanese map atlas. Three hundred- to five hundred-plane raids were common in these final months of the war. When LeMay ran out of the major cities, he

Three B-29s on flight line at Tinian in 1945. (Courtesy of Glen Ralston)

started to burn the smaller ones. Aircraft and engine production went underground to escape the devastation but their output was now only a small fraction of the wartime peak production and could not keep up with the mounting losses.

Russell J. Locandro was a radar bombardier in the 44th Bomb Squadron, 40th Bomb Group, flying out of Tinian. In between his 16 missions to Japan, he was leader of a 7-piece band that would play for anyone, anywhere, anytime — and did. He kept a careful record of his missions to Japan which began in May of 1945:

MISSION: NAGOYA
MAY 17, 1945
LT. COVEY AND CREW
SHIP #541

This was an exciting mission for me as it was my first mission. It was a Primary Visual Target and Primary Radar Target Mission. We had P-51 Fighter escorts from Iwo Jima. It was exciting to see the mainland of Japan for the first time. We dropped the bombs because this was a daylight mission and the target was clearly visual. Had a few fighters make passes at us, but they didn't come in close enough for our gunners to pour lead into them. Results of the mission were excellent. (Flak was light). Combat flying hours logged in at 15:25. #25 BOMBIN BUGGY II.

MISSION: HAMAMATU
MAY 19, 1945
LT. COVEY AND CREW
SHIP #729

Hamamatu was a propeller plant in Japan and this was a night mission and my first combat radar run. The bombs went right into the target area. We had two fighters following us and our left gunner got one as he was coming in at 9 O'Clock. (Flak moderate). Combat Flying Hours logged in at 15:00. #22 NIPPON NIPPER III.

MISSION: KOBE
JUNE 5, 1945
LT. COVEY AND CREW
SHIP #752

This was a Primary Night Radar Mission which was an aircraft factory in Kobe, Japan. Results were excellent again as shown in radar pictures. The flak was moderate - we had damage to our ship, nothing serious however. Saw several planes, but they stayed their distance and we did not get any shots at them. Combat flying hours logged in at 14:35. #15 WICHITA WITCH.

MISSION: OSAKA
JUNE 7, 1945
CAPT. BLEILER AND CREW
SHIP #527

This was another Night Radar Mission to the industrial part of the city as the target. The bombs hit their mark completing another good mission. The Group bombardier flew this mission with us and he commended me for my bomb run. Combat flying hours logged, 15:30. #18 DEVILISH SNOOKS.

MISSION: OMIYA (TOKYO)
JUNE 10, 1945
LT. DOHERTY AND CREW
SHIP #541

We got off OK from Tinian, however when we got as far as Iwo Jima our #4 Engine had given us so much trouble our Engineer said we should return to our base as we couldn't make the mission. Combat flying hours logged in at 5:40. #25 BOMBIN BUGGY II.

MISSION: OMUTA (TOKYO)
JUNE 17, 1945
CAPT. BLEILER AND CREW
SHIP #527

The purpose of this mission was to burn out the industrial urban area which ended in another successful Night Radar run. This was a good mission as far as flak and planes went as we didn't encounter either one. Our landing gear would not come down when we got back to the base; however after about a half hour of working on it, our Engineer was able to get it down. Combat flying hours, 15:15. #18 DEVILISH SNOOKS.

MISSION: TOYOHASHI
JUNE 19, 1945
LT. BUECHLER AND CREW
SHIP #729

This was another Radar Night Mission, of course an excellent run. I had my finger on the bombs-away button about 20 seconds before 'Bombs Away' and we hit some turbulence shaking us and consequently causing me to release the bombs 20 seconds before time. The Bombs however hit the target area, and chalked up another good run. No flak, no fighters. Combat flying hours, 15:25. #22 NIPPON NIPPER.

MISSION: KAWOSAKI
JUNE 26, 1945
LT. BUECHLER AND CREW
SHIP #729

This was a Day Precision Mission, the target was an aircraft plant. The bombardier did an excellent job putting the bombs in the front door, stringing the bombs clear through the back of the building. We had P-51s from Iwo Jima; they did an excellent job of taking care of the enemy planes. They were kept busy all day shooting the planes as it seems the Japs sent out all the Air Force they had. Flak was moderate. Combat flying hours, 15:15. #22 NIPPON NIPPER.

MISSION: OKAYAMA
JUNE 28, 1945
LT. BUECHLER AND CREW
SHIP #729

This was another industrial urban target and was another successful Night Radar Mission. We had little flak on this mission, no planes. My radar set went out before we reached the mainland of Japan; I worked on it and fixed it in time to complete my bomb run. Combat flying hours, 14:45. #22 NIPPON NIPPER.

MISSION: KURE
JULY 1, 1945
LT. BUECHLER AND CREW
SHIP #729

Lt. Buechler and crew did a fine job on this Night Mission which we had a 10/10 undercast, moderate flak & bombs going right in the target area. Yes - that's right, another good bombing mission for the record. Combat flying hours, 14:50. #22 NIPPON NIPPER.

MISSION: CHIBA (TOKYO)
JULY 6, 1945
LT. BUECHLER AND CREW
SHIP #635

There was a lot of sweating before this mission as we were given information that they had mucho and very accurate flak magnet, the flak turned out moderate as were the planes which of course we were happy to see. Combat flying hours 14:10. # & name ???

MISSION: UTSONOMIYA
JULY 13, 1945
LT. BUECHLER AND CREW
SHIP #660

Another Night Radar Mission with 10/10 undercast. Bombardier could not see a thing, and followed my Radar Scope which he also had up front in his compartment. Target was an industrial plant and also the urban area. Post-strike photos showed excellent results. No flak and no planes. Combat flying hours, 15:35. #49 CELESTIAL QUEEN.

MISSION: NUMAZU (SW TOKYO)
JULY 16, 1945
LT. DOHERTY AND CREW
SHIP #139

Something new was added on this mission. Japs were shooting fire balls up at us. No serious damage however. Thank God! We had 8/10 undercast; another Radar run was completed satisfactorily. The flak was light and so were the fighters. Combat flying hours, 14:15. #17 GLOBAL GLAMOUR.

MISSION: FUKUI
JULY 19, 1945
LT. DOHERTY AND CREW
SHIP #752

We saw small arms automatic weapons on this mission for the first time, but we got no serious damage. No fighters were seen on this mission. The target was an urban area where they have a lot of small industries. Another good run chalked up! Combat flying hours, 15:00 #15 WICHITA WITCH.

MISSION: OSAKA
JULY 24, 1945
LT. DOHERTY AND CREW
SHIP #752

Was a daylight raid and we were in the deputy lead. The formation was a very good one, but was almost flubbed up by us. A few minutes before Bombs Away we were hit by flak which caused pressurization to leak out. Co-pilot was flying the ship (without oxygen as we all were). When the Pilot saw us getting out of position and he glanced at the co-pilot and saw he was white as a sheet and almost out. The Pilot immediately put on his oxygen mask and took over the controls and advised us to make sure to put our masks on which we did promptly. Everything from here on turned out to be O.K. We were carrying 4,000 pound bombs for the first time and after I lined the bombardier on course and he visually saw the target, I went to the right blister to see where and what damage the bombs would do. The bombs hit the target and from 20,000 feet in the air you could see the tremendous damage made. The post photos showed surrounding buildings actually down from the terrific explosion it made. after the bombs hit the target I saw the worst flak I ever saw. It looked like a big cloud or blanket of black smoke. Our bomb bay doors were really torn and shattered. We thought that we were going to have to land at Iwo Jima but we did not and made it back to Tinian O.K. Combat flying hours, 15:40. #15 WICHITA WITCH.

B-29s flying by Mount Fujiyama, which was used as the initial point on many missions. (Courtesy of Glen Ralston)

The 19th Bomb Group B-29s pass Mt. Fujiyama on way to target from Guam. (Courtesy of Ray Maguire)

MISSION: TSU
JULY 28, 1945
LT. DOHERTY AND CREW
SHIP #752

We were ready to go on this Mission, however we did not go because one of our engines did not check out. #15 WICHITA WITCH.

MISSION:HACHIOJI (TOKYO)
AUGUST 1,1945
LT. DOHERTY AND CREW
SHIP #752

Ship #752 rides again after being patched up from the Osaka mission, and once again off to bomb Tokyo (West). Target was the urban area and being a night mission, radar was put to work once more. We saw two planes and our left gunner got one of them. He saw him and gave him a few bursts and that was the end of him, and it went down smoking. Was a twin engine plane (Nick). Flak was light. Combat flying hours were 14:25. #15 WICHITA WITCH.

MISSION: IMABARI
AUGUST 5, 1945
MAJ. EIGENMANN AND CREW
SHIP #660

My LAST mission (Thank God) and everything went O.K. on this mission. The bombardier & I dropped the bombs together, radar and bombsight. The tail gunner said he saw the bombs fall directly into the target area.. PERFECT BOMB RUN! No planes, no flak. #49 CELESTIAL QUEEN.

The Bombs of August

It is quite possible that the war could have ended in 1945 — without employing nuclear weapons — due solely to decimation of the home islands by the 20th Air Force and control of the seas by the U. S. Navy. Gen. LeMay was convinced he would do it. Many analysts of the period thought he could, also. The Japanese homeland was at the point of starvation, its industry and transportation and utilities were on the verge of collapse. It had almost no air force, navy or merchant marine left. Its cities were being burned to the ground. Most of its communications with the mainland had been cut. True, its troops in occupied countries could live off the land, but eventually even they would run out of the tools to wage war, for they could no longer be supplied by the mother country.

But that is not the way the war ended. On 6 August 1945 (7 August in Japan) a nuclear bomb was dropped on Hiroshima, Japan. On 9 August a second nuclear device (and the last ever to be so used in anger) was exploded over Nagasaki, Japan. The Empire surrendered five days later on 14 August.

This is not the place to detail the history of the development of a nuclear bomb. Suffice to say that the first sustained nuclear chain reaction was achieved at the University of Chicago on 2 December of 1942. For the next two years a group of the nation's most prestigious scientists and engineers at Los Alamos, New Mexico worked out the details of how to create and control a nuclear explosive device. This effort was the so-called "Manhattan Project." In the spring and summer of 1944 the Army Air Force began putting together the combat team that would deliver the bomb — if one could be made. A very large complex had been created at Oak Ridge, Tennessee to extract and accumulate a considerable quantity of highly radioactive isotopes of the elements uranium and plutonium. Either of these could be used to make a bomb of enormous destructive power; both elements were so used. All this was done in absolute secrecy; very few people in the country knew anything of these events. Some of those that did know had doubts that this device could be controlled in a combat situation. At this time, only two Heads of State knew even of the attempted development of this weapon: President Truman and Prime Minister Churchill.

Col. Paul W. Tibbets, Jr. was chosen to command the team that would deliver the first nuclear bomb on Japan — if the bomb could be made. Paul Tibbets was a B-17 commander in Europe with a "can do" reputation and highly skilled at the controls of the big bomber. He was on the first Flying Fortress strike into Nazi-occupied France in August of 1942; he was at various times the command pilot on highly secret missions of General Mark Clark and General Dwight Eisenhower which initiated the Allied invasion of North Africa in November of 1942. He came back to the States and learned to fly the B-29 in the spring of 1944, first at Grand Island, Nebraska and then at Alamogordo, New Mexico. Tibbets had been around in this war and knew his business. The 393rd Bombardment Squadron was to be the combat unit of the team Tibbets was to lead, and it moved to their new training site at

Wendover Army Air Field in northwest Utah in September of 1944 (from Fairmont Army Air Field in southeastern Nebraska). In December of 1944 the 509th Composite Group was formed, Tibbets commanding, and the 393rd became the only squadron in this Group. Strictly to follow organization rules the 509th was to be a part of Gen. **Frank Armstrong's** 313th Wing on Tinian's North Field, but Gen. Armstrong was not told the mission of the 509th. Stateside however, the Group was assigned to the 2nd Air Force commanded by Gen. **Uzal G. Ent** whose headquarters unit was at Colorado Springs south of Denver. Tibbets and Ent met in September of 1944 together with Navy Captain **William Parsons** who was the ballistics expert in the Manhattan Project.

The 509th was designed to be an almost self-sufficient Group with its own engineering, materiel, and ordinance units and its own air transport system in the form of five C-54s (Douglas four-engine Skymaster). A single combat element in the squadron (there would be five such elements) consisted of three B-29s: one carried the bomb, a second was instrumented to record various parameters of the explosion, and the third plane was loaded with cameras to photograph the blast. As noted above, five such combat elements were formed so the squadron was comprised of 15 Superforts; others would be added later. All guns except the twin .50 caliber tail guns were removed from these planes. The air crews began months of rigorous training at Wendover, much of it aimed at dropping huge 10,000-pound practice bombs shaped like the atomic weapons they *may* drop if the Los Alamos teams could build one. Tibbets and his pilots would practice over and over again a sharp turning maneuver (155 degrees from course) to be executed immediately after bomb release. The turn was designed to put as much distance as possible between the airplane and the blast. Parsons had calculated that the distance *had* to be a minimum of 8 miles from the blast. Closer than 8 miles and the bomber was in jeopardy of suffering severe damage by shock waves of the explosion. The Norden bombsight was to be used so the target had to be clearly visible; no radar bombing on these missions. 1,800 men were required to crew and keep flying these 15 (soon 18) Superforts.

Following the meeting with Ent and Parsons at Colorado Springs, Tibbets went to Wendover in Utah to assume command of what in essence was his private Air

Force. Col. Tibbets was 29 years old at this time, and the only man at Wendover that knew about the nuclear bomb and the highly secret mission of the 509th. Their training began in September of 1944 in Utah and would continue until May of 1945 when their deployment to Tinian Island began. All this enormous effort and organization and no one was absolutely positive that a nuclear bomb could be made work when shackled into the bomb bay of a B-29.

Deployment of the 509th to the Pacific began in May of 1945 and about this time Gen. LeMay was given some bare bones facts about the new weapon and the 509th Bomb Group that was added to his XXIst Bomber Command. All information pertaining to the 509th was on a "need to know" basis. Paul Tibbets arrived on Tinian on the 18th of May and the ground crews showed up on the 29th. Thirteen days later on 11 June their B-29s began to arrive, 18 in all. The 509th occupied a separate area from the 58th and 313th Wings already on Tinian and, by direct order, Tibbet's crews

didn't have much to do with the rest of the XXIst Bomber Command on the island. Various snide remarks about the 509th winning the war all by itself began to circulate because no one knew what they were doing and no one could find out. Before June ended Tibbets had made some trips back to Washington to offer his expertise on target selection — if he ever got to carrying an atomic device in a B-29. At these meetings, three primary targets were finally selected: Hiroshima, Yokohama, and Kokura, along with several secondary targets. All were important to Japan's war effort, either from an industrial or military standpoint.

And now began the hands-on combat training of the 509th, both air crews and ground crews. Training began on 30 June and continued through to the end of July. Navigational training flights to Iwo Jima, now in American hands, and bomb runs on enemy-occupied Rota Island half way between Tinian and Guam. Longer training missions were flown to bomb Truk (650 miles from Tinian) and Marcus Island (about

800 miles from Tinian). All these training missions were with only a few (up to nine) Superforts. With these short flights as an introduction to combat, the air crews now were sent out on a series of twelve bombing missions to Japan using precision (Norden bombsight, therefor visual) procedures. Two to six Superforts went on these missions to Japan, starting on 20 July, and they dropped replicas of the atomic device which they planned to carry but containing conventional high explosives.

During these training missions, on 16 July 1945 near Alamogordo, New Mexico, the United States detonated the world's first atomic bomb, yielding a gigantic explosion with the reported destructive force of 20,000 tons of TNT. The test was so secret that even our most trusted ally, Great Britain, was not told of the impending trial. The device used plutonium as the nuclear explosive. A uranium bomb was not tested simply because the scientists at Los Alamos were positive that the simpler uranium bomb would work. On 26 July a 13-point ultima-

Enola Gay (US Air Force Photo)

tum was sent to the Japanese government by the United States, Great Britain and China demanding Japan's unconditional surrender. The ultimatum was rejected. There was a brief debate in Washington on whether to use this awesome weapon, brief because President Truman wasted little time in sifting through the advice given him and reaching the decision to employ this weapon.

On the same date as the ultimatum to Japan, the cruiser *U.S.S. Indianapolis* arrived at Tinian with elements of the first atomic bomb. One element was a chunk of radioactive uranium — the so-called target chunk. The rest of the necessary uranium would be flown in. This uranium bomb was of a more conventional cylindrical shape than the more round plutonium device. (Four days later the *Indianapolis*, on its way to the Philippines, was torpedoed and sunk by a Japanese submarine with the tragic loss of almost 900 lives). This uranium bomb was called "Little Boy" but it was anything but little. Ten feet long and 28 inches in diameter, it weighed 9,700 pounds of which about 50 pounds was uranium, and special shackles had to be built to mount it into the bomb bay of a B-29. In his book "Superfortress" LeMay recalls that to load the bomb into a Superfort the bomb was placed into a hole in the ground and the plane taxied over it. The bomb was then jacked up into the forward bay; ground crews took an entire afternoon to do this job for one bomb. They were told to be very careful. The fuse necessary to detonate this device was not installed; the bomb was considered far too dangerous to be armed on the ground. The term "atomic bomb" — a by-word today — was not used by the men on Tinian. In fact, almost everybody except Col. Tibbets (and Navy Capt. William "Deke" Parsons who would be on the first atomic mission) thought it was just a big mass of conventional high explosive — roughly 5 tons of it including the massive bomb casing.

Gen. LeMay's orders were to deliver this bomb to a selected target some time after 3 August. The date would be determined by when the airplane and the bomb were ready, and the weather over the target. On 5 August (a Sunday) reconnaissance flights over Japan reported clearing weather and the nuclear mission was then set for the next day. The primary target was Hiroshima, a port city on western Honshu, and the secondary target was Kokura bordering the Shimonoseki Strait in northern Kyushu; the tertiary target was Nagasaki, also on Kyushu. Three Superforts would fly on this mission: Col. Paul Tibbet's *Enola Gay*, plane No. 82, with the bomb; the photographic plane, No. 91, flown by Capt. **George Marquardt**; and the instrument plane *The Great Artiste* flown by Maj. **Charles Sweeney**. Finally a fourth Superfort (pilot **Charles McKnight's** *Top Secret*) would fly as far as Iwo Jima, land there, and act as a back-up to *Enola Gay* if Tibbets should have any trouble on the way to the target.

In Tibbet's crew were co-pilot Capt. **Robert A. Lewis**, bombardier Maj. **Thomas W. Ferebee**, navigator Capt. **Theodore J. Van Kirk**, radar officer Lt. **Jacob Beser**, flight engineer M/Sgt. **Wyatt E. Duzenbury**, radar operator S/Sgt. **Joseph S. Stiborik**, tail gunner Sgt. **George R. Caron**, waist gunner Sgt. **Robert A. Shumard**, radio operator Pfc. **Richard H. Nelson**, Navy Capt. **William S. Parsons** who was responsible for arming the nuclear weapon in flight, and Parson's assistant Lt. **Morris R. Jepperson**. 12 men in all on the *Enola Gay*.

Three weather planes (*Straight Flush, Full House and Jabbitt III*) took off about 0130 hours on 6 August 1945, a Monday, to scout the three targets, and the *Enola Gay* and the two others took off about 0245.

Tibbets eased forward the four throttles and slowly picked up speed into the blackness of the early morning. At about 140 mph the heavily loaded B-29 would fly but Tibbets held it down; 145, 150, 155 mph; there was no more runway left and Tibbets eased back on the yoke and *Enola Gay* lifted off and was over the ocean. Copilot **Bob Lewis** didn't like this hold-down technique of taking off a B-29 but he had learned to live with it.

At 4700 feet Navy Captain **William S. Parsons** and Army Lt. **Maurice Jepperson** entered the bomb bay to arm "Little Boy." They installed a cylindrical slug of uranium backed up with a small charge of TNT. The conventional explosive would ram the slug down a gun barrel tube into 50 pounds of target uranium near the tail fins of the bomb to initiate a chain reaction and the consequent nuclear explosion. The whole arming process took 25 minutes. Approaching Iwo Jima at 0555 at 9300 feet the back-up plane (*Top Secret*) descended to land and the other three closed up in formation. Tibbets started a slow climb to bombing altitude after passing Iwo Jima. They were at bombing altitude well before the three planes crossed the coast of Japan. Parsons had been monitoring the bomb almost continuously since he had armed it; he checked and rechecked everything and then checked again. Everything seemed to be normal. The weather plane over Hiroshima reported 2/10 cloud cover and that was clear enough for a visual run on the target.

Eight minutes before the scheduled drop the target came into view. All concurred that it was Hiroshima. Fifteen and one half miles east of ground zero bombardier **Thomas Ferebee** picked up the I.P. (initial point) and **Tibbets** turned on the target at 264 degrees. **Tom Ferebee** had put in 64 missions in B-17s out of England with the 97th Bomb Group, a lot of them with **Paul Tibbets** as his pilot. They were used to each other. In his autobiography, **Tibbets** describes the bomb run:

"On this important morning, however, the wind was from the south at 10 miles an hour. This was an unpredictable variance, of course. In our planning, we had played the odds and lost.

*"But **Tom Ferebee** was an old hand at dropping bombs with the wind, against it, or in a crosswind. From long experience, he knew what a falling bomb would do under almost any condition, and he knew how to crank all the right information into his Norden bomb sight. It made little difference to him that we were delivering a bomb of tremendous size, unlike any that had ever been dropped in warfare. . .*

*"All that was necessary, upon reaching the I.P., was to fly the predetermined heading, with calculated allowance for the direction (170 degrees) and velocity (8 knots) of the wind. Since we were flying under visual conditions the problem was simplified. The three-minute run gave **Ferebee** time to kill the drift and establish a perfectly stable platform for the release of the bomb.*

*". . . Navigator and bombardier compared notes and agreed that our ground speed was 285 knots (330 mph) and the drift to the right required an 8-degree correction. Adjustments were made to the bomb sight, which was now engaged to the autopilot for the bomb run. **Ferebee**, **Van Kirk**, and I were working as a team, as we had many times before over Europe and North Africa. As we approached the city, we strained our eyes to find the designated aiming point.*

*"At a distance of 10 miles, **Ferebee** suddenly said, 'Okay, I've got the bridge.' . . . The T-shaped bridge was*

easy to spot. Now it was up to Tom and me. We were only 90 seconds from bomb release when I turned the plane over to him on autopilot.

*". . . By this time, **Tom Ferebee** was pressing his left eye against the viewfinder of the bomb sight, using a headrest we had devised at Wendover [Utah] to make sure that he was always in the same position.*

" 'We're on target,' he said, confirming that the sighting and release mechanism were synchronized, so that the drop would take place automatically at the pre-calculated point on our bomb run."

At this point **Ferebee** switched on a radio tone heard by the other B-29s that bomb release was 60 seconds away. It was a warning to get ready to initiate evasive action following the drop. When the tone ceased, "Little Boy" plummeted from the bomb bay of *Enola Gay.* Forty-three seconds later at an altitude of 1,890 feet (sensed and triggered by a bomb-mounted radar altimeter) the bomb exploded and 78,000 citizens of Hiroshima died instantly. Another 62,000 would die later from radiation sickness and burns. Four and a half square miles of the city were destroyed in the blast. The reported power of this bomb was equivalent to 13,000 tons of TNT. It was 0815 plus 17 seconds in Hiroshima and an hour later in the Marianas.

Tibbets turned sharply 155 degrees on bomb release and dived slightly; this much-practiced maneuver was designed to put 8 miles between the plane and the point of the explosion. The 8 miles was calculated to prevent the explosion and the ensuing shock wave from causing serious damage to the *Enola Gay* and to the other planes of the strike group. Less than six hours later at 1458 local time the big B-29s touched down on Tinian, completing the 12 hour and 13 minute mission.

The following first person description of this first drop of an atomic bomb came from a 22 May 1992 interview of bombardier **Thomas Wilson Ferebee.** Tom was a 21 March 1942, class 42-4, graduate of Kirtland Field Bombardier School, Albuquerque, New Mexico. The interview was by Colonel E. C. "Ned" Humphreys, Jr., U.S.A.F. (Ret), during the 7th Annual Reunion of World War II bombardiers.

"I got back from Europe in April 1944, and was told by General Hoyt Vandenberg that they had something for me but he didn't know exactly what it

*was. I loafed around until August when I was told to report to Wendover, Utah. There was really nothing there when I arrived. **Paul [Tibbets]** was being briefed by the atomic officials — Oppenheimer being one.*

"I was briefed on the bomb and was told that it would destroy everything within 8 miles. Having dropped a lot of bombs in Europe, I didn't believe that this was possible, so I kinda' laughed at them.

*"Earlier **Tibbets** had been told that we could get two crews, by name, from any source. I, more or less, selected the bombardier and navigator for the other crews. Tibbets, who had been test flying the B-29, selected the pilots. **Theodore J. "Dutch" Van Kirk**, having flown with us in Europe, was our navigator and **Kermit Beahan** was the other bombardier.*

"As far as training, I flew with a crew from Wright Field [Dayton, Ohio] for about a year, dropping different size and shaped bombs, for at that time we had no idea what the bomb would look like, how long it would be, or what its ballistics would be. We knew more about the second weapon [Fat Man] because it could only be shaped round!

"At the onset of testing, my bomb [Little Boy] was so long that it required both bomb bays but continuing development reduced it to a size where it would fit in one bomb bay.

"I didn't go to Tinian until the 14th of July whereas the ground crew and aircraft went over in May of 1944. Paul joined us three days later, at which time I had only one more required unit drop [involving the fusing mechanism] before the real thing. We all flew this last practice drop.

"We took off after 2 [it was 0245] in the morning and upon reaching 4,000 feet Captain [U.S. Navy, William] Parsons and Lt. [Maurice] Jepperson went back into the bomb bay and fused the weapon. I went back and watched them.

"When we were about 50 or 60 miles from Hiroshima, I could see the target area clearly distinguished by outline of rivers. When Dutch [navigator Capt. Theodore J. Van Kirk] rolled me out on my heading to target, the target area was visible through the bombsight, but was not so clearly defined nor was I close enough to permit placing the rate [lateral] crosshair on the aiming point.

"About two minutes from release point the airplane was turned over to me and I put the crosshairs on the aiming point and let it ride. I just more or less sat there until 'bomb away' since everything else had been 'killed' [drift and target approach speed had been compensated for — synchronized].

"We did a diving turn of 155 degrees immediately after bomb away. When we leveled out, the cloud had nearly reached our altitude. During our turn we felt a bump — like a flak explosion. I turned to Paul and said 'The so and sos are shooting at us!' About that time we both realized that the 'bump' was concussion from the bomb explosion.

"We were supposed to pull down our dark 'welder's glasses' after bomb away, but with Paul flying instruments in the turn and me closely following the bomb in flight, we both forgot. As a result we were momentarily blinded from the flash which was the brightest I had ever seen and possibly will ever see."

As noted above, aircraft escape tactics were implemented after the drop and forty three seconds later, at an altitude of 1,890 feet, the bomb exploded, signifying that **Tom Ferebee's** duty had been successfully fulfilled. Photo experts measured the photographs and concluded — later confirmed by on-site inspection — that the bomb had detonated 700 feet away from the briefed aiming point from a drop altitude of over 30,000 feet. Four and a half square miles of Hiroshima had been destroyed and the world was about to see an end to its most devastating conflict.

President Truman announced to the world, some 16 hours after the drop (but still 6 August in the U. S.) the news of the nuclear strike on Hiroshima. No word came from the government of Japan other than mention of just another incendiary attack. It was learned later that the government was in fact near panic.

LeMay continued with his work. On 7 August he sent 124 Superforts to a Toyokawa naval arsenal with high explosives and another 29 on a mine laying mission to Japanese and Korean waters. On 8 August three missions sent 372 B-29s to Yawata, Fukuyama and Tokyo with high explosives and incendiaries. Since the first of May the XXIst Bomber Command had dropped an average of over 34,000 tons of ordnance *per month* on Japan. Still no word from the Japanese government leaders. They were confused and unable to take action.

The skies over Japan continued to be a dangerous place to make a living. 1st Lt. **Walter R. Ross** of Lenexa, Kansas was a navigator (radar) on the *Nipclipper* on his 16th mission over Japan on 8 August 1945. The target was Yawata on Kyushu Island. The commander of the plane was 2nd Lt. **George Keller** of Fort Wayne, Indiana. **Ross** describes this mission:

MISSION: YAWATA
8 AUG. 1945

*"After 'Bombs Away' the plane received hits from anti-aircraft fire or Japanese fighter planes or both. The right engine caught fire. Damage to the bomb bay doors prevented them from closing. Keller ordered the crew to bail out. Last out of the plane, Keller hit the water before his chute fully opened. The plane crashed over him and he was not seen again. With only four one-man life rafts, the crew grouped together as two B-29s piloted by Capt. **Walter "Scotty" Tulloch** and Capt. **Gordon Nelson** hovered over them, dropping additional (four) one-man rafts.*

"The ten survivors drifted seven days in the Sea of Japan. (The survival rations consisted of four canteens and five cans of water from the life rafts, plus hard candy, chocolate and bouillon cubes from one C-1 vest). Japanese fishermen picked up the crew and brought them to shore where they were beaten and blindfolded. Still blindfolded, they walked, rode in a truck and train to Hiroshima, arriving on August 16th, 1945. They were the first Americans to enter Hiroshima after its destruction by the atomic bomb on August 6th 1945.

*"Placed in a revetment, they slept on the ground. Guards brought in two U. S. airmen, **Norman Brissette** and **Ralph Neal**. They had been recaptured following the destruction of their P.O.W. camp located in Hiroshima. Both died from radiation sickness and injuries on August 19th 1945. A Japanese Christian, Lt. Nobuici Fukui, successfully resisted an order to execute the Keller crew and obtained permission for their safe passage to a P.O.W. camp on the island of Mukaishima, across from Onimichi, Japan. Fukui requisitioned a truck and hid the crew for two nights in the Ujima Military Police headquarters, fearing violence against them. On the way he drove to the center of Hiroshima, he stopped the truck ordering them to remove their blindfolds so they could see, as he stated, 'how inhumane the Americans were.' 'One bomb,' he kept saying, 'One bomb did all this.'*

"At the Mukaishima camp the crews met up with one 106 Americans from Bataan and Corregidor, as well as 75 British prisoners from Singapore. The crew brought them up to date on the progress of the war.

"The crew remained at Hiroshima Camp 2 until repatriation by the Swedish Red Cross on September 14, 1945. Taken to Yokohama, they then flew to Letterman General Hospital in San Francisco, via Guam and Hawaii. By October, 1945 they were on their way to their respective homes."

*Four men of this crew are still alive at this writing: **Carleton M. Holden**, bombardier, Malden, MA; **Walter R. Ross**, navigator (radar), Philadelphia PA; **Stanley H. Levine**, navigator, Hughsville, PA; and **Martin L. Zapf**, right gunner, Skillman, NJ.*

On Tinian there were the makings for one more bomb. A third would not be ready for a month. The second bomb was ordered assembled and loaded; it was to be delivered on a second city as soon as it was practical to do so. This one was called "Fat Man" and was entirely different in shape and contents from the first. This was a plutonium bomb weighing 10,800 pounds, oval in shape, with an implosion-type triggering mechanism. In this weapon, an envelope of TNT drove a hollow sphere of plutonium into a central core of beryllium-plutonium. This was the type that was tested on a tower in New Mexico barely three weeks earlier. "Fat Man" would be delivered to a second Japanese city by a B-29 on 9 August 1945, a Thursday.

Pilot **Chuck Sweeney** - his B-29 was *The Great Artiste* — was chosen by Tibbets to fly the second atomic bomb mission. But *The Great Artiste* was configured as an instrument ship for the Hiroshima mission so Tibbets ordered Sweeney and his entire crew to take over another B-29, *Bockscar*, whose pilot was **Frederick Bock.** Bock and his crew would fly Sweeney's instrument ship for this mission, so Sweeney and Bock simply switched planes and crews. Sweeney's bombardier was Capt. **Kermit K. Beahan,** and it would be he that would drop the second atomic bomb — on his 27th birthday. Nothing went well on this trip: a fuel pump malfunctioned, isolating 600 gallons of fuel that Sweeney couldn't use for the mission; 45 minutes were lost waiting for one of the accompanying planes to show up at the target area; the primary target, Kokura, was obscured by smoke and three bomb runs were attempted and aborted. Fifty minutes were lost there hoping for a clearing; and finally they decided to divert to their secondary target, Nagasaki.

Nagasaki was also found to be partially cloud and smoke covered (8/10), so a radar bomb run was begun. In the final seconds of the coordinated bombardier-radar bombing run, the clouds thinned and parted sufficiently for bombardier Beahan to take over in an attempt to drop visually using the Norden bombsight. He was almost successful in putting his crosshairs on the intended aiming point when the 'Fat Man' was dropped. The time was 1058. *Bockscar* landed safely on Okinawa with nearly empty fuel tanks except for the unavailable 600 gallons. . As soon as the balky fuel pump was repaired Sweeney took off for Tinian, arriving some 20 hours after the start of the mission. (The Soviet Union belatedly declared war on Japan on this day, hoping no doubt to reap some of the spoils for which she had done nothing against Japan to earn). Although this second bomb to be dropped on Japan was wide of the aiming point, 40,000 more Japanese died. Another 30,000 deaths from radiation and burns would later be directly attributable to the blast.

In the two nuclear bombings, there were about an equal number of deaths and injuries. The dropping of two atomic bombs only three days apart apparently convinced the Japanese that we probably had a supply of these deadly weapons. There were no more ready. Five days later on 14 August the Japanese government surrendered without conditions, accepting all points of the Potsdam Declaration which had formulated the surrender terms, and the most destructive war in human history ended. Gen. LeMay and others have written that the use of the atomic bombs probably saved one million American and probably three million Japanese casualties, since an invasion was now not necessary.

Jim Sullivan, Sun City, AZ, was a Corporal in the 200-man engineering unit of the 509th Composite Group, and reflects on the day the *Enola Gay* returned from Hiroshima:

"Initially, the crew and unit had no idea how many thousands of lives were being lost by one bomb. Some of the crew, in months later, saw the intelligence reports and photos and had some misgivings. But they had no choice, they had their duty to do.

".....I thought it was a good idea at the time. It finished off the war, brought our boys home, and saved millions of lives on both sides of the conflict. I hope that type of weapon is never used again, any place, by anyone."

Following the second nuclear strike LeMay got back to business. On 14 August, the last day of missions against Japan for the XXI st Bomber Command, five missions sent 741 Superforts to several Japanese cities including Tokyo, Akita, Hikari, Osaka, Marifu, Kumagaya, Isezaki and Tsuchizakiminato, and on a mine laying mission to Shimonoseki Strait and other waterways. Both high explosives and incendiaries were carried on these final strikes. One of these was certainly the last B-29 mission flown against Japan. Brig. Gen. **Boyd Hubbard, Jr.**, then Colonel and commander of the 315th Wing's 501st Bomb Group, recalls what must have been close to the final Superfort mission of the war in a letter to **Denny Pidhayny**, Recording and Historical Secretary of the 58th Bomb Wing Association. Hubbard was flying the *Fleet Admiral Nimitz* on this mission:

"The last mission of World War II? Certainly the last B-29 mission. President Truman announced the surrender during our return to Guam after dropping a full bomb load on the oil refinery at Akita on northwest Honshu the night of 14-15 August. This was the longest combat strike [from the Marianas], 3740 miles. We met over 300 B-29s and passed thru them as they departed Tokyo leaving it an inferno. All a/c had landing lights on and flying at assigned altitudes, but even so it was a bit unnerving.

"On this mission, as we taxied out, the Fleet Admiral Nimitz *showed a 200 r.p.m. magneto drop on one of the two mags on one engine. When we reached the runway, a jeep drove up in front and an officer signaled 'cut engines.' He climbed in and said, "Admiral Nimitz says the war is over." He had departed and I had just finished 'chiding' my crew chief for the only time the* Nimitz *was short of perfection when another jeep arrived with, "... get going; LeMay hasn't received word that the war is over." We cranked up and took the runway knowing that if we (number 1) didn't get a good power check and runway speed and had to chop throttles and abort, most probably all the a/c would follow us back to the ramp, thinking that the mission was scrubbed. Thankfully, the* **Nimitz** *performed and we lifted off, greatly relieved."*

All this was simply too much for the enemy and he capitulated on the 15th. On 2 September (U.S. time) on board the battleship *U.S.S. Missouri* in Tokyo Bay the surrender document was signed by representatives of the warring parties. According to the recollections of General **Edmundson** of the 468th Bomb Group over 1,000 B-29 Superfortresses sent up from the Marianas thundered over the signing ceremonies — a reminder to all of the source of the near total destruction of the Japanese homeland. The Superforts now

B-29s dropping supplies to prisoners of war in September of 1945, as seen from the Bombardier's position. (Courtesy of Sampson Friedman)

Parachuted supplies dropped to POW camp after the conclusion of the war. (Courtesy of Sampson Friedman)

had one more job to do in the Pacific: supply drops on mercy missions to Prisoner of War camps in Japan and China.

The few accounts of B-29 missions in this story is admittedly woefully inadequate. Many pages could be written, and have been, for example, on the exploits of Major **H. W. "Hap" Good**, colorful pilot of a colorful crew in the 792nd Bomb Squadron, 468th Bomb Group; about "Hap's" mission to Bangkok when his bombs hung up at the target and he dumped them into the jungle, blowing up an enormous (and completely hidden) gasoline dump.

Or, the 16 missions of the *General H. H. Arnold Special* again in the 468th Bomb Group which hit every major target the 58th Wing could reach from India and China (including Palembang, Yawata and Anshan). General Arnold had scrawled his name on this plane on 11 January 1944 at Boeing's Wichita plant, saying: *"This is the plane I want this month."* The *Special* ran low on fuel on a November 11 mission to an aircraft factory at Omura on Kyushu and, unable to reach a friendly base in China, allowed itself to be escorted to the Vladivostok Naval Air Station, 700 miles due north of Omura, by Russian fighters. The crew got out of Russia three months later, but the *Special* just disappeared. (It and a couple of other Russian-captured B-29s were later copied as the Tu-4, rivet for rivet).

XXth BOMBER COMMAND
PRIMARY MISSIONS

JUNE 1944, SORTIES: 145
5 Jun. 1944	Bangkok, Siam
15 Jun. 1944	Yawata, Japan

JULY 1944, SORTIES: 87
7 Jul. 1944	Sasebo, Japan
7 Jul. 1944	Hankow, China
29 Jul. 1944	Anshan, Manchuria

AUGUST 1944, SORTIES: 142
10 Aug. 1944	Palembang, Moese R. Sumatra
10 Aug. 1944	Nagasaki, Yawata, Japan
20 Aug. 1944	Yawata, Japan

SEPTEMBER 1944, SORTIES: 199
8 Sep. 1944	Anshan, Manchuria
26 Sep. 1944	Anshan, Manchuria

OCTOBER 1944, SORTIES: 258
14 Oct. 1944	Okayama, Formosa
16 Oct. 1944	Okayama, Formosa
17 Oct. 1944	Okayama, Formosa
25 Oct. 1944	Omura, Japan

NOVEMBER 1944, SORTIES: 314
3 Nov. 1944	Malagon, Malaya
5 Nov. 1944	Singapore, Malaya
12 Nov. 1944	Omura, Japan
12 Nov. 1944	Nanking, China
21 Nov. 1944	Omura, Japan
21 Nov. 1944	Shanghai, China
27 Nov. 1944	Bangkok, Siam

DECEMBER 1944, SORTIES: 285
7 Dec. 1944	Mukden, Manchuria
14 Dec. 1944	Bangkok, Siam
18 Dec. 1944	Hankow, China
19 Dec. 1944	Omura, Japan
19 Dec. 1944	Shanghai, China
21 Dec. 1944	Mukden, Manchuria

JANUARY 1945, SORTIES: 436
2 Jan. 1945	Bangkok, Siam
6 Jan. 1945	Omura, Japan
6 Jan. 1945	Nanking, China
9 Jan. 1945	Kirun, Formosa
11 Jan. 1945	Singapore, Malaya
14 Jan. 1945	Kagi, Japan
17 Jan. 1945	Shinhiku, Formosa
25 Jan. 1945	Saigon, Singapore
27 Jan. 1945	Saigon, Indochina China

FEBRUARY 1945, SORTIES: 460
1 Feb. 1945	Singapore, Malaya
7 Feb. 1945	Saigon, Bangkok
11 Feb. 1945	Rangoon, Burma
19 Feb. 1945	Kuala Lumpur, Malaya
24 Feb. 1945	Singapore, Malaya
27 Feb. 1945	Penang, Malaya

MARCH 1945, SORTIES: 371
2 Mar. 1945	Singapore, Malaya
4 Mar. 1945	Yangtze River
10 Mar. 1945	Kuala Lumpur, Malaya
12 Mar. 1945	Bakum Island
17 Mar. 1945	Rangoon, Burma
22 Mar. 1945	Rangoon, Burma
28 Mar. 1945	Saigon, Singapore
29 Mar. 1945	Bakum Island
29 Mar. 1945	Singapore, Malaya

XXIst BOMBER COMMAND
PRIMARY MISSIONS

OCTOBER 1944, SORTIES: 26
28 Oct. 1944	Dublon Island
30 Oct. 1944	Dublon Island

NOVEMBER 1944, SORTIES: 282
2 Nov. 1944	Dublon Island
5 Nov. 1944	Iwo Jima
8 Nov. 1944	Iwo Jima
11 Nov. 1944	Dublon Island
24 Nov. 1944	Tokyo, Japan
27 Nov. 1944	Tokyo, Hamamatsu, Japan
29 Nov. 1944	Tokyo, Yokohama, Japan

DECEMBER 1944, SORTIES: 396
3 Dec. 1944	Tokyo, Japan
8 Dec. 1944	Iwo Jima
13 Dec. 1944	Nagoya, Japan
18 Dec. 1944	Nagoya, Japan
18 Dec. 1944	Japan
22 Dec. 1944	Nagoya, Japan
24 Dec. 1944	Iwo Jima
27 Dec. 1944	Tokyo, Japan
27 Dec. 1944	Japan

JANUARY 1945, SORTIES: 531
3 Jan. 1945	Nagoya, Japan
3 Jan. 1945	Japan
9 Jan. 1945	Tokyo, Japan
14 Jan. 1945	Nagoya, Japan
14 Jan. 1945	Japan
16 Jan. 1945	Pagan Island
19 Jan. 1945	Akashi, Japan
19 Jan. 1945	Japan
21 Jan. 1945	Moen Island
23 Jan. 1945	Nagoya, Japan
23 Jan. 1945	Nagoya, Japan
23 Jan. 1945	Japan
24 Jan. 1945	Iwo Jima
27 Jan. 1945	Japan
29 Jan. 1945	Iwo Jima

FEBRUARY 1945, SORTIES: 762
4 Feb. 1945	Kobe, Japan
4 Feb. 1945	Natsusaka, Japan
8 Feb. 1945	Moen Island
9 Feb. 1945	Moen Island
10 Feb. 1945	Ota, Japan
12 Feb. 1945	Iwo Jima
15 Feb. 1945	Nagoya, Japan
15 Feb. 1945	Japan
17 Feb. 1945	Dublon Island
18 Feb. 1945	Moen Island
19 Feb. 1945	Tokyo, Japan
25 Feb. 1945	Tokyo, Japan
25 Feb. 1945	Japan

MARCH 1945, SORTIES: 2,196
4 Mar. 1945	Tokyo, Japan
9 Mar. 1945	Tokyo, Japan
11 Mar. 1945	Nagoya, Japan
13 Mar. 1945	Osaka, Japan
16 Mar. 1945	Kobe, Japan
18 Mar. 1945	Nagoya, Japan
24 Mar. 1945	Nagoya, Japan
27 Mar. 1945	Omura, Kyushu, Japan
27 Mar. 1945	Shimonoseki Strait, Japan
30 Mar. 1945	Nagoya, Japan

30 Mar. 1945	Shimonoseki Strait, Japan
31 Mar. 1945	Omura, Japan

APRIL 1945, SORTIES: 2,895

1 Apr. 1945	Tokyo, Japan
1 Apr. 1945	Hiroshima, Japan
1 Apr. 1945	Kure, Japan
3 Apr. 1945	Shizuoka, Japan
3 Apr. 1945	Tokyo, Koizumi, Japan
3 Apr. 1945	Hiroshima, Japan
3 Apr. 1945	Tachikawa, Kawasaki, Japan
7 Apr. 1945	Nagoya, Japan
7 Apr. 1945	Tokyo, Japan
7 Apr. 1945	Japan
8 Apr. 1945	Kanoya, Kokubu, Japan
9 Apr. 1945	Shimonoseki Strait, Japan
12 Apr. 1945	Tokyo, Japan
12 Apr. 1945	Tokyo, Japan
12 Apr. 1945	Koriyama, Japan
12 Apr. 1945	Japan
12 Apr. 1945	Shimonoseki Strait, Japan
15 Apr. 1945	Tokyo, Japan
17 Apr. 1945	Kyushu and Shikoku Islands, Japan
18 Apr. 1945	Kyushu and Shikoku Islands, Japan
21 Apr. 1945	Kyushu and Shikoku Islands, Japan
22 Apr. 1945	Kyushu and Shikoku Islands, Japan
24 Apr. 1945	Tachikawa, Japan
24 Apr. 1945	Japan
26 Apr. 1945	Kyushu, Shikoku Islands, Japan
27 Apr. 1945	Kyushu, Shikoku Islands, Japan
28 Apr. 1945	Kyushu, Shikoku Islands, Japan
29 Apr. 1945	Kyushu, Shikoku Islands, Japan
30 Apr. 1945	Kyushu, Shikoku Islands, Japan

MAY 1945, SORTIES: 3,931

3 May 1945	Kyushu and Shikoku Islands, Japan
3 May 1945	Shimonoseki Strait, Japan
4 May 1945	Kyushu, Shikoku Islands, Japan
5 May 1945	Kyushu, Shikoku Islands, Japan
5 May 1945	Kure, Japan
5 May 1945	Tokyo, Japan
7 May 1945	Kyushu, Shikuku Islands, Japan
8 May 1945	Kyushu, Shikoku Islands, Japan
10 May 1945	Tokuyama, Otake, Japan
11 May 1945	Kyushu, Shikoku Islands, Japan
11 May 1945	Kobe, Japan
13 May 1945	Shimonoseki Strait, Japan
14 May 1945	Nagoya, Japan
16 May 1945	Shimonoseki Strait, Japan
17 May 1945	Nagoya, Japan
18 May 1945	Shimonoseki Strait, Japan
19 May 1945	Hamamatsu, Japan
20 May 1945	Shimonoseki Strait, Japan
22 May 1945	Shimonoseki Strait, Japan
23 May 1945	Tokyo, Japan
24 May 1945	Shimonoseki Strait, Japan
25 May 1945	Tokyo, Japan
26 May 1945	Shimonoseki.Strait, Japan
27 May 1945	Shimonoseki Strait, Japan
29 May 1945	Yokohama, Japan

JUNE 1945, SORTIES: 4,260

1 Jun. 1945	Osaka, Japan
5 Jun. 1945	Kobe, Japan
7 Jun. 1945	Osaka, Japan
7 Jun. 1945	Shimonoseki Strait, Japan
9 Jun. 1945	Nagoya, Akashi, Japan
10 Jun. 1945	Central Japan
11 Jun. 1945	Shimonoseki Strait, Japan
13 Jun. 1945	Shimonoseki Strait, Japan
15 Jun. 1945	Osaka, Amagasaki, Japan

15 Jun. 1945	Shimonoseki Strait, Japan
17 Jun. 1945	Kagoshima, Omuta, Japan
17 Jun. 1945	Shimonoseki.Strait, Japan
19 Jun. 1945	Toyohashi, Fukuoka, Japan
19 Jun. 1945	Shimonoseki Strait, Japan
21 Jun. 1945	Fushiki, Senzaki,Japan
22 Jun. 1945	Himeji, Kagamigahara, Japan
22 Jun. 1945	Kure, Japan
23 Jun. 1945	Fukuoka, Karatsu,Japan
25 Jun. 1945	Shimonoseki Strait, Japan
26 Jun. 1945	Nagoya, Kagamigahara, Japan
27 Jun. 1945	Hagi, Kobe, Niigata, Japan
28 Jun. 1945	Okayama, Sasebo, Japan
29 Jun. 1945	Kudamatsu, Japan
29 Jun. 1945	Shimonoseki Strai, Japan

JULY 1945, SORTIES: 5,755

1 Jul. 1945	Ube, Kure, Shimonoseki, Japan
1 Jul. 1945	Shimonoseki Strait, Japan
2 Jul. 1945	Minoshima, Japan
3 Jul. 1945	Kochi, Takamatsu, Japan
3 Jul. 1945	Shimonoseki Strait, Japan
6 Jul. 1945	Chiba, Akashi, Shimizu, Japan
6 Jul. 1945	Osaka, Japan
9 Jul. 1945	Sendai, Sakai, Japan
9 Jul. 1945	Yokkaichi, Japan
9 Jul. 1945	Shimonoseki Strait, Japan
11 Jul. 1945	Shimonoseki Strait, Japan; Pusan, Najin, Korea
12 Jul. 1945	Utsonomiyal, Japan
12 Jul. 1945	Kawasaki, Japan
13 Jul. 1945	Shimonoseki Strait, Japan; Seishi, Masan, Korea
15 Jul. 1945	Naoetsu, Niigata, Japan; Najin, Pusan, Korea
15 Jul. 1945	Kudamatsu, Japan
16 Jul. 1945	Numazu, Oita, Kuwana, Japan
17 Jul. 1945	Shimonoseki Strait, Japan; Seishin, Korea
19 Jul. 1945	Fukui, Hitachi, Chosi, Japan
19 Jul.1945	Amagasaki, Japan
19 Jul. 1945	Oyama, Niigata, Tsuruga, Japan; Wonsan, Korea
22 Jul. 1945	Ube, Japan
22 Jul. 1945	Shimonoseki Strait, Japan; Pusan, Masan, Korea
24 Jul. 1945	Handa, Nagoya, Takarazuka. Japan
25 Jul. 1945	Kawasaki, Japan
25 Jul. 1945	Nanao, Fushiki, Tsuruga, Japan; Seishin, Pusan, Korea
26 Jul. 1945	Matsuyama, Tokuyama, Japan
27 Jul. 1945	Shimonoseki Strait, Japan
28 Jul. 1945	Tsu, Aomori, Ichinomiya, Japan
28 Jul. 1945	Shimotsu, Japan
29 Jul. 1945	Shimonoseki Strait; Najin, Korea

1-14 AUGUST 1945, SORTIES: 2,802

1 Aug. 1945	Hachioji, Toyama, Japan
1 Aug. 1945	Kawasaki, Japan
1 Aug. 1945	Shimonoseki Strait, Japan; Najin, Seishin, Korea
5 Aug. 1945	Saga, Mae Bashi, Japan
5 Aug. 1945	Ube, Japan
5 Aug. 1945	Sakai, Yonago, Nakaumi, Japan; Najin, Korea
6 Aug. 1945	Hiroshima, Japan (nuclear)
7 Aug. 1945	Toyokawa, Japan
7 Aug. 1945	Shimonoseki Strait, Japan; Najin, Korea
8 Aug. 1945	Yawata, Japan
8 Aug. 1945	Fukuyama, Japan
8 Aug. 1945	Tokyo, Japan
9 Aug. 1945	Amagasaki, Japan
9 Aug. 1945	Nagasaki, Japan (nuclear)
14 Aug. 1945	Hikari, Osaka, Japan
14 Aug. 1945	Marifu, Japan
14 Aug. 1945	Kumagaya, Isezaki, Japan
14 Aug. 1945	Tsuchizakiminato, Japan
14 Aug. 1945	Shimonoseki Strait, Japan
27 Aug. 1945	(Beginning of supply drops to P.O.W. camps)

Men of a B-29 crew: Moreton, Sprouse, Von Devender, Bodecker, Robert, Gaylon, and Townsend. (Courtesy of Milton Sprouse)

"Hot T' Trot" flight crew, 345th Bomb Sq, 98th Bomb Wing at Yokota AFB Japan. (l. to r.) Standing: Elmer Pahl, Douglas Hassing, Alfred Baker, Dale Allan, and Eugene Hassing. Kneeling: Robert Swift, Pat Dentale, Robert Owings, Robert Forrster, Otha Nelson, and Roland Robitaille. (Courtesy of Robert Owings)

The five-year saga of the Superfortress in World War Two had finally come to a close. It was flown in combat against only one enemy, Japan, for 14 months and 9 days of America's more than 44 months of war. In those 14 months and 9 days air warfare was changed forever. World War II aircraft combat losses numbered 414 Superforts, a loss rate of 1.32% of the total number of aircraft launched (sorties). The table to the right compares various combat data on some of America's attack aircraft, and medium and heavy bombers with the B-29.

An airplane begins as a lifeless machine. Many lives go into its creation but it remains a mute and unknown thing until a crew of men take their stations within it. Then, the airplane seems to come to life, seems to take on the heartbeat of the men who fly it. So it was with the B-29. First it took lives like a wild thing and was hated, even feared; then it was gradually controlled — like an untamed stallion is broken to saddle — and reluctantly did its crew's bidding. Finally, crew and airplane merged into one and it was tested in battle, over and over again, until it became almost revered, almost alive, responding to every whim. The B-29 was among the greatest airplanes ever built, certainly among the greats of World War II. But it was the men who flew and lived and died in the Superfortress that made it so. Still, it would have one more test to meet.

The Superfortress over Korea 1950–1953

The days of the B-29 were not over with the end of World War II. Construction of the Superforts continued well into 1946. For five years after World War II the Superforts were flown in testing, training and transport roles around the world. It continued breaking records: in November 1945 the *Pucosan Dreamboat* was flown 8,198 miles in 35 hours (its tires were filled with helium). It was a B-29, *Dave's Dream*, that dropped a nuclear test bomb on 93 anchored ships at Bikini Atoll in July of 1946 (Operation Crossroads). When the 1940s came to an end, the B-29 was still America's most reliable front-line bomber.

Then, at 0400 hours on 25 June 1950, a Sunday, Communist North Korea crossed, in force, its neighbor's northern border, the

Combat Records

Aircraft	Combat Sorties	Bomb Tonnage	Combat Losses	Combat Loss Rate (losses ÷ sorties)
A-20 Havoc	39,492	31,856	265	0.67%
A-26 Invader	11,567	18,054	67	0.58%
B-25 Mitchell	63,177	84,980	380	0.60%
B-26 Marauder	129,943	169,382	911	0.70%
B-17 Flying Fortress	291,508	640,036	4,688	1.61%
B-24 Liberator	226,775	452,508	3,626	1.60%
B-29 Superfortress	31,387	159,862	414	1.32%

38th parallel (38° North Latitude), into South Korea and the United Nations-waged Korean War was on for the next three years.

By this time the now ageing Superfortress was classed as a long-range *medium* bomber and there would be several B-29 units involved in the Korean War for various times of service. (1) The 19th Bomb Group (28th, 30th and 93rd Squadrons) was based at Andersen Air Base on Guam and, with an attached Strategic Air Command (SAC) unit, the 31st Photo-Reconnaissance Squadron (RB-29s) within two days of the attack, flew into the air base at Kadena on Okinawa (about 10 miles north of Naha, the capital) and operated from there for the duration of the war. (2) The 307th Bomb Group (370th, 371st and 372nd Squadrons) flew into Kadena, Okinawa in August of 1950 and was based there with the 19th Group for the duration of the war. (3) The 98th Bomb Group (343rd, 344th and 345th Squadrons) was based at Yokota, Japan just west of Tokyo and flew its missions from there from August 1950 to the end of the war in July 1953. From Yokota to Seoul is a flight of about 700 miles. Two other B-29 Bomb Groups participated for a shorter time in missions over the Koreas: (4) The 92nd Bomb Group (325th, 326th and 327th Squadrons) flew missions from Yokota, Japan between July and October 1950, and (5) The 22nd Bomb Group (2nd and 33rd Squadrons) based at Kadena, Okinawa also flew missions between July and October 1950. Attached to the 22nd was the 19th Antisubmarine Squadron. It is of some interest that during the Korean conflict the U. S. Air Force began to drop the designation "Bomb Group" in preference for "Bomb Wing," such that all the above Bomb Groups except the 19th became the correspondingly numbered Bomb Wings on 16 June 1952. For ex-

ample, after 16 June 1952 the 307th Bomb Group became the 307th Bomb Wing. The 19th Bomb Group had its name changed to Bomb Wing on 1 June 1953.

A very brief overview of the ground war over the three years in Korea will serve as an orientation to the war in the air.

On 25 June 1950 seven North Korean divisions assaulted across its northern border with South Korea, and within three weeks these troops had engulfed half its southern neighbor. The United Nations (U. N.) condemned the attack and the war became a U. N. war. United Nations forces were powerless to stop the advance in spite of a heroic stand by the 6th Republic of Korea (R.O.K.) Division, and by the middle of September the North Korean divisions had advance to within 30 miles of Pusan on South Korea's southern coast, bottling up U. N. forces in a 40- to 50-mile radius pocket against the Sea of Japan.

Reinforcements (mostly American) were flown in to the Pusan perimeter and the North Korean advance was stopped. And back home, America mobilized — again. Gen. MacArthur was put in charge of all United Nations ground operations and in typical MacArthur fashion, attacked. On 15 September, led by the U. S. 5th Marines, a beachhead assault at Inchon on the Yellow Sea only three miles from Seoul and far behind enemy lines, took the enemy by surprise, and was coordinated with a breakout from Pusan. In a little over a month, U. N. forces had not only pushed the North Koreans back to the 38th parallel but had continued the drive northward to take the entire southern two-thirds of North Korea, only 60 miles from the Yalu River and the Chinese border by the end of October. One U.S. unit actually reached the Yalu on 26 October (17th Regimental Combat Team, 7th Infantry Division). Then 200,000 Chi-

51

The B-29 "Dave's Dream" dropped a nuclear test bomb at Bikini Atoll in July of 1946 during Operation Crossroads. (Courtesy of Milton Sprouse)

nese Communist troops stormed across the Yalu and overwhelmed the U. N. forces. In spite of horrendous losses inflicted by U. N. ground troops and air strikes on the attacking Communists, the Chinese climbed over their own dead troops to push south. By 15 December the front was back to the 38th parallel.

By 1 January 1951 400,000 Chinese troops were on the battlefield and had pushed U. N. forces back to Seoul, which was evacuated for the second time. The enemy advance was finally stopped 50 miles south of Seoul and in February 1951 the U. N. started a slow advance northward back toward Seoul. U. N. and Communist forces now began a war of attrition oscillating back and forth across the 38th parallel, a war that went through the summer of 1951 in offensive after counter-offensive with few decisive victories for either side, although Communist losses were staggering. Cease-fire talks were initiated in July as the Communists needed time to resupply and consolidate their positions. The talks soon broke off as the fighting continued. U. N. forces then attacked northward in September and the Chinese forces slowly gave ground until, unable to stop the U. N. drive, asked for another round of peace talks. On 23 November 1951 a cease fire was declared and all through 1952, while talks continued, a sort of trench warfare resulted in a stalemate punctuated with minor raids by each side.

The Communists took advantage of the talks to build up a force of nearly one million Chinese troops in North Korea by early 1953. Then they attacked in an attempt to end the war with a military victory. Battles raged back and forth across the "cease-fire" line through June and early July 1953, when it became obvious to the Communists that a military victory was not possible. On 27 July an armistice was signed by the belligerents and the fighting ended. No one won, no one surrendered. But Communist expansion was stopped so the U. N. goals were realized. This "limited war" cost six million dead and wounded, about half of this number being South Korean civilians. The peace talks and an uneasy armistice continue at this writing.

1950

From Kadena, Okinawa to Seoul, South Korea is a 750-mile run, about the same distance as from Guam to Iwo Jima during World War II missions from the Mariana Islands, and it was another 250 or so miles to the Yalu River on the North Korea-China border. The Superforts were able to carry maximum bomb loads if they had to, for these relatively short ranges. The first strike of the 19th's B-29s was on the morning of 29 June when, under orders of General MacArthur, nine Superforts hit Seoul's Kimpo Airfield, now in enemy hands, with 500-pound bombs. They shot down a Russian-made Yak-9 fighter and damaged another. The next morning (the 30th of June) 15 B-29s from Okinawa hit enemy troop concentrations along the Han

River, east of Seoul, with 260-pound fragmentation bombs. Early in July two additional B-29 SAC groups, the 22nd and 92nd Bomb Groups were authorized for a move to the Korean theater and, together with the 19th Bomb Group and the 31st Recon Squadron, were organized into the new Far East Air Forces (F. E. A. F.) Bomber Command with Headquarters at Yokota, near Tokyo, and under the command of Major General **Emmet "Rosie" O'Donnell, Jr.** As noted above these two groups would fly missions in this war for only three and a half months.

Fifth Air Force helicopters (Sikorsky H-5s) arrived in Korea in July of 1950 and they soon proved their worth in rescue missions behind enemy lines (the first on 4 September 1951) and in bringing wounded back from the front lines to rear area hospitals — M. A. S. H. units (Mobile Army Surgical Hospital). Army helicopters (Bell H-13s) did not arrive until the near the end of the year.

The B-29 Bomb Groups soon started in on destroying industrial targets and airfields in North Korea. By the first week in August, 1950, the fighters of the 5th and 13th Air Forces (F-80 Shooting Star, F-82 Twin Mustang and P-51 Mustang) and the 1st Marine Air Wing (F4U Corsair and F9F Panther) had destroyed the North Korean Air Force and it was no longer a threat to U. N. air operations. During the summer and fall of 1950 all five of the B-29 Bomb Groups now in the war (19th, 22nd, 92nd, 98th and 307th) hit every worthy target in North Korea and at least 20 secondary industrial targets. The primary target list included aircraft and armaments plants and rail complexes at Pyongyang; oil refineries at the port of Wonsan; chemical and metal industries at Hungnam; iron foundries at Chongjin; and the oil storage facilities and naval yard at Rashin (15 minutes by B-29 from Vladivostok). This last target was missed in the first try and it was decided it was too close to Russia for any more attempts. Rashin became off-limits. (By the time of the big U. N. counterattack northward in the fall of 1950, there were no strategic targets left worth hitting).

The 22nd and 92nd Bomb Groups hit Wonsan on 13 July. These two groups then hit targets near Hungnam on 30 July and 1 and 2 August with raids of 47, 46, and 39 Superforts, destroying 80% of the city's industries. Marshalling yards at Seoul were taken out by the 19th, 22nd and 92nd Groups on 4 and 5 August, and the 22nd 92nd and 98th did the same to Pyongyang on 8 August. Then they turned to bridges and in the week following 12 August these Groups destroyed or badly damaged 44 key bridges in North Korea. The 5th Air Force and Navy carrier and Marine pilots on low level strikes, did the same to bridges even deeper into North Korea. At this time the Communist forces were gobbling up South Korea so O'Donnell's bombers turned to supporting the the hard-pressed U. N. ground forces. Tactical use of the B-29s was not always encouraging; a 98-plane raid on 16 August on a suspected concentration of Communist troops later showed not a single enemy soldier or vehicle in the recon photos. But this was not always the case. **Charles F. Beard** was a T/Sgt., and instrument repairman on B-29s on Okinawa and he remembers these early days of the war:

"I was on Guam with the 28th Bomb Squadron. . . . Then came the Korean War in June of 1950 and our planes flew out to Okinawa the next day. The rest of the squadron soon followed in troop carrier planes. Duty on Okinawa was usually 12 or more hours a day, seven days a week, repairing, servicing and loading armament on bombers for the daily mass raids on Korea in an attempt to disrupt the invasion from the North. There were several bomb Wings with a total of about 90 B-29s on the base. Some planes returned with battle damage, dead and wounded aboard, and some never made it back. I know of one loaded plane that lost power on take off, rolled into a big ravine, burned and exploded,

jolting us out of our bunks in a concrete barracks two miles away. Four or five men died in that one including some fire fighters.

"The ground crews endured the blazing sun, heating the planes like ovens inside, cool rainy nights, annoying winds, high humidity, mosquitos and even typhoons. Mess hall meals were only fair at best and mattresses always hard and damp. But through it all they always managed to get the scheduled flights in the air the next day — no small achievement even under the best of living and working conditions.

"One of the memorable combat missions was the day when emergency orders were received to down load all heavy bombs and reload many of the planes with 100 pound bombs. They were strung on thin wire cables and hung on the bomb shackles in clusters of six. Each plane carried nearly 20,000 pounds of bombs and every man available was sent to assist the armament crews. They took off after dark and returned the next morning with crews tired but jubilant. The flight crews told us that they had attacked a large heavily armed force of North Korean troops massed in a narrow valley described as about half a mile wide and a few miles long. They [the North Korean troops] were poised to punch through the desperate defenders of the Pusan perimeter at daybreak to flank and overrun the line. 'We caught them and wiped them out! Hardly enough survivors to form a cooks company,' so boasted one of the plane commanders. Since then I've found scant mention of that raid in my military history books but it's very unlikely that so many pilots and crewmen would have been deceiving us about it. I think that raid was in mid-August and probably helped forestall the fall of Pusan, [South] Korea, until General McArthur's decisive seaborne invasion at Inchon on the 15th of September which reversed the course of the Korean War. . . "

But eventually the bridge, communication and perhaps even the strategic attacks were telling. The enemy thrust southward was stopped at Pusan and the air war had helped. Through to the end of October 1950 O'Donnell's Bomber Command had rained 30,000 tons of bombs on North Korean targets. The damage resulting from these high explosive and incendiary attacks was appalling, but it was precision bombing and few civilian lives were lost.

For four days prior to the landings at Inchon (on 15 September) the B-29 Groups were called in to cut all rail and road lines

in the area to reduce the movement of enemy reinforcements into the beachhead. They did a superb job. The 92nd and 98th Groups then turned to help the breakout from Pusan on 16 September and again did some incredibly precise bombing cutting bridges and bottling up enemy troop columns which were then destroyed by advancing U. N. troops. At the end of October 1950 the 22nd and 92nd Bomb Groups had been ordered out to the Korean theater, leaving the 19th, 98th and 307th to continue the bombing campaign.

Losses of B-29s were light up to this point but that would soon change; on 1 November 1950 the first Soviet-made MiG-15 jet fighter (code named *Fagot*) appeared in North Korean skies; and Chinese Communist troops began pouring across the Yalu River from Manchuria. On 5 November the F. E. A. F. Bomber Command was ordered to 'take off the gloves' and hit everything and anything that might be useful to the Communists, and never mind how close the target may be to China. The 19th Group went up to Kanggye, a bare 20 miles from the Yalu River and the Chinese border and dropped 170 tons of bombs on the city. Within days the Superforts of the 19th, 98th and 307th were hitting the bridges spanning the Yalu and with good results and they continued this through November. The enemy threw across pontoon bridges and soon the river froze over and no bridges were needed. The inflow of Communist troops from China was barely slowed. But targets close to Russia were to remain off-limits. By the middle of December a Wing each of F-86A Sabres and F-84E Thunderjets were operating from South Korean bases and they began terrorizing the Chinese pilots flying MiG-15s. Sabre pilots were to shoot down almost 800 MiG-15s in the next 2 1/2 years, boasting a kill ratio of about 10 to 1.

1951

The Chinese launched their attack southward in December. Through December of 1950 the B-29s were employed essentially as a tactical force, bombing advancing enemy troop concentrations in North Korea. By the end of January 1951 the Communist offensive had dried up near the 38th parallel from Allied forces having inflicted on them almost 40,000 casualties, and there began a disastrous war of attrition in which men would die in taking an almost useless hill or ridge or valley. In the middle of January Brig. Gen. **James E. Briggs** took over leadership of the Bomber Command from Maj. Gen. O'Donnell. MiG versus Sabre dogfights heated up over the Yalu as 5th Air Force Thunderjets flew north to attack new Communist airfields in far northern North Korea.

Late February and March 1951 saw interdiction missions by the B-29s back at the Yalu River. By the middle of April as many as 70 MiG-15s were climbing to attack B-29 formations of 20 to 40 planes. The number would grow to 100 and even 150 MiGs in an attack on a single B-29 formation. The Sabre and Thunderjet escorting fighters couldn't prevent them all from breaking through and B-29 losses began to mount. More Allied fighters were put up as protection and the MiG pilots became more cautious about attacking the Superfort formations, usually choosing unprotected flights. Through 14 April the Bomber Command had destroyed 48 bridges on their list of 60. But they paid a price. Between 15 March and 15 April 1951, eight B-29s and their crews were lost and 25 Superforts were so badly damaged that they were out of the war for a long time. But B-29 gunners were getting their share of the attacking MiGs. The B-29's gun system had not been designed to protect the bomber against a fast-moving jet fighter with a fly-by speed of 600 m.p.h., but the gunners were adapting to the challenge and doing well.

By 1 May 1951 another Chinese offensive had stalled just north of Seoul with 70,000 casualties versus 7,000 for the U. N. side. But with new wing tanks mounted, the MiG-15s were now flying south almost to the 38th parallel and the B-29s and Allied fighters again went after their airfields in North Korea. By July the U. N. fighters and bombers had so thoroughly shot up the Chinese-flown MiG-15s that the Chinese backed off and mounted very few attacks during the rest of 1951. But increasing numbers of enemy antiaircraft batteries and the MiGs forced the B-29s to do their bombing from higher and higher altitudes. Hitting bridges from 20,000 feet became a sometime thing and something had to change. Late in 1950 the 19th Bomb Group had tried out a radio-controlled 1,000-pound 'Razon' bomb. They were not new; they had been used in World War II. The bombardiers got better and better at controlling the flight of these bombs, and had actually destroyed 15 bridges with them. But they were too small; it usually took at least four direct hits to destroy a bridge. Enter the

'Tarzon' bomb, again radio-controlled, but weighing 12,000 pounds. These did a fair job. One hit, dead center (and the 19th got several good hits in January of 1951 and following) and a bridge disappeared. But they were far from perfect. When their use was discontinued in August of 1951, 30 bombs had been dropped with only six bridges destroyed and one damaged; three bombs were duds. Most of the rest simply missed the target.

The beginning of June 1951 saw the B-29s concentrating on bombing enemy communications between the front lines and the 39th parallel in North Korea as the ground fighting headed toward a stalemate at and around the 38th parallel. Everything was hit: roads and truck convoys, rail lines and freight trains, radio communications towers and bridges. These missions continued through July, and enemy troops at the front were now being starved of the tools to make war. But this type of interdiction was becoming costly as the enemy brought in more and varied types of antiaircraft weapons to protect themselves. An enemy offensive that had begun in May suffered a vicious series of counterattacks by U. N. divisions in June, and by the end of the month all Communist forces had been driven out of South Korea except for a small sector on the west coast. They had suffered 90,000 casualties. But during the summer and early fall the Chinese MiG pilots, who were getting better, made an attempt to gain control of the air over North Korea. They lost a large number of their fighters to U. N. Sabres, Thunderjets, British Meteors and even the older Shooting Stars, and the attempt failed.

In October it was observed that the Communists were rebuilding their airfields in North Korea, from which their jet fighters could range all the way to the 38th parallel. Consequently it was decided to hit the airfields again. The first attack was by the 19th and 98th Groups on 18 October. The 98th was diverted to a secondary target ; the 19th hit its airfield squarely but one Superfort of the 19th Group was lost to an aggressive MiG pilot. Its crew bailed out and was rescued. Another airfield attack was mounted on the 23rd by eight Superforts of the 307th Bomb Group with and escort of 89 Sabres and Thunderjets. They were hit by 150 MiG-15s that came in from Manchuria. Three B-29 were blown out of the sky; the crew of one bailed out and was rescued. The remaining five Superforts limped home, all badly damaged, and with dead and wounded aboard. Three of four MiGs shot down were claimed by B-29

gunners. It was the Bomber Command's worst day of the war. The next day 60 MiGs attacked eight more 98th Group B-29s; one more Superfort went down, but its crew was rescued. Four days later eight Superforts of the 19th Group were jumped by 95 MiGs. The Group's 48-plane flight escort was quickly scattered by the MiGs and four B-29s suffered severe damage although all made it home. B-29 gunners claimed three more MiGs. October 1951 ended with a total loss of five B-29s to Communist pilots. And MiG-15s were now staging from North Korean airfields.

During the last two months of 1951 the Bomber Command switched to night bombing missions using newly outfitted Shoran radar. This proved eminently successful as the Chinese had little night fighter capability. The North Korean airfields were quickly being destroyed.

1952

Although the Communists early in 1952 continued to increase the number of MiG-15s it was sending across the Yalu — up to 200 on a single flight — their pilots seemed to be less aggressive and would not come down from their 40,000 feet altitude to mix it up with U. N. fighters. When they did come down, they lost heavily. But in May and June of 1952 it became obvious that enemy antiaircraft batteries and searchlights were being directed by radar and the Superforts were no longer immune to night attacks. B-29 losses began to climb again. Bomber Command went back to daylight bombing of bridges — road and rail. These "interdiction" missions never stopped the flow of men and materiel to the enemy front, but they were effective enough so that he could not mount an all-out offensive against U. N. forces.

Strategic targets in North Korea became more rare as the war — and the peace talks — wore on. But one type of target that had not been on anyone's list to this point was North Korea's hydro-electric plants. The Joint Chiefs in Washington had until the spring of 1952 placed them off-limits to air attack, not wishing to jeopardize the talks at Panmunjom. The Joint Chiefs finally gave permission in April for the bombing when the North Koreans became intransigent at the peace table. The Navy was called in; it would be a joint Navy-Fifth Air Force effort. Four sites were selected at which there were five major hydro-electric installations. Fifth Air Force and Navy fighters would hit these by day and the B-29s would continue the attack by night, using their

Shoran radar. A total of eight plants were singled out for destruction: a major complex at Suiho, one at Kyosen, two plants at Choshin and a four-plant complex at Fusen.

The daylight attack got off on 23 June at 1600 hours, delayed because of cloud cover over the targets. With F-86 Sabres flying top cover, Navy F9F Panthers took out the flak guns at Suiho and then A-1 Skyraiders, F-84 Thunderjets and F-80 Shooting Stars dropped 145 tons of bombs on the plant and scooted for home. The hydro-electric plant was completely destroyed. Almost at the same time, Fifth Air Force Mustangs struck two of Fusen's plants and Marine Panthers hit two of Choshin's plants. Then the Navy came in again with Skyraiders, Corsairs and Panthers to strike two other plants at Fusen and the plant at Kyosen. The next day (the 24th) all plants got a working over again, and Superforts that night dropped tons of bombs on the Choshin complex, bombing by Shoran. The Fifth Air Force knew they had a good thing going so they hit Fusen and Choshin again on the 26th and 27th of June. When it was all over, the Fifth had lost two fighters to ground fire (both pilots were rescued) and some 90% (!) of North Korea's electricity-generating capacity was in ruins. June 1952 was a bad month for the North Korean Reds.

Throughout the summer of 1952 Bomber Command's Superforts hit strategic targets north of the 38th parallel including the hydro-electric plant at Choshin again, cement plants at Sungho-ri, a light metals plant at Sinuiju, a heavy metals fabrication plant at Sindok and a munitions plant at Nakwon. But the Communists had brought in from China state-of-the-art radar control systems earlier in the year, including a night fighter squadron, and B-29 night raids were getting more dangerous. With constant Fifth Air Force and Navy carrier attacks by day and B-29 raids by night, North Korea's industry was in ruins by the end of September. The crowning blow was delivered by 45 Superforts on the night of 30 September which, via pin-point radar bombing, completely leveled the Namsan-ni chemical plant.

Still, the peace talks were going nowhere, so the bombing kept up. The trouble now was there wasn't anything left worth hitting in North Korea. So, the Navy, Fifth Air Force, and Bomber Command's B-29s turned to hitting Communist troop concentrations near the front lines. It wasn't nearly as satisfying as bridge-busting or emptying bomb bays on strategic targets but it kept everyone, including the Communists, on their toes. And this was the way 1952 came to a close.

1953

But enemy defense measures were becoming a serious problem to the B-29s of the 19th, 98th and 307th Groups. From the middle of November 1952 to the end of January 1953. Red night fighters shot down five Superforts and damaged several more. Electronic counter-measures kept the number from rising, but it was still too many. The answer came in the form of escorting night fighters — F-94B Starfires, and Marine F$_3$D-2 Skynights. With this cover at night against Communist night patrols, the B-29 crews started to breath a little easier on their missions. Various industrial targets, including the hydro-electric plants, now partially rebuilt by the North Koreans, went on the Superfort list again in February. In March of 1953 bridge-busting was again given priority to slow enemy troop movements to the front lines. The North Koreans were still dragging their feet at Panmunjom but it was now obvious that this war was not going to last much longer.

Looking around for targets, U. N. planners settled on a group of structures that had been avoided in the past — dams. These were part of a complex irrigation system that supplied water to North Korea's rice crop, about 20 such dams supplying some three-fourths of the water for all of the country's rice fields. On 13 May 1953, 59 Thunderjets each dropped a 1,000-pound bomb on the Toksan dam. It had been so weakened by this pummeling that it gave way the next morning, causing enormous flood devastation. Five square miles of rice crops destroyed along with roads, rail lines and an airfield, all under water. On the 15th and 16th of May the Thunderjets hit another dam at Chasan and it too crumbled with devastating results downstream. On the night of 21 May the B-29s got into the act. Seven Superforts hit the Kuwonga dam using Shoran, but the enemy learned fast; he had lowered the water level behind this dam to reduce the pressure and so prevent its collapsing. After the bomb hits, he was forced to drain completely the reservoir behind the structure to prevent its collapse. The result was the same as if the dam had been destroyed, however: The rice crop down river dried up from lack of irrigation water. With 17 more dams to go, this was going to take a lot of missions.

But the fighting was not over yet. The Communists launched an attack on 28 May on the west side of the front. Air strikes from every available unit, including the Navy and Superfort units on Okinawa and Japan, helped contain the

offensive. But the ground fighting continued through June and into July of 1953. All air units were also targeting enemy airfields during this latest Red offensive; recon photos showed that the North Koreans were bring in large numbers of aircraft from China in anticipation of an armistice that would have prohibited such stockpiling. By the third week in June, after constant bombardment by the Fifth Air Force and the B-29s, 34 of these airfields (out of 35 on the target list) had been made unusable for flight operations. The North Koreans went about repairing these fields and so the Fifth and the B-29s hit them again in July, and by the 27th, they were all in a shambles again.

And this was the day that an armistice was signed at Panmunjom. A final Communist offensive that had been launched on 13 July had been stopped on the 20th with 70,000 enemy casualties, all unnecessary. The armistice was effective as of 2201 hours on the 27th of July 1953 ending three years and a month of bloody fighting on the ground and in the air.

The combat days of the B-29 Superfortress came to an end in the skies over Korea. That war had shown the inadequacy of a conventional, piston-engine bomber to wage a jet aircraft war. When MiG-15s broke through the fighter protection, even if the MiGs were flown by inexperienced pilots, the Superfort formations suffered. By 1955 all combat B-29s had been replaced by six-jet B-47s and the propeller/jet hybrid B-36s were replaced by mammoth eight-jet B-52s.

During its 21,328 sorties in the Korean war, B-29s dropped 167,000 tons of bombs in flying all but 26 days of the three-year war. Its crews shot down at least 30 enemy fighters, but 34 Superforts were lost over the Koreas (a one-tenth per cent sortie/ loss ratio). The B-29 survived for a few years both as the B-29, and as the B-50 variant with more powerful (3500 horsepower, 28-cylinder) Pratt and Whitney R-4360 engines, as an aerial tanker and transport, and the mother ship for the Bell X-1 rocket plane (flown by "Chuck" Yeager to Mach 1). But the B-29 had had its day in the sun. It had been a major factor in bringing a first rate military power to its knees in 1945, but it made only a modest contribution in halting the aggression of a fourth rate power only five years later. But what it did, it did as usual, superbly. The last flight of an operational Air Force B-29 Superfortress was on 21 June 1960 on a radar evaluation mission. So passed one of the greatest airplanes ever to fly.

REFERENCES

Anderson, Kenneth. **History of U.S. Military Operations Since World War II.** Crescent Books, New York. 1992.

Atlas of the World (6th Edition). National Geographic Society, Washington, D.C. 1992.

Churchill, Winston. **The Second World War.** Volumes 1 through 6. Houghton Mifflin Co., Boston. 1948—1953.

Dorr, Robert F. **U.S. Bombers of World War Two.** Arms and Armour Press, London (Sterling Publishing Co., New York). 1989.

Edoin, Hoito. **The Night Tokyo Burned.** St. Martin's Press, New York. 1987.

Fahey, James C., (Editor). **U.S. Army Aircraft (Heavier Than Air) 1908-1946.** Ships and Aircraft, New York. 1946.

Gurney, Gene. **Journey of the Giants.** Coward-McCann, Inc. New York. 1961.

Hammond's Complete World Atlas. C. S. Hammond & Co., New York. 1953.

Jackson, Robert. **Air War over Korea.** Charles Scribner's Sons, New York. 1973.

LeMay, Curtis and Bill Yenne. **Superfortress. The B-29 and American Air Power.** McGraw-Hill Book Company, New York. 1988.

Lloyd, Alwyn T. **B-29 Superfortress in Detail and Scale** (Vol. 10). Airlife Publishing Ltd., England (Tab Books Inc., Blue Ridge Summit, PA) 1983.

Messenger, Charles. **The Chronological Atlas of World War Two.** Macmillan Publishing Co., New York. 1989.

Murphy, Edward F. **Heroes of World War II.** Presidio Press, Novato, CA. 1990.

Spencer, Otha C. **Flying the Hump.** Texas A & M University Press, College Station. 1992.

World Book Encyclopedia, Vol 20. Field Enterprises Educational Corp., Chicago. 1970.

Maurer Maurer, (Editor). **World War II Combat Squadrons of the United States Air Force.** Smithmark Publishers Inc., New York. 1992.

SQUADRONS THAT FLEW THE B-29
"SUPERFORTRESS"

A B-29 (upper left corner) flies over one of the many islands won in the battle for the Pacific. (Courtesy of Jim Sullivan)

1st BOMB SQUADRON

Lineage
Organized as 1st Provisional Aero Sq on 5 Mar 1913. Redesignated: 1st Aero SQ on 8 Dec 1913; 1st Sq on 14 Mar 1921; 1st Observation SQ on 25 Jan 1923; 1st Bomb Sq on 1 Mar 1935; 1st Bomb Sq (Medium) on 6 Dec 1939; 1st Bomb Sq (Heavy) on 20 Nov 1940; 1st Bomb Sq (Very Heavy) on 28 Mar 1944; 1st Strategic Recon Sq (Photographic) on 10 Oct 1948; 1st Bomb Sq (Heavy) on 1 Apr 1950; 1st Bomb Sq (Medium) on 2 Oct 1950.

Assignments
Unkn, 5 Mar 1913–Apr 1918; I Corps Observation Grp, Apr–Nov 1918; unkn, Nov 1918–1 Oct 1919; 1st Army Observation (later 7th Observation) Grp, 1 Oct 1919 (attached to 1st Provisional Air Brigade for operations, 6 May–3 Oct 1921); 2d Wing, 30 Aug 1921; Second Corps Area, 30 Sept 1921; 9th Observation (later Bomb) Grp, assigned on 1 Aug 1922, attached on 24 Mar 1923, and assigned on 15 Feb 1929; 311th Air Division, 10 Oct 1948 (attached to 55th Strategic Recon Wing on 10 Oct 1948, and to 55th Strategic Recon Grp on 27 Oct 1948); 9th Strategic Recon (later Bomb) Grp, 1 June 1949; 9th Bomb (later Strategic Aerospace) Wing, 16 June 1952–.

Stations
Texas City, TX, 5 Mar 1913; San Diego, CA, c. 28 Nov 1913 (detachment operated from Ft Crockett, TX, 30 Apr–13 July 1914; from Brownsville, TX, 17 Apr–c. 24 May 1915); Ft Sill, OK, 29 July 1915 (detachment operated from Brownsville, TX, 18 Aug–c. Dec 1915); Ft Sam Houston, TX, 26 Nov 1915; Columbus, NM, 15 Mar 1916; Casas Grandes, Mexico (operated from Colonia Dublan), 19 Mar 1916; San Geronimo, Mexico 5 Apr 1916; San Antonio, Mexico 9 Apr 1916; Satevo, Mexico, 11 Apr 1916; Namiquipa, Mexico, 17 Apr 1916; Columbus, NM, 22 Apr 1916–5 Aug 1917 (detachments operated from Colonia Dublan and El Valle, Mexico, until c. Jan 1917); Avord, France, 13 Sept 1917; Issoudun, France, 29 Sept 1917; Amanty, France, 19 Oct 1917; Ourches, France, 4 Apr 1918; Saints, France, 29 June 1918; Francheville, France, 6 July 1918; Moras Ferme (near La Ferte-sous Jouarre), France, c. 22 July 1918; May-en-Multien, France, 5 Aug 1918; Coincy, France, 10 Aug 1918; Chailly-en-Brie, France, 13 Aug 1918; Toul, France, 22 Aug 1918; Remicourt, France, 21 Sept 1918; Julvecourt, France, 5 Nov 1918; Mercy-le-Bas, France, 21 Nov 1918; Trier, Germany, 6 Dec 1918; Weissenthurm, Germany, 21 Jan–14 July 1919; Park Field, TN, 4 Aug 1919; Mitchel Field, NY, 10 Oct 1919–6 Nov 1940 (operated from Langley Field, VA, 6 May–26 Oct 1921); Rio Hato, Panma, 13 Nov 1940; Piarco Aprt, Trinidad, 24 Apr 1941; Waller Field, Trinidad, 29 Oct 1941; Edinburgh Field, Trinidad, 23 Aug 1942; Orlando AB, FL, 31 Oct 1942; Brooksville, FL, 15 Dec 1942; Orlando AB, FL, 25 Feb 1944; Dalhart AAFld, TX, c. 3 Mar 1944; McCook AAFld, NE, 19 May–18 Nov 1944; North Field, Tinian, 28 Dec 1944 Mar 1946; Clark Field, Luzon, 14 Mar 1946; Harmon Field, Guam, 9 June 1947; Topeka AFB, KS, 10 Oct 1948; Fairfield-Suisun AFB, CA, 1 June 1949; Mountain Home AFB, ID, 1 May 1953–.

Aircraft
In addition to Wright C, 1913–1914, and Burgess H, 1913–1915, included Wright B, Burgess F, Burgess I-Scout, Burgess J-Scout, Curtiss D, Curtiss E, Curtiss H, Martin TT, and apparently Wright D-Scout, during period 1913–1915; JN-2 (JN-3), 1915–1916; N-8, 1916; in addition to R-2, 1916–1917, included (for field testing) H-2, H-3, Twin JN, R-Land, Sturtevant Adv Tr, V-1, D-5, and JN-4 during period 1916–1917; AR 1, 1917–1918; Spad XI, 1918; Salmson 2, 1918–1919; in addition to DH-4 apparently included O-2 during period 1919–1928; in addition to O-1, c. 1928–1936, included O-13, Y1O-31, Y1O-35, O-39, Y1O-40, and B-6, during period 1930–1936; B-10, 1936–1938; B-18, 1938–1942; B-17, 1942–1944, 1948–1949; B-29, 1944–1947, 1948–1949, 1950–1954; RB-17, 1948–1949; RB-29, 1948–1949; B-36, 1949–1950; B-47, 1954–.

Operations
Organized in response to Mexican revolution of Feb 1913; deployed detachments to Texas, for projected foreign service during Tampico-Vera Cruz crisis, Apr–July 1914, and for border patrol duty, Apr–May 1915, Aug–c. Dec 1915; served as reconnaissance and liaison unit with Punitive Expedition to Mexico, Mar 1916–c. Jan 1917; patroled border until c. May 1917. Combat as corps observation unit with French XXXVIII Army Corps and American I Army Corps, 11 Apr–8 Nov 1918; served with III Army Corps as part of occupation forces, Nov 1918–Jul 1919. Participated in demonstrations of effectiveness of aerial bombardment on warships, June–Sept 1921. Antisubmarine patrols, and reconnaissance of Vichy French fleet at Martinique, Dec 1941–Oct 1942. Trained cadres for bombardment units, Nov 1942–Feb 1944. Combat in Western Pacific, 25 Jan–14 Aug 1945. Unmanned, Apr 1947–10 Oct 1948.

Service Streamers
None

Campaigns
Mexico 1916–1917. World War I: Lorraine; Ile-de-France; Champagne; Champagne-Marne; Aisne-Marne; St Mihiel; Meuse-Argonne. World War II: Antisubmarine, American Theater; Air Offensive, Japan; Eastern Mandates; Western Pacific.

Decorations
Distinguished Unit Citations: Kawasaki, Japan, 15-16 Apr 1945; Japan, 13-28 May 1945. Air Force Outstanding Unit Award: 1 Jan 1957–31 Jan 1958.

2d BOMB SQUADRON

Lineage
Constituted 2d Bomb Sq on 1 Jan 1938. Redesignated 2d Bomb Sq (Medium). Activated on 1 Feb 1940. Redesignated: 2d Bomb Sq (heavy) on 3 Feb 1944; 2d Bomb Sq (Very Heavy) on 30 Apr 1946; 2d Bomb Sq (Medium) on 28 July 1948.

Assignments
22d Bomb Grp, 1 Feb 1940; 22d Bomb Wing, 16 June 1952–.

Stations
Bolling Field, DC, 1 Feb 1940; Langley Field, VA, 14 Nov 1940; Muroc, CA, c. 9 Dec 1941-29 Jan 1942; Brisbane, Australia, 25 Feb 1942; Ipswich, Australia, 2 Mar 1942; Townsville, Australia, 7 Apr 1942; Reid River, Australia, 9 Apr 1942; Dobodura, New Guinea, 9 Oct 1943; Nadzab, New Guinea, 19 Dec 1943; Owi, Schouten Islands, 11 Aug 1944; Leyte, c. 19 Nov 1944; Angaur, c. 28 Nov 1944; Samar, 20 Jan 1945; Clark Field, Luzon, Mar 1945; Okinawa, 18 Aug 1945; Ft William McKinley, Luzon, 23 Nov 1945; Okinawa, 15 May 1946; Smoky Hill AFB, KS, 18 May 1948; March AFB, CA, 10 May 1949 (operated from Kadena AFB, Okinawa, c. 9 July–c. 30 Oct 1950)–.

Aircraft
B-18, 1940–1941; B-26, 1941–1943; B-25, 1943–1944; B-24, 1944–1945; B-29, 1946–1953; B-47, 1953–.

Operations
Antisubmarine patrols, Dec 1941–Jan 1942; combat in Southwest and Western Pacific, 8 Apr 1942–3 Jan 1943, 5 Oct 1943–24 July 1945. Not manned, 23 Nov 1945–15 June 1946. Combat in Korea, 13 July–19 Oct 1950.

Service Streamers
None

Campaigns
World War II: Antisubmarine, American Theater; East Indies; Air Offensive, Japan; China Defensive; Papua; New Guinea; Northern Solomons; Bismarck Archipelago; Western Pacific; Leyte; Luzon; Southern Philippines; China Offensive; Air Combat, Asiatic-Pacific Theater. Korean War: UN Defensive; UN Offensive.

Decorations
Distinguished Unit Citations: Papua, 23 July 1942–[3] Jan 1943; New Guinea, 5 Nov 1943. Philippine Presidential Unit Citation. Republic of Korea Presidential Unit Citation: 10 July–24 Oct 1950.

5th BOMB SQUADRON

Lineage
Organized as 5th Aero Sq on 5 May 1917. Redesignated Sq A, Souther Field, GA, on 15 July 1918. Demobilized on 11 Nov 1918. Reconstituted and consolidated (1924) with 5th Aero Sq which was organized on 24 Oct 1919. Redesignated: 5th Sq on 14 Mar 1921; 5th Observation Sq on 25 Jan 1923; 5th Bomb Sq on 1 Mar 1935; 5th Bomb Sq on 1 Mar 1935; 5th Bomb Sq (Medium) on 6 Dec 1939; 5th Bomb Sq (heavy) on 20 Nov 1940; 5th Bomb Sq (Very Heavy) on 28 Mar 1944. Inactivated on 20 Oct 1948. Redesignated 5th Strategic Recon Sq (Photographic), and activated, on 1 May 1949. Redesignated 5th Bomb Sq (Heavy) on 1 Apr 1950; 5th Bomb Sq (Medium) on 2 Oct 1950.

Assignments
Unkn, 1917-1918. 3d Observation Grp (attached to Eastern Dept) 24 Oct 1919; Eastern Dept, 24 Mar 1920; Second Corps Area, 20 Aug 1920

(attached to 1st Provisional Air Brigade for operations, 6 May–3 Oct 1921); 9th Observation (later Bombardment) Grp, assigned on 1 Aug 1922, attached on 24 Mar 1923, and assigned 15 Feb 1929–20 Oct 1948. 9th Strategic Recon (later Bomb) Grp, 1 May 1949; 9th Bomb (later Strategic Aerospace) Wing, 16 June 1952–.

Stations
San Antonio, TX, 5 May 1917; Souther Field, GA, 1 May–11 Nov 1918. Hazelhurst Field, NY, 24 Oct 1919; Mitchel Field, NY, Nov 1919 (operated from Langley Field, VA, 6 May–26 Oct 1921); Rio Hato, Panama, 13 Nov 1940; Beane Field, St Lucia, c. 28 Sept 1941; Orlando AB, FL, 31 Oct 1942; Pinecastle AAFld, FL, 15 Apr 1943; Brooksville AAFld, FL, 7 Jan 1944; Pinecastle AAFld, FL 13 Feb 1944; Dalhart AAFld, TX, c. 9 Mar 1944; McCook AAFld, KS, 19 May–18 Nov 1944; North Field, Tinian, 28 Dec 1944–6 Mar 1946; Clark Field, Luzon, 14 March 1946; Harmon Field, Guam, 9 June 1947–20 Oct 1948. Fairfield-Suisun AFB, CA, 1 May 1949; Mountain Home AFB, ID, 1 May 1953.

Aircraft
Apparently included JN-4 during period 1917–1918. Included DH-4 and O-2 during period 1919–1928; in addition to O-1, O-11, and O-25, included O-31, Y1O-35, O-39, A-3, B-6, and C-8 during period 1928–1936; B-10, 1936–1938; B-18, 1938–1942; B-24, 1942–1943; B-25, 1943; B-26, 1943–1944; B-17, 1944; B-29, 1944–1947. B/RB-17, 1949–1950; RB-29, 1949–1950; B-29, 1949–1954; B-47, 1954.

Operations
Flying training unit, 1917–1918. Demonstrations of effectiveness of aerial bombardment on warships, June–Sept 1921. Antisubmarine patrols, and reconnaissance of Vichy French fleet at Martinique, Dec 1941–Oct 1942. Trained cadres for bombardment units, Nov 1942–Feb 1944. Combat in Western Pacific, 25 Jan–15 Aug 1945. Unmanned, Apr 1947–20 Oct 1948.

Service Streamers
None

Campaigns
Antisubmarine, American Theater; Air Offensive, Japan; Eastern Mandates; Western Pacific.

Decorations
Distinguished Unit Citations: Kawasaki, Japan, 15–16 Apr 1945; Japan, 13–28 May 1945. Air Force Outstanding Unit Award: 1 Jan 1957–31 Jan 1958.

6th BOMB SQUADRON
Lineage
Constituted 6th Bomb Sq (Heavy) on 22 Dec 1939. Activated on 1 Feb 1940. Inactivated on 1 Apr 1944. Redesignated 6th Bomb Sq (Very Heavy). Activated on 1 Apr 1944. Inactivated on 20 May 1946. Activated in the reserve on 15 June 1947. Inactivated on 27 June 1949.

Assignments
29th Bomb Grp, 1 Feb 1940–1 Apr 1944. 29th Bomb Grp, 1 Apr 1944–20 May 1946. Tenth Air

Force, 15 June 1947; 482d Bomb Grp, 30 Sept 1947–27 June 1949.

Stations
Langley Field, VA, 1 Feb 1940; MacDill Field, FL, 21 May 1940; Gowen Field, ID, 25 June 1942–1 Apr 1944. Pratt AAFld, KS, 1 Apr–c. 6 Dec 1944; North Field, Guam, 17 Jan 1945–20 May 1946. Barksdale Field, LA, 15 June 1947–27 June 1949.

Aircraft
YB-17, 1940; B-18, 1940–1941; B-17, 1940–1943; B-24, 1943–1944. B-17, 1944; B-29, 1944–1946.

Operations
Antisubmarine patrols, Jan–June 1942. Operational and later replacement training unit, 1942–1944. Combat in Western Pacific, c. 16 Feb–15 Aug 1945.

Service Streamers
None

Campaigns
Antisubmarine, American Theater; Air Offensive, Japan; Western Pacific.

Decorations
Distinguished Unit Citations: Japan, 31 Mar 1945; Japan, 19–26 June 1945.

9th BOMB SQUADRON
Lineage
Organized as 9th Aero Sq on 14 June 1917. Redesignated: 9th Sq on 14 Mar 1921. Inactivated on 29 June 1922. Redesignated: 9th Observation Sq on 25 Jan 1923; 9th Bomb Sq on 24 Mar 1923. Activated on 1 Apr 1931. Redesignated 9th Bomb Sq (Heavy) on 6 Dec 1939. Inactivated on 6 Jan 1946. Redesignated 9th Bomb Sq (Very Heavy), and activated, on 1 Oct 1946. Redesignated 9th Bomb Sq (Heavy) on 20 July 1948.

Assignments
Unkn, 14 June 1917–Sep 1918; First Army Observation Grp, Sept–Nov 1918; unkn, Nov 1918–July 1919; Western Department, July 1919; Ninth Corps Area, 20 Aug 1920–29 June 1922. 7th Bomb Grp, 1 Apr 1931–6 Jan 1946 (attached to United States Army Middle East Air Force for operations, 28 June–c. 4 Oct 1942). 7th Bomb Grp, 1 Oct 1946; 7th Bomb Wing, 16 June 1952–.

Stations
Camp Kelly, TX, 14 June 1917; Selfridge Field, MI, 8 July 1917; Garden City, NY, 28 Oct–22 Nov 1917; Winchester, England, c. 8 Dec 1917; Grantham, England, c. 28 Dec 1917–7 Aug 1918; Colombey-les-Belles, France, 23 Aug 1918; Amanty, France, 28 Aug 1918; Vavincourt, France, 21 Sept 1918; Preutin, France, 21 Nov 1918; Trier, Germany, 5 Dec 1918; Colombey-les-Belles, France 18 May 1919; Marseille, France 25 May–7 June 1919, Mitchel Field, NY, 23 June 1919; Park Field, TN, 12 July 1919; March Field, CA, 22 July 1919; Rockwell Field, CA, 2 Aug 1919 (flight operated from Calexico,

CA, to Apr 1920); March Field, CA, 15 Nov 1919; Rockwell Field, CA, 11 Dec 1919; Mather Field, CA, 27 Apr 1920–29 June 1922 (detachments operated from several places in northern and central CA, May–Sept 1920, c. June–c. Oct 1921; detachment operated from Rockwell Field, CA, c. Jan–29 July 1921). March Field, CA, 1 Apr 1931; Hamilton Field, CA, 5 Dec 1934; Ft Douglas, UT, 7 Sept 1940; Salt Lake City, UT, 13 Jan–13 Nov 1941; Brisbane, Australia, 22 Dec 1941–4 Feb 1942 (operated from Muroc, CA, 8–c. 12 Dec 1941; Singosari, Java, 13–19 Jan 1942; and Jogjakarta, Java, 19 Jan–c. 1 Mar 1942); Karachi, India, 14 Mar 1942; Allahabad, India, (air echelon at Baumrauli, India) 27 Apr–29 June 1942; Lydda, Palestine, 2 July–4 Oct 1942; Karachi, India, 5 Oct 1942 (operated from Gaya, India, 14 Nov–12 Dec 1942); Pandaveswar, India, 12 Dec 1942; Kurmitola, India, c. 11 June 1944; Pandaveswar, India, 1 Oct 1944; Tezpur, India, 1 June–7 Dec 1945; Camp Kilmer, NJ, 5–6 Jan 1946. Ft Worth AAFld, TX, 1 Oct 1946–.

Aircraft
In addition to Breguet 14, included DH-4 and Sopwith FE-2 during period 1918–1919; included DH-4 during period 1919–1922. Included B-3, B-4, O-19, O-38 during period 1931–1934; primarily B-12, 1934–1936, and B-10, 1936–1937; B-18, 1937–1940; B-17, 1939–1942; LB-30, 1942; B-24, 1942–1945. B-29, 1946–1948; B-36, 1948–1958; B-52, 1958–.

Operations
Combat with First Army as observation unit specializing in night reconnaissance, 2 Sept–11 Nov 1918, and subsequently served with Third Army as part of occupation forces until May 1919. Mexican border patrol, Aug 1919–Apr 1920, c. Jan–July 1921; forest fire patrol, 16 May–30 Sept 1920, c. June–c. Sept 1921. Antisubmarine patrols off California coast, 8–c. 12 Dec 1941. Combat in Southwest Pacific, c. 13 Jan–c. 1 Mar 1942; CBI, 2 Apr–4 June 1942, 22 Nov 1942–10 June 1944, and 19 Oct 1944–10 May 1945; and MTO, c. 4 July–1 Oct 1942; transportation of gasoline to forward bases in China, 20 June–30 Sept 1944, and June–Sept 1945.

Service Streamers
None

Campaigns
World War I: Lorraine; St Mihiel; Meuse-Argonne. World War II: Antisubmarine, American Theater; Philippine Islands, East Indies; Egypt-Libya; Burma; India-Burma; China Defensive; Central Burma; China Offensive.

Decorations
Distinguished Unit Citations: Netherlands Indies, 14 Jan–1 Mar 1942; Thailand, 19 Mar 1945. Philippine Presidential Unit Citation.

15th BOMB SQUADRON
Lineage
Constituted 15th Bomb Sq (Very Heavy) on 28 Mar 1944. Activated on 1 Apr 1944. Inactivated on 15 Apr 1946. Activated in the reserve on 1 Aug 1947. Inactivated on 27 June 1949.

Assignments
16th Bomb Grp, 1 Apr 1944–15 Apr 1946. 445th Bomb Grp, 1 Aug 1947–27 June 1949.

Stations
Dalhart AAFld, TX, 1 Apr 1944; Fairmont AAFld, NB, 15 Aug 1944–7 Mar 1945; Northwest Field, Guam, 14 Apr 1945–15 Apr 1946. Hill Field, UT, 1 Aug 1947–27 June 1949.

Aircraft
B-17, 1944–1945; B-29, 1944–1946.

Operations
Combat in Western Pacific, 16 June–14 Aug 1945.

Service Streamers
None

Campaigns
Air Offensive, Japan; Eastern Mandates; Western Pacific.

Decorations
Distinguished Unit Citation: Japan, 29 July–6 Aug 1945.

16th BOMB SQUADRON
Lineage
Constituted 16th Bomb Sq (Very Heavy) on 28 Mar 1944. Activated on 1 Apr 1944. Inactivated on 15 Apr 1946.

Assignments
16th Bomb Grp, 1 Apr 1944–15 Apr 1946.

Stations
Dalhart AAFld, TX, 1 Apr 1944; Fairmont AAFld, NB, 15 Aug 1944–7 Mar 1945; Northwest Field, Guam, 14 Apr 1945–15 Apr 1946.

Aircraft
B-17, 1944–1945; B-29, 1944–1946.

Operations
Combat in Western Pacific, 16 June–14 Aug 1945.

Service Streamers
None

Campaigns
Air Offensive, Japan; Eastern Mandates; Western Pacific.

Decorations
Distinguished Unit Citation: Japan, 29 July–6 Aug 1945.

17th BOMB SQUADRON
Lineage
Constituted 17th Bomb Sq (Very Heavy) on 28 Mar 1944. Activated on 1 Apr 1944. Inactivated on 15 Apr 1946.

Assignments
16th Bomb Grp, 1 Apr 1944–15 Apr 1946.

Stations
Dalhart AAFld, TX, 1 Apr 1944; Fairmont AAFld, NB, 15 Aug 1944–7 Mar 1945; Northwest Field, Guam, 14 Apr 1945–15 Apr 1946.

Aircraft
B-17, 1944–1945; B-29, 1944–1946.

Operations
Combat in Western Pacific, 16 June–14 Aug 1945.

Service Streamers
None

Campaigns
Air Offensive, Japan; Eastern Mandates; Western Pacific.

Decorations
Distinguished Unit Citation: Japan, 29 July–6 Aug 1945.

19th BOMB SQUADRON
Lineage
Constituted 19th Bomb Sq (Medium) on 22 Dec 1939. Activated on 1 Feb 1940. Redesignated: 19th Bomb Sq (Heavy) on 3 Feb 1944; 19th Bomb Sq (Very Heavy) on 30 Apr 1946; 19th Bomb Sq (Medium) on 28 July 1948.

Assignments
22d Bomb Grp, 1 Feb 1940; 22d Bomb Wing, 16 June 1952–.

Stations
Patterson Field, OH, 1 Feb 1940; Langley Field, VA, 16 Nov 1940; Muroc, CA, 9 Dec 1941–28 Jan 1942; Brisbane, Australia, 25 Feb 1942; Ipswich, Australia, 2 Mar 1942; Townsville, Australia,, 29 Mar 1942; Woodstock, Australia, 4 July 1942; Iron Range, Australia, 15 Sept 1942; Woodstock, Australia, 4 Feb 1943; Dobodura, New Guinea, 11 July 1943; Nadzab, New Guinea, c. 24 Jan 1944; Owi, Schouten Islands, 22 July 1944; Leyte, c. 10 Nov 1944; Anguar, 2 Dec 1944; Samar, 27 Jan 1945; Clark Field, Luzon, c. 15 Mar 1945; Okinawa, 14 Aug 1945; Ft William McKinley, Luzon, 23 Nov 1945; Okinawa, 15 May 1946; Smoky Hill AFB, KS, 18 May 1948; March AFB, CA, 10 May 1949 (operated from Kadena, Okinawa, c. 9 July–c. 30 Oct 1950)–.

Aircraft
B-18, 1940–1941; B-26, 1941–1944; B-24, 1944–1945; B-29, 1946–1953; B-47, 1953–.

Operations
Antisubmarine patrols, Dec 1941–Jan 1942; combat in Southwest and Western Pacific, 6 Apr 1942–9 Jan 1943, 27 July 1943–3 Aug 1945. Not manned, 23 Nov 1945–15 June 1946. Combat in Korea, 13 July–19 Oct 1950.

Service Streamers
None

Campaigns
World War II: Antisubmarine, American Theater; East Indies; Air Offensive, Japan; China Defensive; Papua; New Guinea; Bismarck Archipelago; Western Pacific; Leyte; Luzon; Southern Philippines; China Offensive; Air Combat, Asiatic-Pacific Theater. Korean War: UN Defensive; UN Offensive.

Decorations
Distinguished Unit Citations: Papua, 23 July 1942–[9] Jan 1943; New Guinea, 5 Nov 1943. Philippine Presidential Unit Citation. Republic of Korea Presidential Unit Citation: 10 July–24 Oct 1950.

20th BOMB SQUADRON
Lineage
Organized as 20th Aero Sq on 26 June 1917. Redesignated: 20th Sq on 14 Mar 1921; 20th Bomb Sq on 25 Jan 1923; 20th Bomb Sq (Heavy) on 6 Dec 1939. Inactivated on 28 Feb 1946. Redesignated 20th Bomb Sq (Very Heavy) on 5 Apr 1946. Activated on 1 July 1947. Redesignated 20th Bomb Sq (Medium) on 28 May 1948.

Assignments
Unkn, 26 June 1917–Sept 1918; 1st Day Bomb Grp, Sept–Nov 1918; unkn, Nov 1918–18 Sept 1919; 1st Day Bomb (later 2d Bomb) Grp, 18 Sept 1919–28 Feb 1946. 2d Bomb Grp, 1 July 1947; 2d Bomb Wing, 16 June 1952–.

Stations
Camp Kelly, TX, 26 June 1917; Wilbur Wright Field, OH, 31 July 1917; Garden City, NY, 1 Nov–17 Dec 1917; Stamford, England, 7 Jan–7 Aug 1918; Delouze, France, 26 Aug 1918; Amanty, France, 7 Sept 1918; Maulan, France, 23 Sept 1918; Colombey-les-Belles, France, 16 Jan 1919; Guitres, France, 1 Feb 1919; St Denis de Pile, France, 5 Feb 1919; Libourne, France, 27 Feb–Apr 1919; Mitchel Field, NY, 2 May 1919; Ellington Field, TX, June 1919; Kelly Field, TX, c. 25 Sept 1919; Langley Field, VA, 30 June 1922 (operated from Mitchel Field, NY, 8 Dec 1941–24 Jan 1942); Ephrata, WA, 29 Oct 1942; Great Falls AAB, MT, 28 Nov 1942–13 Mar 1943; Navarin, Algeria, 25 Apr 1943; Chateaudun-du-Rhumel, Algeria, 27 Apr 1943; Ain M'lila, Algeria, 17 June 1943; Massicault, Tunisia, 31 July 1943; Amendola, Italy, 8 Dec 1943; Foggia, Italy, c. 10 Oct 1945–28 Feb 1946. Andrews Field, MD, 1 July 1947; Davis-Monthan Field, AZ, 24 Sept 1947; Chatham AFB, GA, 1 May 1949; Hunter AFB, GA, 29 Sept 1950–.

Aircraft
DH-4, 1918; included DH-4 and MB-2 (NBS-1) during period 1919–1929; included LB-5, LB-7, B-3, and B-5, during period 1928–1932; in addition to B-6, 1931–1936, included Y1B-9 during period 1932–1936; in addition to B-10, B-17, B-18, and B-25, included A-17, A-20, B-23, and B-34, during period 1936–1942; B-17, 1942–1945. B-29, 1947–1950; B-50, 1949–1954; B-47, 1954–.

Operations
Combat as day bombardment unit with First Army, 14 Sept–5 Nov 1918. Participated in demonstration of effectiveness of aerial bom-

bardment on warships, 5 Sept 1923; flew mercy mission in relief of flood victims in Pennsylvania, 20-22 Mar 1936; participated in good-will flights to Argentina, 15–27 Feb 1938, Colombia, 3–12 Aug 1938, and Brazil, 10–26 Nov 1939. Antisubmarine patrols, 8 Dec 1941–c. 28 Oct 1942; combat in MTO and ETO, 28 Apr 1943–1 May 1945. Electronic countermeasures testing and evaluation, May 1950–May 1952.

Service Streamers
None

Campaigns
World War I: St Mihiel; Lorraine; Meuse-Argonne. World War II: Antisubmarine, American Theater; Air Offensive, Europe; Tunisia; Sicily; Naples-Foggia; Anzio; Rome-Arno; Normandy; Northern France; Southern France; North Apennines; Rhineland; Central Europe; Po Valley; Air Combat, EAME Theater.

Decorations
Distinguished Unit Citations: Steyr, Austria, 24 Feb 1944; Germany, 25 Feb 1944. Air Force Outstanding Unit Award: 1 Nov 1956–1 Apr 1957.

21st BOMB SQUADRON
Lineage
Constituted 21st Bomb Sq (Very Heavy) on 28 Mar 1944. Activated on 1 Apr 1944. Inactivated on 10 May 1944. Activated on 1 June 1944. Inactivated on 10 June 1946.

Assignments
16th Bomb Grp, 1 Apr–10 May 1944. 501st Bomb Grp, 1 June 1944–10 June 1946.

Stations
Dalhart AAFld, TX, 1 Apr–10 May 1944. Dalhart AAFld TX, 1 June 1944; Harvard AAFld, NE, 23 Aug 1944–7 Mar 1945; Northwest Field, Guam, 14 Apr 1945–10 June 1946.

Aircraft
B-29, 1944–1946.

Operations
Apparently not manned, 1 Apr–10 May 1944. Combat in Western Pacific, 16 June–14 Aug 1945.

Service Streamers
None.

Campaigns
Air Offensive, Japan; Eastern Mandates; Western Pacific.

Decorations
Distinguished Unit Citation: Japan, 6–13 July 1945.

24th BOMB SQUADRON
Lineage
Constituted 24th Bomb Sq (Very Heavy) on 28 Mar 1944. Activated on 1 Apr 1944. Inactivated on 18 Oct 1948. Redesignated 24th Bomb Sq

(Medium) on 20 Dec 1950. Activated on 2 Jan 1951. Redesignated 24th Bomb Sq (Heavy) on 16 June 1952.

Assignments
6th Bomb Grp, 1 Apr 1944–18 Oct 1948. 6th Bomb Grp, 2 Jan 1951; 6th Bomb (later Strategic Aerospace) Wing, 16 June 1952–.

Stations
Dalhart AAFld, TX, 1 Apr 1944; Grand Island AAFld, NE, 26 May–18 Nov 1944; North Field, Tinian, 28 Dec 1945; Clark Field, Luzon, 13 Mar 1946; Kadena, Okinawa, 1 June 1947–18 Oct 1948. Walker AFB, NM, 2 Jan 1951–.

Aircraft
B-17, 1944; B-29, 1944–1947. B-29, 1951–1952; B-36, 1952–1957; B-52, 1957–.

Operations
Combat in Western Pacific, 27 Jan–14 Aug 1945. No personnel assigned, 25 Apr 1947–18 Oct 1948. While retaining combat capability, trained B-52 crews for Strategic Air Command, 15 July 1959–.

Service Streamers
None

Campaigns
Air Offensive, Japan; Eastern Mandates; Western Pacific.

Decorations
Distinguished Unit Citations: Tokyo, Japan, 25 May 1945; Japanese Empire, 9–19 July 1945. Air Force Outstanding Unit Award: 1 May 1960–31 May 1962.

25th BOMB SQUADRON
Lineage
Organized as 20th Aero Sq on 13 Jun 1917. Redesignated 25th Aero Sq on 22 June 1917. Demobilized on 17 June 1919. Reconstituted and consolidated (1924) with 25th Sq which was authorized on 30 Aug 1921. Organized on 1 Oct 1921. Redesignated: 25th Bomb Sq on 25 Jan 1923; 25th Bomb Sq (Medium) on 6 Dec 1939; 25th Bomb Sq (Heavy) on 20 Nov 1940; 25th Bomb Sq (Very Heavy) on 20 Nov 1943. Inactivated on 1 Oct 1946. Redesignated 25th Bomb Sq (Medium) on 9 May 1952. Activated on 28 May 1952.

Assignments
Unkn, 13 June 1917–Nov 1918; 4th Pursuit Group, Nov 1918–Apr 1919; unkn, Apr–17 June 1919. Second Corps Area, 1 Oct 1921; Panama Canal Dept, 30 Apr 1922; 6th Observation (later Composite; Bomb) Grp, 27 May 1922; 40th Bomb Grp, 12 May 1943–1 Oct 1946. 40th Bomb Wing, 28 May 1952.

Stations
Camp Kelly, TX, 13 June–28 Dec 1917; Ayr, Scotland, 31 Jan 1918; Marske, England, 23 Apr–7 Aug 1918; St Maxient, France, 20 Aug 1918; Romorantin, France, 29 Aug 1918; Colombey-les-Belles, France, 18 Sept 1918; Toul, France, 24 Oct 1918; Colombey-les-Belles,

France, 15 Apr 1919; Le Mans, France 5–19 May 1919; Mitchel Field, NY, 6–17 Jun 1919. Mitchel Field, NY, 1 Oct 1921–22 Apr 1922; France Field, CZ, 30 Apr 1922; Rio Hato, Panama, 8 Dec 1941; Salinas, Ecuador, c. 21 Jan 1942; Howard Field, CZ, 22 May–16 June 1943; Pratt AAFld, KS, 1 July 1943–12 Mar 1944; Chakulia, India, c. 11 Apr 1944–Apr 1945; West Field, Tinian, Apr–7 Nov 1945; March Field, CA, 27 Nov 1945; Davis-Monthan Field, AZ c. 8 May–1 Oct 1946. Smoky Hill AFB, KS, 28 May 1952; Forbes AFB, KS, 20 June 1960.

Aircraft
SE-5, 1918–1919. Unkn, 1921–1922; included NBS-1 during period 1922–1929; included LB-5, LB-6 and LB-7 during period 1928–1932; B-3, 1931–1936; B-6, 1936–1937; B-10, 1937–1939; B-18, 1938 –1942; B-24, 1942–1943; LB-30, 1942–1943; B-26, 1943; B-17, 1943–1944; YB-29, 1943–1944; B-29, 1944–1946. B-29, 1953–1954; B-47, 1954.

Operations
Combat as pursuit unit with Second Army, 10–11 Nov 1918. Good-will flights to El Salvador and Nicaragua, 13–19 May 1935, to Guatemala, 8–11 Feb 1938, and to El Salvador, 19–22 Apr 1938; mercy mission to Chile following devastating earthquake, 28 Jan–13 Feb 1939. Antisubmarine patrols, Dec 1941–May 1943. Combat in CBI, 5 June 1944–29 Mar 1945, and Western Pacific, 5 May–14 Aug 1945.

Service Streamers
None

Campaigns
World War I: Meuse-Argonne. World War II: Antisubmarine, American Theater; India-Burma; Air Offensive, Japan; China Defensive; Western Pacific; Central Burma.

Decorations
Distinguished Unit Citations: Yawata, Japan, 20 Aug 1944; Japan, 5–14 May 1945; Japan, 24 July 1945.

28th BOMB SQUADRON
Lineage
Organized as 28th Aero Sq on 22 June 1917. Demobilized on 16 June 1919. Reconstituted and consolidated (9 Jan 1922) with 28th Sq which was authorized on 30 Aug 1921. Organized on 20 Sept 1921. Inactivated on 28 June 1922. Activated on 1 Sept 1922. Redesignated: 28th Bomb Sq on 25 Jan 1923; 28th Bomb Sq (Medium) on 6 Dec 1939; 28th Bomb Sq (Heavy) on 16 Nov 1941; 28th Bomb Sq (Very Heavy) on 28 Mar 1944. Inactivated on 1 Apr 1944. Activated on 1 Apr 1944. Redesignated: 28th Bomb Sq (Medium) on 10 Aug 1948; 28th Bomb Sq (Heavy) on 1 July 1961.

Assignments
Unkn, 22 June 1917–Mar 1918; attached to RAF for operations and training, Mar–June 1918; unkn, June–Aug 1918; 3d Pursuit Grp, Aug 1918; 2d Pursuit Grp, Dec 1918–Apr 1919. Ninth Corps Area, 20 Sept 1921–28 June 1922. Philippine Dept, 1 Sept 1922; 4th Composite

Grp, 2 Dec 1922; 19th Bomb Grp, 16 Nov 1941–1 Apr 1944 (ground echelon attached to the 5th Interceptor Command, c. 24 Dec 1941–May 1942). 19th Bomb Grp, 1 Apr 1944; 19th Bomb Wing, 1 June 1953–.

Stations
Camp Kelly, TX, 22 June 1917; Toronto, Ont, Canada, 25 Aug 1917; Deseronto, Ont, Canada, 1 Sept 1917; Taliaferro Field No. 1, TX, 5 Nov 1917; Garden City, NY, 25 Jan–25 Feb 1918; St Marie-Cappel, France, 20 Mar 1918 (flights operated from various stations in Nord, Pas-de-Calais, and Somme, until squadron reassembled at St Omer on 24 June: headquarters and B flights located in Flanders; C flight in Picardy; A flight in Flanders until 6 June when it moved to Picardy and joined C flight at Rousseauville in the Amiens sector); Boisdinghem, France, 13 Apr 1918; Alquines, France, 15 Apr 1918; St Omer, France 24 June 1918; Issoudun, France, 26 June 1918; Orly, France, 8 July 1918; Vaucouleurs, France, 16 Aug 1918; Lisle-en-Barrois, France, 20 Sept 1918; Foucaucourt, France, 6 Nov 1918; Grand, France, 15 Feb 1919; Colombey-les-Belles, France, 15 Apr 1919; Le Mans, France, 4–19 May 1919; Mitchel Field, NY, 31 May–16 June 1919. Mather Field, CA, 20 Sept 1921–28 June 1922. Clark Field, Luzon, 1 Sept 1922; Kindley Field, Corregidor, Sept 1922; Camp Nichols, Luzon, Nov 1922; Clark Field, Luzon, Dec 1922; Camp Nichols, Luzon, 4 June 1923; Clark Field, Luzon, 16 June 1938; Batchelor, Australia, c. 24 Dec 1941 (ground echelon in Luzon and Mindanao, c. 24 Dec 1941–May 1942); Singosari, Java, 30 Dec 1941; Melbourne, Australia, c. 4 Mar 1942; Cloncurry, Australia, c. 28 Mar 1942 (detachment operated from Perth, Australia, c. 28 Mar–18 May 1942); Longreach, Australia, c. 5 May 1942; Mareeba, Australia, 24 July–c. 18 Nov 1942; Pocatello, ID, c. 30 Dec 1942; Pyote AAB, TX 24 Jan 1943–1 Apr 1944. Great Bend AAFld, KS, 1 Apr–8 Dec 1944; North Field, Guam, 16 Jan 1945; Kadena, Okinawa, 27 June 1950–14 May 1954; Pinecastle AFB, FL, c. 28 May 1954; Homestead AFB, FL, c. 25 June 1956–.

Aircraft
JN-4, 1917; in addition to Spad XIII, briefly included Spad VII during period 1918-1919. Apparently included DH-4, 1921-1922. In addition to DH-4, 1922–c. 1928, and NBS-1, 1924–1930, included LB-5 and OA-1 during period 1929-1931; B-3, c. 1931–1937; B-10, 1937–1941; B-18 and B-17, successively during 1941; B-17s, LB-30s, and probably B-24s, 7 Dec 1941–1942; B-17, 1942–1944. B-29, 1944–1954; B-47, 1954-1961; B-52, 1962–.

Operations
Flying training unit, Nov–Dec 1917; maintained aircraft and underwent combat training while attached by flights to tactical units of RAF serving on front with British Second and Fifth Armies, 20 Mar–c. 24 June 1918 (C flight, attached to 25 Squadron, RAF, at Villers-Brettonneux, Beauvais, and Rousseauville, participated in Somme Defensive, 21 Mar–6 Apr 1918); combat as pursuit unit with American First Army, 2 Sept–10 Nov 1918. Combat in Southwest Pacific, 7 Dec 1941–c. 16 Nov 1942;

ground echelon fought with infantry units in Philippine Islands, c. 24 Dec 1941–May 1942; replacement training, 1 Feb 1943–1 Apr 1944. Combat in Western Pacific, c. 12 Feb–15 Aug 1945. Combat in Korea, 28 June 1950–25 July 1953.

Service Streamers
American Theater.

Campaigns
World War I: Flanders; Lys; Picardy; Lorraine; St Mihiel; Meuse-Argonne. World War II: Philippine Islands; East Indies; Air Offensive, Japan; Papua; Guadalcanal; Western Pacific; Air Combat, Asiatic-Pacific Theater; Korean War: UN Defensive; UN Offensive; CCF Intervention; First UN Counteroffensive; CCF Spring Offensive; UN Summer-Fall Offensive; Second Korean Winter; Korea Summer-Fall 1952; Third Korean Winter; Korea Summer-Fall, 1953.

Decorations
Distinguished Unit Citations: Philippine Islands, 7 Dec 1941–10 May 1942; Philippine Islands, 8–22 Dec 1941; Philippines and Netherlands Indies, 1 Jan–1 Mar 1942; Philippine Islands, 6 Jan–8 Mar 1942; Papua, 23 July–c. 16 Nov 1942; New Britain, 7–12 Aug 1942; Japan, 9–19 Mar 1945; Kobe, Japan, 5 June 1945; Korea, 28 June–15 Sept 1950. Philippine Presidential Unit Citation. Republic of Korea Presidential Unit Citation: 7 July 1950–27 July 1953.

30th BOMB SQUADRON
Lineage
Organized as 30th Aero Sq on 13 June 1917. Demobilized on 14 April 1919. Reconstituted, and redesignated 30th Bomb Sq on 24 Mar 1923. Activated on 24 June 1932. Redesignated 30th Bomb Sq (Heavy) on 6 Dec 1939. Inactivated on 1 Apr 1944. Redesignated 30th Bomb Sq (Very Heavy). Activated on 1 Apr 1944. Redesignated: 30th Bomb Sq (Medium) on 10 Aug 1948; 30th Bomb Sq (Heavy) on 1 July 1961. Discontinued, and inactivated on 1 Feb 1963.

Assignments
Unkn, 13 June–Sept 1917; Third Aviation Instruction Center, Sept 1917–Jan 1919; unkn, Jan–14 Apr 1919. 19th Bomb Grp, 24 June 1932–1 Apr 1944 (ground echelon attached to the 5th Interceptor Command, c. 20 Dec 1941–May 1942). 19th Bomb Grp, 1 Apr 1944; 19th Bomb Wing, 1 June 1953; 4133d Strategic Wing, 1 Jan 1962–1 Feb 1963.

Stations
Camp Kelly, TX, 13 June –11 Aug 1917; Etampes, France, 19 Sept 1917; Issoudun, France, 23 Sept 1917; Bordeaux, France, c. 6 Jan–c. 18 Mar 1919; Mitchel Field, NY, c. 5–14 Apr 1919. Rockwell Field, CA, 24 June 1932; March Field, CA, 25 Oct 1935; Albuquerque, NM, June–27 Sept 1941; Clark Field, Luzon, c. 23 Oct 1941; Batchelor, Australia, c. 20 Dec 1941 (ground echelon in Luzon and Mindanao, c. 20 Dec 1941–May 1942); Singosari, Java, c. 31 Dec 1941; Melbourne, Australia, c. 5 Mar 1942; Cloncurry, Australia, c. 27 Mar 1942; Longreach, Australia, c. 13 May 1942; Mareeba, Australia, c. 24 July–c. 10 Nov 1942; Pocatello,

ID, c. 9 Dec 1942; Pyote AAB, TX 24 Jan 1943–1 Apr 1944. Great Bend AAFld, KS, 1 Apr–8 Dec 1944; North Field, Guam, 16 Jan 1945; Kadena, Okinawa, 27 June 1950–16 May 1954; Pinecastle AFB, FL, 30 May 1954; Homestead AFB, FL, c. 25 June 1956; Grand Forks AFB, ND, 1 Jan 1962–1 Feb 1963.

Aircraft
Included O-27, OA-4, YOA-5, B-3, and B-12 during period 1932–1936; included B-10, B-18, and B-17, successively, during period 1935–1941; B-17s, and probably B-24s and LB-30', 7 Dec 1941–1942; B-17, 1942–1944. B-29, 1944–1954; B-47, 1954–1961; B-52, 1962–1963.

Operations
Repaired and overhauled aircraft engines, 1917–1918. Combat in Southwest Pacific, 7 Dec 1941–c. 16 Nov 1942; ground echelon fought with infantry units in Philippine Islands, c. 20 Dec 1941–May 1942; replacement training, 1 Feb 1943–1 Apr 1944. Combat in Western Pacific, c. 12 Feb–15 Aug 1945. Combat in Korea, 28 June 1950–25 July 1953.

Service Streamers
Theater of Operations..

Campaigns
World War II: Philippine Islands; East Indies; Air Offensive, Japan; Papua; Guadalcanal; Western Pacific; Air Combat, Asiatic-Pacific Theater; Korean War: UN Defensive; UN Offensive; CCF Intervention; First UN Counteroffensive; CCF Spring Offensive; UN Summer-Fall Offensive; Second Korean Winter; Korea Summer-Fall 1952; Third Korean Winter; Korea Summer-Fall, 1953.

Decorations
Distinguished Unit Citations: Philippine Islands, 7 Dec 1941–10 May 1942; Philippine Islands, 8–22 Dec 1941; Philippines and Netherlands Indies, 1 Jan–1 Mar 1942; Philippine Islands, 6 Jan–8 Mar 1942; Papua, 23 July–c. 10 Nov 1942; New Britain, 7–12 Aug 1942; Japan, 9–19 Mar 1945; Kobe, Japan, 5 June 1945; Korea, 28 June–15 Sept 1950. Philippine Presidential Unit Citation. Republic of Korea Presidential Unit Citation: 7 July 1950–27 July 1953.

32d BOMB SQUADRON
Lineage
Organized as 32d Aero Sq on 13 June 1917. Demobilized on 14 Apr 1919. Reconstituted, and redesignated 32d Bomb Sq, on 24 Mar 1923. Activated on 24 June 1932. Redesignated: 32d Bomb Sq (Heavy) on 6 Dec 1949; 32d Bomb Sq (Very Heavy) on 5 Aug 1945. Inactivated on 15 Oct 1945. Activated on 4 Aug 1946. Redesignated 32d Bomb Sq (Medium) on 28 May 1948.

Assignments
Unkn, 13 June–Sept 1917; Third Aviation Instruction Center, Sept 1917–Jan 1919; unkn, Jan–14 Apr 1919. 19th Bomb Grp, 24 June 1932 (attached to IV Bomber Command, 22 Oct 1941; apparently attached to 7th Bomb Grp for opera-

tions, c. 8 Dec 1941); Sierra Bomb Grp, 16 Dec 1941; Fourth Air Force, 17 Jan 1942 (attached to IV Bomber Command, 26 Jan 1942); Second Air Force (attached to 301st Bomb Grp), 16 Mar 1942; 301st Bomb Grp, 31 Mar 1942–15 Oct 1945. 301st Bomb Grp, 4 Aug 1946; 301st Bomb Wing, 16 June 1952–.

Stations
Camp Kelly, TX, 13 June–11 Aug 1917; Etampes, France, 20 Sept 1917; Issoudun, France, 28 Sept 1917; Bordeau, France, c. 6 Jan–c. 18 Mar 1919; Mitchel Field, NY, c. 5–14 Apr 1919; Rockwell Field, CA, 24 June 1932; March Field, CA, 25 Oct 1935; Albuquerque, NM, c. 4 June–22 Nov 1941 (air echelon, which was at Hamilton Field, CA, under orders for movement to Philippine Islands at time of Japanese attack on Hawaii on 7 Dec 1941, apparently moved to Muroc, CA, c. 8 Dec 1941; ground echelon departed San Francisco aboard ship on 6 Dec 1941 and returned on 9 Dec 1941); Bakersfield, CA, 17 Dec 1941 (air echelon evidently departed for Southwest Pacific, c. late Dec 1941; concurrently dissolved and personnel assigned to other units); Geiger Field, WA, c. 14 Mar 1942; Alamogordo, NM, 27 May 1942 (operated from Muroc, CA, c. 28 May–14 June 1942); Richard E Byrd Field, VA, 21 June –19 July 1942; Chelveston, England, 18 Aug 1942; Tafaraoui, Algeria, 26 Nov 1942; Maison Blanche, Algeria, 6 Dec 1942; Biskra, Algeria, 16 Dec 1942; Ain M'lila, Algeria, 16 Jan 1943; St-Donat, Algeria, 8 Mar 1943; Oudna, Tunisia, 6 Aug 1943; Cerignola, Italy, 11 Dec 1943; Lucera, Italy, 2 Feb 1944–July 1945; Sioux Falls AAFld, SD, 28 July 1945; Mountain Home AAFld, ID, 17 Aug 1945; Pyote AAFld, TX, 23 Aug–15 Oct 1945. Clovis AAFld, NM, 4 Aug 1946; Smoky Hill AAFld, KS, 16 July 1947; Barksdale AFB, LA, 7 Nov 1949; Lockbourne AFB, OH, 15 Apr 1958–.

Aircraft
Included C-26, O-27, B-12, and apparently B-3 during period 1932–1935; included B-10, B-18, and B-17, successively, during period 1935–1941; B-17, 1942–1945. B-29, 1947–1953; B-47, 1953–1958; RB-47, 1958; B-47, 1958–1961; E-47, 1961–.

Operations
Aircraft repair, 1917–1918. Antisubmarine patrols off California coast, mid–Dec 1941, and c. late may–c. early June 1942. Combat in ETO and MTO, 2 Oct 1942–c. 26 Apr 1945. Electronics countermeasures, 1958–.

Service Streamers
Theater of Operations.

Campaigns
Antisubmarine, American Theater; Air Offensive, Europe; Egypt-Libya; Tunisia; Sicily; Naples-Foggia; Anzio; Rome-Arno; Normandy; Northern France; Southern France; North Apennines; Rhineland; Central Europe; Po Valley; Air Combat, EAME Theater.

Decorations
Distinguished Unit Citations: Tunisia, 6 Apr 1943; Germany, 25 Feb 1944. Air Force Outstanding Unit Award: 1 Jan 1961–31 Dec 1962.

33d BOMB SQUADRON

Lineage
Constituted 33d Bomb Sq (Medium) on 22 Dec 1939. Activated on 1 Feb 1940. Redesignated: 33d Bomb Sq (Heavy) on 3 Feb 1944; 33d Bomb Sq (Very Heavy) on 30 Apr 1946; 33d Bomb Sq (Medium) on 28 July 1948.

Assignments
22d Bomb Grp, 1 Feb 1940; 22d Bomb Wing, 16 June 1952–.

Stations
Patterson Field, OH, 1 Feb 1940; Langley Field, VA, 16 Nov 1940; Muroc, CA, 9 Dec 1941-28 Jan 1942; Brisbane, Australia, 25 Feb 1942; Ipswich, Australia, 1 Mar 1942; Antil Plains, Australia, 7 Apr 1942; Woodstock, Australia, 20 July 1942; Iron Range, Australia, 29 Sept 1942; Woodstock, Australia, 4 Feb 1943; Dobodura, New Guinea, 15 Oct 1943; Nadzab, New Guinea, c. 10 Jan 1944; Owi, Schouten Islands, 14 Aug 1944; Leyte, c. 10 Nov 1944; Angaur, 26 Nov 1944; Samar, 21 Jan 1945; Clark Field, Luzon, 12 Mar 1945; Okinawa, 15 Aug 1945; Ft William McKinley, Luzon, 23 Nov 1945; Okinawa, 15 June 1946; Smoky Hill AFB, KS, June 1948; March AFB, CA, 10 May 1949 (operated from Kadena AFB, Okinawa, c. 9 July–c. 30 Oct 1950)–.

Aircraft
B-18, 1940–1941; B-26, 1941–1943; B-25, 1943–1944; B-24, 1944–1945; B-29, 1946–1953; B-47, 1953–.

Operations
Antisubmarine patrols, Dec 1941–Jan 1942; combat in Southwest and Western Pacific, 6 Apr 1942–7 Jan 1943, 7 Oct 1943–3 Aug 1945. Not manned, 23 Nov 1945–15 June 1946. Combat in Korea, 13 July–1 Oct 1950.

Service Streamers
None

Campaigns
World War II: Antisubmarine, American Theater; East Indies; Air Offensive, Japan; China Defensive; Papua; New Guinea; Bismarck Archipelago; Western Pacific; Leyte; Luzon; Southern Philippines; China Offensive; Air Combat, Asiatic-Pacific Theater. Korean War: UN Defensive; UN Offensive.

Decorations
Distinguished Unit Citations: Papua, 23 July 1942–[7] Jan 1943; New Guinea, 5 Nov 1943. Philippine Presidential Unit Citation. Republic of Korea Presidential Unit Citation: 10 July–24 Oct 1950.

39th BOMB SQUADRON

Lineage
Constituted 39th Bomb Sq (Very Heavy) on 28 Mar 1944. Activated on 1 Apr 1944. Inactivated on 18 Oct 1948. Redesignated 39th Bomb Sq (Medium) on 20 Dec 1950. Activated on 2 Jan 1951. Redesignated 39th Bomb Sq (Heavy) on 16 June 1952.

Assignments
6th Bomb Grp, 1 Apr 1944–18 Oct 1948. 6th Bomb Grp, 2 Jan 1951; 6th Bomb (later Strategic Aerospace) Wing, 16 June 1952–.

Stations
Dalhart AAFld, TX, 1 Apr 1944; Grand Island AAFld, NE, 26 May–18 Nov 1944; North Field, Tinian, 28 Dec 1945; Clark Field, Luzon, 13 Mar 1946; Kadena, Okinawa, 1 June 1947–18 Oct 1948. Walker AFB, NM, 2 Jan 1951–.

Aircraft
B-17, 1944; B-29, 1944–1947. B-29, 1951–1952; B-36, 1952–1957; B-52, 1957–.

Operations
Combat in Western Pacific, 27 Jan–14 Aug 1945. No personnel assigned, 25 Apr 1947–18 Oct 1948. While retaining combat capability, trained B-52 crews for Strategic Air Command, 15 July 1959–.

Service Streamers
None

Campaigns
Air Offensive, Japan; Eastern Mandates; Western Pacific.

Decorations
Distinguished Unit Citations: Tokyo, Japan, 25 May 1945; Japanese Empire, 9–19 July 1945. Air Force Outstanding Unit Award: 1 May 1960–31 May 1962.

40th BOMB SQUADRON

Lineage
Constituted 40th Bomb Sq (Very Heavy) on 28 Mar 1944. Activated on 1 Apr 1944. Inactivated on 18 Oct 1948. Redesignated 40th Bomb Sq (Medium) on 20 Dec 1950. Activated on 2 Jan 1951. Redesignated 40th Bomb Sq (Heavy) on 16 June 1952.

Assignments
6th Bomb Grp, 1 Apr 1944–18 Oct 1948. 6th Bomb Grp, 2 Jan 1951; 6th Bomb (later Strategic Aerospace) Wing, 16 June 1952.

Stations
Dalhart AAFld, TX, 1 Apr 1944; Grand Island AAFld, NE, 26 May–18 Nov 1944; North Field, Tinian, 28 Dec 1945; Clark Field, Luzon, 13 Mar 1946; Kadena, Okinawa, 1 June 1947–18 Oct 1948. Walker AFB, NM, 2 Jan 1951–.

Aircraft
B-17, 1944; B-29, 1944–1947. B-29, 1951–1952; B-36, 1952–1957; B-52, 1957–.

Operations
Combat in Western Pacific, 27 Jan–14 Aug 1945. No personnel assigned, 25 Apr 1947–18 Oct 1948. While retaining combat capability, trained B-52 crews for Strategic Air Command, 10 June 1960–1 Jan 1962.

Service Streamers
None

Campaigns
Air Offensive, Japan; Eastern Mandates; Western Pacific.

Decorations
Distinguished Unit Citations: Tokyo, Japan, 25 May 1945; Japanese Empire, 9–19 July 1945. Air Force Outstanding Unit Award: 1 May 1960–31 May 1962.

41st BOMB SQUADRON
Lineage
Constituted 41st Bomb Sq (Very Heavy) on 28 Mar 1944. Activated on 1 Apr 1944. Inactivated on 10 May 1944. Activated on 1 June 1944. Inactivated on 10 June 1946. Activated in the reserve on 12 July 1947. Inactivated on 27 June 1949.

Assignments
6th Bomb Grp, 1 Apr–10 May 1944. 501st Bomb Grp, 1 June 1944–10 June 1946. 448th Bomb Grp, 12 July 1947–27 June 1949.

Stations
Dalhart AAFld, TX, 1 Apr–10 May 1944. Dalhart AAFld TX, 1 June 1944; Harvard AAFld, NE, 23 Aug 1944–7 Mar 1945; Northwest Field, Guam, 14 Apr 1945–10 June 1946. Long Beach Mun Aprt, CA, 12 July 1947–27 June 1949.

Aircraft
B-29, 1944–1946.

Operations
Combat in Western Pacific, 16 June–14 Aug 1945.

Service Streamers
None.

Campaigns
Air Offensive, Japan; Eastern Mandates; Western Pacific.

Decorations
Distinguished Unit Citation: Japan, 6–13 July 1945.

42d BOMB SQUADRON
Lineage
Organized as 42d Aero Sq on 13 June 1917. Redesignated Sq I, Wilbur Wright Field, OH, on 1 Oct 1918. Demobilized on 21 Feb 1919. Reconstituted and consolidated (1924) with 42d Sq which was authorized on 10 June 1922. Organized on 5 July 1922. Redesignated: 42d School Sq on 25 Jan 1923; 42d Bomb Sq on 1 Mar 1935. Inactivated on 1 Sept 1936. Redesignated 42d Bomb Sq (Medium) on 22 Dec 1939. Activated on 1 Feb 1940. Redesignated 42d Bomb Sq (Heavy) on 11 Dec 1940; 42d Bomb Sq (Very Heavy) on 30 Apr 1946. Inactivated on 20 Oct 1948. Redesignated 42d Bomb Sq (Heavy), and activated, on 1 Dec 1948. Discontinued, and inactivated, on 1 Feb 1963.

Assignments
Unkn, 1917–1919. 10th School Grp, 5 July 1922; Air Corps Advanced Flying School, 16 July 1931; 3d Wing (attached to Air Corps Advanced Flying School), 1 Mar 1935–1 Sept 1936. 11th Bomb Grp, 1 Feb 1940–20 Oct 1948. 11th Bomb Grp, 1 Dec 1948; 11th Bomb Wing, 16 June 1952; 4043d Strategic Wing, 1 June 1960–1 Feb 1963.

Stations
Camp Kelly, TX, 13 June 1917; Wilbur Wright Field, OH, 25 Aug 1917–21 Feb 1919. Kelly Field, TX, 5 July 1922–1 Sept 1936. Hickam Field, TH, 1 Feb 1940; Kualoa Point, TH, 5 June 1942; Mokuleia, TH, 8 July 1942; Plaines des Gaiacs, New Caledonia, 22 July 1942; Espiritu Santo, 23 Nov 1942 (forward echelon operated from Guadalcanal, Dec 1942); Kualoa Point, TH, 8 Apr 1943; Funafuti, 9 Nov 1943; Mokuleia, TH, 9 Jan 1944; Kahuku, TH, 19 Mar 1944; Mokuleia, TH, 23 June 1944; Guam, 22 Sept 1944; Okinawa, 2 July 1945; Manila, Luzon, Dec 1945; Guam, 15 May 1946–20 Oct 1948. Carswell AFB, TX, 1 Dec 1948; Altus AFB, OK, 13 Dec 1957; Wright-Patterson AFB, OH, 1 June 1960–1 Feb 1963.

Aircraft
Apparently included SJ-1, JN-4, and possibly DH-4 during period 1917–1919. In addition to DH-4 , c. 1922–1931, and O-2, c. 1926–1933, included O-11 and O-19 during period 1930–1932; primarily O-19 and O-25 during period 1933–1935; included B-3, B-4, and B-5 during period 1935–1936. B-18, 1940–1941; B-17, 1941–1943; B-24, 1943–1945; B-29, 1946. B-36, 1949–1957; B-52, 1958–1963.

Operations
Evidently flying training unit during period 1917–1919. Search missions from Hawaii, 7 Dec 1941–July 1942; May–Oct 1943. Combat in South and Southwest Pacific, 24 July 1942–7 Feb 1943; in Central Pacific, May, June, July, Sept 1943; and in Central and Western Pacific, 13 Nov–20 Dec 1943, and 24 Oct 1944–12 Aug 1945. Operational training unit, Jan–June 1944. Non-operational, 1947–1948.

Service Streamers
None

Campaigns
Central Pacific; Air Offensive, Japan; Papua; Guadalcanal; Eastern Mandates; Western Pacific; Ryukyus; China Offensive; Air Combat, Asiatic-Pacific Theater.

Decorations
Distinguished Unit Citation: South Pacific, 31 July–30 Nov 1942. Presidential Unit Citation, [1942]. Air Force Outstanding Unit Awards: 6 Aug 1954–15 July 1957; 27 Oct 1958–[1 June] 1960.

43d BOMB SQUADRON
Lineage
Constituted 29th Bomb Sq (Heavy) on 22 Dec 1939. Activated on 1 Feb 1940. Redesignated 43d Bomb Sq (Heavy) on 13 Mar 1940. Inactivated on 1 Apr 1944. Redesignated 43d Bomb Sq (Very Heavy). Activated on 1 Apr 1944. Inactivated on 20 May 1946.

Assignments
29th Bomb Grp, 1 Feb 1940–1 Apr 1944. 29th Bomb Grp, 1 Apr 1944–20 May 1946.

Stations
Langley Field, VA, 1 Feb 1940; MacDill Field, FL, 21 May 1940; Pope Field, NC, c. 7 Dec 1941; MacDill Field, FL, c. 1 Jan 1942; Gowen Field, ID, 25 June 1942–1 Apr 1944. Pratt AAFld, KS, 1 Apr–c. 6 Dec 1944; North Field, Guam, 17 Jan 1945–20 May 1946.

Aircraft
B-18, 1940–1941; B-17, 1940–1943; B-24, 1943–1944. B-17, 1944; B-29, 1944–1946.

Operations
Antisubmarine patrols, Dec 1941–June 1942. Operational and later replacement training unit, 1942–1944. Combat in Western Pacific, c. 16 Feb–15 Aug 1945.

Service Streamers
None

Campaigns
Antisubmarine , American Theater; Air Offensive, Japan; Western Pacific.

Decorations
Distinguished Unit Citations: Japan, 31 Mar 1945; Japan, 19–26 June 1945.

44th BOMB SQUADRON
Lineage
Constituted 44th Bomb Sq (Medium) on 22 Nov 1940. Activated on 1 Apr 1941. Redesignated 44th Bomb Sq (Heavy) on 7 May 1942; 44th Bomb Sq (Very Heavy) on 20 Nov 1943. Inactivated on 1 Oct 1946. Redesignated 44th Bomb Sq (Medium) on 9 May 1952. Activated on 28 May 1952.

Assignments
40th Bomb Grp, 1 Apr 1941–1 Oct 1946. 40th Bomb Wing, 28 May 1952–.

Stations
Borinquen Field, PR, 1 Apr 1941; Howard Field, CZ, 16 June 1942; Guatemala City, Guatemala, 6 July 1942; Howard Field, CZ, c. 4–15 June 1943; Pratt AAFld, KS, 1 July 1943–12 Mar 1944; Chakulia, India, c. 11 Apr 1944°Apr 1945; West Field, Tinian, Apr–7 Nov 1945; March Field, CA, 27 Nov 1945; Davis-Monthan Field, AZ, 13 May–1 Oct 1946. Smoky Hill AFB, KS, 28 May 1952; Forbes AFB, KS, 20 June 1960.

Aircraft
B-18, 1941 –1942; B-17, 1942–1944; B-24, 1942–1943; B-26, 1943–1944; YB-29, 1943–1944; B-29, 1944–1946. B-29, 1953–1954; B-47, 1954–.

Operations
Antisubmarine patrols, Dec 1941–May 1943. Combat in CBI, 5 June 1944–29 Mar 1945, and Western Pacific, 5 May–14 Aug 1945.

Service Streamers
None

Campaigns
Antisubmarine, American Theater; India-Burma; Air Offensive, Japan; China Defensive; Western Pacific; Central Burma.

Decorations
Distinguished Unit Citations: Yawata, Japan, 20 Aug 1944; Japan, 5–14 May 1945; Japan, 24 July 1945.

45th BOMB SQUADRON

Lineage
Constituted 45th Bomb Sq (Medium) on 22 Nov 1940. Activated on 1 Apr 1941. Redesignated: 45th Bomb Sq (Heavy) on 7 May 1942; 45th Bomb Sq (Very Heavy) on 20 Nov 1943. Inactivated on 1 Oct 1946. Redesignated 45th Bomb Sq (Medium) on 9 May 1952. Activated on 28 May 1952.

Assignments
40th Bomb Grp, 1 Apr 1941–1 Oct 1946. 40th Bomb Wing, 28 May 1952–.

Stations
Borinquen Field, PR, 1 Apr 1941; France Field, CZ, 17 June 1942; David, Panama, 13 Nov 1942; Galapagos Islands, 18 Feb 1943; Howard Field, CZ, c. 22 May–15 June 1943; Pratt AAFld, KS, 1 July 1943–11 Mar 1944; Chakulia, India, c. 9 Apr 1944–Apr 1945; West Field, Tinian, Apr–7 Nov 1945; March Field, CA, 27 Nov 1945; Davis-Monthan Field, AZ, c. 13 May–1 Oct 1946. Smoky Hill AFB, KS, 28 May 1952; Forbes AFB, KS 20 June 1960–.

Aircraft
B-18, 1941 –1942; LB-30, 1942–1943; B-24, 1943; B-17, 1943–1944; B-26, 1943; YB-29, 1943–1944; B-29, 1943–1946. B-29, 1953–1954; B-47, 1954–.

Operations
Antisubmarine patrols, Dec 1941–May 1943. Combat in CBI, 5 June 1944–29 Mar 1945, and Western Pacific, 5 May–14 Aug 1945.

Service Streamers
None

Campaigns
Antisubmarine, American Theater; India-Burma; Air Offensive, Japan; China Defensive; Western Pacific; Central Burma.

Decorations
Distinguished Unit Citations: Yawata, Japan, 20 Aug 1944; Japan, 5–14 May 1945; Japan, 24 July 1945.

49th BOMB SQUADRON

Lineage
Organized as 49th Aero Sq on 6 Aug 1917. Demobilized on 22 Mar 1919. Reconstituted and consolidated (16 Oct 1936) with 166th Aero Sq which was organized on 18 Dec 1917 and redesignated 49th Sq on 14 Mar 1921. Redesignated: 49th Bomb Sq on 25 Jan 1923; 49th Bomb Sq (Heavy) on 6 Dec 1939. Inactivated on 28 Feb 1946. Redesignated 49th Bomb Sq (Very Heavy) on 5 Apr 1946. Activated on 1 July 1947. Redesignated 49th Bomb Sq (Medium) on 28 May 1948.

Assignments
2d Bomb Grp, from consolidation in 1936 to 28 Feb 1946 (attached to Newfoundland Base Command, Dec 1941–June 1942). 2d Bomb Grp, 1 July 1947; 2d Bomb Wing, 16 June 1952–.

Stations
Langley Field, VA, from consolidation in 1936 to 23 Nov 1941; Newfoundland AB, Newfoundland, 13 Dec 1941 (air echelon, en route to Newfoundland, arrived Mitchel Field, NY, 1 Dec 1941; ordered to west coast for emergency duty, 8 Dec 1941; operated from Geiger Field, WA, in conjunction with 12th Recon Sq until echelon dissolved in late Dec 1941); Argentia, Newfoundland, 16 Jan–June 1942; Langley Field, VA, 24 June 1942; Ephrata, WA, 29 Oct 1942; Lewistown, MT, 28 Nov 1942–c. 13 Mar 1943; Navarin, Algeria, 25 Apr 1943; Chateaudun-du-Rhumel, Algeria, 27 Apr 1943; Ain M'lila, Algeria, 17 June 1943; Massicault, Tunisia, 31 July 1943; Amendola, Italy, c. 10 Dec 1943; Foggia, Italy, 29 Oct 1945–28 Feb 1946. Andrews Field, MD, 1 July 1947; Davis-Monthan Field, AZ, 24 Sept 1947; Chatham AFB, GA, 1 May 1949; Hunter AFB, GA, 29 Sept 1950–.

Aircraft
In addition to B-10, B-17, and B-18, included A-20, XB-15, and B-23, during period 1936–1942; B-17, 1942–1945. B-29, 1947–1950; B-50, 1949–1954; B-47, 1954–.

Operations
Participated in good-will flights to Argentina, 15–27 Feb 1938, Colombia, 3–12 Aug 1938, Mexico, 9–15 June 1939, and Brazil, 10–28 Nov 1939; in a famous demonstration of the long-range capabilities of the B-17, intercepted Italian liner Rex 725 miles at sea, 12 May 1938; mercy mission in relief of earthquake victims in Santiago, Chile, 4–14 Feb 1939. Anti-submarine patrols off Pacific coast, Dec 1941, and Atlantic coast, 25 July–c. 28 Oct 1942; combat in MTO and ETO, 28 Apr 1943–1 May 1945.

Service Streamers
None

Campaigns
World War I, credits of consolidated squadron: Lorraine (earned by 49th Aero); St Mihiel (earned by 49th Aero); Meuse-Argonne (earned by 49th Aero and 166th Aero). World War II: Antisubmarine, American Theater; Air Offensive, Europe; Tunisia; Sicily; Naples-Foggia; Anzio; Rome-Arno; Normandy; Northern France; Southern France; North Apennines; Rhineland; Central Europe; Po Valley; Air Combat, EAME Theater.

Decorations
Distinguished Unit Citations: Steyr, Austria, 24 Feb 1944; Germany, 25 Feb 1944. Air Force Outstanding Unit Award: 1 Nov 1956–1 Apr 1957.

52d BOMB SQUADRON

Lineage
Constituted 52d Bomb Sq (Heavy) on 22 Dec 1939. Activated on 1 Feb 1940. Inactivated on 1 Apr 1944. Redesignated 52d Bomb Sq (Very Heavy). Activated on 1 Apr 1944. Inactivated on 20 May 1946.

Assignments
29th Bomb Grp, 1 Feb 1940–1 Apr 1944. 29th Bomb Grp, 1 Apr 1944–20 May 1946.

Stations
Langley Field, VA, 1 Feb 1940; MacDill Field, FL, 21 May 1940; Gowen Field, ID, 25 June 1942–1 Apr 1944. Pratt AAFld, KS, 1 Apr–c. 6 Dec 1944; North Field, Guam, 17 Jan 1945–20 May 1946.

Aircraft
B-18, 1940–1941; B-17, 1940–1943; B-24, 1943–1944. B-17, 1944; B-29, 1944–1946.

Operations
Antisubmarine patrols, Jan–June 1942. Operational and later replacement training unit, 1942–1944. Combat in Western Pacific, c. 16 Feb–15 Aug 1945.

Service Streamers
None

Campaigns
Antisubmarine , American Theater; Air Offensive, Japan; Western Pacific.

Decorations
Distinguished Unit Citations: Japan, 31 Mar 1945; Japan, 19–26 June 1945.

60th BOMB SQUADRON

Lineage
Constituted 60th Bomb Sq (Heavy) on 20 Nov 1940. Activated on 15 Jan 1941. Inactivated on 1 April 1944. Redesignated 60th Bomb Sq (Very Heavy). Activated on 1 Apr 1944. Inactivated on 27 Dec 1945.

Assignments
39th Bomb Grp, 15 Jan 1941–1 Apr 1944. 39th Bomb Grp, 1 Apr 1944–27 Dec 1945.

Stations
Ft Douglas, UT, 15 Jan 1941; Geiger Field, WA, 2 July 1941; Davis-Monthan Field, AZ, 5 Feb 1942–1 Apr 1944. Smoky Hill AAFld, KS, 1 Apr 1944; Dalhart AAFld, TX, 27 May 1944; Smoky Hill AAFld, KS, 17 July 1944–8 Jan 1945; North Field, Guam, 18 Feb–16 Nov 1945; Camp Anza, CA, 15–27 Dec 1945.

Aircraft
B-17, 1941–1942; B-24, 1942–1944. B-29, 1944–1945.

Operations
Operational and later replacement training unit, 1942–1944. Combat in Western Pacific, c. 6 Apr–14 Aug 1945.

Service Streamers
American Theater

Campaigns
Air Offensive, Japan; Western Pacific.

Decorations
Distinguished Unit Citations: Japan, 10 May 1945; Tokyo and Yokohama, Japan, 23–29 May 1945.

61st BOMB SQUADRON
Lineage
Constituted 61st Bomb Sq (Heavy) on 20 Nov 1940. Activated on 15 Jan 1941. Inactivated on 1 April 1944. Redesignated 61st Bomb Sq (Very Heavy). Activated on 1 Apr 1944. Inactivated on 27 Dec 1945.

Assignments
39th Bomb Grp, 15 Jan 1941–1 Apr 1944. 39th Bomb Grp, 1 Apr 1944–27 Dec 1945.

Stations
Ft Douglas, UT, 15 Jan 1941; Geiger Field, WA, 2 July 1941; Davis-Monthan Field, AZ, 5 Feb 1942–1 Apr 1944. Smoky Hill AAFld, KS, 1 Apr 1944; Dalhart AAFld, TX, 27 May 1944; Smoky Hill AAFld, KS, 17 July 1944–8 Jan 1945; North Field, Guam, 18 Feb–16 Nov 1945; Camp Anza, CA, 15–27 Dec 1945.

Aircraft
B-17, 1941–1942; B-24, 1942–1944. B-29, 1944–1945.

Operations
Operational and later replacement training unit, 1942–1944. Combat in Western Pacific, c. 6 Apr–14 Aug 1945.

Service Streamers
American Theater

Campaigns
Air Offensive, Japan; Western Pacific.

Decorations
Distinguished Unit Citations: Japan, 10 May 1945; Tokyo and Yokohama, Japan, 23–29 May 1945.

62d BOMB SQUADRON
Lineage
Constituted 62d Bomb Sq (Heavy) on 20 Nov 1940. Activated on 15 Jan 1941. Inactivated on 1 April 1944. Redesignated 62d Bomb Sq (Very Heavy). Activated on 1 Apr 1944. Inactivated on 27 Dec 1945. Redesignated 62d Bomb Sq (Heavy), and activated, on 15 Nov 1962. Organized on 1 Feb 1963.

Assignments
39th Bomb Grp, 15 Jan 1941–1 Apr 1944. 39th Bomb Grp, 1 Apr 1944–27 Dec 1945. Strategic Air Command, 15 Nov 1962; 39th Bomb Wing, 1 Feb 1963–.

Stations
Ft Douglas, UT, 15 Jan 1941; Geiger Field, WA, 2 July 1941; Davis-Monthan Field, AZ, 5 Feb

1942–1 Apr 1944. Smoky Hill AAFld, KS, 1 Apr 1944; Dalhart AAFld, TX, 27 May 1944; Smoky Hill AAFld, KS, 17 July 1944–8 Jan 1945; North Field, Guam, 18 Feb–16 Nov 1945; Camp Anza, CA, 14–27 Dec 1945. Eglin AFB, FL, 1 Feb 1963–.

Aircraft
B-17, 1941–1942; B-24, 1942–1944. B-29, 1944–1945. B-52, 1963–.

Operations
Operational and later replacement training unit, 1942–1944. Combat in Western Pacific, c. 6 Apr–14 Aug 1945.

Service Streamers
American Theater

Campaigns
Air Offensive, Japan; Western Pacific.

Decorations
Distinguished Unit Citations: Japan, 10 May 1945; Tokyo and Yokohama, Japan, 23–29 May 1945.

63d BOMB SQUADRON
Lineage
Constituted 63d Bomb Sq (Heavy) on 20 Nov 1940. Activated on 15 Jan 1941. Inactivated on 29 Apr 1946. Redesignated 63d Bomb Sq (Very Heavy), and activated, on 1 Oct 1946. Redesignated 63d Bomb Sq (Medium) on 2 July 1948.

Assignments
43d Bomb Grp, 15 Jan 1941–29 Apr 1946. 43d Bomb Grp, 1 Oct 1946; 43d Bomb Wing 16 June 1952–.

Stations
Langley Field, VA, 15 Jan 1941; Bangor, ME, 28 Aug 1941–17 Feb 1942; Sydney, Australia, 28 Mar 1942; Charleville, Australia, 15 June 1942; Torrens Creek, Australia, 3 Aug 1942; Mareeba, Australia, 20 Aug 1942; Port Moresby, New Guinea, 23 Jan 1943; Dobodura, New Guinea, 29 Oct 1943; Nadzab, New Guinea, Apr 1944; Owi, Schouten Islands, 20 July 1944; Tacloban, Leyte, 23 Nov 1944; Clark Field, Luzon, 19 Mar 1945; Ie Shima, 25 July 1945; Ft William McKinley, Luzon, 10 Dec 1945–29 Apr 1946. Davis-Monthan Field, AZ, 1 Oct 1946; Carswell AFB, TX, 15 Mar 1960–.

Aircraft
B-18, B-25, and B-17 for training, and LB-30 for antisubmarine operations, 1941–1942; B-17, 1942–1943; B-24, 1943–1945. B-29, 1946–1950; B-50, 1948–1954; B-47, 1954–1960; B-58, 1960–.

Operations
Antisubmarine, Dec 1941–Feb 1942; combat in Southwest and Western Pacific, 14 Aug 1942–14 Aug 1945, using airborne radar after Oct 1943 for many low-level attacks at night, or for pathfinder operations; not fully manned or equipped, 23 Nov 1945–29 Apr 1946.

Service Streamers
None

Campaigns
Antisubmarine, American Theater; Air Offensive, Japan; China Defensive, Papua; Guadalcanal; New Guinea; Northern Solomons; Bismarck Archipelago; Western Pacific; Leyte; Luzon; Ryukyus; China Offensive.

Decorations
Distinguished Unit Citations: Papua, [14 Aug] 1942–23 Jan 1943; Bismarck Sea, 2–4 Mar 1943. Philippine Presidential Unit Citation. Air Force Outstanding Unit Award: 1 Aug 1960–1 Aug 1962.

64th BOMB SQUADRON
Lineage
Constituted 64th Bomb Sq (Heavy) on 20 Nov 1940. Activated on 15 Jan 1941. Inactivated on 29 Apr 1946. Redesignated: 64th Bomb Sq (Very Heavy), and activated, on 1 Oct 1946. Redesignated 64th Bomb Sq (Medium) on 2 July 1948.

Assignments
43d Bomb Grp, 15 Jan 1941–29 Apr 1946. 43d Bomb Grp, 1 Oct 1946; 43d Bomb Wing 16 June 1952–.

Stations
Langley Field, VA, 15 Jan 1941; Bangor, ME, 29 Aug 1941–17 Feb 1942; Sydney, Australia, c. 16 Mar 1942; Daly Waters, Australia, c. 16 May 1942; Fenton Field, Australia, 2 Aug–25 Sept 1942; Iron Range, Australia, 12 Oct 1942; Mareeba, Australia, c. 8 Nov 1942; Port Moresby, New Guinea, 20 Jan 1943; Dobodura, New Guinea, 10 Dec 1943; Nadzab, New Guinea, 11 Mar 1944; Owi, Schouten Islands, c. 10 July 1944; Taclobon, Leyte, 23 Nov 1944; Clark Field, Luzon, c. 22 Mar 1945; Ie Shima, 26 July 1945; Ft William McKinley, Luzon, 10 Dec 1945–29 Apr 1946. Davis-Monthan Field, AZ, 1 Oct 1946; Carswell AFB, TX, 15 Mar 1960–.

Aircraft
B-18, 1941–1942; B-17, 1942–1943; B-24, 1943–1945. B-29, 1946–1950; B-50, 1948–1954; B-47, 1954–1960; B-58, 1960–.

Operations
Antisubmarine, Dec 1941–Feb 1942; combat in Southwest and Western Pacific, c. 13 Aug 1942–12 Aug 1945. Not fully manned or equipped, 23 Nov 1945–29 Apr 1946.

Service Streamers
None

Campaigns
Antisubmarine, American Theater; East Indies; Air Offensive, Japan; China Defensive, Papua; Guadalcanal; New Guinea; Northern Solomons; Bismarck Archipelago; Western Pacific; Leyte; Luzon; Southern Philippines; China Offensive.

Decorations
Distinguished Unit Citations: Papua, [c. 13 Aug] 1942–23 Jan 1943; Bismarck Sea, 2–4 Mar

1943. Philippine Presidential Unit Citation. Air Force Outstanding Unit Award: 1 Aug 1960–1 Aug 1962.

65th BOMB SQUADRON

Lineage
Constituted 65th Bomb Sq (Heavy) on 20 Nov 1940. Activated on 15 Jan 1941. Inactivated on 29 Apr 1946. Redesignated: 65th Bomb Sq (Very Heavy), and activated, on 1 Oct 1946. Redesignated 65th Bomb Sq (Medium) on 2 July 1948.

Assignments
43d Bomb Grp, 15 Jan 1941–29 Apr 1946. 43d Bomb Grp, 1 Oct 1946; 43d Bomb Wing 16 June 1952–.

Stations
Langley Field, VA, 15 Jan 1941; Bangor, ME, 29 Aug 1941–17 Feb 1942; Sydney, Australia, 28 Mar 1942; Williamstown, Australia, 23 June 1942; Torrens Creek, Australia, 15 Aug 1942; Iron Range, Australia, 13 Oct 1942; Mareeba, Australia, 7 Nov 1942; Port Moresby, New Guinea, 20 Jan 1943; Dobodura, New Guinea, c. 11 Dec 1943; Nadzab, New Guinea, Mar 1944; Owi, Schouten Islands, c. 11 July 1944; Tacloban, Leyte, c. 24 Nov 1944; Clark Field, Luzon, c. 16 Mar 1945; Ie Shima, c. 24 July 1945; Ft William McKinley, Luzon, 10 Dec 1945–29 Apr 1946. Davis-Monthan Field, AZ, 1 Oct 1946; Carswell AFB, TX, 15 Mar 1960–.

Aircraft
B-25, 1941; B-17, 1941–1943; B-24, 1942–1945. B-29, 1946–1950; B-50, 1948–1954; B-47, 1954–1960; B-58, 1960–.

Operations
Antisubmarine, Dec 1941–Jan 1942; combat in Southwest and Western Pacific, 12 Nov 1942–12 Aug 1945. Not fully manned or equipped, 23 Nov 1945–29 Apr 1946.

Service Streamers
None

Campaigns
Antisubmarine, American Theater; Central Pacific; Air Offensive, Japan; China Defensive, Papua; Guadalcanal; New Guinea; Bismarck Archipelago; Western Pacific; Leyte; Luzon; Southern Philippines; China Offensive.

Decorations
Distinguished Unit Citations: Papua, [12 Nov] 1942–23 Jan 1943; Bismarck Sea, 2–4 Mar 1943. Philippine Presidential Unit Citation. Air Force Outstanding Unit Award: 1 Aug 1960–1 Aug 1962.

66th BOMB SQUADRON

Lineage
Constituted 66th Bomb Sq (Heavy) on 20 Nov 1940. Activated on 15 Jan 1941. Redesignated 66th Bomb Sq (Very Heavy) on 5 Aug 1945. Inactivated on 12 July 1946. Activated on 1 July 1947. Inactivated on 6 Sept 1948. Redesignated 66th Bomb Sq (Medium) on 20 Dec 1950. Activated on 2 Jan 1951. Discontinued on 15 June 1960. Redesignated 66th Strategic Missile Sq on 24 Jan 1962. Organized on 1 July 1962.

Assignments
44th Bomb Grp, 15 Jan 1941–12 July 1946. 44th Bomb Grp, 1 July 1947–6 Sept 1948. 44th Bomb Grp, 2 Jan 1951; 44th Bomb Wing, 16 June 1952; Department of the Air Force, 15 June 1960; Strategic Air Command, 24 Jan 1962; 44th Strategic Missile Wing, 1 July 1962–.

Stations
MacDill Field, FL, 15 Jan 1941; Barksdale Field, LA, 9 Feb 1942; Will Rogers Field, OK, 26 July–25 Aug 1942; Cheddington, England, 12 Sept 1942; Shipdham, England, 10 Oct 1942–c. 15 June 1945 (detachments operated from Benina, Libya, 28 June–c. 31 Aug 1943, and Tunis, Tunisia, 19 Sept–c. 9 Oct 1943); Sioux Falls AAFld, SD, 26 June 1945; Great Bend AAFld, KS, 24 July 1945; Smoky Hill AAFld, KS, c. 12 Oct 1945–12 July 1946. Andrews Field, MD, 1 July 1947–6 Sept 1948. March AFB, CA, 2 Jan 1951; Lake Charles AFB, LA, c. 7 Aug 1951–15 June 1960. Ellsworth AFB, SD, 1 July 1962–.

Aircraft
B-18, 1941–1942; B-24, 1942–1945; B-29, 1945–1946. B-29, 1951–1953; B-47, 1953–1960.

Operations
Operational training unit, Feb–June 1942; antisubmarine operations, 28 Jan–22 July 1942; combat in ETO and MTO, 7 Nov 1942–25 Apr 1945, including pathfinder missions, 8 May–c. Nov 1944. Apparently not manned, 1 July 1947–6 Sept 1948. Operational and replacement training unit, 1 Oct 1951–c. 31 Aug 1952. Trained for operations with Minuteman, 1 July 1962–.

Service Streamers
None

Campaigns
Antisubmarine, American Theater; Air Offensive, Europe; Sicily; Naples-Foggia; Normandy; Northern France; Rhineland; Ardennes-Alsace; Central Europe; Air Combat, EAME Theater.

Decorations
Distinguished Unit Citations: Kiel, Germany, 14 May 1943; Ploesti, Rumania, 1 Aug 1943.

67th BOMB SQUADRON

Lineage
Constituted 67th Bomb Sq (Heavy) on 20 Nov 1940. Activated on 15 Jan 1941. Redesignated 67th Bomb Sq (Very Heavy) on 5 Aug 1945. Inactivated on 12 July 1946. Activated on 1 July 1947. Inactivated on 6 Sept 1948. Redesignated 67th Bomb Sq (Medium) on 20 Dec 1950. Activated on 2 Jan 1951. Discontinued on 15 June 1960. Redesignated 67th Strategic Missile Sq on 26 Feb 1962. Organized on 1 Aug 1962.

Assignments
44th Bomb Grp, 15 Jan 1941–12 July 1946. 44th Bomb Grp, 1 July 1947–6 Sept 1948. 44th Bomb Grp, 2 Jan 1951; 44th Bomb Wing, 16 June 1952; Department of the Air Force, 15 June 1960; Strategic Air Command, 26 Feb 1962; 44th Strategic Missile Wing, 1 Aug 1962–.

Stations
MacDill Field, FL, 15 Jan 1941; Barksdale Field, LA, 9 Feb 1942; Will Rogers Field, OK, c. 21 July–25 Aug 1942; Cheddington, England, 10 Sept 1942; Shipdham, England, c. 10 Oct 1942–c. 15 June 1945 (detachments operated from Benina, Libya, 28 June–c. 13 Aug 1943, and Tunis, Tunisia, 19 Sept–c. 9 Oct 1943); Sioux Falls AAFld, SD, 26 June 1945; Great Bend AAFld, KS, 24 July 1945; Smoky Hill AAFld, KS, c. 12 Dec 1945–12 July 1946. Andrews Field, MD, 1 July 1947–6 Sept 1948. March AFB, CA, 2 Jan 1951; Lake Charles AFB, LA, c. 8 Aug 1951–15 June 1960. Ellsworth AFB, SD, 1 Aug 1962–.

Aircraft
B-24, 1942–1945; B-29, 1945–1946. B-29, 1951–1953; B-47, 1953–1960.

Operations
Operational training unit, Feb–June 1942; antisubmarine operations, 28 Jan–22 July 1942; combat in ETO and MTO, 20 Dec 1942–25 Apr 1945. Apparently not manned, 1 July 1947–6 Sept 1948. Operational and replacement training unit, 1 Oct 1951–31 Aug 1952. Trained for operations with Minuteman, 1 Aug 1962–.

Service Streamers
None

Campaigns
Antisubmarine, American Theater; Air Offensive, Europe; Sicily; Naples-Foggia; Normandy; Northern France; Rhineland; Ardennes-Alsace; Central Europe; Air Combat, EAME Theater.

Decorations
Distinguished Unit Citations: Kiel, Germany, 14 May 1943; Ploesti, Rumania, 1 Aug 1943.

68th BOMB SQUADRON

Lineage
Constituted 68th Bomb Sq (Heavy) on 20 Nov 1940. Activated on 15 Jan 1941. Redesignated 68th Bomb Sq (Very Heavy) on 5 Aug 1945. Inactivated on 12 July 1946. Activated on 1 July 1947. Inactivated on 6 Sept 1948. Redesignated 68th Bomb Sq (Medium) on 20 Dec 1950. Activated on 2 Jan 1951. Discontinued on 15 June 1960. Redesignated 68th Strategic Missile Sq on 19 Mar 1962. Organized on 1 Sept 1962.

Assignments
44th Bomb Grp, 15 Jan 1941–12 July 1946. 44th Bomb Grp, 1 July 1947–6 Sept 1948. 44th Bomb Grp, 2 Jan 1951; 44th Bomb Wing, 16 June 1952; Department of the Air Force, 15 June 1960; Strategic Air Command, 19 Mar 1962; 44th Strategic Missile Wing, 1 Sept 1962–.

Stations
MacDill Field, FL, 15 Jan 1941; Barksdale Field, LA, c. 7 Feb 1942; Will Rogers Field, OK, c. 25 July–3 Sept 1942; Cheddington, England, c. 12 Sept 1942; Shipdham, England, c. 10 Oct 1942–c. 15 June 1945 (detachments operated from Benina, Libya, c. 26 June–c. 31 Aug 1943, and Tunis, Tunisia, 19 Sept–c. 9 Oct 1943); Sioux Falls AAFld, SD, 26 June 1945; Great Bend AAFld, KS, 24 July 1945; Smoky Hill AAFld, KS, c. 12 Dec 1945–12 July 1946. Andrews Field, MD, 1 July 1947–6 Sept 1948. March AFB, CA, 2 Jan 1951; Lake Charles AFB, LA, c. 3 Aug 1951–15 June 1960. Ellsworth AFB, SD, 1 Sept 1962–.

Aircraft
B-24, 1942–1945; B-29, 1945–1946. B-29, 1951–1953; B-47, 1953–1960.

Operations
Operational training unit, Feb–June 1942; antisubmarine operations, 28 Jan–22 July 1943; combat in ETO and MTO, 7 Nov 1942–25 Apr 1945. Apparently not manned, 1 July 1947–6 Sept 1948. Operational and replacement training unit, 1 Oct 1951–c. 31 Aug 1952. Trained for operations with Minuteman, 1 Sept 1962–.

Service Streamers
None

Campaigns
Antisubmarine, American Theater; Air Offensive, Europe; Sicily; Naples-Foggia; Normandy; Northern France; Rhineland; Ardennes-Alsace; Central Europe; Air Combat, EAME Theater.

Decorations
Distinguished Unit Citations: Kiel, Germany, 14 May 1943; Ploesti, Rumania, 1 Aug 1943.

72d BOMB SQUADRON
Lineage
Organized as 72d Aero Sq on 18 Feb 1918. Demobilized on 11 July 1919. Reconstituted and consolidated (1924) with the 72d Bomb Sq which was constituted on 6 Feb 1923. Activated on 1 May 1923. Redesignated: 72d Bomb Sq (Medium) on 6 Dec 1939; 72d Bomb Sq (Heavy) on 20 Nov 1940; 72d Bomb Sq (Very Heavy) on 30 Apr 1946. Inactivated on 10 Mar 1947. Redesignated 72d Recon Sq (Very Long Range, Photographic) on 16 Sept 1947. Activated on 13 Oct 1947. Redesignated: 72d Strategic Recon Sq (Photographic) on 23 Feb 1949; 72d Strategic Recon Sq (Heavy) on 14 Nov 1950; 72d Bomb Sq (Heavy) on 1 Oct 1955. Discontinued, and inactivated, on 1 Feb 1963.

Assignments
Unkn, 18 Feb–Sept 1918; 1st Air Depot, Sept 1918–June 1919; unkn, June–11 July 1919. 5th Composite Group, assigned on 1 May 1923, and attached on 8 May 1929; 19th Bomb Grp (attached to 5th Grp), 24 June 1932; 5th Bomb (later Recon) Grp, 12 Oct 1938–10 Mar 1947. Alaskan Air Command, 13 Oct 1947; 311th Air Division, 1 Apr 1949; 5th Strategic Recon Grp, 28 June 1949; 5th Strategic Recon (later Bomb) Wing, 16 June 1952; 4134th Strategic Wing, 1 July 1958–1 Feb 1963.

Stations
Waco, TX, 18 Feb 1918; Rich Field, TX, 23 Feb 1918; Garden City, NY, 16 July–13 Aug 1918; St Maixent, France, 4 Sept 1918; Delouze, France, 20 Sept 1918; Colombey-les-Belles, France, 30 Sept 1918–June 1919 (detachment at Bar-le Duc, 4 Oct–1 Dec 1918); Mitchel Field, NY, c. 29 June–11 July 1919. Luke Field, TH, 1 May 1923; Hickam Field, TH, 4 Jan 1939; Bellows Field, TH, 11 Dec 1941–18 Sept 1942; Espiritu Santo, 24 Sept 1942 (operated from Guadalcanal, 4 Oct 1942–8 Aug 1943; 7 Oct–15 Nov 1943; 13 Dec 1943–27 Jan 1944); Munda, New Georgia, 9 Jan 1944; Momote Airfield, Los Negros, 15 Apr 1944; Wakde, c. 19 Aug 1944; Noemfoor, 27 Sept 1944; Morotai, 24 Oct 1944; Samar, 20 Mar 1945; Clark Field, Luzon, Dec 1945–10 Mar 1947. Ladd Field, AK, 13 Oct 1947; Mountain Home AFB, ID, 28 June 1949; Fairfield-Suisun AFB, CA, 9 Nov 1949; Mather AFB, CA, 1 July 1958–1 Feb 1963.

Aircraft
In addition to DH–4, included NBS-1 and LB-5 during period 1923–1929; primarily B-4, B-5, and LB-6 during period 1929–1936; B-12, 1936–1938; B-18, 1938–1942; B-17, 1941, 1942–1943; B-24, 1943–1945. B-29, 1947–1951; F-13, 1947–1948; RB-36, 1951–1955; B/RB-36, 1955–1958; B-52, 1958–1963.

Operations
Air park in Zone of Advance, 1918–1919. Bombed lava flowing from Mauna Loa, thus diverting it from the city of Hilo, 27 Dec 1935. Patrols over the Pacific, 7 Dec 1941–Sept 1942; 8 Aug–2 Oct 1943; combat in South and Southwest Pacific, 26 Sept 1942–6 Aug 1943; 4 Oct–15 Nov 1943; 24 Dec 1943–2 Apr 1944, and in Southwest and Western Pacific, 18 Apr 1944–12 Aug 1945. Non-operational, 1946–1947.

Service Streamers
Theater of Operations.

Campaigns
Central Pacific; Guadalcanal; China Defensive; New Guinea; Northern Solomons; Eastern Mandates; Bismarck Archipelago; Western Pacific; Leyte; Luzon; Southern Philippines; China Offensive; Air Combat, Asiatic-Pacific Theater.

Decorations
Distinguished Unit Citations: Woleai Island, 18 Apr–15 May 1944; Borneo, 30 Sept 1944. Presidential Unit Citation: [1942]. Philippine Presidential Unit Citation.

74th BOMB SQUADRON
Lineage
Organized as 74th Aero Sq on 22 Feb 1918. Demobilized on 28 Jan 1919. Organized on 17 June 1919. Demobilized on 25 Sept 1919. Reconstituted and consolidated (1936) with 74th Attack Sq which was constituted on 18 Oct 1927. Redesignated 74th Pursuit Sq on 8 May 1929. Activated on 1 Oct 1933. Redesignated: 74th Attack Sq on 1 Sept 1937; 74th Bomb Sq on 1 Nov 1939; 74th Bomb Sq (Medium) on 6 Dec 1939; 74th Bomb Sq (Heavy) on 20 Nov 1940. Inactivated on 1 Nov

1946. Redesignated 135th Bomb Sq (Medium) on 27 Mar 1951. Activated on 1 May 1951. Inactivated on 1 Dec 1952.

Assignments
Unkn, 1918–1919. 16th Pursuit Grp, 1 Oct 1933; 6th Bomb Grp, 1 Feb 1940; 40th Bomb Grp, 9 Aug 1942; 6th Bomb Grp, 12 May 1943; VI Bomber Command, 1 Nov 1943–1 Nov 1946. 106th Bomb Grp, 1 May 1951; 106th Bomb Wing, 16 June–1 Dec 1952.

Stations
Waco, TX, 22 Feb 1918; Call Field, TX, 1 Mar 1918; Hazelhurst Field, NY, 29 July 1918; Roosevelt Field, NY, Sept 1918; Garden City, NY, unkn–28 Jan 1919. Langley Field, VA, 17 June–25 Sept 1919. Albrook Field, CZ, 1 Oct 1933; Howard Field, CZ, 14 July 1941; Aguadulce, Panama, 8 Nov 1941; Rio Hato, Panama, c. 11 Dec 1941; Guatemala City, Guatemala, 9 Jan 1942; Rio Hato, Panama, c. 7 Apr 1944; Galapagos Islands, c. 21 Aug 1944; Aguadulce, Panama, 13 Feb 1945; Rio Hato, Panama, 1 May 1945–1 Nov 1946. March AFB, CA, 1 May 1951–1 Dec 1952.

Aircraft
Probably included DH-4, 1918–1919. In addition to P–12, included OA-3 and B-6 during period 1933–1937; in addition to A-17, included Y10A-8 and OA-9 during period 1937–1940; B-18, 1939–1942; B-17, 1942–1943; B-24, 1942–1946. B-29, 1951–1952.

Operations
Presumably a tactical defense unit, 1918–1919. Good-will flight to Guatemala, 7–12 Feb 1938. Antisubmarine patrols in the Pacific and Caribbean, 1941–1943. Replacement training, 1943–1945 and 1951–1952.

Service Streamers
None.

Campaigns
Antisubmarine, American Theater.

Decorations
None.

77th BOMB SQUADRON
Lineage
Constituted 77th Bomb Sq (Medium) on 20 Nov 1940. Activated on 15 Jan 1941. Inactivated on 5 Nov 1945. Redesignated 77th Bomb Sq (Very Heavy) on 15 July 1946. Activated on 4 Aug 1946. Redesignated: 77th Bomb Sq (Medium) on 28 May 1948; 77th Bomb Sq (Heavy) on 16 May 1949; 77th Strategic Recon Sq (Photographic) on 1 Apr 1950; 77th Strategic Recon Sq (Heavy) on 16 July 1950; 77th Bomb Sq (Heavy) on 1 Oct 1955.

Assignments
42d Bomb Grp, 15 Jan 1941; 28th Composite (later Bomb) Grp, 2 Jan 1942; Eleventh Air Force, 20 Oct–5 Nov 1945. 28th Bomb (later Strategic Recon) Grp, 4 Aug 1946; 28th Strategic Recon (later Bomb) Wing, 16 June 1952–

Stations
Salt Lake City, UT, 15 Jan 1941; Boise, ID, 4 June–14 Dec 1941; Elmendorf Field, AK, 29 Dec 1941 (operated from Umnak beginning 30 May 1942); Adak, 3 Oct 1942 (operated from Adak beginning 12 Dec 1942 and from Attu beginning 22 July 1943); Amchitka, 11 Sept 1943; Attu, 11 Feb 1944–19 Oct 1945; Ft Lawton, WA, 29 Oct–5 Nov 1945. Grand Island AAFld, NE, 4 Aug–6 Oct 1946; Elmendorf Field, AK, 20 Oct 1946–24 Apr 1947; Rapid City AAFld, SD, 3 May 1947–.

Aircraft
B-18, 1941, 1942–1943; B-26, 1941–1943; B-25, 1942–1945. B-29, 1946–1950; RB-29, 1950; RB-36, 1949–1955; B-36, 1955–1957; B-52, 1957–.

Operations
Combat in Northern Pacific, c. Feb 1942–17 July 1945.

Service Streamers
None.

Campaigns
Aleutian Islands; Air Offensive, Japan; Air Combat, Asiatic-Pacific Theater.

Decorations
Distinguished Unit Citation: Kuril Islands, 1 Apr 1944–[17 July] 1945. Air Force Outstanding Unit Award: 1 Sept 1957–30 June 1958.

93d BOMB SQUADRON
Lineage
Organized as 93d Aero Sq on 21 Aug 1917. Demobilized on 31 Mar 1919. Reconstituted, and consolidated (1936) with 93d Bomb Sq which was constituted on 1 Mar 1935. Redesignated 93d Bomb Sq (Heavy), and activated, on 20 Oct 1939. Inactivated on 1 Apr 1944. Redesignated 93d Bomb Sq (Very Heavy). Activated on 1 Apr 1944. Redesignated: 93d Bomb Sq (Medium) on 10 Aug 1948; 93d Bomb Sq (Heavy) on 1 July 1961. Discontinued, and inactivated on 1 Feb 1963.

Assignments
Unkn, 21 Aug 1917–Aug 1918; 3d Pursuit Grp, Aug–Dec 1918; unkn, Dec 1918–31 Mar 1919. 19th Bomb Grp, 20 Oct 1939–1 Apr 1944 (ground echelon attached to the 5th Interceptor Command, c. 19 Dec 1941–May 1942). 19th Bomb Grp, 1 Apr 1944; 19th Bomb Wing, 1 June 1953; 4239th Strategic Wing, 1 Aug 1961–1 Feb 1963.

Stations
Kelly Field, TX, 21 Aug–29 Sept 1917; England, 29 Oct 1917; Beaulieu, England, Jan–24 June 1918; Issoudun, France, c. 7 July 1918; Vaucouleurs, France, 28 July 1918; Lisle-en-Barrois, France, 24 Sept 1918; Foucaucourt, France, 6 Nov 1918; Colombey-les-Belles, France, c. 15 Dec 1918–unkn; Garden City, NY, c. 14–31 Mar 1919. March Field, CA, 20 Oct 1939; Albuquerque, NM, June–27 Sept 1941; Clark Field, Luzon, c. 23 Oct 1941; Batchelor Field, Australia, c. 19 Dec 1941 (ground echelon in Luzon and Mindanao, c. 19 Dec 1941–May 1942); Singosari, Java, c. 1 Jan 1942;

Melbourne, Australia, c. 1 Mar 1942; Cloncurry, Australia, 29 Mar 1942; Longreach, Australia, 18 May 1942; Mareeba, Australia, 23 July–c. 25 Oct 1942; Pocatello, ID, c. 28 Dec 1942; Pyote, TX c. 18 Jan 1943–1 Apr 1944. Great Bend AAFld, KS, 1 Apr–7 Dec 1944; North Field, Guam, 16 Jan 1945; Kadena, Okinawa, 27 June 1950–18 May 1954; Pinecastle AFB, FL, c. 2 June 1954; Homestead AFB, FL, c. 25 June 1956; Kincheloe AFB, MI, 1 Aug 1961–1 Feb 1963.

Aircraft
In addition to Spad XIII, briefly included Spad VII, 1918. B-18 and B-17, successively 1939–1941; B-17, and probably B-24 and LB-30, during period 7 Dec 1941–Oct 1942; B-17, 1942–1944. B-29, 1944–1954; B-47, 1954-1961; B-52, 1961–1963.

Operations
Combat as pursuit unit with First Army, 11 Aug–10 Nov 1918. Combat in Southwest Pacific, 7 Dec 1941–c. 24 Oct 1942; ground echelon fought with infantry units in Philippine Islands, c. 19 Dec 1941–May 1942; replacement training unit, 1 Feb 1943–1 Apr 1944. Combat in Western Pacific, c. 12 Feb–15 Aug 1945. Combat in Korea, 28 June 1950–25 July 1953.

Service Streamers
American Theater.

Campaigns
World War I: Lorraine; St Mihiel; Meuse-Argonne. World War II: Philippine Islands; East Indies; Air Offensive, Japan; Papua; Guadalcanal; Western Pacific; Air Combat, Asiatic-Pacific Theater; Korean War: UN Defensive; UN Offensive; CCF Intervention; First UN Counteroffensive; CCF Spring Offensive; UN Summer-Fall Offensive; Second Korean Winter; Korea Summer-Fall 1952; Third Korean Winter; Korea Summer-Fall, 1953.

Decorations
Distinguished Unit Citations: Philippine Islands, 7 Dec 1941–10 May 1942; Philippine Islands, 8–22 Dec 1941; Philippines and Netherlands Indies, 1 Jan–1 Mar 1942; Philippine Islands, 6 Jan–8 Mar 1942; Papua, 23 July–24 Oct 1942; New Britain, 7–12 Aug 1942; Japan, 9–19 Mar 1945; Kobe, Japan, 5 June 1945; Korea, 28 June–15 Sept 1950. Philippine Presidential Unit Citation. Republic of Korea Presidential Unit Citation: 7 July 1950–27 July 1953.

96th BOMB SQUADRON
Lineage
Organized as 96th Aero Sq on 20 Aug 1917. Redesignated: 96th Sq on 14 Mar 1921; 96th Bomb Sq on 25 Jan 1923. 96th Bomb Sq (Heavy) on 6 Dec 1939. Inactivated on 28 Feb 1946. Redesignated 96th Bomb Sq (Very Heavy) on 5 Apr 1946. Activated on 1 July 1947. Redesignated 96th Bomb Sq (Medium) on 28 May 1948.

Assignments
Unkn, 20 Aug 1917–Sept 1918; 1st Day Bomb Grp, Sept–Nov 1918; unkn, Nov 1918–Sept 1919; 1st Day Bomb (later 2d Bomb) Grp, 18 Sept

1919–28 Feb 1946 (attached to 1st Surveillance Grp, 12 Nov 1919–10 Jan 1921, and to 1st Provisional Air Brigade, May–Oct 1921). 2d Bomb Grp, 1 July 1947; 2d Bomb Wing, 16 June 1952–.

Stations
Kelly Field, TX, 20 Aug–7 Oct 1917; Clermont-Ferrand, France, 16 Nov 1917; Amanty, France, 18 May 1918; Maulan, France, 23 Sept 1918; Colombey-les-Belles, France, 10 Jan 1919; St Denis de Pile, France, 13 Feb 1919; Libourne, France, 12–16 Apr 1919; Mitchel Field, NY, 2 May 1919; Ellington Field, TX, 26 May 1919; Camp Furlong, NM, c. 28 June 1919; Fort Bliss, TX, 3 July 1919 (flight operated from Douglas, AZ, c. 10 Aug 1919–10 Jan 1920); Kelly Field, TX, 12 Jan 1920 (operated from Langley Field, VA, 20 May–26 Oct 1921); Langley Field, VA, 30 June 1922; Ephrata, WA, 29 Oct 1942; Glasgow, MT, 29 Nov 1942–14 Mar 1943; Navarin, Algeria, 25 Apr 1943; Chateaudun-du-Rhumel, Algeria, 27 Apr 1943; Ain M'lila, Algeria, 17 June 1943; Massicault, Tunisia, 30 July 1943; Amendola, Italy, c. 10 Dec 1943; Foggia, Italy, c. 20 Oct 1945–28 Feb 1946. Andrews Field, MD, 1 July 1947; Davis-Monthan Field, AZ, 24 Sept 1947; Chatham AFB, GA, 1 May 1949; Hunter AFB, GA, 29 Sept 1950–.

Aircraft
In addition to Breguet 14 included DH-4, 1918; included DH-4, Caproni bomber, HP 0/400, and MB-2 (NBS-1) during period 1919–1928; included LB-5, LB-7, B-3, and apparently B-5 during period 1928–1932; primarily B-6 during period 1932–1936; in addition to B-10, B-17, and B-18, included B-25 during period 1936–1942; B-17, 1942–1945. B-29, 1947–1950; B-50, 1949–1954; B-47, 1954–.

Operations
Combat as day bombardment unit with French Eighth and American First Army, 12 June–4 Nov 1918. Mexican border patrol, Aug 1919–10 Jan 1920; participated in demonstrations of effectiveness of aerial bombardment on warships, June–Sept 1921, and 5 Sept 1923; mercy missions in relief of marooned inhabitants of islands in the frozen Chesapeake, 9 Feb 1936, and of flood victims in Pennsylvania, 20 Mar 1936; good-will flights to Argentina, 15–27 Feb 1938, Colombia, 3–12 Aug 1938, and Brazil, 10–26 Nov 1939. Antisubmarine patrols, 8 Dec 1941–c. 28 Oct 1942; combat in MTO and ETO, 28 Apr 1943–1 May 1945.

Service Streamers
None

Campaigns
World War I: Lorraine; St Mihiel; Meuse-Argonne. World War II: Antisubmarine, American Theater; Air Offensive, Europe; Tunisia; Sicily; Naples-Foggia; Anzio; Rome-Arno; Normandy; Northern France; Southern France; North Apennines; Rhineland; Central Europe; Po Valley; Air Combat, EAME Theater.

Decorations
Distinguished Unit Citations: Steyr, Austria, 24 Feb 1944; Germany, 25 Feb 1944. Air Force Outstanding Unit Award: 1 Nov 1956–1 Apr 1957.

98th BOMB SQUADRON

Lineage

Constituted 98th Bomb Sq (Heavy) on 2 Dec 1941. Activated on 16 Dec 1941. Redesignated 98th Bomb Sq (Very Heavy) on 30 Apr 1946. Inactivated on 20 Oct 1948. Redesignated 98th Bomb Sq (Heavy), and activated, on 1 Dec 1948. Discontinued, and inactivated on 1 Feb 1963.

Assignments

11th Bomb Grp, 16 Dec 1941–20 Oct 1948. 11th Bomb Grp, 1 Dec 1948; 11th Bomb Wing, 16 June 1952; 4123d Strategic Wing, 10 Dec 1957–1 Feb 1963.

Stations

Hickam Field, TH, 16 Dec 1941; Espiritu Santo, 11 Aug 1942 (operated from New Caledonia, 21 July–11 Aug 1942, and Guadalcanal, Nov 1942); Mokuleia, TH, 8 Apr 1943; Nukufetau, 11 Nov 1943; Tarawa, 20 Jan 1944; Kwajalein, 3 Apr 1944; Guam, 21 Oct 1944; Okinawa, 2 July 1945; Manila, Luzon, Dec 1945; Guam, 15 May 1945–20 Oct 1948. Carswell AFB, TX, 1 Dec 1948; Clinton-Sherman AFB, OK, 1 Mar 1959–1 Feb 1963.

Aircraft

B-18, 1942; B-17, 1942–1943; B-24, 1943–1945; B-29, 1946. B-36, 1949–1957; B-52, 1958–1963.

Operations

Search missions from Hawaii, c. May–June 1942; May–Oct 1943. Combat in South and Southwest Pacific, 31 July 1942–c. 14 Feb 1943; in Central Pacific; June, July, Sept 1943; and in Central and Western Pacific, 14 Nov 1943–12 Aug 1945. Non-operational, 1947–1948.

Service Streamers

None

Campaigns

Central Pacific; Air Offensive, Japan; Papua; Guadalcanal; Eastern Mandates; Western Pacific; Ryukyus; China Offensive; Air Combat, Asiatic-Pacific Theater.

Decorations

Distinguished Unit Citation: South Pacific, 31 July–30 Nov 1942. Presidential Unit Citation: [1942]. Air Force Outstanding Unit Awards: 6 Aug 1954–15 July 1957; 6 Oct 1959–15 July 1960.

99th BOMB SQUADRON

Lineage

Organized as 99th Aero Sq on 21 Aug 1917. Redesignated: 99th Sq on 14 Mar 1921; 99th Observation Sq on 25 Jan 1923. Inactivated on 31 July 1927. Activated on 9 Nov 1928. Redesignated: 99th Bomb Sq on 1 Mar 1935; 99th Bomb Sq (Medium) on 6 Dec 1939; 99th Bomb Sq (Heavy) on 20 Nov 1940; 99th Bomb Sq (Very Heavy) on 28 Mar 1944. Inactivated on 20 Oct 1948. Redesignated 99th Strategic Recon Sq (Photographic), and activated, on 1 May 1949. Redesignated: 99th Bomb Sq (Heavy) on 1 Apr 1950; 99th Bomb Sq (Medium) on 2 Oct 1950.

Assignments

Unkn, 21 Aug 1917–7 Aug 1918; V Corps Observation Group, 7 Aug–Dec 1918; unkn, Dec 1918–May 1919; Eastern Dept, May 1919; Third Corps Area, 20 Aug 1920; District of Washington, c. Jan 1922; Air Corps Training Center, June–31 July 1927. 9th Observation (later Bomb) Grp, attached on 9 Nov 1928, and assigned 15 Feb 1929–20 Oct 1948. 9th Strategic Recon (later Bomb) Grp, 1 May 1949; 9th Bomb (later Strategic Aerospace) Wing, 16 June 1952–.

Stations

Kelly Field, TX, 21 Aug 1917; Garden City, NY, 3–14 Nov 1917; Tour, France, 12 Dec 1917; Haussimont, France, 11 Mar 1918; Amanty, France, 31 May 1918; Luxeuil-les-Bains, France, 1 July 1918 (flight operated from Corcieux, 19–24 July 1918, and Dogneville, 24 July–26 Aug 1918); Souilly, France, 7 Sept 1918; Foucaucourt, France, 20 Sept 1918; Parois, France, 4 Nov 1918; Belrain, France, 31 Nov 1918; Chaumont-sur-Aire, France, 13 Dec 1918; Chaumont, France, c. 25 Dec 1918 (flights operated from Prauthoy, Bourbonne-les-Bains, and Montigny-le-Roi, until c. 1 Feb 1919); Colombey-les-Belles, France, 19 Feb 1919; Sadirac, France, c. 2 Mar–8 May 1919; Mitchel Field, NY, 24 May 1919; Hazelhurst Field, NY, 25 May 1919; Camp Alfred Vail, NJ, July 1919; Bolling Field, DC, 17 Aug 1919; Kelly Field, TX, 23 June–31 July 1927. Mitchel Field, NY, 9 Nov 1928–6 Nov 1940; Rio Hato, Panama, 13 Nov 1940; Zandery Field, Surinam, 3 Dec 1941; Orlando AB, FL, 31 Oct 1942; Montbrook AAFld, FL, 5 Feb 1943; Kissimmee AAFld, FL 14 Nov 1943; Brooksville AAFld, FL, 5 Jan 1944; Orlando AB, FL, 25 Feb 1944; Dalhart AAFld, TX, c. 9 Mar 1944; McCook AAFld, KS, 19 May–18 Nov 1944; North Field, Tinian, 28 Dec 1944–7 Mar 1946; Clark Field, Luzon, 14 Mar 1946; Harmon Field, Guam, 9 June 1947–20 Oct 1948. Fairfield-Suisun AFB, CA, 1 May 1949; Mountain Home AFB, ID, 1 May 1954–.

Aircraft

Sopwith 1, 1918; Salmson 2, 1918–1919; included DH-4 and SE-5 during period 1919–1927. In addition to O-1, O-11, and O-25, included OA-2, O-31, Y1O-35, O-38, O-39, Y1O-40, O-40, and O-43, during period 1928–1936; B-10, 1936–1938; B-18, 1938–1942; B-25, 1943; B-26, 1943; B-17, 1943–1944; B-29, 1944–1947. B/RB-17, 1949–1950; RB-29, 1949–1950; B-29, 1949–1954; B-47, 1954–.

Operations

Combat as corps observation unit with French Eighth Army and American V Army Corps, 22–23 June, 9 Sept–10 Nov 1918; school squadron with V Army Corps Infantry Liaison School, 1 July–7 Sept 1918, during which time one flight of unit, operating in Vosges region of Alsace and Lorraine, participated in combat with French XXXIII Corps and American 5th Division, 19 July–26 Aug 1918. Antisubmarine patrols, and reconnaissance of Vichy French fleet at Martinique, Dec 1941–Oct 1942. Unmanned, Nov 1942–Feb 1943. Trained cadres for bombardment units, Feb 1943–Feb 1944. Combat in Western Pacific, 25 Jan–15 Aug 1945. Unmanned, Apr 1947–20 Oct 1948.

Service Streamers

None

Campaigns

World War I: Lorraine; Alsace; St Mihiel; Meuse-Argonne. World War II: Antisubmarine, American Theater; Air Offensive, Japan; Eastern Mandates; Western Pacific.

Decorations

Distinguished Unit Citations: Kawasaki, Japan, 15-16 Apr 1945; Japan, 13-28 May 1945. Air Force Outstanding Unit Award: 1 Jan 1957–31 Jan 1958.

325th BOMB SQUADRON

Lineage

Constituted 325th Bomb Sq (Heavy) on 28 Jan 1942. Activated on 1 Mar 1942. Inactivated on 28 Feb 1946. Redesignated 325th Bomb Sq (Very Heavy) on 15 July 1946. Activated on 4 Aug 1946. Redesignated: 325th Bomb Sq (Medium) on 28 May 1948; 325th Bomb Sq (Heavy) on 16 June 1951.

Assignments

92d Bomb Grp, 1 Mar 1942–28 Feb 1946. 92d Bomb Grp, 4 Aug 1946; 92d Bomb (later Strategic Aerospace) Wing, 16 June 1952–.

Stations

Barksdale Field, LA, 1 Mar 1942; MacDill Field, FL, 26 Mar 1942; Sarasota, FL, 18 May–18 July 1942; Bovington, England, 18 Aug 1942; Alconbury, England, 6 Jan 1943; Podington, England, 15 Sept 1943; Istres, France, 12 June 1945–28 Feb 1946. Fort Worth AAFld, TX, 4 Aug 1946; Smoky Hill AAFld, KS, 26 Oct 1946; Spokane AAFld, WA, 20 June 1947 (operated from Yokota, Japan, 9 July–29 Oct 1950)–.

Aircraft

B-17, 1942–1946. B-29, 1946, 1947–1951; B-36, 1951–1957; B-52, 1957–.

Operations

Antisubmarine duty while training in Florida. Four combat missions while training replacement crews in England, 18 Aug 1942–6 Jan 1943; after reorganization, combat in ETO, 15 May 1943–25 Apr 1945. Transported personnel from ETO to North Africa for deployment to US, 15 June–9 Sept 1945. Combat in Korea, 13 July–20 Oct 1950.

Service Streamers

None

Campaigns

World War II: Antisubmarine, American Theater; Air Offensive, Europe; Normandy; Northern France; Rhineland; Ardennes-Alsace; Central Europe; Air Combat, EAME Theater. Korean War: UN Defensive; UN Offensive

Decorations

Distinguished Unit Citations: Germany, 11 Jan 1944; Germany, 11 Sept 1944. Air Force Outstanding Unit Awards: 22 Aug–11 Sept 1953; 3 Mar–6 Oct 1959; 1 Jan 1961–31 Mar 1962. Republic of Korea Presidential Unit Citation: 10 July–24 Oct 1950.

326th BOMB SQUADRON

Lineage
Constituted 326th Bomb Sq (Heavy) on 28 Jan 1942. Activated on 1 Mar 1942. Inactivated on 28 Feb 1946. Redesignated 326th Bomb Sq (Very Heavy) on 15 July 1946. Activated on 4 Aug 1946. Redesignated: 326th Bomb Sq (Medium) on 28 May 1948; 326th Bomb Sq (Heavy) on 16 June 1951. Discontinued, and inactivated, on 1 Feb 1963.

Assignments
92d Bomb Grp, 1 Mar 1942–28 Feb 1946. 92d Bomb Grp, 4 Aug 1946; 92d Bomb Wing, 16 June 1952; 4141st Strategic Wing, 1 Apr 1961–1 Feb 1963.

Stations
Barksdale Field, LA, 1 Mar 1942; MacDill Field, FL, 26 Mar 1942; Sarasota, FL, 18 May–18 July 1942; Bovington, England, 18 Aug 1942; Alconbury, England, 6 July 1943; Podington, England, 15 Sept 1943; Istres, France, June 1945–28 Feb 1946. Fort Worth AAFld, TX, 4 Aug 1946; Smoky Hill AAFld, KS, 25 Oct 1946; Spokane AAFld, WA, 20 June 1947 (operated from Yokota, Japan, 9 July–26 Oct 1950); Glasgow AFB, MT, 1 Apr 1961–1 Feb 1963.

Aircraft
B-17, 1942–1946. B-29, 1946, 1947–1951; B-36, 1951–1957; B-52, 1957–1963.

Operations
Antisubmarine duty while training in Florida. Four combat missions while training replacement crews in England, 18 Aug 1942–1 Jan 1943; after reorganization, combat in ETO, 17 July 1943–25 Apr 1945. Transported personnel from ETO to North Africa for deployment to US, 28 June–10 Sept 1945. Combat in Korea, 13 July–20 Oct 1950.

Service Streamers
None

Campaigns
World War II: Antisubmarine, American Theater; Air Offensive, Europe; Normandy; Northern France; Rhineland; Ardennes-Alsace; Central Europe; Air Combat, EAME Theater. Korean War: UN Defensive; UN Offensive

Decorations
Distinguished Unit Citations: Germany, 11 Jan 1944; Germany, 11 Sept 1944. Air Force Outstanding Unit Awards: 22 Aug–11 Sept 1953; 3 Mar–6 Oct 1959. Republic of Korea Presidential Unit Citation: 10 July–24 Oct 1950.

327th BOMB SQUADRON

Lineage
Constituted 327th Bomb Sq (Heavy) on 28 Jan 1942. Activated on 1 Mar 1942. Inactivated on 28 Feb 1946. Redesignated 327th Bomb Sq (Very Heavy) on 15 July 1946. Activated on 4 Aug 1946. Redesignated: 327th Bomb Sq (Medium) on 28 May 1948; 327th Bomb Sq (Heavy) on 16 June 1951. Discontinued, and inactivated, on 1 Feb 1963.

Assignments
92d Bomb Grp, 1 Mar 1942–28 Feb 1946. 92d Bomb Grp, 4 Aug 1946; 92d Bomb Wing, 16 June 1952; 4170th Strategic Wing, 1 June 1960–1 Feb 1963.

Stations
Barksdale Field, LA, 1 Mar 1942; MacDill Field, FL, 26 Mar 1942; Sarasota, FL, 18 May–18 July 1942; Bovington, England, 18 Aug 1942; Alconbury, England, 6 Jan 1943; Podington, England, 15 Sept 1943; Port Lyautey, French Morocco, 13 May 1945; Istres, France, 9 Sept 1945–28 Feb 1946. Fort Worth AAFld, TX, 4 Aug 1946; Smoky Hill AAFld, KS, 25 Oct 1946; Spokane AAFld, WA, 20 June 1947 (operated from Yokota, Japan, 9 July–27 Oct 1950); Larson AFB, WA, 15 July 1960–1 Feb 1963.

Aircraft
B-17, 1942–1946. YB-40, 1943. B-29, 1946, 1947–1951; B-36, 1951–1957; B-52, 1957–1963.

Operations
Antisubmarine duty while training in Florida. Three combat missions while training replacement crews in England, 18 Aug 1942–6 Jan 1943; after reorganization, combat in ETO, 29 May 1943–25 Apr 1945. Serviced aircraft of units which were transporting redeployed personnel from Europe to North Africa, 13 May–9 Sept 1945. Combat in Korea, 13 July–20 Oct 1950.

Service Streamers
None

Campaigns
World War II: Antisubmarine, American Theater; Air Offensive, Europe; Normandy; Northern France; Rhineland; Ardennes-Alsace; Central Europe; Air Combat, EAME Theater. Korean War: UN Defensive; UN Offensive

Decorations
Distinguished Unit Citations: Germany, 11 Jan 1944; Germany, 11 Sept 1944. Air Force Outstanding Unit Awards: 22 Aug–11 Sept 1953; 3 Mar–6 Oct 1959. Republic of Korea Presidential Unit Citation: 10 July–24 Oct 1950.

328th BOMB SQUADRON

Lineage
Constituted 328th Bomb Sq (Heavy) on 28 Jan 1942. Activated on 1 Mar 1942. Redesignated 328th Bomb Sq (Very Heavy) on 23 May 1945: 328th Bomb Sq (Medium) on 28 May 1948; 328th Bomb Sq (Heavy) on 1 Feb 1955.

Assignments
93d Bomb Grp, 1 Mar 1942; 93d Bomb Wing, 16 June 1952–.

Stations
Barksdale Field, LA, 1 Mar 1942; Ft Myers, FL, 18 May–13 Aug 1942; Alconbury, England, 7 Sept 1942; Hardwick, England, c. 6 Dec 1942–15 June 1945 (operated from Tafaraoui, Algeria, 7–15 Dec 1942; Gambut, Libya, 16 Dec 1942–25 Feb 1943; Bengasi, Libya, 27 June–26 Aug 1943; Oudna, Tunisia, 18 Sept–3 Oct 1943); Sioux Falls AAFld, SD, 26 June 1945; Pratt AAFld, KS, 24 July 1945; Clovis AAFld, NM, 13 Dec 1945; Castle Field, CA, 21 June 1946–.

Aircraft
B-24, 1942–1945; B-29, 1945–1949; B-50, 1949–1954; B-47, 1954–1955; B-52, 1955–.

Operations
Antisubmarine patrols May–30 July 1942; combat in ETO and MTO, 9 Oct 1942–25 Apr 1945.

Service Streamers
None

Campaigns
Antisubmarine, American Theater; Egypt-Libya; Air Offensive, Europe; Tunisia; Sicily; Naples-Foggia; Normandy; Northern France; Rhineland; Ardennes-Alsace; Central Europe; Air Combat, EAME Theater.

Decorations
Distinguished Unit Citations: North Africa, 17 Dec 1942–20 Feb 1943; Ploesti, Rumania, 1 Aug 1943. Air Force Outstanding Unit Awards: 1 Jan 1956–1 July 1959; 1 June 1962–1 Apr 1963.

329th BOMB SQUADRON

Lineage
Constituted 329th Bomb Sq (Heavy) on 28 Jan 1942. Activated on 1 Mar 1942. Redesignated 329th Bomb Sq (Very Heavy) on 23 May 1945: 329th Bomb Sq (Medium) on 28 May 1948; 329th Bomb Sq (Very Heavy) on 1 Feb 1955.

Assignments
93d Bomb Grp, 1 Mar 1942; 93d Bomb Wing, 16 June 1952–.

Stations
Barksdale Field, LA, 1 Mar 1942; Ft Myers, FL, 18 May 1942–13 Aug 1942; Alconbury, England, 7 Sept 1942; Hardwick, England, c. 6 Dec 1942; Bungay, England, c. 14 Dec 1942; Hardwick England, c. 15 June 1943–15 June 1945 (operated from Bengasi, Libya, 27 June–26 Aug 1943; Oudna, Tunisia, 18 Sept–3 Oct 1943); Sioux Falls AAFld, SD, 26 June 1945; Pratt AAFld, KS, 24 July 1945; Clovis AAFld, NM, 13 Dec 1945; Castle Field, CA, 21 June 1946–.

Aircraft
B-24, 1942–1945; B-29, 1945–1949; B-50, 1949–1954; B-47, 1954–1955; B-52, 1955–.

Operations
Antisubmarine patrols 7–30 July 1942; combat in ETO and MTO, 9 Oct 1942–25 Apr 1945.

Service Streamers
None

Campaigns
Antisubmarine, American Theater; Air Offensive, Europe; Sicily; Naples-Foggia; Normandy; Rhineland; Ardennes-Alsace; Central Europe; Air Combat, EAME Theater.

Decorations
Distinguished Unit Citation: Ploesti, Rumania, 1 Aug 1943. Air Force Outstanding Unit Awards: 1 Jan 1956–1 July 1959; 1 June 1962–1 Apr 1963.

330th BOMB SQUADRON

Lineage
Constituted 330th Bomb Sq (Heavy) on 28 Jan 1942. Activated on 1 Mar 1942. Redesignated 330th Bomb Sq (Very Heavy) on 23 May 1945: 330th Bomb Sq (Medium) on 28 May 1948; 330th Bomb Sq (Heavy) on 1 Feb 1955.

Assignments
93d Bomb Grp, 1 Mar 1942; 93d Bomb Wing, 16 June 1952–.

Stations
Barksdale Field, LA, 1 Mar 1942; Ft Myers, FL, 18 May–13 Aug 1942; Alconbury, England, 7 Sept 1942; (operated from Holmsley, England, 22 Oct–Nov 1942); Hardwick, England, c. 6 Dec 1942–15 June 1945 (operated from Tafaraoui, Algeria, 7–15 Dec 1942; Gambut, Libya, 16 Dec 1942–25 Feb 1943; Bengasi, Libya, 27 June–26 Aug 1943; Oudna, Tunisia, 18 Sept–3 Oct 1943); Sioux Falls AAFld, SD, 26 June 1945; Pratt AAFld, KS, 24 July 1945; Clovis AAFld, NM, 13 Dec 1945; Castle Field, CA, 21 June 1946–.

Aircraft
B-24, 1942–1945; B-29, 1945–1949; B-50, 1949–1954; B-47, 1954–1955; B-52, 1955–.

Operations
Antisubmarine patrols, May–30 July 1942; combat in ETO and MTO, 9 Oct 1942–25 Apr 1945.

Service Streamers
None

Campaigns
Antisubmarine, American Theater; Egypt-Libya; Air Offensive, Europe; Tunisia; Sicily; Naples-Foggia; Normandy; Northern France; Rhineland; Ardennes-Alsace; Central Europe; Air Combat, EAME Theater.

Decorations
Distinguished Unit Citations: North Africa, 17 Dec 1942–20 Feb 1943; Ploesti, Rumania, 1 Aug 1943. Air Force Outstanding Unit Awards: 1 Jan 1956–1 July 1959; 1 June 1962–1 Apr 1963.,

340th BOMB SQUADRON

Lineage
Constituted 340th Bomb Sq (Heavy) on 28 Jan 1942. Activated on 3 Feb 1942. Inactivated on 29 Oct 1945. Redesignated 340th Bomb Sq (Very Heavy) on 15 July 1946. Activated on 4 Aug 1946. Redesignated: 340th Bomb Sq (Medium) on 28 May 1948; 340th Bomb Sq (Heavy) on 1 Oct 1959.

Assignments
97th Bomb Grp, 3 Feb 1942–29 Oct 1945. 97th Bomb Grp, 4 Aug 1946; 97th Bomb Wing, 16 June 1952–.

Stations
MacDill Field, FL, 3 Feb 1942; Sarasota, FL, 29 Mar–16 May 1942; Polebrook, England, 11 June–10 Nov 1942; Maison Blanche, Algeria, c. 13 Nov 1942; Tafaraoui, Algeria, c. 22 Nov 1942; Biskra, Algeria, 26 Dec 1942; Chateaudun-du-Rhumel, Algeria, 8 Feb 1943; Pont-du-Fahs, Tunisia, 12 Aug 1943; Depienne, Tunisia, 14 Aug 1943; Cerignola, Italy, c. 14 Dec 1943; Amendola, Italy, 17 Jan 1944; Marcianise, Italy, c. Oct–29 Oct 1945. Smoky Hill AAFld, KS, 4 Aug 1946; Biggs AFB, TX, 17 May 1948 (detachments at Lakenheath, England, and Yokota, Japan, for operations, Apr 1954–1 Apr 1955); Blytheville AFB, AR, 1 July 1959–.

Aircraft
B-17, 1942–1945. B-29, 1946–1950; B-50, 1950–1954; RB-50 and KB-29, 1954–1955; B-47, 1955–1959; B-52, 1960–.

Operations
Antisubmarine, Mar–Apr 1942; combat in ETO and MTO, 17 Aug 1942–26 Apr 1945. Electronic reconnaissance, Apr 1954-1 Apr 1955.

Service Streamers
None

Campaigns
Antisubmarine, American Theater; Egypt-Libya; Air Offensive, Europe; Tunisia; Sicily; Naples-Foggia; Anzio; Rome-Arno; Normandy; Northern France; Southern France; North Apennines; Rhineland; Central Europe; Po Valley; Air Combat, EAME Theater.

Decorations
Distinguished Unit Citations: Steyr, Austria, 24 Feb 1944; Ploesti, Romania, 18 Aug 1944. Air Force Outstanding Unit Awards: Apr 1954–1 Apr 1955; 2 July–3 Nov 1957; 23 Oct–22 Nov 1962.

341st BOMB SQUADRON

Lineage
Constituted 341st Bomb Sq (Heavy) on 28 Jan 1942. Activated on 3 Feb 1942. Inactivated on 29 Oct 1945. Redesignated 341st Bomb Sq (Very Heavy) on 15 July 1946. Activated on 4 Aug 1946. Redesignated: 341st Bomb Sq (Medium) on 28 May 1948; 341st Bomb Sq (Heavy) on 1 Oct 1959. Discontinued, and inactivated, on 1 Feb 1963.

Assignments
97th Bomb Grp, 3 Feb 1942–29 Oct 1945. 97th Bomb Grp, 4 Aug 1946; 97th Bomb Wing, 16 June 1952; 4038th Strategic Wing, 15 Feb 1960–1 Feb 1963.

Stations
MacDill Field, FL, 3 Feb 1942; Sarasota, FL, 29 Mar–16 May 1942; Polebrook, England, 12 June 1942; Algeria, c. 16 Nov 1942; Tafaraoui, Algeria, c. 22 Nov 1942; Biskra, Algeria, 27 Dec 1942; Chateaudun-du-Rhumel, Algeria, 8 Feb 1943; Pont-du-Fahs, Tunisia, 11 Aug 1943; Depienne, Tunisia, 14 Aug 1943; Cerignola, Italy, 12 Dec 1943; Amendola, Italy, 17 Jan 1944; Marcianise, Italy, c. Oct–29 Oct 1945. Smoky Hill AAFld, KS, 4 Aug 1946; Biggs AFB, TX, 24 May 1948; Blytheville AFB, AR, 1 July 1959; Dow AFB, ME, c. 15 Feb 1960–1 Feb 1963.

Aircraft
B-17, 1942–1945. B-29, 1946–1950; B-50, 1950–1955; B-47, 1955–1959; B-52, 1960–1963.

Operations
Antisubmarine, Mar–Apr 1942; combat in ETO and MTO, 17 Aug 1942–26 Apr 1945.

Service Streamers
None

Campaigns
Antisubmarine, American Theater; Egypt-Libya; Air Offensive, Europe; Tunisia; Sicily; Naples-Foggia; Anzio; Rome-Arno; Normandy; Northern France; Southern France; North Apennines; Rhineland; Central Europe; Po Valley.

Decorations
Distinguished Unit Citations: Steyr, Austria, 24 Feb 1944; Ploesti, Romania, 18 Aug 1944. Air Force Outstanding Unit Awards: 2 July–3 Nov 1957.

342d BOMB SQUADRON

Lineage
Constituted 342d Bomb Sq (Heavy) on 28 Jan 1942. Activated on 3 Feb 1942. Inactivated on 29 Oct 1945. Redesignated 342d Bomb Sq (Very Heavy) on 15 July 1946. Activated on 4 Aug 1946. Redesignated: 342d Bomb Sq (Medium) on 28 May 1948; 342d Bomb Sq (Heavy) on 1 Oct 1959. Discontinued, and inactivated, on 1 Feb 1963.

Assignments
97th Bomb Grp, 3 Feb 1942–29 Oct 1945. 97th Bomb Grp, 4 Aug 1946; 97th Bomb Wing, 16 June 1952; 4137th Strategic Wing, 1 May 1960–1 Feb 1963.

Stations
MacDill Field, FL, 3 Feb 1942; Sarasota, FL, 29 Mar–16 May 1942; Grafton Underwood, England, 9 June 1942; Polebrook, England, 8 Sept 1942; Algeria, c. 19 Nov 1942; Tafaraoui, Algeria, c. 22 Nov 1942; Biskra, Algeria, 27 Dec 1942; Chateaudun-du-Rhumel, 18 Feb 1943; Pont-du-Fahs, Tunisia, 10 Aug 1943; Depienne, Tunisia, 14 Aug 1943; Cerignola, Italy, c. 9 Dec 1943; Amendola, Italy, 16 Jan 1944; Marcianise, Italy, c. Oct–29 Oct 1945. Smoky Hill AAFld, KS, 4 Aug 1946; Biggs AFB, TX, 18 May 1948; Blytheville AFB, AR, 1 July 1959; Robins AFB, GA, 1 May 1960–1 Feb 1963.

Aircraft
B-17, 1942–1945. B-29, 1946–1950; B-50, 1950–1955; B-47, 1955–1959; B-52, 1960–1963.

Operations
Antisubmarine, Mar–Apr 1942; combat in ETO and MTO, 17 Aug 1942–26 Apr 1945.

Service Streamers
None

Campaigns

Antisubmarine, American Theater; Egypt-Libya; Air Offensive, Europe; Tunisia; Sicily; Naples-Foggia; Anzio; Rome-Arno; Normandy; Northern France; Southern France; North Apennines; Rhineland; Central Europe; Po Valley; Air Combat, EAME Theater.

Decorations

Distinguished Unit Citations: Steyr, Austria, 24 Feb 1944; Ploesti, Romania, 18 Aug 1944. Air Force Outstanding Unit Awards: 2 July–3 Nov 1957; 2 Feb 1961–31 Mar 1962.

343d BOMB SQUADRON

Lineage

Constituted 343d Bomb Sq (Heavy) on 28 Jan 1942. Activated on 3 Feb 1942. Redesignated 343d Bomb Sq (Very Heavy) on 23 May 1945. Inactivated on 27 Mar 1946. Activated on 1 July 1947. Redesignated 343d Bomb Sq (Medium) on 28 May 1948.

Assignments

98th Bomb Grp, 3 Feb 1942; 40th Bomb Grp, 10 Nov 1945–27 Mar 1946. 98th Bomb Grp, 1 July 1947; 98th Bomb Wing, 16 June 1952–.

Stations

MacDill Field, FL, 3 Feb 1942; Barksdale Field, LA, 16 Feb 1942; Ft Myers, FL, 30 Mar 1942; Drane Field, FL, 15 May–3 July 1942; Ramat David, Palestine, 7 Aug 1942; St Jean, Palestine, 21 Aug 1942; Kabrit, Egypt, 10 Nov 1942; Gambut, Libya, 31 Jan 1943; Lete, Libya, 3 Mar 1943; Hergla, Tunisia, 25 Sept 1943; Brindisi, Italy, 18 Nov 1943; Manduria, Italy, 19 Dec 1943: Lecce, Italy, 17 Jan 1944–19 Apr 1945; Fairmont AAFld, NE, 8 May 1945; McCook AAFld, NE, 25 June 1945; March Field, CA, 10 Nov 1945–27 Mar 1946. Andrews Field, MD, 1 July 1947; Spokane AAFld, WA, 24 Sept 1947; Yokota, Japan, 5 Aug 1950; Lincoln AFB, NE, 25 July 1954–.

Aircraft

B-24, 1942–1945. B-29, 1945. B-29, 1947–1954; B-47, 1954–.

Operations

Combat in MTO and ETO, Aug 1942–15 Apr 1945. Combat in Korea, 7 Aug 1950–25 July 1953.

Service Streamers

American Theater.

Campaigns

World War II: Egypt-Libya; Air Offensive, Europe; Tunisia; Sicily; Naples-Foggia; Anzio; Rome-Arno; Normandy; Northern France; Southern France; North Apennines; Rhineland; Central Europe; Po Valley; Air Combat, EAME Theater. Korean War: UN Defensive; UN Offensive; CCF Intervention; First UN Counteroffensive; CCF Spring Offensive; UN Summer-Fall Offensive; Second Korean Winter; Korea Summer-Fall, 1952; Third Korean Winter; Korea Summer-Fall 1953.

Decorations

Distinguished Unit Citations: North Africa and Sicily, Aug 1942–17 Aug 1943; Ploesti, Romania, 1 Aug 1943. Korea, 1 Dec 1952–30 Apr 1953. Republic of Korea Presidential Unit Citation: [7 Aug] 1950–27 July 1953.

344th BOMB SQUADRON

Lineage

Constituted 344th Bomb Sq (Heavy) on 28 Jan 1942. Activated on 3 Feb 1942. Redesignated 344th Bomb Sq (Very Heavy) on 23 May 1945. Inactivated on 27 Mar 1946. Activated on 1 July 1947. Redesignated 344th Bomb Sq (Medium) on 28 May 1948.

Assignments

98th Bomb Grp, 3 Feb 1942; 444th Bomb Grp, 10 Nov 1945–27 Mar 1946. 98th Bomb Grp, 1 July 1947; 98th Bomb Wing, 16 June 1952–.

Stations

MacDill Field, FL, 3 Feb 1942; Barksdale Field, LA, c. 9 Feb 1942; Ft Myers, FL, 30 Mar 1942; Drane Field, FL, 17 May–3 July 1942; Ramat David, Palestine, 25 July 1942; St Jean, Palestine, 21 Aug 1942; Kabrit, Egypt, 11 Nov 1942; Lete, Libya, 4 Mar 1943; Hergla, Tunisia, 24 Sept 1943; Brindisi, Italy, 18 Nov 1943; Manduria, Italy, 19 Dec 1943: Lecce, Italy, 18 Jan 1944–19 Apr 1945; Fairmont AAFld, NE, 8 May 1945; McCook AAFld, NE, 25 June 1945; Merced AAFld, CA, 10 Nov 1945–27 Mar 1946. Andrews Field, MD, 1 July 1947; Spokane AAFld, WA, 24 Sept 1947; Yokota, Japan, 5 Aug 1950; Lincoln AFB, NE, 24 July 1954–.

Aircraft

B-24, 1942–1945. B-29, 1945. B-29, 1947–1954; B-47, 1954–.

Operations

Combat in MTO and ETO, 1 Aug 1942–15 Apr 1945. Combat in Korea, 7 Aug 1950–25 July 1953.

Service Streamers

American Theater.

Campaigns

World War II: Egypt-Libya; Air Offensive, Europe; Tunisia; Sicily; Naples-Foggia; Anzio; Rome-Arno; Normandy; Northern France; Southern France; North Apennines; Rhineland; Central Europe; Po Valley; Air Combat, EAME Theater. Korean War: UN Defensive; UN Offensive; CCF Intervention; First UN Counteroffensive; CCF Spring Offensive; UN Summer-Fall Offensive; Second Korean Winter; Korea Summer-Fall, 1952; Third Korean Winter; Korea Summer-Fall 1953.

Decorations

Distinguished Unit Citations: North Africa and Sicily, Aug 1942–17 Aug 1943; Ploesti, Romania, 1 Aug 1943. Korea, 1 Dec 1952–30 Apr 1953. Republic of Korea Presidential Unit Citation: [7 Aug] 1950–27 July 1953.

345TH BOMB SQUADRON

Lineage

Constituted 345th Bomb Sq (Heavy) on 28 Jan 1942. Activated on 3 Feb 1942. Redesignated 345th Bomb Sq (Very Heavy) on 23 May 1945. Inactivated on 5 July 1946. Activated on 1 July 1947. Redesignated 345th Bomb Sq (Medium) on 28 May 1948.

Assignments

98th Bomb Grp, 3 Feb 1942; 462d Bomb Grp, 10 Nov 1945; Strategic Air Command, 31 Mar–5 July 1946. 98th Bomb Grp, 1 July 1947; 98th Bomb Wing, 16 June 1952–.

Stations

MacDill Field, FL, 3 Feb 1942; Barksdale Field, LA, c. 9 Feb 1942; Ft Myers, FL, 30 Mar 1942; Drane Field, FL, 16 May–3 July 1942; Ramat David, Palestine, 5 Aug 1942; Fayid, Egypt, 16 Nov 1942; Tobruk, Libya, 25 Jan 1943; Benina, Libya, 16 Feb 1943; Hergla, Tunisia, 26 Sept 1943; Brindisi, Italy, 18 Nov 1943; Manduria, Italy, 20 Dec 1943: Lecce, Italy, 18 Jan 1944–19 Apr 1945; Fairmont AAFld, NE, 8 May 1945; McCook AAFld, NE, 25 June 1945; MacDill Field, FL, 10 Nov 1945–5 July 1946. Andrews Field, MD, 1 July 1947; Spokane AAFld, WA, 24 Sept 1947; Yokota, Japan, 5 Aug 1950; Lincoln AFB, NE, 24 July 1954–.

Aircraft

B-24, 1942–1945. B-29, 1945. B-29, 1947–1954; B-47, 1954–.

Operations

Combat in MTO and ETO, 12 Aug 1942–15 Apr 1945. Combat in Korea, 7 Aug 1950–25 July 1953.

Service Streamers

American Theater.

Campaigns

World War II: Egypt-Libya; Air Offensive, Europe; Tunisia; Sicily; Naples-Foggia; Anzio; Rome-Arno; Normandy; Northern France; Southern France; North Apennines; Rhineland; Central Europe; Po Valley; Air Combat, EAME Theater. Korean War: UN Defensive; UN Offensive; CCF Intervention; CCF Spring Offensive; UN Summer-Fall Offensive; Second Korean Winter; Korea Summer-Fall, 1952; Third Korean Winter; Korea Summer-Fall 1953.

Decorations

Distinguished Unit Citations: North Africa and Sicily, Aug 1942–17 Aug 1943; Ploesti, Romania, 1 Aug 1943. Korea, 1 Dec 1952–30 Apr 1953. Republic of Korea Presidential Unit Citation: [7 Aug] 1950–27 July 1953.

352d BOMB SQUADRON

Lineage

Constituted 352d Bomb Sq (Heavy) on 28 Jan 1942. Activated on 3 Feb 1942. Redesignated 352d Bomb Sq (Very Heavy) on 5 Aug 1945. Inactivated on 15 Oct 1945. Activated on 4 Aug 1946. Redesignated 352d Bomb Sq (Medium) on 28 May 1948.

Assignments
301st Bomb Grp, 3 Feb 1942–15 Oct 1945. 301st Bomb Grp, 4 Aug 1946; 301st Bomb Wing, 16 June 1952–.

Stations
Geiger Field, WA, 3 Feb 1942; Alamogordo, NM, 28 May 1942 (operated from Muroc and San Diego, CA, c. 28 May–14 June 1942); Richard E Byrd Field, VA, 21 June–19 July 1942; Podington, England, 20 Aug 1942; Chelveston, England, 4 Sept 1942; Tafaraoui, Algeria, 24 Nov 1942; Biskra, Algeria, 13 Dec 1942; Ain M'lila, Algeria, 16 Jan 1943; St-Donat, Algeria, 7 Mar 1943; Oudna, Tunisia, 8 Aug 1943; Cerignola, Italy, 9 Dec 1943; Lucera, Italy, 2 Feb 1944–July 1945; Sioux Falls AAFld, SD, 28 July 1945; Mountain Home AAFld, ID, 17 Aug 1945; Pyote AAFld, TX 23 Aug–15 Oct 1945. Clovis AAFld, NM, 4 Aug 1946; Smoky Hill AAFld, KS, 16 July 1947; Barksdale AFB, LA, 7 Nov 1949; Lockbourne AFB, OH, 15 Apr 1958–.

Aircraft
B-17, 1942–1945. B-29, 1947–1953; B-47, 1953–1958; RB-47, 1958; B-47, 1958–1961; E-47, 1961–.

Operations
Antisubmarine patrols off California coast, late May–c. mid-June 1942. Combat in ETO and MTO, 5 Sept 1942–c. 26 Apr 1945. Electronic countermeasures, 1958–.

Service Streamers
None

Campaigns
Antisubmarine, American Theater; Air Offensive, Europe; Egypt-Libya; Tunisia; Sicily; Naples-Foggia; Anzio; Rome-Arno; Normandy; Northern France; Southern France; North Apennines; Rhineland; Central Europe; Po Valley; Air Combat, EAME Theater.

Decorations
Distinguished Unit Citations: Tunisia, 6 Apr 1943; Germany, 25 Feb 1944. Air Force Outstanding Unit Award: 1 Jan 1961–31 Dec 1962.

353d BOMB SQUADRON
Lineage
Constituted 353d Bomb Sq (Heavy) on 28 Jan 1942. Activated on 3 Feb 1942. Redesignated 353d Bomb Sq (Very Heavy) on 5 Aug 1945. Inactivated on 15 Oct 1945. Activated on 4 Aug 1946. Redesignated 353d Bomb Sq (Medium) on 28 May 1948.

Assignments
301st Bomb Grp, 3 Feb 1942–15 Oct 1945. 301st Bomb Grp, 4 Aug 1946; 301st Bomb Wing, 16 June 1952–.

Stations
Geiger Field, WA, 3 Feb 1942; Alamogordo, NM, 27 May 1942 (operated from Muroc and San Diego, CA, c. 28 May–14 June 1942); Richard E Byrd Field, VA, 21 June–20 July 1942; Chelveston, England, 19 Aug 1942; Tafaraoui, Algeria, 26 Nov 1942; Maison Blanche, Algeria, 6 Dec 1942; Biskra, Algeria,

16 Dec 1942; Ain M'lila, Algeria, 17 Jan 1943; St-Donat, Algeria, 8 Mar 1943; Oudna, Tunisia, 6 Aug 1943; Cerignola, Italy, 10 Dec 1943; Lucera, Italy, 2 Feb 1944–July 1945; Sioux Falls AAFld, SD, 28 July 1945; Mountain Home AAFld, ID, 17 Aug 1945; Pyote AAFld, TX 23 Aug–15 Oct 1945. Clovis AAFld, NM, 4 Aug 1946; Smoky Hill AAFld, KS, 16 July 1947; Barksdale AFB, LA, 7 Nov 1949; Lockbourne AFB, OH, 15 Apr 1958–.

Aircraft
B-17, 1942–1945. B-29, 1947–1953; B-47, 1953–1958; RB-47, 1958; B-47, 1958–1961; E-47, 1961–.

Operations
Antisubmarine patrols off California coast, late May–c. mid-June 1942. Combat in ETO and MTO, 2 Oct 1942–c. 26 Apr 1945. Electronic countermeasures, 1958–.

Service Streamers
None

Campaigns
Antisubmarine, American Theater; Air Offensive, Europe; Egypt-Libya; Tunisia; Sicily; Naples-Foggia; Anzio; Rome-Arno; Normandy; Northern France; Southern France; North Apennines; Rhineland; Central Europe; Po Valley; Air Combat, EAME Theater.

Decorations
Distinguished Unit Citations: Tunisia, 6 Apr 1943; Germany, 25 Feb 1944. Air Force Outstanding Unit Award: 1 Jan 1961–31 Dec 1962.

355th BOMB SQUADRON
Lineage
Constituted 355th Bomb Sq (Heavy) on 28 Jan 1942. Activated on 1 June 1942. Inactivated on 10 Apr 1944. Redesignated 355th Bomb Sq (Very Heavy) on 27 June 1944. Activated on 7 July 1944. Inactivated on 15 Apr 1946. Redesignated 355th Troop Carrier Sq (Medium) on 16 May 1949. Activated in the reserve on 27 June 1949. Redesignated 355th Troop Carrier Sq (Heavy) on 28 Jan 1950. Ordered to active service on 1 June 1951. Inactivated on 8 June 1951. Redesignated 355th Troop Carrier Sq (Medium) on 26 May 1952. Activated in the reserve on 14 June 1952. Ordered to active service on 28 Oct 1962. Relieved from active duty on 28 Nov 1962.

Assignments
302d Bomb Grp, 1 June 1942–10 Apr 1944. 331st Bomb Grp, 7 July 1944–15 Apr 1946. 302d Troop Carrier Grp, 27 June 1949–8 June 1951. 302d Troop Carrier Grp, 14 June 1952; 302d Troop Carrier Wing, 14 Apr 1959; 906th Troop Carrier Grp, 11 Feb 1963–.

Stations
Geiger Field, WA, 1 June 1942; Davis-Monthan Field, AZ, 23 June 1942; Wendover Field, UT, 30 July 1942; Pueblo AAB, CO, 30 Sept 1942; Davis-Monthan Field, AZ, 1 Dec 1942; Clovis, NM, 29 Jan 1943; Langley Field, VA, 17 Dec 1943; Chatham AAFld, GA, 9 Mar–10 Apr

1944. Dalhart AAFld, TX, 7 July 1944; McCook AAFld, NE, 22 Nov 1944–8 Apr 1945; Northwest Field, Guam, 12 May 1945–15 Apr 1946. McChord AFB, WA, 27 June 1949–8 June 1951. Clinton County AFB, OH, 14 June 1952–.

Aircraft
B-24, 1942–1944. B-17, 1944; B-29, 1945–1946. C-119, 1962.

Operations
Operational and later replacement training unit, 1943–1944. Combat in Western Pacific, c. 7 July–14 Aug 1945.

Service Streamers
American Theater.

Campaigns
Air Offensive, Japan; Eastern Mandates; Western Pacific.

Decorations
Distinguished Unit Citation: Japan, 22–29 July 1945.

356th BOMB SQUADRON
Lineage
Constituted 356th Bomb Sq (Heavy) on 28 Jan 1942. Activated on 1 June 1942. Inactivated on 10 Apr 1944. Redesignated 356th Bomb Sq (Very Heavy) on 27 June 1944. Activated on 7 July 1944. Inactivated on 15 Apr 1946. Redesignated 356th Troop Carrier Sq (Medium) on 16 May 1949. Activated in the reserve on 27 June 1949. Inactivated on 28 Jan 1950. Activated in the reserve on 14 June 1952. Ordered to active service on 28 Oct 1962. Relieved from active duty on 28 Nov 1962.

Assignments
302d Bomb Grp, 1 June 1942–10 Apr 1944. 331st Bomb Grp, 7 July 1944–15 Apr 1946. 302d Troop Carrier Grp, 27 June 1949–28 Jan 1950. 302d Troop Carrier Grp, 14 June 1952; 302d Troop Carrier Wing, 14 Apr 1959; 907th Troop Carrier Grp, 11 Feb 1963–.

Stations
Geiger Field, WA, 1 June 1942; Davis-Monthan Field, AZ, 23 June 1942; Wendover Field, UT, 30 July 1942; Pueblo AAB, CO, 30 Sept 1942; Davis-Monthan Field, AZ, 1 Dec 1942; Clovis, NM, 29 Jan 1943; Langley Field, VA, 17 Dec 1943; Chatham AAFld, GA, 27 Jan–10 Apr 1944. Dalhart AAFld, TX, 7 July 1944; McCook AAFld, NE, 22 Nov 1944–8 Apr 1945; Northwest Field, Guam, 12 May 1945–15 Apr 1946. McChord AFB, WA, 27 June 1949–28 Jan 1950. Clinton County AFB, OH, 14 June 1952–.

Aircraft
B-24, 1942–1944. B-17, 1944; B-29, 1945–1946. C-119, 1962.

Operations
Operational and later replacement training unit, 1942–1944. Combat in Western Pacific, c. 1 July–14 Aug 1945.

Service Streamers
American Theater.

Campaigns
Air Offensive, Japan; Eastern Mandates; Western Pacific.

Decorations
Distinguished Unit Citation: Japan, 22–29 July 1945.

357th BOMB SQUADRON
Lineage
Constituted 357th Bomb Sq (Heavy) on 28 Jan 1942. Activated on 1 June 1942. Inactivated on 10 Apr 1944. Redesignated 357th Bomb Sq (Very Heavy) on 27 June 1944. Activated on 7 July 1944. Inactivated on 15 Apr 1946. Redesignated 357th Troop Carrier Sq (Medium) on 26 May 1952. Activated in the reserve on 14 June 1952. Ordered to active service on 28 Oct 1962. Relieved from active duty on 28 Nov 1962.

Assignments
302d Bomb Grp, 1 June 1942–10 Apr 1944. 331st Bomb Grp, 7 July 1944–15 Apr 1946. 302d Troop Carrier Grp, 14 June 1952; 445th Troop Carrier Group, 16 Nov 1957; 446th Troop Carrier Group, 25 Mar 1958; 306th Troop Carrier Wing, 8 May 1961; 908th Troop Carrier Group, 11 Feb 1963–.

Stations
Geiger Field, WA, 1 June 1942; Davis-Monthan Field, AZ, 23 June 1942; Wendover Field, UT, 30 July 1942; Pueblo AAB, CO, 30 Sept 1942; Davis-Monthan Field, AZ, 1 Dec 1942; Clovis, NM, 29 Jan 1943; Langley Field, VA, 17 Dec 1943; Chatham AAFld, GA, 9 Mar–10 Apr 1944. Dalhart AAFld, TX, 7 July 1944; McCook AAFld, NE, 22 Nov 1944–8 Apr 1945; Northwest Field, Guam, 12 May 1945–15 Apr 1946. Clinton County AFB, OH, 14 June 1952; Donaldson AFB, SC, 16 Nov 1957; New Orleans NAS, LA, 25 Mar 1958; Bates Field, AL, 8 May 1961–.

Aircraft
B-24, 1942–1944. B-17, 1944; B-29, 1945–1946. C-119, 1962.

Operations
Operational and later replacement training unit, 1942–1944. Combat in Western Pacific, c. 7 July–14 Aug 1945.

Service Streamers
American Theater.

Campaigns
Air Offensive, Japan; Eastern Mandates; Western Pacific.

Decorations
Distinguished Unit Citation: Japan, 22–29 July 1945.

358th BOMB SQUADRON
Lineage
Constituted 358th Bomb Sq (Heavy) on 28 Jan 1942. Activated on 3 Feb 1942. Inactivated on 25 July 1945. Redesignated 358th Bomb Sq (Very Heavy) on 11 June 1947. Activated on 1 July 1947. Inactivated on 6 Sept 1948. Redesignated 358th Bomb Sq (Medium) on 27 Aug 1951. Activated on 4 Sept 1951.

Assignments
303d Bomb Grp, 3 Feb 1942–25 July 1945. 303d Bomb Grp, 1 July 1947–6 Sept 1948. 303d Bomb Grp, 4 Sept 1951; 303d Bomb Wing, 16 June 1952–.

Stations
Pendleton Field, OR, 3 Feb 1942; Gowen Field, ID, 11 Feb 1942 (operated from Muroc, CA, 28 May–early June 1942); Alamogordo, NM, 18 June 1942; Biggs Field, TX, 6–22 Aug 1942; Molesworth, England, 12 Sept 1942; Casablanca, French Morocco, c. 31 May–25 July 1945. Andrews Field, MD, 1 July 1947–6 Sept 1948. Davis-Monthan AFB, AZ, 4 Sept 1951–.

Aircraft
B-17, 1942–1945; B-29, 1951–1953; B-47, 1953–.

Operations
Antisubmarine patrols off California coast, late May–early June 1942. Combat in ETO, 17 Nov 1942–25 Apr 1945. Apparently not manned, 1947–1948.

Service Streamers
None

Campaigns
Antisubmarine, American Theater; Air Offensive, Europe; Normandy; Northern France; Rhineland; Ardennes-Alsace; Central Europe; Air Combat, EAME Theater.

Decorations
Distinguished Unit Citations: Germany, 11 Jan 1944. Air Force Outstanding Unit Award: 1 Jan 1961–31 Mar 1962.

359th BOMB SQUADRON
Lineage
Constituted 359th Bomb Sq (Heavy) on 28 Jan 1942. Activated on 3 Feb 1942. Inactivated on 25 July 1945. Redesignated 359th Bomb Sq (Very Heavy) on 11 June 1947. Activated on 1 July 1947. Inactivated on 6 Sept 1948. Redesignated 359th Bomb Sq (Medium) on 27 Aug 1951. Activated on 4 Sept 1951.

Assignments
303d Bomb Grp, 3 Feb 1942–25 July 1945. 303d Bomb Grp, 1 July 1947–6 Sept 1948. 303d Bomb Grp, 4 Sept 1951; 303d Bomb Wing, 16 June 1952–.

Stations
Pendleton Field, OR, 3 Feb 1942; Gowen Field, ID, 16 Feb 1942 (operated from Muroc, CA, 28 May–June 1942); Alamogordo, NM, 18 June 1942; Biggs Field, TX, 5–24 Aug 1942; Molesworth, England, 12 Sept 1942; Casablanca, French Morocco, c. 31 May–25 July 1945. Andrews Field, MD, 1 July 1947–6 Sept 1948. Davis-Monthan AFB, AZ, 4 Sept 1951–.

Aircraft
B-17, 1942–1945; B-29, 1951–1953; B-47, 1953–.

Operations
Antisubmarine patrols off California coast, late May–early June 1942. Combat in ETO, 17 Nov 1942–25 Apr 1945. Apparently not manned, 1947–1948.

Service Streamers
None

Campaigns
Antisubmarine, American Theater; Air Offensive, Europe; Normandy; Northern France; Rhineland; Ardennes-Alsace; Central Europe; Air Combat, EAME Theater.

Decorations
Distinguished Unit Citations: Germany, 11 Jan 1944. Air Force Outstanding Unit Award: 1 Jan 1961–31 Mar 1962.

360th BOMB SQUADRON
Lineage
Constituted 360th Bomb Sq (Heavy) on 28 Jan 1942. Activated on 3 Feb 1942. Inactivated on 25 July 1945. Redesignated 360th Bomb Sq (Very Heavy) on 11 June 1947. Activated on 1 July 1947. Inactivated on 6 Sept 1948. Redesignated 360th Bomb Sq (Medium) on 27 Aug 1951. Activated on 4 Sept 1951.

Assignments
303d Bomb Grp, 3 Feb 1942–25 July 1945. 303d Bomb Grp, 1 July 1947–6 Sept 1948. 303d Bomb Grp, 4 Sept 1951; 303d Bomb Wing, 16 June 1952–.

Stations
Pendleton Field, OR, 3 Feb 1942; Gowen Field, ID, 11 Feb 1942 (operated from Muroc, CA, 28 May–c. 14 June 1942); Alamogordo, NM, 17 June 1942; Biggs Field, TX, 7–24 Aug 1942; Molesworth, England, 12 Sept 1942; Casablanca, French Morocco, c. 31 May–25 July 1945. Andrews Field, MD, 1 July 1947–6 Sept 1948. Davis-Monthan AFB, AZ, 4 Sept 1951–.

Aircraft
B-17, 1942–1945; B-29, 1951–1953; B-47, 1953–.

Operations
Antisubmarine patrols off California coast, c. late May–early June 1942. Combat in ETO, 17 Nov 1942–25 Apr 1945. Apparently not manned, 1947–1948.

Service Streamers
None

Campaigns
Antisubmarine, American Theater; Air Offensive, Europe; Normandy; Northern France; Rhineland; Ardennes-Alsace; Central Europe; Air Combat, EAME Theater.

Decorations
Distinguished Unit Citations: Germany, 11 Jan 1944. Air Force Outstanding Unit Award: 1 Jan 1961–31 Mar 1962.

364th BOMB SQUADRON
Lineage
Constituted 364th Bomb Sq (Heavy) on 28 Jan 1942. Activated on 1 Mar 1942. Inactivated on 29 June 1946. Redesignated 364th Bomb Sq (Very Heavy) on 11 June 1947. Activated on 1 July 1947. Inactivated on 6 Sept 1948. Redesignated 364th Bomb Sq (Medium) on 20 Dec 1950. Activated on 2 Jan 1951.

Assignments
305th Bomb Grp, 1 Mar 1942–29 June 1946. 305th Bomb Grp, 1 July 1947–6 Sept 1948. 305th Bomb Grp, 2 Jan 1951; 305th Bomb Wing, 16 June 1952–.

Stations
Salt Lake City, UT, 1 Mar 1942; Geiger Field, WA, 11 June 1942; Muroc, CA, 4 July–23 Aug 1942; Grafton Underwood, England, 11 Sept 1942; Chelveston, England, 11 Dec 1942; St Trond, Belgium, 25 July 1945 (operated principally from Meeks Frield, Iceland, 16 Aug–13 Oct 1945); Lechfeld, Germany, 19 Dec 1945–29 June 1946. Andrews Field, MD, 1 July 1947–6 Sept 1948. MacDill AFB, Fl, 2 Jan 1951; Bunker Hill AFB, IN, 1 June 1959–.

Aircraft
B-17, 1942–1946; B-29, 1951–1953; B-47, 1952–1961; B-58, 1961–.

Operations
Combat in ETO, 17 Nov 1942–25 Apr 1945. Photo-mapping, June 1945–c. June 1946. Apparently not manned, 1947–1948.

Service Streamers
None

Campaigns
Air Offensive, Europe; Normandy; Northern France; Rhineland; Ardennes-Alsace; Central Europe; Air Combat, EAME Theater.

Decorations
Distinguished Unit Citations: France, 4 Apr 1943; Germany, 11 Jan 1944. Air Force Outstanding Unit Award: 1 Jan 1954–1 Mar 1957.

365th BOMB SQUADRON
Lineage
Constituted 365th Bomb Sq (Heavy) on 28 Jan 1942. Activated on 1 Mar 1942. Inactivated on 25 Dec 1946. Redesignated 365th Bomb Sq (Very Heavy) on 11 June 1947. Activated on 1 July 1947. Inactivated on 6 Sept 1948. Redesignated 365th Bomb Sq (Medium) on 20 Dec 1950. Activated on 2 Jan 1951.

Assignments
305th Bomb Grp, 1 Mar 1942; XII Tactical Air Command, 1 Nov–25 Dec 1946. 305th Bomb Grp, 1 July 1947–6 Sept 1948. 305th Bomb Grp, 2 Jan 1951; 305th Bomb Wing, 16 June 1952–.

Stations
Salt Lake City, UT, 1 Mar 1942; Geiger Field, WA, 11 June 1942; Muroc, CA, 4 July–23 Aug 1942; Grafton Underwood, England, 11 Sept 1942; Chelveston, England, 11 Dec 1942; St Trond, Belgium, 25 July 1945; Lechfeld, Germany, Dec 1945–25 Dec 1946 (operated principally from Tripoli, Libya, Jan–Oct 1946; Port Lyautey, French Morocco, Oct–Dec 1946). Andrews Field, MD, 1 July 1947–6 Sept 1948. MacDill AFB, Fl, 2 Jan 1951; Bunker Hill AFB, IN, 1 June 1959–.

Aircraft
B-17, 1942–1946; B-29, 1951–1953; B-47, 1952–1961; B-58, 1961–.

Operations
Combat in ETO, 17 Nov 1942–25 Apr 1945. Photo-mapping, 17 June 1945–Dec 1946. Apparently not manned, 1947–1948.

Service Streamers
None

Campaigns
Air Offensive, Europe; Normandy; Northern France; Rhineland; Ardennes-Alsace; Central Europe; Air Combat, EAME Theater.

Decorations
Distinguished Unit Citations: France, 4 Apr 1943; Germany, 11 Jan 1944. Air Force Outstanding Unit Award: 1 Jan 1954–1 Mar 1957.

366th BOMB SQUADRON
Lineage
Constituted 366th Bomb Sq (Heavy) on 28 June 1942. Activated on 1 Mar 1942. Inactivated on 25 Dec 1946. Redesignated 366th Bomb Sq (Very Heavy) on 11 June 1947. Activated on 1 July 1947. Inactivated on 6 Sept 1948. Redesignated 366th Bomb Sq (Medium) on 20 Dec 1950. Activated on 2 Jan 1951.

Assignments
305th Bomb Grp, 1 Mar 1942–25 Dec 1946. 305th Bomb Grp, 1 July 1947–6 Sept 1948. 305th Bomb Grp, 2 Jan 1951; 305th Bomb Wing, 16 June 1952–.

Stations
Salt Lake City, UT, 1 Mar 1942; Geiger Field, WA, 11 June 1942; Muroc, CA, 4 July–23 Aug 1942; Grafton Underwood, England, 12 Sept 1942; Chelveston, England, 11 Dec 1942; St Trond, Belgium, 25 July 1945; (operated principally from Foggia, Italy, and Tunis, Tunisia, Sept–Nov 1945); Lechfeld, Germany, 19 Dec 1945–25 Dec 1946 (operated principally from Roberts Field, Liberia, Jan–Apr 1946; Gibraltar and Port Lyautey, French Morocco, Sept–Oct 1946). Andrews Field, MD, 1 July 1947–6 Sept 1948. MacDill AFB, Fl, 2 Jan 1951; Bunker Hill AFB, IN, 1 June 1959–.

Aircraft
B-17, 1942–1946; B-29, 1951–1953; B-47, 1952–1961; B-58, 1961–.

Operations
Combat in ETO, 17 Nov 1942–25 Apr 1945. Photo-mapping, June 1945–Oct 1946. Apparently not manned, 1947–1948.

Service Streamers
None

Campaigns
Air Offensive, Europe; Normandy; Northern France; Rhineland; Ardennes-Alsace; Central Europe; Air Combat, EAME Theater.

Decorations
Distinguished Unit Citations: France, 4 Apr 1943; Germany, 11 Jan 1944. Air Force Outstanding Unit Award: 1 Jan 1954–1 Mar 1957.

367th BOMB SQUADRON
Lineage
Constituted 367th Bomb Sq (Heavy) on 28 Jan 1942. Activated on 1 Mar 1942. Inactivated on 25 Dec 1946. Redesignated 367th Bomb Sq (Very Heavy) on 11 June 1947. Activated on 1 July 1947. Redesignated 367th Bomb Sq (Medium) on 11 Aug 1948.

Assignments
306th Bomb Grp, 1 Mar 1942–25 Dec 1946. 306th Bomb Grp, 1 July 1947; 306th Bomb Wing, 16 June 1952–.

Stations
Gowen Field, ID, 1 Mar 1942; Wendover Field, UT, c. 6 Apr–1 Aug 1942; Thurleigh, England, c. 6 Sept 1942 (detachments operated from Lagens, Azores, 20 Aug–Oct 1945; Dakar, French West Africa, Sept 1945; Marrakech, French Morocco, Oct 1945); Giebelstadt, Germany, 25 Dec 1945; Istres, France, 26 Feb 1946; Furstenfeldbruck, Germany, 16 Aug 1946; Lechfeld, Germany, 13 Sept–25 Dec 1946. Andrews Field, MD, 1 July 1947; MacDill AFB, FL, 1 Aug 1948–.

Aircraft
B-17, 1942–1946. B-29, 1948–1951; B-50, 1950–1951; B-47, 1951–.

Operations
Combat in ETO, 9 Oct 1942–19 Apr 1945. Photo-mapping, Europe and Africa, June 1945–Mar 1946; later, courier missions to aid photo-mapping operations of the group. Apparently not manned, 1 July 1947–1 Aug 1948.

Service Streamers
None

Campaigns
Air Offensive, Europe; Normandy; Northern France; Rhineland; Ardennes-Alsace; Central Europe; Air Combat, EAME Theater.

Decorations
Distinguished Unit Citations: Germany, 11 Jan 1944; Germany, 22 Feb 1944. Air Force Outstanding Unit Award: 22 Jan 1953–8 Dec 1956.

368th BOMB SQUADRON

Lineage
Constituted 368th Bomb Sq (Heavy) on 28 Jan 1942. Activated on 1 Mar 1942. Inactivated on 25 Dec 1946. Redesignated 368th Bomb Sq (Very Heavy) on 11 June 1947. Activated on 1 July 1947. Redesignated 368th Bomb Sq (Medium) on 11 Aug 1948.

Assignments
306th Bomb Grp, 1 Mar 1942–25 Dec 1946. 306th Bomb Grp, 1 July 1947; 306th Bomb Wing, 16 June 1952–.

Stations
Gowen Field, ID, 1 Mar 1942; Wendover Field, UT, c. 6 Apr–1 Aug 1942; Thurleigh, England, c. 6 Sept 1942 (detachment operated from Gibraltar, 18 Aug 1945–Jan 1946; Port Lyautey, French Morocco, Feb–15 July 1946); Giebelstadt, Germany, 25 Dec 1945; Istres, France, 24 Feb 1946 (detachment operated from Dakar, West Africa, Jan–Mar 1946); Furstenfeldbruck, Germany, 16 Aug 1946; Lechfeld, Germany, 13 Sept–25 Dec 1946. Andrews Field, MD, 1 July 1947; MacDill AFB, FL, 1 Aug 1948–.

Aircraft
B-17, 1942–1946. B-29, 1948–1951; B-50, 1950–1951; B-47, 1951–.

Operations
Combat in ETO, 9 Oct 1942–19 Apr 1945. Photo-mapping, Europe and Africa, June 1945–July 1946. Apparently not manned, 1 July 1947–1 Aug 1948.

Service Streamers
None

Campaigns
Air Offensive, Europe; Normandy; Northern France; Rhineland; Ardennes-Alsace; Central Europe; Air Combat, EAME Theater.

Decorations
Distinguished Unit Citations: Germany, 11 Jan 1944; Germany, 22 Feb 1944. Air Force Outstanding Unit Award: 22 Jan 1953–8 Dec 1956.

369th BOMB SQUADRON

Lineage
Constituted 369th Bomb Sq (Heavy) on 28 Jan 1942. Activated on 1 Mar 1942. Inactivated on 29 June 1946. Redesignated 369th Bomb Sq (Very Heavy) on 11 June 1947. Activated on 1 July 1947. Redesignated 369th Bomb Sq (Medium) on 11 Aug 1948.

Assignments
306th Bomb Grp, 1 Mar 1942–29 June 1946. 306th Bomb Grp, 1 July 1947; 306th Bomb Wing, 16 June 1952–.

Stations
Gowen Field, ID, 1 Mar 1942; Wendover Field, UT, c. 6 Apr–1 Aug 1942; Thurleigh, England, 6 Sept 1942 (detachment operated from Istres, France, 31 Aug–Sept 1945; Marrakech, French Morocco, 6 Sept 1945–Jan 1946); Giebelstadt, Germany, 25 Dec 1945; Istres, France, 26 Feb–29 June 1946. Andrews Field, MD, 1 July 1947; MacDill AFB, FL, 1 Aug 1948–.

Aircraft
B-17, 1942–1946. B-29, 1948–1951; B-50, 1950–1951; B-47, 1951–.

Operations
Combat in ETO, 9 Oct 1942–19 Apr 1945. Photo-mapping, Europe and Africa, June 1945–June 1946. Apparently not manned, 1 July 1947–1 Aug 1948.

Service Streamers
None

Campaigns
Air Offensive, Europe; Normandy; Northern France; Rhineland; Ardennes-Alsace; Central Europe; Air Combat, EAME Theater.

Decorations
Distinguished Unit Citations: Germany, 11 Jan 1944; Germany, 22 Feb 1944. Air Force Outstanding Unit Award: 22 Jan 1953–8 Dec 1956.

370th BOMB SQUADRON

Lineage
Constituted 370th Bomb Sq (Heavy) on 28 Jan 1942. Activated on 15 Apr 1942. Inactivated on 18 Jan 1946. Redesignated 370th Bomb Sq (Very Heavy) on 15 July 1946. Activated on 4 Aug 1946. Redesignated 370th Bomb Sq (Medium) on 28 May 1948.

Assignments
307th Bomb Grp, 15 Apr 1942–18 Jan 1946. 307th Bomb Grp, 4 Aug 1946; 307th Bomb Wing, 16 June 1952–.

Stations
Geiger Field, WA, 15 Apr 1942; Ephrata, WA, 27 May 1942; Sioux City AAB, IA, 29 Sept–21 Oct 1942; Kipapa Field, TH, 2 Nov 1942 (operated from Midway, 22–24 Dec 1942, and from Espiritu Santo, c. 6 Feb–c. 18 Mar 1943); Guadalcanal, 18 Mar 1943; Munda, New Georgia, 22 Feb 1944; Los Negros, 13 May 1944; Wakde, 22 Aug 1944 (operated from Noemfoor, c. 20 Sept–12 Nov 1944); Morotai, 14 Nov 1944; Clark Field, Luzon, 10 Sept–27 Dec 1945; Camp Stoneman, CA, 16–18 Jan 1946. MacDill Field, FL, 4 Aug 1946 (operated from Kadena, Okinawa, beginning c. 4 Aug 1950); Kadena, Okinawa, 15 Aug 1953; Lincoln AFB, NE, 19 Nov 1954–.

Aircraft
B-17, 1942; B-24, 1942–1945. B-29, 1946–1954; B-47, 1955–.

Operations
Sea search missions from Hawaii, Nov 1942–Jan 1943. Combat in Central Pacific, 22–23 Dec 1942; South and Southwest Pacific, 16 Feb 1943–11 Aug 1945. Training unit for antisubmarine warfare, Sept 1947–c. May 1948. Combat in Korea, 8 Aug 1950–27 July 1953.

Service Streamers
None

Campaigns
World War II: Central Pacific; Guadalcanal; New Guinea; Northern Solomons; Eastern Mandates; Bismarck Archipelago; Western Pacific; Leyte; Luzon; Southern Philippines; China Offensive; Air Combat, Asiatic-Pacific Theater. Korean War: UN Defensive; UN Offensive; CCF Intervention; First UN Counteroffensive; CCF Spring Offensive; UN Summer-Fall Offensive; Second Korean Winter; Korean Summer-Fall, 1952; Third Korean Winter; Korea Summer-Fall, 1953.

Decorations
Distinguished Unit Citations: Truk, 29 Mar 1944; Borneo, 3 Oct 1944; Korea, 11-27 July 1953. Philippine Presidential Unit Citation. Republic of Korea Presidential Unit Citation: [Aug] 1950–27 July 1953.

371st BOMB SQUADRON
Lineage
Constituted 371st Bomb Sq (Heavy) on 28 Jan 1942. Activated on 15 Apr 1942. Inactivated on 18 Jan 1946. Redesignated 371st Bomb Sq (Very Heavy) on 15 July 1946. Activated on 4 Aug 1946. Redesignated 371st Bomb Sq (Medium) on 28 May 1948.

Assignments
307th Bomb Grp, 15 Apr 1942–18 Jan 1946. 307th Bomb Grp, 4 Aug 1946; 307th Bomb Wing, 16 June 1952–.

Stations
Geiger Field, WA, 15 Apr 1942; Ephrata, WA, 28 May 1942; Sioux City AAB, IA, 30 Sept–20 Oct 1942; Wheeler Field, TH, 2 Nov 1942 (operated from Midway, 21–24 Dec 1942 and 20–25 Jan 1943; Canton, 6–12 Feb 1943; Funafuti, 18–23 Apr 1943 and 27 July–1 Aug 1943); Espiritu Santo, 13 June 1943 (operated from Guadalcanal, 25 Aug–14 Oct 1943; 24 Nov–31 Dec 1943); Munda, New Georgia, 9 Jan 1944; Los Negros, 13 May 1944; Wakde, 22 Aug 1944 (operated from Noemfoor, c. 18 Sept–c. 20 Nov 1944); Morotai, 10 Nov 1944; Clark Field, Luzon, 1 Sept–27 Dec 1945; Camp Stoneman, CA, 16–18 Jan 1946. MacDill Field, FL, 4 Aug 1946 (operated from Kadena, Okinawa, beginning c. 5 Aug 1950); Kadena, Okinawa, 15 Aug 1953; Lincoln AFB, NE, 19 Nov 1954–.

Aircraft
B-17, 1942; B-24, 1942–1945. B-29, 1946–1954; B-47, 1955–.

Operations
Sea search from Hawaii, Nov 1942–Jan 1943. Combat in Central Pacific, 22–23 Dec 1942; 20–25 Jan 1943; 6–12 Feb 1943, 18–23 Apr 1943, 27 July–1 Aug 1943; South and Southwest Pacific, 26 Aug 1943–11 Aug 1945. Training unit for antisubmarine warfare, Sept 1947–c. May 1948. Combat in Korea, 9 Aug 1950–27 July 1953.

Service Streamers
None

Campaigns
World War II: Central Pacific; New Guinea; Northern Solomons; Eastern Mandates; Bismarck Archipelago; Western Pacific; Leyte; Luzon; Southern Philippines; Air Combat, Asiatic-Pacific Theater. Korean War: UN Defensive; UN Offensive; CCF Intervention; First UN Counteroffensive; CCF Spring Offensive; UN Summer-Fall Offensive; Second Korean Winter; Korean Summer-Fall, 1952; Third Korean Winter; Korea Summer-Fall, 1953.

Decorations
Distinguished Unit Citations: Borneo, 3 Oct 1944; Korea, 11-27 July 1953. Philippine Presidential Unit Citation. Republic of Korea Presidential Unit Citation: [Aug] 1950–27 July 1953.

372d BOMB SQUADRON
Lineage
Constituted 372d Bomb Sq (Heavy) on 28 Jan 1942. Activated on 15 Apr 1942. Inactivated on 26 Dec 1945. Redesignated 372d Bomb Sq (Very Heavy) on 15 July 1946. Activated on 4 Aug 1946. Redesignated 372d Bomb Sq (Medium) on 28 May 1948.

Assignments
307th Bomb Grp, 15 Apr 1942–26 Dec 1945. 307th Bomb Grp, 4 Aug 1946; 307th Bomb Wing, 16 June 1952–.

Stations
Geiger Field, WA, 15 Apr 1942; Ephrata, WA, 28 May 1942; Sioux City AAB, IA, 1–20 Oct 1942; Kahuku, TH, 2 Nov 1942 (operated from Midway, 22–24 Dec 1942; Funafuti, 18–23 Apr 1943); Espiritu Santo, 13 June 1943 (operated from Guadalcanal, 5 Aug–15 Sept 1943 and 25 Oct–3 Dec 1943); Munda, New Georgia, 9 Jan 1944; Los Negros, 13 May 1944; Wakde, c. 22 Aug 1944 (operated from Noemfoor, c. 20 Sept–c. 9 Nov 1944); Morotai, c. 10 Nov 1944; Clark Field, Luzon, c. 1 Sept–7 Dec 1945; Camp Stoneman, CA, 26 Dec 1945. MacDill Field, FL, 4 Aug 1946 (operated from Kadena, Okinawa, beginning c. 7 Aug 1950); Kadena, Okinawa, 15 Aug 1953; Lincoln AFB, NE, 19 Nov 1954–.

Aircraft
B-17, 1942; B-24, 1942–1945. B-29, 1946–1954; B-47, 1955–.

Operations
Sea search from Hawaii, Nov 1942–May 1945. Combat in Central Pacific, 22–23 Dec 1942 and 18–23 Apr 1943; South and Southwest Pacific, 7 Aug 1943–11 Aug 1945. Training unit for antisubmarine warfare, Sept 1947–May 1948. Combat in Korea, 9 Aug 1950–27 July 1953.

Service Streamers
None

Campaigns
World War II: Central Pacific; New Guinea; Northern Solomons; Eastern Mandates; Bismarck Archipelago; Western Pacific; Leyte;

Luzon; Southern Philippines; China Offensive; Air Combat, Asiatic-Pacific Theater. Korean War: UN Defensive; UN Offensive; CCF Intervention; First UN Counteroffensive; CCF Spring Offensive; UN Summer-Fall Offensive; Second Korean Winter; Korean Summer-Fall, 1952; Third Korean Winter; Korea Summer-Fall, 1953.

Decorations
Distinguished Unit Citations: Borneo, 3 Oct 1944; Korea, 11-27 July 1953. Philippine Presidential Unit Citation. Republic of Korea Presidential Unit Citation: [Aug] 1950–27 July 1953.

373d BOMB SQUADRON
Lineage
Constituted 373d Bomb Sq (Heavy) on 28 Jan 1942. Activated on 15 Apr 1942. Inactivated on 7 Jan 1946. Redesignated 373d Recon Sq (Very Long Range, Weather) on 16 Sept 1947. Activated on 15 Oct 1947. Inactivated on 21 Feb 1951. Redesignated 373d Bomb Sq (Medium) on 4 Oct 1951. Activated on 10 Oct 1951. Discontinued, and inactivated, on 25 June 1961. Redesignated 373d Strategic Missile Sq, and activated, on 29 Nov 1961. Organized on 1 Apr 1962.

Assignments
308th Bomb Grp, 15 Apr 1942; 494th Bomb Grp, 21 July 1945; 11th Bomb Grp, 11 Oct 1945–7 Jan 1946. 8th Weather (later 2108th Air Weather) Grp, 15 Oct 1947–21 Feb 1951. 308th Bomb Grp, 10 Oct 1951 (attached to 21st Air Division, 10 Oct 1951–17 Apr 1952); 308th Bomb Wing, 16 June 1952–25 June 1961. Strategic Air Command, 29 Nov 1961; 308th Strategic Missile Wing, 1 Apr 1962–.

Stations
Gowen Field, ID, 15 Apr 1942; Davis-Monthan Field, AZ, 20 June 1942; Alamogordo, NM, 23 July 1942; Davis-Monthan Field, AZ, 28 Aug 1942; Wendover Field, UT, 1 Oct 1942; Pueblo AAB, CO, 30 Nov 1942–2 Jan 1943; Yangkai, China, 20 Mar 1943; Luliang, China, 14 Sept 1944; Yontan, Okinawa, 21 July–19 Dec 1945; Vancouver, WA, 4–7 Jan 1946. Kindley Field, Bermuda, 15 Oct 1947–21 Feb 1951. Forbes AFB, KS, 10 Oct 1951; Hunter AFB, GA, 17 Apr 1952; Plattsburgh AFB, NY, 15 July 1959–25 June 1961. Little Rock AFB, AR, 1 Apr 1962–.

Aircraft and Missiles
B-18, 1942; B-24, 1942–1945. TB-17, 1947–1948; B/RB/WB-29, 1947–1951. B-29, 1951–1953; B-47, 1954–1959. Titan, 1963–.

Operations
Combat in CBI and Western Pacific, 4 May 1943–3 June 1945 and 21 July–14 Aug 1945. Not manned, 15 July 1959–25 June 1961.

Service Streamers
None

Campaigns
India-Burma; Air Offensive, Japan; China Defensive; New Guinea; Western Pacific; China Offensive; Air Combat, Asiatic-Pacific Theater.

Decorations
Distinguished Unit Citation: East and South China Seas, Straits of Formosa, and Gulf of Tonkin, 24 May 1944–28 Apr 1945. Air Force Outstanding Unit Award: 1 Nov 1956–1 Apr 1957.

374th BOMB SQUADRON
Lineage
Constituted 374th Bomb Sq (Heavy) on 28 Jan 1942. Activated on 15 Apr 1942. Inactivated on 6 Jan 1946. Redesignated 374th Recon Sq (Very Long Range, Weather) on 16 Sept 1947. Activated on 15 Oct 1947. Inactivated on 21 Feb 1951. Redesignated 374th Bomb Sq (Medium) on 4 Oct 1951. Activated on 10 Oct 1951. Discontinued, and inactivated, on 25 June 1961. Redesignated 374th Strategic Missile Sq, and activated, on 24 Jan 1962. Organized on 1 Sept 1962.

Assignments
308th Bomb Grp, 15 Apr 1942–6 Jan 1946. 308th Recon Grp, 15 Oct 1947; Air Weather Service, 19 Dec 1950–21 Feb 1951. 308th Bomb Grp, 10 Oct 1951 (attached to 21st Air Division, 10 Oct 1951–17 Apr 1952); 308th Bomb Wing, 16 June 1952–25 June 1961. Strategic Air Command, 24 Jan 1962; 308th Strategic Missile Wing, 1 Sept 1962–.

Stations
Gowen Field, ID, 15 Apr 1942; Davis-Monthan Field, AZ, 18 June 1942; Alamogordo, NM, 24 July 1942; Davis-Monthan Field, AZ, 28 Aug 1942; Wendover Field, UT, 1 Oct 1942; Pueblo AAB, CO, 30 Nov 1942–2 Jan 1943; Chengkung, China, 20 Mar 1943: Kwanghan, China, 18 Feb 1945; Rupsi, India, 27 June–14 Oct 1945; Camp Kilmer, NJ, 5–6 Jan 1946. Fairfield-Suisun AAFld, CA, 15 Oct 1947 (one flight operated from Lincolnshire, England, 22 Nov 1948–6 July 1949); McClellan AFB, CA, 28 Oct 1949–21 Feb 1951 (one flight operated from Dhahran Airfield, Saudi Arabia, 8 May–4 Dec 1950, and another from Eielson AFB, AK, 3 July–28 Sept 1950). Forbes AFB, KS, 10 Oct 1951; Hunter AFB, GA, 17 Apr 1952; Plattsburgh AFB, NY, 15 July 1959–25 June 1961. Little Rock AFB, AR, 24 Jan 1962–.

Aircraft
B-18, 1942; B-24, 1942–1945. B/RB/WB-29, 1947–1951. C-47, 1947–1951. B-29, 1951–1953; B-47, 1953–1959.

Operations
Combat in CBI and Western Pacific, 4 May 1943–11 May 1945. Not manned, 15 July 1959–25 June 1961. Training for operations with Titan missiles, 1 Sept 1962–.

Service Streamers
None

Campaigns
India-Burma; China Defensive; New Guinea; Western Pacific; China Offensive; Air Combat, Asiatic-Pacific Theater.

Decorations
Distinguished Unit Citation: China, 21 Aug 1943; East and South China Seas, Straits of

Formosa, and Gulf of Tonkin, 24 May 1944–28 Apr 1945. Air Force Outstanding Unit Award: 1 Nov 1956–1 Apr 1957.

375th BOMB SQUADRON
Lineage
Constituted 375th Bomb Sq (Heavy) on 28 Jan 1942. Activated on 15 Apr 1942. Inactivated on 6 Jan 1946. Redesignated 375th Recon Sq (Very Long Range, Weather) on 16 Sept 1947. Activated on 15 Oct 1947. Inactivated on 21 Feb 1951. Redesignated 375th Bomb Sq (Medium) on 4 Oct 1951. Activated on 10 Oct 1951. Discontinued, and inactivated, on 25 June 1961.

Assignments
308th Bomb Grp, 15 Apr 1942–6 Jan 1946. 7th Weather (later 2107th Air Weather) Grp, 15 Oct 1947–21 Feb 1951. 308th Bomb Grp, 10 Oct 1951 (attached to 21st Air Division, 10 Oct 1951–17 Apr 1952); 308th Bomb Wing, 16 June 1952–25 June 1961.

Stations
Gowen Field, ID, 15 Apr 1942; Davis-Monthan Field, AZ, 18 June 1942; Alamogordo, NM, 24 July 1942; Davis-Monthan Field, AZ, 28 Aug 1942; Wendover Field, UT, 1 Oct 1942; Pueblo AAB, CO, 1 Dec 1942–2 Jan 1943; Chengkung, China, 20 Mar 1943; Hsinching, China, 18 Feb 1945; Rupsi, India, 27 June–14 Oct 1945; Camp Kilmer, NJ, 5–6 Jan 1946. Ladd Field, AK, 15 Oct 1947 (one flight operated from Fairfield-Suisun AAFld, CA and later from Shemya AFB, AK, 15 Oct 1947–15 May 1949); Eielson AFB, AK, 6 Mar 1949–21 Feb 1951. Forbes AFB, KS, 10 Oct 1951; Hunter AFB, GA, 17 Apr 1952; Plattsburgh AFB, NY, 15 July 1959–25 June 1961.

Aircraft
B-18, 1942; B-24, 1942–1945. B/RB/WB-29, 1947–1951. C-47, 1947–1951. B-29, 1951–1952; B-47, 1953–1959.

Operations
Combat in CBI and Western Pacific, 4 May 1943–19 Apr 1945. Not manned, 15 July 1959–25 June 1961.

Service Streamers
None

Campaigns
India-Burma; China Defensive; New Guinea; Western Pacific; China Offensive; Air Combat, Asiatic-Pacific Theater.

Decorations
Distinguished Unit Citation: China, 21 Aug 1943; East and South China Seas, Straits of Formosa, and Gulf of Tonkin, 24 May 1944–[19] Apr 1945. Air Force Outstanding Unit Award: 1 Nov 1956–1 Apr 1957.

379th BOMB SQUADRON
Lineage
Constituted 379th Bomb Sq (Medium) on 28 Jan 1942. Activated on 15 Mar 1942. Inactivated on 12 Sept 1945. Redesignated 379th Bomb Sq (Light) on 11 Mar 1947. Activated in the reserve on 11 June 1947. Inactivated on 27 June 1949. Redesignated 379th Bomb Sq (Medium) on 15 Mar 1952. Activated on 28 Mar 1952.

Assignments
310th Bomb Grp, 15 Mar 1942–12 Sept 1945 (attached to 235 Wing, RAF, c. 2 Nov 1943–c. 26 Feb 1944). 310th Bomb Grp, 11 June 1947–27 June 1949. 310th Bomb (later Strategic Aerospace) Wing, 28 Mar 1952–.

Stations
Davis-Monthan Field, AZ, 15 Mar 1942; Jackson AAB, MS, 15 Mar 1942; Key Field, MS, 25 Apr 1942; Columbia AAB, SC, c. 18 May 1942; Walterboro, SC, 14 Aug 1942; Greenville AAB, SC, 18 Sept–17 Oct 1942; Mediouna, French Morocco, 19 Nov 1942; Telergma, Algeria, 21 Dec 1942; Berteaux, Algeria, 1 Jan 1943; Dar el Koudia, Tunisia, 6 June 1943; Menzel Temime, Tunisia, 5 Aug 1943 (operated from Oudna, Tunisia, c. 13–c. 31 Oct 1943); Philippeville, Algeria, c. 9 Nov 1943 (operated from El Adem, Libya, 2–26 Nov 1943, and from Gambit, Libya, 26 Nov 1943–26 Feb 1944); Ghisonaccia, Corsica, c. 26 Feb 1944; Fano Italy, c. 9 Apr 1943; Pomigliano, Italy, c. 15 Aug–12 Sept 1945. Bedford AAFld, MA, 11 June 1947–27 June 1949. Forbes AFB, KS, 28 Mar 1952; Smoky Hill AFB, KS, 3 Sept 1952–.

Aircraft
B-25, 1942–1945. B-29, 1952–1954; B-47, 1954–.

Operations
Combat in MTO and ETO, 2 Dec 1942–3 May 1945.

Service Streamers
None

Campaigns
Tunisia; Sicily; Naples-Foggia; Rome-Arno; Southern France; North Apennines; Rhineland; Central Europe; Po Valley; Air Combat, EAME Theater.

Decorations
Distinguished Unit Citations: Italy, 27 Aug 1943; Ora, Italy, 10 Mar 1945. Air Force Outstanding Unit Award: 1 Jan 1956–1 Jan 1959.

380th BOMB SQUADRON
Lineage
Constituted 380th Bomb Sq (Medium) on 28 Jan 1942. Activated on 15 Mar 1942. Inactivated on 12 Sept 1945. Redesignated 380th Bomb Sq (Light) on 11 Mar 1947. Activated in the reserve on 9 Aug 1947. Inactivated on 27 June 1949. Redesignated 380th Bomb Sq (Medium) on 15 Mar 1952. Activated on 28 Mar 1952.

Assignments
310th Bomb Grp, 15 Mar 1942–12 Sept 1945. 310th Bomb Grp, 9 Aug 1947–27 June 1949. 310th Bomb (later Strategic Aerospace) Wing, 28 Mar 1952–.

Stations
Davis-Monthan Field, AZ, 15 Mar 1942; Jackson AAB, MS, 15 Mar 1942; Key Field, MS, 25 Apr 1942; Columbia AAB, SC, c. 16 May 1942; Walterboro, SC, 14 Aug 1942; Greenville AAB, SC, 18 Sept–17 Oct 1942; Mediouna, French Morocco, 17 Nov 1942; Telergma, Algeria, c. 13 Dec 1942; Berteaux, Algeria, 1 Jan 1943; Dar el Koudia, Tunisia, 6 June 1943; Menzel Temime, Tunisia, 5 Aug 1943 (detachment operated from Oudna, Tunisia, 10 Oct–19 Nov 1943); Philippeville, Algeria, 10 Nov 1943; Ghisonaccia, Corsica, 4 Jan 1944; Fano, Italy, 7 Apr 1945; Pomigliano, Italy, c. 15 Aug–12 Sept 1945. Bedford AAFld, MA, 9 Aug 1947; Providence, RI, 4 Mar 1948–27 June 1949. Forbes AFB, KS, 28 Mar 1952; Smoky Hill AFB, KS, 3 Sept 1952–.

Aircraft
B-25, 1942–1945. B-29, 1952–1954; B-47, 1954–.

Operations
Combat in MTO and ETO, 13 Dec 1942–3 May 1945.

Service Streamers
None

Campaigns
Tunisia; Sicily; Naples-Foggia; Rome-Arno; Southern France; North Apennines; Rhineland; Central Europe; Po Valley; Air Combat, EAME Theater; Antisubmarine, EAME Theater.

Decorations
Distinguished Unit Citations: Italy, 27 Aug 1943. Ora. Italy, 10 Mar 1945. Air Force Outstanding Unit Award: 1 Jan 1956–1 Jan 1959.

381st BOMB SQUADRON
Lineage
Constituted 381st Bomb Sq (Medium) on 28 Jan 1942. Activated on 15 Mar 1942. Inactivated on 12 Sept 1945. Redesignated 381st Bomb Sq (Light) on 11 Mar 1947. Activated in the reserve on 9 Aug 1947. Inactivated on 27 June 1949. Redesignated 381st Bomb Sq (Medium) on 15 Mar 1952. Activated on 28 Mar 1952.

Assignments
310th Bomb Grp, 15 Mar 1942–12 Sept 1945. 310th Bomb Grp, 9 Aug 1947–27 June 1949. 310th Bomb (later Strategic Aerospace) Wing, 28 Mar 1952–.

Stations
Davis-Monthan Field, AZ, 15 Mar 1942; Jackson AAB, MS, 15 Mar 1942; Key Field, MS, 25 Apr 1942; Columbia AAB, SC, 18 May 1942; Walterboro, SC, 14 Aug 1942; Greenville AAB, SC, 18 Sept–17 Oct 1942; Mediouna, French Morocco, 18 Nov 1942; Telergma, Algeria, 21 Dec 1942; Berteaux, Algeria, 1 Jan 1942; Dar el Koudia, Tunisia, c. 6 Jan 1943; Menzel Temime, Tunisia, 5 Aug 1943 (operated from Oudna, Tunisia, 11 Oct–17 Nov 1943); Philippeville, Algeria, 18 Nov 1943; Ghisonaccia, Corsica, 21 Jan 1944; Fano, Italy, 7 Apr 1945; Pomigliano, Italy, c. 15 Aug–12 Sept 1945. Bedford AAFld, MA, 9 Aug 1947–27 June 1949. Forbes AFB, KS, 28 Mar 1952; Smoky Hill AFB, KS, 3 Sept 1952–.

Aircraft
B-25, 1942–1945. B-29, 1952–1954; B-47, 1954–.

Operations
Combat in MTO and ETO, 18 Dec 1942–3 May 1943.

Service Streamers
None

Campaigns
Tunisia; Sicily; Naples-Foggia; Rome-Arno; Southern France; North Apennines; Rhineland; Central Europe; Po Valley; Air Combat, EAME Theater.

Decorations
Distinguished Unit Citation: Italy, 27 Aug 1943. Air Force Outstanding Unit Award: 1 Jan 1956–1 Jan 1959.

393d BOMB SQUADRON (NUCLEAR)

Lineage
Constituted 393d Bomb Sq (Very Heavy) on 28 Feb 1944. Activated on 11 Mar 1944. Redesignated 393d Bomb Sq (Medium) on 2 July 1948.

Assignments
504th Bomb Grp, 11 Mar 1944; Second Air Force, 25 Nov 1944; 509th Composite (later Bomb) Grp, 17 Dec 1944; 509th Bomb Wing, 16 June 1952–.

Stations
Dalhart AAFld, TX, 11 Mar 1944; Fairmont AAFld, NE, 12 Mar 1944; Wendover Field, UT, 14 Sept 1944–26 Apr 1945; North Field, Tinian, 30 May–17 Oct 1945; Roswell AAFld, NM, 6 Nov 1945; Pease AFB, NH, 1 July 1958–.

Aircraft
B-17, 1944; B-29, 1944–1952; B-50, 1949–1955; B-47, 1955.

Operations
Combat in Western Pacific, 1 July–14 Aug 1945. This squadron, the only unit trained for atomic warfare in World War II, dropped the first atomic bomb, on Hiroshima, Japan, 6 Aug 1945, from the B-29, "Enola Gay", piloted by Col Paul W Tibbets Jr, and the second atomic bomb, on Nagasaki, Japan, 9 Aug 1945, from the B-29 "Bock's Car", piloted by Maj Charles W Sweeney. Participated in atomic bomb tests on Bikini Atoll, Jul 1946, while temporarily stationed on Kwajalein.

Service Streamers
American Theater

Campaigns
Air Offensive, Japan; Eastern Mandates; West-ern Pacific.

Decorations
None

395th BOMB SQUADRON

Lineage
Constituted 5th Recon Sq (Medium) on 22 Nov 1940. Activated on 1 Apr 1941. Redesignated: 395th Bomb Sq (Medium) on 22 Apr 1942; 395th Bomb Sq (Heavy) 7 May 1942; 395th Bomb Sq (Very Heavy) on 20 Nov 1943. Disbanded on 20 Oct 1944.

Assignments
40th Bomb Grp, attached on 1 Apr 1941, and assigned on 25 Feb 1942; 6th Bomb Grp, 9 Aug 1942; 40th Bomb Grp, 12 May 1943–20 Oct 1944.

Stations
Borinquen Field, PR, 1 Apr 1941; Rio Hato, Panama, 17 June 1942–16 June 1943; Pratt AAFld, KS, 1 Aug 1943–12 Mar 1944; Chakulia, India, c. 11 Apr–20 Oct 1944.

Aircraft
B-18, 1941–1943; A-17, 1942–1943; B-24, 1942–1943; LB-30, 1942–1943; B-17, 1942–1944; B-26, 1943; YB-29, 1943; B-29, 1943-1944.

Operations
Antisubmarine patrols, Dec 1941–Feb 1943. Replacement and later operational training unit, June 1942-May 1943. Combat in CBI, 5 June–17 Oct 1944.

Service Streamers
None

Campaigns
Antisubmarine, American Theater; India-Burma; Air Offensive, Japan; China Defensive; Western Pacific.

Decorations
Distinguished Unit Citations: Yawata, Japan, 20 Aug 1944.

398th BOMB SQUADRON

Lineage
Constituted 398th Bomb Sq (Very Heavy) on 28 Feb 1944. Activated on 11 Mar 1944. Inacti-vated on 15 June 1946.

Assignments
504th Bomb Grp, 11 Mar 1944–15 June 1946.

Stations
Dalhart AAFld, TX, 11 Mar 1944; Fairmont AAFld, NE, 12 Mar–5 Nov 1944; North Field, Tinian, 23 Dec 1944; Clark Field, Luzon, 13 Mar–15 June 1946.

Aircraft
B-17, 1944; B-29, 1944–1946.

Operations
Combat in Western Pacific, 16 June–14 Aug 1945.

Service Streamers
None

Campaigns
Air Offensive, Japan; Eastern Mandates; West-ern Pacific.

Decorations
Distinguished Unit Citations: Yokohama, Japan, 28 May 1945; Japan and Korea, 27 July–14 Aug 1945.

402d BOMB SQUADRON

Lineage
Constituted 12th Recon Sq (Heavy) on 20 Nov 1940. Activated on 15 Jan 1941. Redesignated: 402d Bomb Sq (heavy) on 22 Apr 1942; 402d Bomb Sq (Very Heavy) on 28 Mar 1944. Inactivated on 1 Apr 1944. Activated on 1 Apr 1944. Inactivated on 10 May 1944. Activated on 1 June 1944. Inactivated on 15 Apr 1946.

Assignments
39th Bomb Grp, attached on 15 Jan 1941, and assigned 25 Feb 1942–1 Apr 1944. 39th Bomb Grp, 1 Apr–10 May 1944. 502d Bomb Grp, 1 June 1944–15 Apr 1946.

Stations
Ft Douglas, UT, 15 Jan 1941; Geiger Field, WA, 2 July 1941; Davis-Monthan Field, AZ, 5 Feb 1942–1 Apr 1944. Smoky Hill AAFld, KS, 1 Apr–10 May 1944. Davis-Monthan Field, AZ, 1 June 1944; Dalhart AAFld, TX, 5 June 1944; Grand Island AAFld, NE, 26 Sept 1944–7 Apr 1945; Northwest Field, Guam, 12 May 1945–15 Apr 1946.

Aircraft
B-25, 1941; B-17, 1941–1942; B-24, 1942–1944. B-29, 1944–1946.

Operations
Antisubmarine patrols, Dec 1941–Jan 1942. Operational and later replacement training unit, 1942–1944. Combat in Western Pacific, 30 June–15 Aug 1945.

Service Streamers
None.

Campaigns
Antisubmarine, American Theater; Air Offensive, Japan; Eastern Mandates; Western Pacific.

Decorations
Distinguished Unit Citation: Japan, 5–15 Aug 1945.

409th BOMB SQUADRON

Lineage
Constituted 19th Recon Sq (Heavy) on 28 Jan 1942. Activated on 1 Mar 1942. Redesignated 409th Bomb Sq (Heavy) on 22 Apr 1942. Inactivated on 6 July 1945. Redesignated 409th Bomb Sq (Very Heavy) on 5 Aug 1945. Activated on 20 Aug 1945. Inactivated on 1 Oct 1946.

Assignments
93d Bomb Grp, 1 Mar 1942–6 July 1945. 93d Bomb Grp, 20 Aug 1945; 444th Bomb Grp, 6 May–1 Oct 1946.

Stations
Barksdale Field, LA, 1 Mar 1942. Ft Myers, FL, 18 May–13 Aug 1942; Alconbury, England, 7

Sept 1942; Hardwick, England, c. 6 Dec 1942–15 June 1945 (operated from Tafaraoui, Algeria, 7–15 Dec 1942; Gambut, Libya, 16 Dec 1942–25 Feb 1943; Bengasi, Libya, 27 June–26 Aug 1943; Oudna, Tunisia, 18 Sept–3 Oct 1943); Sioux Falls AAFld, SD, 26 June–6 July 1945. Pratt AAFld, KS, 20 Aug 1945; Clovis AAFld, NM, 13 Dec 1945; Davis-Monthan Field AZ, 18 June–1 Oct 1946.

Aircraft
B-24, 1942–1945; B-29, 1945–1946.

Operations
Antisubmarine patrols, May–30 July 1942. Combat in ETO and MTO, 9 Oct 1942–25 Apr 1945.

Service Streamers
None

Campaigns
Antisubmarine, American Theater; Egypt-Libya; Air Offensive, Europe; Tunisia; Sicily; Naples-Foggia; Normandy; Northern France; Rhineland; Ardennes-Alsace; Central Europe; Air Combat, EAME Theater.

Decorations
Distinguished Unit Citations: North Africa, 17 Dec 1942–20 Feb 1943; Ploesti, Rumania, 1 Aug 1943.

411th BOMB SQUADRON
Lineage
Organized as 16th Aero Sq in May 1917. Redesignated 21st Aero Sq on 13 June 1917. Demobilized on 14 Apr 1919. Reconstituted and redesignated 21st Observation Sq on 24 Mar 1923. Disbanded on 1 Oct 1933. Reconstituted and consolidated (2 Dec 1936) with 21st Observation Sq (Long Range, Amphibian) which was constituted and activated on 1 Mar 1935. Redesignated: 21st Recon Sq on 1 Sept 1936; 21st Recon Sq (Long Range) on 6 Dec 1929; 21st Recon Sq (Heavy) on 20 Nov 1940; 411th Bomb Sq (Heavy) on 22 Apr 1942; 411th Bomb Sq (Very Heavy) on 28 Mar 1944. Inactivated on 1 Apr 1944. Activated on 1 Apr 1944. Inactivated on 10 May 1944. Activated on 1 June 1944. Inactivated on 15 Apr 1946.

Assignments
Third Aviation Instruction Center, 1918, 2d (later 2d Bomb) Wing, 1 Mar 1935 (attached to 2d Bomb Grp, 1 Sept 1936; 7th Naval District, Sept 1939–Aug 1940); 3d Bomb Wing, 15 Nov 1940 (attached to Newfoundland Base Command, May–Aug 1941); 29th Bomb Grp, attached on 5 Sept 1941, and assigned 25 Feb 1942–1 Apr 1944. 29th Bomb Grp, 1 Apr–10 May 1944. 502d Bomb Grp, 1 June 1944–15 Apr 1946.

Stations
San Antonio, TX, May 1917; Scott Field, IL, 11 Aug 1917; Garden City, NY, 23 Dec 1917–c. 4 Jan 1918; St Maxient, France, 23 Jan 1918; Issoudun, France, 21 Feb 1918; Bordeaux, France, c. 6 Jan–c. 18 Mar 1919; Hazelhurst Field, NY, c. 5–14 Apr 1919. Bolling Field, DC,

1 Mar 1935; Langley Field, VA, 1 Sept 1936; Miami Mun Aprt, FL, 9 Sept 1939–22 Apr 1941; Newfoundland Aprt, Newfoundland, 1 May–30 Aug 1941; MacDill Field, FL, c. 3 Sept 1941; Gowen Field, ID, 25 June 1942–1 Apr 1944. Pratt AAFld, KS, 1 Apr–10 May 1944. Davis-Monthan Field, AZ, 1 June 1944; Dalhart AAFld, TX, 5 June 1944; Grand Island AAFld, NE, 26 Sept 1944–7 Apr 1945; Northwest Field, Guam, 12 May 1945–15 Apr 1946.

Aircraft
In addition to Nieuport 27 and Nieuport 80, apparently included Avro 504-K, 1918. Included O-38 during period 1935–1936; OA-4, YOA-5, and B-10, 1936–1937; B-18, 1937–1941 (additionally included A-17, B-17, Y1OA-8, OA-9, and apparently OA-10, during period 1939–1941); B-17, 1939–1943; A-29, 1941–1942; B-24, 1943–1944. B-29, 1944–1946.

Operations
Flying training unit, Feb–c. Dec 1918. Neutrality, sea-search, and weather reconnaissance missions, 1 Oct 1939–21 Aug 1940, June–Aug 1941. Antisubmarine patrols, Jan–June 1942. Operational and later replacement training unit, 1942–1944. Combat in Western Pacific, 15 July–15 Aug 1945.

Service Streamers
Theater of Operations

Campaigns
Antisubmarine, American Theater; Air Offensive, Japan; Eastern Mandates; Western Pacific.

Decorations
Distinguished Unit Citation: Japan, 5–15 Aug 1945.

420th BOMB SQUADRON
Lineage
Constituted 30th Recon Sq (Heavy) on 28 Jan 1942. Redesignated 420th Bomb Sq (Heavy) on 22 Apr 1942. Activated on 1 June 1942. Inactivated on 10 Apr 1944. Redesignated 420th Bomb Sq (Very Heavy) on 4 Aug 1944. Activated on 19 Sept 1944. Inactivated on 4 Jan 1946.

Assignments
302d Bomb Grp, 1 June 1942–10 Apr 1944. 382d Bomb Grp, 19 Sept 1944–4 Jan 1946.

Stations
Geiger Field, WA, 1 June 1942; Davis-Monthan Field, AZ, 23 June 1942; Wendover Field, UT, 30 July 1942; Pueblo AAB, CO, 1 Oct 1942; Davis-Monthan Field, AZ, 1 Dec 1942; Clovis, NM, 29 Jan 1943; Langley Field, VA, 17 Dec 1943; Chatham AAFld, GA, 10 Feb–10 Apr 1944. Dalhart AAFld, TX, 19 Sept 1944; Smoky Hill AAFld, KS, 11 Dec 1944–1 Aug 1945; Guam, 9 Sept–16 Dec 1945 (ground echelon only; air echelon remained in US); Camp Anza, CA, 30 Dec 1945–4 Jan 1946.

Aircraft
B-24, 1942–1944; B-29, 1945–1946.

Operations
Operational and later replacement training unit, Oct 1942–Mar 1944.

Service Streamers
American Theater; Asiatic-Pacific Theater.

Campaigns
None.

Decorations
None

421st BOMB SQUADRON
Lineage
Constituted 421st Bomb Sq (Very Heavy) on 28 Feb 1944. Activated on 11 Mar 1944. Inactivated on 15 June 1946.

Assignments
504th Bomb Grp, 11 Mar 1944–15 June 1946.

Stations
Dalhart AAFld, TX, 11 Mar 1944; Fairmont AAFld, NE, 12 Mar–5 Nov 1944; North Field, Tinian, 23 Dec 1944; Clark Field, Luzon, 13 Mar–15 June 1946.

Aircraft
B-17, 1944; B-29, 1944–1946.

Operations
Combat in Western Pacific, 16 Jan–14 Aug 1945.

Service Streamers
None

Campaigns
Air Offensive, Japan; Eastern Mandates; Western Pacific.

Decorations
Distinguished Unit Citations: Yokohama, Japan, 28 May 1945; Japan and Korea, 27 July–14 Aug 1945.

430th BOMB SQUADRON
Lineage
Organized as 44th Aero Sq on 30 June 1917. Redesignated: Sq K, Wilbur Wright Field, OH, in Oct 1918; SQ P, Wilbur Wright Field, OH, in Nov 1918, Demobilized on 30 Apr 1919. Reconstituted and consolidated (1924) with 44th Sq which was authorized on 10 June 1922. Organized on 26 June 1922. Redesignated 44th Observation Sq on 25 Jan 1923. Inactivated on 31 July 1927. Activated on 1 Apr 1931. Redesignated: 44th Recon Sq on 1 Sept 1937; 44th Recon Sq (medium Range) on 6 Dec 1939; 44th Recon Sq (Heavy) on 20 Nov 1940; 430th Bomb Sq (heavy) on 22 Apr 1942; 430th Bomb Sq (Very Heavy) on 28 Mar 1944. Inactivated on 10 May 1944. Activated on 1 June 1944. Inactivated on 15 Apr 1946.

Assignments
Unkn, 1917–1919. Eighth Corps Area, 26 June 1922 (attached to Field Artillery School, c. Aug 1922); Air Corps Training Center, June–31 July

1927. 6th Composite Grp, 1 Apr 1931 (attached to 16th Pursuit Grp, c. Dec 1932); 16th Pursuit Grp, assigned on 1 Sept 1937, and attached on 1 Feb 1940; 9th Bomb Grp, attached on 20 Nov 1940, and assigned 25 Feb 1942–10 May 1944. 502d Bomb Grp, 1 June 1944–15 Apr 1946.

Stations
Camp Kelly, TX, 30 June 1917; Wilbur Wright Field, OH, 25 Aug 1917–30 Apr 1919. Post Field, OK, 26 June 1922; March Field, CA, 25 June–31 July 1927. France Field, CZ, 1 Apr 1931; Albrook Field, CZ, 13 May 1932; Howard Field, CZ, 8 July–27 Oct 1941; Atkinson Field, British Guiana, 4 Nov 1941; Orlando AB, FL, 31 Oct 1942; Brooksville AAFld, FL, 6 Jan 1944; Orlando AB, FL, 25 Feb 1944; Dalhart AAFld, TX, 6 Mar–10 May 1944. Davis-Monthan Field, AZ, 1 June 1944; Dalhart AAFld, TX, 5 June 1944; Grand Island AAFld, NE, 26 Sept 1944–7 Apr 1945; Northwest Field, Guam, 12 May 1945–15 Apr 1946.

Aircraft
Apparently included SJ-1, JN-4, and possibly DH-4 during period 1917–1919. Included DH-4 and evidently O-2 during period 1922–1927. In addition to O-19, 1932–1927. In addition to O-19, 1932–1937, and B-10, 1936–1939, included OA-4 during period 1931–1939; B-18, 1938–1942; B-17, 1943–1944; B-24, 1943–1944; B-25, 1943–1944; B-26, 1943–1944; C-73, 1943–1944. B-29, 1944–1946.

Operations
Evidently flying training unit during period 1917–1919. Good-will flight to Guatemala, 7–12 Feb 1938. Antisubmarine patrols, and reconnaissance of Vichy French fleet at Martinique, Dec 1941–Oct 1942. Unmanned, Nov 1942–Mar 1943. Tested equipment, Apr 1943–Feb 1944. Combat in Western Pacific, c. 1 Aug–15 Aug 1945.

Service Streamers
None

Campaigns
Antisubmarine, American Theater; Air Offensive, Japan; Eastern Mandates; Western Pacific.

Decorations
Distinguished Unit Citation: Japan, 5–15 Aug 1945.

435th BOMB SQUADRON
Lineage
40th Recon Sq formed on 14 Mar 1942 by authority of War Department but apparently without formal constitution and activation. Redesignated 435th Bomb Sq (Heavy) on 22 Apr 1942. Inactivated on 1 Apr 1944. Redesignated 435th Bomb Sq (Very Heavy). Activated on 1 Apr 1944. Inactivated on 10 May 1944. Activated on 7 July 1944. Inactivated on 28 May 1946.

Assignments
19th Bomb Grp, 14 Mar 1942–1 Apr 1944 (attached to Allied Air Forces, c. 17 July–c. 24 Sept 1942). 19th Bomb Grp, 1 Apr–10 May 1944. 333d Bomb Grp, 7 July 1944–28 May 1946.

Stations
Townsville, Australia, 14 Mar–c. 15 Nov 1942; Pocatello, ID, c. 30 Dec 1943; Pyote AAB, TX, 5 Jan 1943–1 Apr 1944. Great Bend AAFld, TX, 1 Apr–10 May 1944. Dalhart AAFld, TX, 7 July 1944; Great Bend AAFld, KS, 10 Dec 1944–19 June 1945; Kadena, Okinawa, 5 Aug 1945–28 May 1946.

Aircraft
LB-30, 1942, B-17, 1942–1943. B-29, 1944–1946.

Operations
Evacuated General Douglas MacArthur and President Manuel Quezon from the Philippine Islands, Mar 1942; combat in Southwest Pacific, 14 Mar–c. 13 Nov 1942; replacement training, 1 Feb–29 Oct 1943; not manned, 29 Oct 1943–1 Apr 1944. After training for B-29 operations, deployed to Pacific too late for combat before end of war in 1945.

Service Streamers
American Theater.

Campaigns
Philippine Islands; East Indies, Papua; Guadalcanal.

Decorations
Distinguished Unit Citations: New Britain, 7–12 Aug 1942; Papua, 23 July–[c. 13 Nov 1942]; New Guinea, New Britain, New Ireland, and Solomon Islands, 10 Sept–10 Oct 1942. Philippine Presidential Unit Citation.

436th BOMB SQUADRON
Lineage
Organized as 88th Aero Sq on 18 Aug 1917. Redesignated: 88th Sq 14 Mar 1921; 88th Observation Sq on 25 Jan 1923. Inactivated on 1 Aug 1927. Activated on 1 June 1928. Redesignated: 88th Observation Sq (Long Range, Amphibian) on 1 Mar 1935; 88th Recon Sq on 1 Sept 1936; 88th Recon Sq (Long Range) on 6 Dec 1939; 88th Recon Sq (Heavy) on 20 Nov 1940; 436th Bomb Sq (Heavy) on 22 Apr 1942. Inactivated on 6 Jan 1946. Redesignated 436th Bomb Sq (Very Heavy), and activated, on 1 Oct 1946. Redesignated 436th Bomb Sq (Heavy) on 20 July 1948.

Assignments
Unkn, 18 Aug 1917–May 1918; I Corps Observation Grp, May 1918; III Corps Observation Grp, Aug–Nov 1918 (attached to V Corps Observation Grp, 12–17 Sept 1918); unkn, Nov 1918–Sept 1919; 2d Wing, Sept 1919 (attached to 1st Army Observation Group c. Oct 1919); 1st Army Observation Grp, 24 Mar 1920; Air Service Field Officers' School, 10 Feb 1921 (attached to 1st Provisional Air Brigade for operations, 6 May–3 Oct 1921); Fifth Corps Area, 15 Oct 1921; Air Corps Training Center, May–1 Aug 1927. Eighth Corps Area, 1 June 1928 (attached to Field Artillery School to c. Nov 1931); 12th Observation Grp, 30 June 1931; 1st Wing, 1 Mar 1935; 7th Bomb Grp; attached 1 Sept 1936 (air echelon attached to 31st Bomb Sq, 10 Dec 1941–c. 8 Feb 1942, and to USN, c. 8 Feb–14 Mar 1942), and assigned 25 Feb 1942–6 Jan 1946. 7th Bomb Grp, 1 Oct 1946; 7th Bomb Wing, 16 June 1952; 4238th Strategic Wing, 1 Aug 1958–.

Stations
Kelly Field, TX, 18 Aug 1917; Garden City, NY, 11–27 Oct 1917; Colombey-les-Belles, France, 16 Nov 1917; Amanty, France, 1 Feb 1918; Ourches, France, 28 May 1918; Francheville, France, 7 July 1918; Ferme-de-Greves, France, 4 Aug 1918; Goussancourt, France, 4 Sept 1918; Ferme-de-Greves, France, 9 Sept 1918; Souilly, France, 12 Sept 1918; Pretz-en-Argonne, France, 14 Sept 1918; Souilly, France, 20 Sept 1918; Bethelainville, France, 4 Nov 1918; Villers-la-Chevre, France, 29 Nov 1918; Trier, Germany, 6 Dec 1918; Le Mans, France, 1–10 June 1919; Mitchel Field, NY, 27 June 1919; Scott Field, IL, 11 July 1919; Langley Field, VA, 5 Sept 1919 (operated from Charleston, WV, 3–8 Sept 1921); detachment at Charleston until Oct 1921); Godman Field, KY, 15 Oct 1921; Wilbur Wright Field, OH, 11 Oct 1922; Brooks Field, TX, 7 May–1 Aug 1927. Post Field, OK, 1 June 1928; Brooks Field, TX, 5 Nov 1931; Hamilton Field, CA, 28 Sept 1935; Ft Douglas, UT, 7 Sept 1940; Salt Lake City, UT, c. 15 Jan–11 Nov 1941; Brisbane, Australia, 22 Dec 1941–4 Feb 1942 (operated from Hickam Field, Hawaii, 7 Dec 1941–10 Feb 1942, Nandi Airport, Fiji Islands, 12–17 Feb 1942, Townsville, Australia, 20 Feb–c. 14 Mar 1942); Karachi, India, 12 Mar 1942; Allahabad, India, 1 June 1942; Gaya, India, 14 Nov 1942; Bishnupur, India, 25 Feb 1943; Panagarh, India, 25 Sept 1943; Madhaiganj, India, 13 Dec 1943; Tezgaon, India, 14 June 1944; Madhaiganj, India, 6 Oct 1944 (detachment based at Luliang, China, ferrying gasoline to Suichwan, China, Dec 1944–Jan 1945); Tezpur, India, 1 June–7 Dec 1945; Camp Kilmer, NJ, 5–6 Jan 1946. Ft Worth AAFld, TX, 1 Oct 1946; Barksdale AAB, LA, 1 Aug 1958–.

Aircraft
AR type, 1918; Sopwith 1, 1918; Salmson 2, 1918–1919; included DH-4 and O-2 during period 1919–1927; O-2, 1928–1930; in addition to O-19, 1930–1935, included O-31 and C-1 during period 1930–1933; O-43, 1934–1935; in addition to O-35, 1935–1937, and B-12, 1936–c. 1937, included O-27, OA-4, Y1OA-8, B-7, and B-10 during period 1935–1938; B-18, 1937–1940; B-17, 1939–1942; B-24, 1942–1945. B-29, 1946–1948; B-36, 1948–1958; B-52, 1958–.

Operations
Combat as corps observation squadron with I, III, IV, and V Army Corps, 30 May–10 Nov 1918; Subsequently served with VII Army Corps in occupation force, Nov 1918–May 1919. Participated in demonstrations of effectiveness of aerial bombardment on warships, June–Sept 1921. Deployed for service in connection with civil disorders arising from West Virginia coal strike, Sept 1921. Dropped food and supplies and flew photographic missions in connection with flood-

relief operations in central California, 12–13 Dec 1937. Air echelon under attack during its arrival in Hawaii, 7 Dec 1941; air echelon in combat while operating from Hawaii, Fiji Islands, and Australia, 9 Dec 1941–c. 14 Mar 1942; combat in CBI, 4 June 1942–10 June 1944 and 19 Oct 1944–10 May 1945; transported gasoline to China, 20 June–30 Sept 1944 and 17 June–18 Sept 1945.

Service Streamers
None

Campaigns
World War I: Lorraine; Ile-de-France; Champagne-Marne; Aisne-Marne; Champagne; Oise-Aisne; St Mihiel; Meuse-Argonne. World War II: Central Pacific; East Indies; Burma; India-Burma; China Defensive; Central Burma; China Offensive; Air Combat, Asiatic-Pacific Theater.

Decorations
Distinguished Unit Citation: Thailand, 19 Mar 1945.

441st BOMB SQUADRON
Lineage
Constituted 441st Bomb Sq (Medium) on 19 June 1942. Activated on 1 July 1942. Inactivated on 7 Dec 1945. Redesignated 441st Bomb Sq (Light) on 26 May 1947. Activated in the reserve on 9 July 1947. Inactivated on 27 June 1949. Redesignated 441st Bomb Sq (Medium), and activated, on 1 Dec 1952. Discontinued on 15 Sept 1960. Redesignated 441st Bomb Sq (Heavy) on 15 Nov 1962. Organized on 1 Feb 1963.

Assignments
320th Bomb Grp, 1 July 1942–4 Dec 1945. 320th Bomb Grp, 9 July 1947–27 June 1949. 320th Bomb Wing, 1 Dec 1952; Department of the Air Force, 15 Sept 1960; Strategic Air Command, 15 Nov 1962; 320th Bomb Wing, 1 Feb 1963–.

Stations
MacDill Field, FL, 1 July 1942; Drane Field, FL, 8–28 Aug 1942; Hethel, England, 12 Sept 1942; Tibenham, England, 1 Oct 1942; La Senia, Algeria, 9 Jan 1943; Tafaraoui, Algeria, 28 Jan 1943; Montesquieu, Algeria, 14 Apr 1943; Massicault, Tunisia, 29 June 1943; El Bathan, Tunisia, 29 July 1943; Decimomannu, Sardinia, c. 9 Nov 1943; Alto, Corsica, c. 19 Sept 1944; Dijon/Longvic, France, 11 Nov 1944; Dole/Tavaux, France, 2 Apr 1945; Pfriemd, Germany, 20 June 1945; Clastres, France, c. Oct–28 Nov 1945; Camp Kilmer, NJ, c. 5–7 Dec 1945. Mitchel Field, NY, 9 July 1947–27 June 1949. March AFB, CA, 1 Dec 1952–15 Sept 1960. Mather AFB, CA, 1 Feb 1963–.

Aircraft
B-26, 1942–1945. B-29, 1952–1953; YRB-47, 1953; B-47, 1953–1960. B-52, 1963–.

Operations
Antisubmarine patrols in Mediterranean, Feb–Mar 1943; combat in MTO and ETO, 22 Apr 1943–1 May 1945.

Service Streamers
None.

Campaigns
Tunisia; Sicily; Naples-Foggia; Anzio; Rome-Arno; Northern France; Southern France; North Apennines; Rhineland; Central Europe; Air Combat, EAME Theater; Antisubmarine, EAME Theater.

Decorations
Distinguished Unit Citations: Italy, 12 May 1944; ETO, 15 Mar 1945. French Croix de Guerre with Palm: Apr, May, and June 1944.

442d BOMB SQUADRON
Lineage
Constituted 442d Bomb Sq (Medium) on 19 June 1942. Activated on 1 July 1942. Inactivated on 6 Dec 1945. Redesignated 442d Bomb Sq (Light) on 26 May 1947. Activated in the reserve on 9 July 1947. Inactivated on 27 June 1949. Redesignated 442d Bomb Sq (Medium) and activated, on 1 Dec 1952. Discontinued on 15 Sept 1960.

Assignments
320th Bomb Grp, 1 July 1942–4 Dec 1945. 320th Bomb Grp, 9 July 1947–27 June 1949. 320th Bomb Wing, 1 Dec 1952; Department of the Air Force, 15 Sept 1960–.

Stations
MacDill Field, FL, 1 July 1942; Drane Field, FL, 8–28 Aug 1942; Hethel, England, 12 Sept 1942; Tibenham, England, 1 Oct 1942; La Senia, Algeria, 9 Jan 1943; Tafaraoui, Algeria, 28 Jan 1943; Montesquieu, Algeria, 14 Apr 1943; Massicault, Tunisia, 29 June 1943; El Bathan, Tunisia, 29 July 1943; Decimomannu, Sardinia, c. 9 Nov 1943; Alto, Corsica, 20 Sept 1944; Dijon/Longvic, France, 11 Nov 1944; Dole/Tavaux, France, 2 Apr 1945; Herzogenaurach, Germany, 22 June 1945; Clastres, France, c. Oct–27 Nov 1945; Camp Shanks, NY, c. 4–6 Dec 1945. Mitchel Field, NY, 9 July 1947–27 June 1949. March AFB, CA, 1 Dec 1952–15 Sept 1960.

Aircraft
B-26, 1942–1945. B-29, 1952–1953; YRB-47, 1953; B-47, 1953–1960.

Operations
Antisubmarine patrols in Mediterranean, Feb–Mar 1943; combat in MTO and ETO, 22 Apr 1943–1 May 1945.

Service Streamers
None.

Campaigns
Tunisia; Sicily; Naples-Foggia; Anzio; Rome-Arno; Northern France; Southern France; North Apennines; Rhineland; Central Europe; Air Combat, EAME Theater; Antisubmarine, EAME Theater.

Decorations
Distinguished Unit Citations: Italy, 12 May 1944; ETO, 15 Mar 1945. French Croix de Guerre with Palm: Apr, May, and June 1944.

443d BOMB SQUADRON
Lineage
Constituted 443d Bomb Sq (Medium) on 19 June 1942. Activated on 1 July 1942. Inactivated on 7 Dec 1945. Redesignated 443d Bomb Sq (Light) on 26 May 1947. Activated in the reserve on 9 July 1947. Inactivated on 27 June 1949. Redesignated 443d Bomb Sq (Medium) and activated, on 1 Dec 1952. Discontinued on 15 Sept 1960.

Assignments
320th Bomb Grp, 1 July 1942–4 Dec 1945. 320th Bomb Grp, 9 July 1947–27 June 1949. 320th Bomb Wing, 1 Dec 1952; Department of the Air Force, 15 Sept 1960–.

Stations
MacDill Field, FL, 1 July 1942; Drane Field, FL, 8–28 Aug 1942; Hethel, England, 12 Sept 1942; Tibenham, England, 1 Oct 1942; La Senia, Algeria, 8 Jan 1943; Tafaraoui, Algeria, 28 Jan 1943; Montesquieu, Algeria, 9 Apr 1943; Massicault, Tunisia, 29 June 1943; El Bathan, Tunisia, 28 July 1943; Decimomannu, Sardinia, c. 9 Nov 1943; Alto, Corsica, 20 Sept 1944; Dijon/Longvic, France, 11 Nov 1944; Dole/Tavaux, France, 2 Apr 1945; Furth, Germany, 20 June 1945; Clastres, France, c. Oct–28 Nov 1945; Camp Myles Standish, MA, c. 5–7 Dec 1945. Mitchel Field, NY, 9 July 1947–27 June 1949. March AFB, CA, 1 Dec 1952–15 Sept 1960.

Aircraft
B-26, 1942–1945. B-29, 1952–1953; YRB-47, 1953; B-47, 1953–1960.

Operations
Antisubmarine patrols in Mediterranean, Feb–Mar 1943; combat in MTO and ETO, 22 Apr 1943–1 May 1945.

Service Streamers
None.

Campaigns
Tunisia; Sicily; Naples-Foggia; Anzio; Rome-Arno; Northern France; Southern France; North Apennines; Rhineland; Central Europe; Air Combat, EAME Theater; Antisubmarine, EAME Theater.

Decorations
Distinguished Unit Citations: Italy, 12 May 1944; ETO, 15 Mar 1945. French Croix de Guerre with Palm: Apr, May, and June 1944.

457th BOMB SQUADRON
Lineage
Constituted 457th Bomb Sq (Heavy) on 1 Jul 1942. Activated on 6 July 1942. Inactivated on 1 Apr 1944. Redesignated 457th Bomb Sq (Very Heavy). Activated on 1 Apr 1944. Inactivated on 27 Dec 1945. Redesignated 457th Bomb Sq (Medium) on 16 May 1949. Activated in the reserve on 27 June 1949. Ordered to active service on 1 May 1951. Inactivated on 16 June 1951. Redesignated 457th Troop Carrier Sq (Medium) on 26 May 1952. Activated in the reserve on 14 June 1952. Inactivated on 14 July 1952.

Assignments

330th Bomb Grp, 6 July 1942–1 Apr 1944. 330th Bomb Grp, 1 Apr 1944–27 Dec 1945. 330th Bomb Grp, 27 June 1949–16 June 1951. 330th Troop Carrier Grp, 14 June–14 July 1952.

Stations

Salt Lake City AAB, UT, 6 July 1942; Alamogordo, NM, 1 Aug 1942; Biggs Field, TX, c. 2 Sept 1942; Alamogordo, NM, 29 Nov 1942; Biggs Field, TX, 5 Mar 1943–1 Apr 1944. Walker AAFld, KS, 1 Apr 1944; Dalhart AAFld, TX, 25 May 1944; Walker AAFld, KS, 1 Aug 1944–7 Jan 1945; North Field, Guam, 18 Feb–21 Nov 1945; Camp Anza, CA, c. 19–27 Dec 1945. March AFB, CA, 27 June 1949–16 June 1951. Greater Pittsburgh Aprt, PA, 14 June–14 July 1952.

Aircraft

B-17, 1942; B-24, 1942–1944. B-17, 1944; B-29, 1944–1945.

Operations

Replacement training, 1942–1944. Combat in Western Pacific, c. 12 Apr–14 Aug 1945.

Service Streamers

American Theater

Campaigns

Air Offensive, Japan; Western Pacific.

Decorations

Distinguished Unit Citations: Japan, 3–9 July 1945; Tokyo, Japan, 8 Aug 1945.

458th BOMB SQUADRON

Lineage

Constituted 458th Bomb Sq (Heavy) on 1 Jul 1942. Activated on 6 July 1942. Inactivated on 1 Apr 1944. Redesignated 458th Bomb Sq (Very Heavy). Activated on 1 Apr 1944. Inactivated on 27 Dec 1945. Redesignated 458th Troop Carrier Sq (Medium) on 26 May 1952. Activated in the reserve on 14 June 1952. Inactivated on 14 July 1952.

Assignments

330th Bomb Grp, 6 July 1942–1 Apr 1944. 330th Bomb Grp, 1 Apr 1944–27 Dec 1945. 330th Troop Carrier Grp, 14 June 1952–14 July 1952.

Stations

Salt Lake City AAB, UT, 6 July 1942; Alamogordo, NM, 1 Aug 1942; Biggs Field, TX, 1 Sept 1942; Alamogordo, NM, 29 Nov 1942; Biggs Field, TX, 5 Apr 1943–1 Apr 1944. Walker AAFld, KS, 1 Apr 1944; Dalhart AAFld, TX, 25 May 1944; Walker AAFld, KS, 1 Aug 1944–7 Jan 1945; North Field, Guam, 18 Feb–21 Nov 1945; Camp Anza, CA, c. 22–27 Dec 1945. Greater Pittsburgh Aprt, PA, 14 June–14 July 1952.

Aircraft

B-17, 1942; B-24, 1942–1944. B-17, 1944; B-29, 1944–1946.

Operations

Replacement training, 1942–1944. Combat in Western Pacific, c. 12 Apr–14 Aug 1945.

Service Streamers

American Theater

Campaigns

Air Offensive, Japan; Western Pacific.

Decorations

Distinguished Unit Citations: Japan, 3–9 July 1945; Tokyo, Japan, 8 Aug 1945.

459th BOMB SQUADRON

Lineage

Constituted 459th Bomb Sq (Heavy) on 1 Jul 1942. Activated on 6 July 1942. Inactivated on 1 Apr 1944. Redesignated 459th Bomb Sq (Very Heavy). Activated on 1 Apr 1944. Inactivated on 27 Dec 1945. Redesignated 459th Troop Carrier Sq (Medium) on 26 May 1952. Activated in the reserve on 14 June 1952. Inactivated on 14 July 1952.

Assignments

330th Bomb Grp, 6 July 1942–1 Apr 1944. 330th Bomb Grp, 1 Apr 1944–27 Dec 1945. 330th Troop Carrier Grp, 14 June–14 July 1952.

Stations

Salt Lake City AAB, UT, 6 July 1942; Alamogordo, NM, 1 Aug 1942; Biggs Field, TX, 2 Sept 1942; Alamogordo, NM, 29 Nov 1942; Biggs Field, TX, 5 Apr 1943–1 Apr 1944. Walker AAFld, KS, 1 Apr 1944; Dalhart AAFld, TX, 25 May 1944; Walker AAFld, KS, 1 Aug 1944–7 Jan 1945; North Field, Guam, 18 Feb–19 Nov 1945; Camp Anza, CA, c. 18–27 Dec 1945. Greater Pittsburgh Aprt, PA, 14 June–14 July 1952.

Aircraft

B-17, 1942; B-24, 1942–1944. B-17, 1944; B-29, 1944–1945.

Operations

Replacement training, 1942–1944. Combat in Western Pacific, c. 12 Apr–14 Aug 1945.

Service Streamers

American Theater

Campaigns

Air Offensive, Japan; Western Pacific.

Decorations

Distinguished Unit Citations: Japan, 3–9 July 1945; Tokyo, Japan, 8 Aug 1945.

460th BOMB SQUADRON

Lineage

Constituted 460th Bomb Sq (Heavy) on 1 July 1942. Activated on 6 July 1942. Inactivated on 1 Apr 1944. Redesignated 460th Bomb Sq (Very Heavy). Activated on 1 Apr 1944. Inactivated on 10 May 1944. Activated on 7 July 1944. Inactivated on 28 May 1946.

Assignments

330th Bomb Grp, 6 July 1942–1 Apr 1944. 330th Bomb Grp, 1 Apr 1944–10 May 1944. 333d Bomb Grp, 7 July 1944–28 May 1946.

Stations

Salt Lake City AAB, UT, 6 July 1942; Alamogordo, NM, 1 Aug 1942; Biggs Field, TX, 2 Sept 1942; Alamogordo, NM, 1 Dec 1942; Biggs Field, TX, 5 Apr 1943–1 Apr 1944. Walker AAFld, KS, 1 Apr–10 May 1944. Dalhart AAFld, TX, 7 July 1944; Great Bend AAFld, KS, 10 Dec 1944–18 June 1945; Kadena, Okinawa, 5 Aug 1945–28 May 1946.

Aircraft

B-24, 1942–1944. B-29, 1944–1946.

Operations

Replacement training, 1 Aug 1942–c. 1 Mar 1944.

Service Streamers

American Theater; Asiatic-Pacific Theater.

Campaigns

None.

Decorations

None.

461st BOMB SQUADRON

Lineage

Constituted 461st Bomb Sq (Heavy) on 1 July 1942. Activated on 6 July 1942. Inactivated on 1 Apr 1944. Redesignated 461st Bomb Sq (Very Heavy) on 4 Aug 1944. Activated on 18 Aug 1944. Inactivated on 30 June 1946.

Assignments

331st Bomb Grp, 6 July 1942–1 Apr 1944. 346th Bomb Grp, 18 Aug 1944–30 June 1946.

Stations

Salt Lake City AAB, UT, 6 July 1942; Casper AAFld, WY, 15 Sept 1942–1 Apr 1944. Dalhart AAFld, TX, 18 Aug 1944; Pratt AAFld, KS, 12 Dec 1944–29 June 1945; Kadena, Okinawa, 13 Aug 1945–30 June 1946.

Aircraft

B-17, 1942–1943; B-24, 1943–1944. B-17, 1945; B-29, 1945–1946; C-46, 1946.

Operations

Replacement training, 1942–1944.

Service Streamers

American Theater; Asiatic-Pacific Theater.

Campaigns

None.

Decorations

None.

462d BOMB SQUADRON

Lineage

Constituted 462d Bomb Sq (Heavy) on 1 July 1942. Activated on 6 July 1942. Inactivated on 1 Apr 1944. Redesignated 462d Bomb Sq (Very Heavy) on 4 Aug 1944. Activated on 18 Aug 1944. Inactivated on 30 June 1946.

Assignments

331st Bomb Grp, 6 July 1942–1 Apr 1944. 346th Bomb Grp, 18 Aug 1944–30 June 1946.

Stations
Salt Lake City AAB, UT, 6 July 1942; Casper AAFld, WY, 15 Sept 1942–1 Apr 1944. Dalhart AAFld, TX, 18 Aug 1944; Pratt AAFld, KS, 12 Dec 1944–29 June 1945; Kadena, Okinawa, 13 Aug 1945–30 June 1946.

Aircraft
B-17, 1942–1943; B-24, 1943–1944. B-17, 1945; B-29, 1945–1946; C-46, 1946.

Operations
Replacement training, 1942–1944.

Service Streamers
American Theater; Asiatic-Pacific Theater.

Campaigns
None.

Decorations
None.

463d BOMB SQUADRON
Lineage
Constituted 463d Bomb Sq (Heavy) on 1 July 1942. Activated on 6 July 1942. Inactivated on 1 Apr 1944. Redesignated 463d Bomb Sq (Very Heavy) on 4 Aug 1944. Activated on 18 Aug 1944. Inactivated on 30 June 1946.

Assignments
331st Bomb Grp, 6 July 1942–1 Apr 1944. 346th Bomb Grp, 18 Aug 1944–30 June 1946.

Stations
Salt Lake City AAB, UT, 6 July 1942; Casper AAFld, WY, 15 Sept 1942–1 Apr 1944. Dalhart AAFld, TX, 18 Aug 1944; Pratt AAFld, KS, 12 Dec 1944–29 June 1945; Kadena, Okinawa, 13 Aug 1945–30 June 1946.

Aircraft
B-17, 1942–1943; B-24, 1943–1944. B-17, 1945; B-29, 1945–1946; C-46, 1946.

Operations
Replacement training, 1942–1944.

Service Streamers
American Theater; Asiatic-Pacific Theater.

Campaigns
None.

Decorations
None.

464th BOMB SQUADRON
Lineage
Constituted 464th Bomb Sq (Heavy) on 1 July 1942. Activated on 6 July 1942. Inactivated on 1 Apr 1944. Redesignated 464th Bomb Sq (Very Heavy) on 4 Aug 1944. Activated on 19 Sept 1944. Inactivated on 4 Jan 1946.

Assignments
331st Bomb Grp, 6 July 1942–1 Apr 1944. 382d Bomb Grp, 19 Sept 1944–4 Jan 1946.

Stations
Salt Lake City AAB, UT, 6 July 1942; Casper AAFld, WY, 15 Sept 1942–1 Apr 1944. Dalhart AAFld, TX, 19 Sept 1944; Smoky Hill AAFld, KS, 11 Dec 1944–1 Aug 1945; Guam, 8 Sept 1945 (ground echelon only; air echelon remained in US); Tinian, c. Oct–15 Dec 1945; Camp Anza, CA, 28 Dec 1945–4 Jan 1946.

Aircraft
B-17, 1942–1943; B-24, 1943–1944. B-29, 1945–1946.

Operations
Replacement training, Nov 1942–Mar 1944.

Service Streamers
American Theater; Asiatic-Pacific Theater.

Campaigns
None.

Decorations
None.

482d BOMB SQUADRON
Lineage
Organized as 70th Aero Sq on 13 Aug 1917. Redesignated 482d Aero Sq on 1 Feb 1918. Demobilized on 18 Mar 1919. Reconstituted and consolidated (1936) with 482d Bomb Sq which was constituted and allotted to the reserve on 31 Mar 1924. Activated, date unkn (personnel assigned, Mar 1925). Disbanded on 31 May 1942. Reconstituted and consolidated (21 Apr 1944) with 482d Bomb Sq (Very Heavy) which was constituted on 28 Feb 1944. Activated on 11 Mar 1944. Inactivated on 30 June 1946.

Assignments
Unkn, 13 Aug 1917–Mar 1918; Advance Section, Service of Supply, Mar–Dec 1918; unkn, Dec 1918–18 Mar 1919. Third Corps Area 1924–31 May 1942. 505th Bomb Grp, 11 Mar 1944–30 June 1946.

Stations
Kelly Field, TX, 13 Aug 1917; Camp Morrison, VA, 21 Dec 1917–4 Mar 1918; Colombey-les-Belles, France, 27 Mar 1918; Autreville, France, 28 Mar 1918; Trampot, France, c. 9 July 1918; Longeaux, France, 22 Sept 1918; Trampot, France, c. 24 Oct 1918; Braux, France, c. 22 Nov 1918; Pont Rousseau, France, 25 Dec 1918–unkn; Garden City, NY, c. 8–18 Mar 1919. Baltimore, MD, 1924–31 May 1942. Dalhart AAFld, TX, 11 Mar 1944; Harvard AAFld, NE, 12 Mar–6 Nov 1944; North Field, Tinian, 24 Dec 1944–5 Mar 1946; Clark Field, Luzon, 14 Mar–30 June 1946.

Aircraft
B-17, 1944; B-29, 1944–1946.

Operations
Constructed airfields and related facilities in Zone of Advance, 28 Mar–Dec 1918. Combat in Western Pacific, c. 30 Dec 1944–14 Aug 1945.

Service Streamers
Theater of Operations.

Campaigns
Air Offensive, Japan; Eastern Mandates; Western Pacific.

Decorations
Distinguished Unit Citations: Ota, Japan, 10 Feb 1945; Japan, 17 June–1 July 1945.

483d BOMB SQUADRON
Lineage
Constituted 483d Bomb Sq (Very Heavy) on 28 Feb 1944. Activated on 11 Mar 1944. Inactivated on 30 June 1946.

Assignments
505th Bomb Grp, 11 Mar 1944–30 June 1946.

Stations
Dalhart AAFld, TX, 11 Mar 1944; Harvard AAFld, NE, 12 Mar–6 Nov 1944; North Field, Tinian, 24 Dec 1944–5 Mar 1946; Clark Field, Luzon, 14 Mar–30 June 1946.

Aircraft
B-17, 1944; B-29, 1944–1946.

Operations
Combat in Western Pacific, c. 30 Dec 1944–14 Aug 1945.

Service Streamers
None

Campaigns
Air Offensive, Japan; Eastern Mandates; Western Pacific.

Decorations
Distinguished Unit Citations: Ota, Japan, 10 Feb 1945; Japan, 17 June–1 July 1945.

484th BOMB SQUADRON
Lineage
Organized as 72d Aero Sq on 15 Aug 1917. Redesignated 484th Aero Sq on 1 Feb 1918. Demobilized on 8 Feb 1919. Reconstituted and consolidated (1936) with 484th Bomb Sq which was constituted and allotted to the reserve on 31 Mar 1924. Activated, date unkn. Disbanded on 31 May 1942. Reconstituted and consolidated (21 Apr 1944) with 484th Bomb Sq (Very Heavy) which was constituted on 28 Feb 1944. Activated on 11 Mar 1944. Inactivated on 30 June 1946.

Assignments
Unkn, 15 Aug 1917–Mar 1918; Advance Section, Service of Supply, Mar 1918; First Army, 23 Aug 1918; Second Army, 28 Oct–Nov 1918; unkn, Nov 1918–8 Feb 1919. Seventh Corps Area 1924–1942. 505th Bomb Grp, 11 Mar 1944–30 June 1946.

Stations
Kelly Field, TX, 15 Aug 1917; Camp Morrison, VA, 1 Feb–4 Mar 1918; Vinets-sur-Aube, France, 26 Mar 1918; Longeaux, France, 15 July 1918; Lay-St Remy, France, c. 26 Aug 1918 (detachments operated from several points

in Toul and Verdun sectors, 1–11 Sept 1918; unit from Noviant-aux-Pres and Grosrouvres after 14 Sept 1918); Saizerais, France, c. 10 Oct 1918 (unit operated from Noviant-aux-Pres and Grosrouvres to 13 Oct 1918; detachments from Toul and Manonville, c. 5–c. 21 Nov 1918); Colombey-les-Belles, France, 24 Nov 1918; Brest, France, 16 Dec 1918–2 Jan 1919; Washington, DC, unkn–8 Feb 1919. Unkn, 1924-1942. Dalhart AAFld, TX, 11 Mar 1944; Harvard AAFld, NE, 12 Mar–6 Nov 1944; North Field, Tinian, 24 Dec 1944–5 Mar 1946; Clark Field, Luzon, 14 Mar–30 June 1946.

Aircraft
B-17, 1944; B-29, 1944–1946.

Operations
Constructed airfields and related facilities in Zone of Advance, 1 Apr–Nov 1918. Combat in Western Pacific, c. 30 Dec 1944–14 Aug 1945.

Service Streamers
None

Campaigns
World War I: St Mihiel. World War II: Air Offensive, Japan; Eastern Mandates; Western Pacific.

Decorations
Distinguished Unit Citations: Ota, Japan, 10 Feb 1945; Japan, 17 June–1 July 1945.

485th BOMB SQUADRON
Lineage
Organized as 73d Aero Sq on 14 Aug 1917. Redesignated 485th Aero Sq on 1 Feb 1918. Demobilized on 20 May 1919. Reconstituted and consolidated (1936) with 485th Bomb Sq which was constituted and allotted to the reserve on 31 Mar 1924. Activated, date unkn (personnel assigned, Sept 1925). Disbanded on 31 May 1942. Reconstituted and consolidated (21 Apr 1944) with 485th Bomb Sq (Very Heavy) which was constituted on 28 Feb 1944. Activated on 11 Mar 1944. Inactivated on 10 May 1944. Activated on 1 June 1944. Inactivated on 10 June 1946.

Assignments
Unkn, 14 Aug 1917–Mar 1918; Air Service Production Center No. 2, Mar 1918; Air Service Spares Depot, Sept 1918–Jan 1919; unkn, Jan–20 May 1919. Fifth Corps Area, (1925–31 May 1942). 505th Bomb Grp, 11 Mar–10 May 1944. 501st Bomb Grp, 1 June 1944–10 June 1946.

Stations
Kelly Field, TX, 14 Aug 1917; Camp Morrison, VA, 21 Dec 1917–4 Mar 1918; Romorantin, France, 25 Mar 1918 (detachment operated from St Nazaire to 3 Apr 1918; unit from Gievres, 17 May–9 June 1918; detachment from Chatenay-sur-Seine from 11 Sept 1918); Chatenay-sur-Seine, 21 Sept 1918; Bordeaux, France, c. 1 Feb 1919–unkn; Mitchel Field, NY, c. 2–20 May 1919. Dayton, OH 1925–31 May 1942. Dalhart AAFld, TX, 11 Mar 1944; Harvard

AAFld, NE, 12 Mar–10 May 1944. Dalhart AAFld, TX, 1 June 1944; Harvard AAFld, NE, 23 Aug 1944–7 Mar 1945; Northwest Field, Guam, 14 Apr 1945–10 June 1946.

Aircraft
B-29, 1944–1946.

Operations
Constructed and maintained facilities (in Zone of Advance after Sept 1918), Mar–c. Dec 1918. Combat in Western Pacific, 23 June–14 Aug 1945.

Service Streamers
Theater of Operations

Campaigns
Air Offensive, Japan; Eastern Mandates; Western Pacific.

Decorations
Distinguished Unit Citation: Japan, 6–13 July 1945.

492d BOMB SQUADRON
Lineage
Organized as 80th Aero Sq on 15 Aug 1917. Redesignated 492d Aero Sq on 1 Feb 1918. Demobilized on 13 Feb 1919. Reconstituted and consolidated (1936) with 492d Bomb Sq which was constituted and allotted to the reserve on 31 Mar 1924. Disbanded on 31 May 1942. Consolidated (1960) with 492d Bomb Sq (Heavy) which was constituted on 19 Sept 1942. Activated on 25 Oct 1942. Inactivated on 6 Jan 1946. Redesignated 492d Bomb Sq (Very Heavy), and activated, on 1 Oct 1946. Redesignated 492d Bomb Sq (Heavy) on 20 July 1948. Discontinued, and inactivated, on 1 Feb 1963.

Assignments
Unkn, 15 Aug 1917–Feb 1918; Headquarters, Air Service, Service of Supply, Feb–Dec 1918 (detachment attached to Second Aviation Instruction Center, 25 Apr–9 Dec 1918); unkn, Dec 1918–13 Feb 1919. 7th Bomb Grp, 25 Oct 1942–6 Jan 1946. 7th Bomb Grp, 1 Oct 1946; 7th Bomb Wing, 16 June 1952; 4228th Strategic Wing, 15 June 1959–1 Feb 1963.

Stations
Kelly Field, TX, 15 Aug 1917; Garden City, NY, 3–22 Nov 1917; Tours, France, 17 Dec 1917; Brest, France, c. 30 Dec 1918–c. 19 Jan 1919; Garden City, NY, c. 31 Jan–13 Feb 1919. Karachi, India, 25 Oct 1942; Gaya, India, 14 Nov 1942; Bishnupur, India, 26 Feb 1943; Panagarh, India, 25 Apr 1943; Madhaiganij, India, 22 Jan 1944; Tezgaon, India, 17 June 1944; Madhaiganij, India, 6 Oct 1944 (detachment at Luliang, China, ferrying gasoline to Suichwan, China, 20 Dec 1944–30 Jan 1945); Tezpur, India, 1 June–7 Dec 1945; Camp Kilmer, NJ, 5–6 Jan 1946. Ft Worth AAFld, TX, 1 Oct 1946; Columbus AFB, MS, 15 June 1959–1 Feb 1963.

Aircraft
B-24, 1942–1945. B-29, 1946–1948; B-36, 1948–1958; B-52, 1958–1963.

Operations
Constructed and maintained facilities, Jan–Dec 1918. Apparently never active during period 1924–1942 when allotted to the reserve with assignment to Ninth Corps Area and designated station at Seattle, WA. Combat in CBI, 24 Jan 1943–10 June 1944 and 19 Oct 1944–10 May 1945; transported gasoline to forward bases in China, 20 June–30 Sept 1944 and 20 June–18 Sept 1945.

Service Streamers
Theater of Operations.

Campaigns
India-Burma; China Defensive; Central Burma; China Offensive.

Decorations
Distinguished Unit Citation: Thailand, 19 Mar 1945. Air Force Outstanding Unit Award: 6 Oct 1959–15 July 1960.

506th BOMB SQUADRON
Lineage
Constituted 506th Bomb Sq (Heavy) on 24 Sept 1942. Activated on 1 Oct 1942. Redesignated 506th Bomb Sq (Very Heavy) on 5 Aug 1945. Inactivated on 4 Aug 1946. Redesignated 506th Bomb Sq (Medium) on 20 Aug 1958. Activated on 1 Dec 1958. Discontinued on 15 June 1960.

Assignments
44th Bomb Grp, 1 Oct 1942 (attached to 308th Bomb Grp for training, 1 Oct 1942–c. 16 Jan 1943); 485th Bomb Grp, 7 Mar–4 Aug 1946. 44th Bomb Wing, 1 Dec 1958; Department of the Air Force, 15 June 1960–.

Stations
Salt Lake City AAB, UT, 1 Nov 1942; Pueblo AAB, CO, 1 Oct 1942; Wendover Field, UT, 29 Oct 1942; Pueblo AAB, CO, c. 29 Nov 1942–7 Feb 1943; Shipdham, England, 17 Mar 1943–c. 15 June 1945 (detachments operated from Benina, Libya, c. 27 June–c. 1 Sept 1943, and Tunis, Tunisia, c. 19 Sept–c. 9 Oct 1943); Sioux Falls AAFld, SD, 26 June 1945; Great Bend AAFld, KS, 25 July 1945; Smoky Hill AAFld, KS, 14 Dec 1945–4 Aug 1946. Lake Charles AFB, LA, 1 Dec 1958–15 June 1960.

Aircraft
B-24, 1942–1945; B-29, 1945–1946. B-47, 1958–1960.

Operations
Combat in ETO and MTO, 22 Mar 1943–25 Apr 1945.

Service Streamers
American Theater.

Campaigns
Air Offensive, Europe; Sicily; Naples-Foggia; Normandy, Northern France; Rhineland; Ardennes-Alsace; Central Europe; Air Combat EAME Theater.

Decorations
Distinguished Unit Citations: Kiel, Germany 14 May 1943; Ploesti; Rumania, 1 Aug 1943.

507th BOMB SQUADRON

Lineage

Constituted 507th Bomb Sq (Very Heavy) on 28 Feb 1944. Activated on 11 Mar 1944. Inactivated on 10 May 1944. Activated on 7 July 1944. Inactivated on 28 May 1946.

Assignments

504th Bomb Grp, 11 Mar–10 May 1944. 333d Bomb Grp, 7 July 1944–28 May 1946.

Stations

Dalhart AAFld, TX, 11 Mar 1944; Fairmont AAFld, NE, 12 Mar–10 May 1944. Dalhart AAFld, TX, 7 July 1944; Great Bend AAFld, 10 Dec 1944–18 June 1945; Kadena, Okinawa, 5 Aug 1945–28 May 1946.

Aircraft

B-29, 1944-1946.

Operations

Not manned, 11 Mar–10 May 1944.

Service Streamers

American Theater; Asiatic-Pacific Theater.

Campaigns

None.

Decorations

None.

512th BOMB SQUADRON

Lineage

Constituted 512th Bomb Sq (Heavy) on 19 Oct 1942. Activated on 31 Oct 1942. Redesignated 512th Bomb Sq (Very Heavy) on 23 May 1945. Inactivated on 26 Mar 1946. Redesignated 512th Recon Sq (Very Long Range, Weather) on 6 May 1947. Activated on 23 May 1947. Inactivated on 20 Sept 1948. Activated on 13 Feb 1949. Inactivated on 20 Feb 1951. Redesignated 512th Bomb Sq (Medium) on 25 May 1951. Activated on 1 June 1951.

Assignments

376th Bomb Grp, 31 Oct 1942; 468th Bomb Grp, 10 Nov 1945–26 Mar 1946. 376th Recon Grp, 23 May 1947; Air Weather Service, 16 Sept 1947; 308th Recon Grp, 14 Oct 1947–20 Sept 1948. 308th Recon Grp, 13 Feb 1949; 2143d Air Weather Wing, 14 Nov 1949–20 Feb 1951. 376th Bomb Grp, 1 June 1951; 376th Bomb Wing, 16 June 1952–.

Stations

Lydda, Palestine, 31 Oct 1942; Abu Sueir, Egypt, 9 Nov 1942; Gambut Libya, 10 Feb 1943; Soluch, Libya, 25 Feb 1943; Bengasi, Libya, 16 Apr 1943; Enfidaville, Tunisia, c. 26 Sept 1943 (detachment operated from Bengasi, Libya, 3–11 Oct 1943); San Pancrazio, Italy, c. 19 Nov 1943–19 Apr 1945; Harvard AAFld, NE, 8 May 1945; Grand Island AAFld, NE, 25 June 1945; Tarrant Field, TX, 10 Nov 1945; Roswell AAFld, NM, 9 Jan–26 Mar 1946. Gravelly Point, VA, 23 May 1947–20 Sept 1948. Fairfield-Suisun AFB, CA, 13 Feb 1949–9 Jan 1950; Yokota, Japan, 27 Jan 1950; Misawa, Japan, 11 Aug 1950–20 Feb 1951. Forbes AFB, KS, 1 June 1951; Barksdale AFB, LA, 10 Oct 1951; Lockbourne AFB, OH, 1 Dec 1957–.

Aircraft

B-17, 1942; B-24, 1942–1945; B-29, 1945. B/RB/WB-29, 1949–1951; C-47, 1949–1950. C-54, 1950-1951. B-29, 1951–1954; B-47, 1954–1961; E-47, 1961–.

Operations

Combat in MTO and ETO, 1 Nov 1942–15 Apr 1943; not fully manned or equipped, 10 Nov 1945–26 Mar 1946. Not manned, 23 May 1947–20 Sept 1948. Served in Korean War, c. 1 July 1950–Feb 1951. Primarily electronic countermeasures, c. Nov 1952–.

Service Streamers

None

Campaigns

World War II: Egypt-Libya; Air Offensive, Europe; Tunisia; Sicily; Naples-Foggia; Anzio; Rome-Arno; Normandy, Northern France; Southern France; North Apennines; Rhineland; Central Europe; Po Valley; Air Combat, EAME Theater. Korean War: UN Defensive; UN Offensive; CCF Intervention; First UN Counter-offensive.

Decorations

Distinguished Unit Citations: North Africa and Sicily, [Nov] 1942–17 Aug 1943; Ploesti, Rumania, 1 Aug 1943; Bratislava, Czechoslovakia, 16 June 1944. Air Force Outstanding Unit Award: 27 June–27 Dec 1950.

513th BOMB SQUADRON

Lineage

Constituted 513th Bomb Sq (Heavy) on 19 Oct 1942. Activated on 31 Oct 1942. Redesignated 513th Bomb Sq (Very Heavy) on 23 May 1945. Inactivated on 31 Mar 1946. Redesignated 513th Recon Sq (Very Long Range, Weather) on 6 May 1947. Activated on 23 May 1947. Inactivated on 20 Sept 1948. Activated on 10 Aug 1949. Inactivated on 20 Feb 1951. Redesignated 513th Bomb Sq (Medium) on 25 May 1951. Activated on 1 June 1951.

Assignments

376th Bomb Grp, 31 Oct 1942; 497th Bomb Grp, 1 Nov 1945–31 Mar 1946. 376th Recon Grp, 23 May 1947; Air Weather Service, 26 Sept 1947; 308th Recon Grp, 14 Oct 1947–20 Sept 1948. 308th Recon Grp, 10 Aug 1949; Air Weather Service, 19 Dec 1950–20 Feb 1951. 376th Bomb Grp, 1 June 1951; 376th Bomb Wing, 16 June 1952–.

Stations

Lydda, Palestine, 31 Oct 1942; Abu Sueir, Egypt, 8 Nov 1942; Gambut Libya, 10 Feb 1943; Soluch, Libya, 25 Feb 1943; Bengasi, Libya, 16 Apr 1943; Enfidaville, Tunisia, c. 26 Sept 1943 (detachment operated from Bengasi, Libya, 3–11 Oct 1943); San Pancrazio, Italy, 19 Nov 1943–19 Apr 1945; Harvard AAFld, NE, 8 May 1945; Grand Island AAFld, NE, 25 June 1945; March Field, CA, 1 Nov 1945; MacDill Field, Fl, c. 5 Jan–31 Mar 1946. Gravelly Point, VA, 23 May 1947–20 Sept 1948. Fairfield-Suisun AFB, CA, 10 Aug 1949; Tinker AFB, OK, 10 Nov 1949–20 Feb 1951 (detachment operated from Dhahran Airfield, Saudi Arabia, c. 6 Mar–May 1950). Forbes AFB, KS, 1 June 1951; Barksdale AFB, LA, 10 Oct 1951; Lockbourne AFB, OH, 1 Dec 1957–.

Aircraft

B-17, 1942–1943; B-24, 1943–1945; B-29, 1945. B/RB/WB-29, 1950–1951; C-47, 1950; C-54, 1950-1951. B-29, 1951–1954; B-47, 1954–1961; E-47, 1961–.

Operations

Combat in ETO, c. 1 Nov 1942–15 Apr 1943; not fully manned or equipped, 1 Nov 1945–31 Mar 1946. Not manned, 23 May 1947–20 Sept 1948. Primarily electronic countermeasures, c. Nov 1952–.

Service Streamers

None

Campaigns

Egypt-Libya; Air Offensive, Europe; Tunisia; Sicily; Naples-Foggia; Anzio; Rome-Arno; Normandy, Northern France; Southern France; North Apennines; Rhineland; Central Europe; Po Valley; Air Combat, EAME Theater.

Decorations

Distinguished Unit Citations: North Africa and Sicily, [Nov] 1942–17 Aug 1943; Ploesti, Rumania, 1 Aug 1943; Bratislava, Czechoslovakia, 16 June 1944.

514th BOMB SQUADRON

Lineage

Constituted 514th Bomb Sq (Heavy) on 19 Oct 1942. Activated on 31 Oct 1942. Redesignated 514th Bomb Sq (Very Heavy) on 23 May 1945. Inactivated on 7 Mar 1946. Redesignated 514th Recon Sq (Very Long Range, Weather) on 16 Sept 1947. Activated on 15 Oct 1947. Inactivated on 20 Feb 1951. Redesignated 514th Bomb Sq (Medium) on 25 May 1951. Activated on 1 June 1951.

Assignments

376th Bomb Grp, 31 Oct 1942; 498th Bomb Grp, 10 Nov 1945–7 Mar 1946. 43d (later 2143d Air) Weather Wing, 15 Oct 1947–20 Feb 1951. 376th Bomb Grp, 1 June 1951; 376th Bomb Wing, 16 June 1952–.

Stations

Lydda, Palestine, 31 Oct 1942; Abu Sueir, Egypt, 8 Nov 1942; Gambut Libya, 10 Feb 1943; Soluch, Libya, 25 Feb 1943; Bengasi, Libya, c. 6 Apr 1943; Enfidaville, Tunisia, 26 Sept 1943 (detachment operated from Bengasi, Libya, 3–11 Oct 1943); San Pancrazio, Italy, 18 Nov 1943–19 Apr 1945; Harvard AAFld, NE, 8 May 1945; Grand Island AAFld, NE, 25 June 1945; March Field, CA, 10 Nov 1945; MacDill Field, FL, 22 Dec 1945–7 Mar 1946. North Field, Guam, 15 Oct 1947–20 Feb 1951. Forbes AFB, KS, 1 June 1951; Barksdale AFB, LA, 10 Oct 1951; Lockbourne AFB, OH, 1 Dec 1957–.

Aircraft
B-17, 1942; B-24, 1942–1945; B-29, 1945. B/
TB/RB/WB-29, 1947–1951; C-54, 1948–1951;
C-47, 1949–1950. B-29, 1951–1954; B-47,
1954–1961; E-47, 1961–.

Operations
Combat in MTO and ETO, c. 1 Nov 1942–15
Apr 1945; not fully manned or equipped, 10 Nov
1945–7 Mar 1946. Weather reconnaissance in
support of Korean War, July 1950–10 Feb 1951.
Primarily electronic countermeasures, c. Nov
1952–.

Service Streamers
Korean Theater.

Campaigns
Egypt-Libya; Air Offensive, Europe; Tu-
nisia; Sicily; Naples-Foggia; Anzio; Rome-
Arno; Normandy, Northern France; Southern
France; North Apennines; Rhineland; Central
Europe; Po Valley; Air Combat, EAME The-
ater.

Decorations
Distinguished Unit Citations: North Africa and
Sicily, [Nov} 1942–17 Aug 1943; Ploesti, Rumania, 1 Aug 1943; Bratislava, Czechoslovakia, 16 June 1944.

654th BOMB SQUADRON
Lineage
Constituted 654th Bomb Sq (Heavy, Recon,
Special) on 17 July 1944. Activated on 9 Aug
1944. Redesignated: 54th Recon Sq (Long
Range, Weather) on 4 Sept 1945; 54th Recon Sq
(Very Long Range, Weather) on 27 Nov 1945.
Inactivated on 15 Oct 1947. Redesignated 54th
Strategic Recon Sq (Medium, Weather) on 22
Jan 1951. Activated on 21 Feb 1951.
Redesignated 54th Weather Recon Sq on 15 Feb
1954. Discontinued on 18 Mar 1960. Organized
on 18 Apr 1962.

Assignments
25th Bomb Grp (Recon), 9 Aug 1944; Third Air
Force, 8 Sept 1945; 311th Recon Wing, 27 Nov
1945 (attached to Twentieth Air Force, 8 Dec
1945–28 Feb 1946); Air Weather Service, 13
Mar 1946; 43d Weather Wing, 1 Aug–15 Oct
1947. 2143d Air Weather Wing, 21 Feb 1951;
1st Weather Wing, 8 Feb 1954; Department of
the Air Force, 18 Mar 1960; Military Air Transport Service, 8 Feb 1962; 9th Weather Recon
Grp, 18 Apr 1962–.

Stations
Watton, England, 9 Aug 1944–25 July 1945;
Drew Field, FL, c. 6 Aug 1945; Guam, 27 Nov
1945; Buckley Field, CO, 28 Feb 1946; Langley
Field, VA, 2 June 1946; Morrison Field, FL, 19
July 1946–11 June 1947; North AB, Guam, 7
July–15 Oct 1947. Anderson AFB, Guam, 21
Feb 1951–18 Mar 1960. Andersen AFB, Guam,
18 Apr 1962–.

Aircraft
B-25, 1944; Mosquito XVI, 1944–1945; B-26,
1944–1945; P-38, 1944–1945; B-29, 1946-1947;

C-47, 1946-1947. WB-29, 1951-1956; C-54,
1951–1960; YC-97, 1952-1953; TB-50, 1955;
WB-50, 1955–1960. WB-50, RB-57, and C-
130, 1962–.

Operations
Photographic and weather reconnaissance in
ETO, 9 Aug 1944–4 May 1945. Weather recon-
naissance in support of the Korean War.

Service Streamers
Asiatic-Pacific Theater; Korean Theater.

Campaigns
Northern France; Rhineland; Ardennes-Alsace;
Central Europe; Air Combat, EAME Theater.

Decorations
Air Force Outstanding Unit Award, Mar–Oct
1956.

676th BOMB SQUADRON
Lineage
Constituted 676th Bomb Sq (Heavy) on 15 Feb
1943. Activated on 1 Mar 1943. Redesignated
676th Bomb Sq (Very Heavy) on 20 Nov 1943.
Inactivated on 1 Oct 1946.

Assignments
444th Bomb Grp, 1 Mar 1943–1 Oct 1946.

Stations
Davis-Monthan Field, AZ, 1 Mar 1943; Great
Bend AAFld, KS, 2 Aug 1943–12 Mar 1944;
Charra, India, c. 11 Apr 1944; Dudhkundi, In-
dia, 1 July 1944–Apr 1945; West Field, Tinian,
Apr–27 Oct 1945; Merced AAFld, CA, 15 Nov
1945; Davis-Monthan Field, AZ, c. 9 May–1·
Oct 1946.

Aircraft
B-26, 1943; B-17, 1943–1944; YB-29, 1943–
1944; B-29, 1943–1946.

Operations
Combat in CBI, 5 June 1944–28 Mar 1945, and
Western Pacific, 10 May–14 Aug 1945.

Service Streamers
American Theater

Campaigns
India-Burma; Air Offensive, Japan; China Defensive; Western Pacific; Central Burma.

Decorations
Distinguished Unit Citations: Yawata, Japan,
20 Aug 1944; Japan, 10–14 May 1945; Japan, 24
July 1945.

677th BOMB SQUADRON
Lineage
Constituted 677th Bomb Sq (Heavy) on 15 Feb
1943. Activated on 1 Mar 1943. Redesignated
677th Bomb Sq (Very Heavy) on 20 Nov 1943.
Inactivated on 1 Oct 1946.

Assignments
444th Bomb Grp, 1 Mar 1943–1 Oct 1946.

Stations
Davis-Monthan Field, AZ, 1 Mar 1943; Great
Bend AAFld, KS, 2 Aug 1943–12 Mar 1944;
Charra, India, c. 13 Apr 1944; Dudhkundi, In-
dia, 1 July 1944–Apr 1945; West Field, Tinian,
Apr–27 Oct 1945; Merced AAFld, CA, 15 Nov
1945; Davis-Monthan Field, AZ, 10 May–1 Oct
1946.

Aircraft
B-26, 1943; B-17, 1943–1944; YB-29, 1943–
1944; B-29, 1944–1946.

Operations
Combat in CBI, 5 June 1944–28 Mar 1945, and
Western Pacific, 10 May–14 Aug 1945.

Service Streamers
American Theater

Campaigns
India-Burma; Air Offensive, Japan; China Defensive; Western Pacific; Central Burma.

Decorations
Distinguished Unit Citations: Yawata, Japan,
20 Aug 1944; Japan, 10–14 May 1945; Japan, 24
July 1945.

678th BOMB SQUADRON
Lineage
Constituted 678th Bomb Sq (Heavy) on 15 Feb
1943. Activated on 1 Mar 1943. Redesignated
678th Bomb Sq (Very Heavy) on 20 Nov 1943;
10th Recon Sq (Very Long Range, Photographic)
on 17 Dec 1945. Inactivated on 31 Mar 1946.
Redesignated 10th Recon Sq (Photographic) on
8 Oct 1947. Activated in the reserve on 6 Nov
1947. Redesignated 10th Tactical Recon Sq
(Photographic) on 27 June 1949. Inactivated on
28 Jan 1950. Redesignated 10th Strategic Recon
Sq (Medium) on 9 May 1952. Activated on 28
May 1952. Inactivated on 1 July 1958.

Assignments
444th Bomb Grp, 1 Mar 1943; 311th Recon
Wing, 7–31 Mar 1946. 26th Recon Grp, 6 Nov
1947; Ninth Air Force, 27 June 1949–28 Jan
1950. 26th Strategic Recon Wing, 28 May 1952–
1 July 1958.

Stations
Davis-Monthan Field, AZ, 1 Mar 1943; Great
Bend AAFld, KS, 3 Aug 1943–12 Mar 1944;
Charra, India, c. 13 Apr 1944; Dudhkundi, In-
dia, 1 July 1944–Apr 1945; West Field, Tinian,
Apr–27 Oct 1945; Merced AAFld, CA, 15 Nov
1945–31 Mar 1946. Rochester, NY, 6 Nov 1947;
Langley AFB, VA, 27 June 1949–28 Jan 1950.
Lockbourne AFB, OH, 28 May 1952–1 July
1958.

Aircraft
B-24, 1943; B-26, 1943; B-17, 1943–1944; YB-
29, 1943–1944; B-29, 1943–1946. YRB-47,
1954; RB-47, 1954–1958.

Operations
Combat in CBI, 5 June 1944–28 Mar 1945, and
Western Pacific, 10 May–14 Aug 1945.

Campaigns
India-Burma; Air Offensive, Japan; China Defensive; Western Pacific; Central Burma.

Decorations
Distinguished Unit Citations: Yawata, Japan, 20 Aug 1944; Japan, 10–14 May 1945; Japan, 24 July 1945. Air Force Outstanding Unit Award: 21 Mar–9 May 1956.

679th BOMB SQUADRON
Lineage
Constituted 679th Bomb Sq (Heavy) on 15 Feb 1943. Activated on 1 Mar 1943. Redesignated 679th Bomb Sq (Very Heavy) on 20 Nov 1943. Disbanded on 12 Oct 1944.

Assignments
444th Bomb Grp, 1 Mar 1943–12 Oct 1944.

Stations
Davis-Monthan Field, AZ, 1 Mar 1943; Great Bend AAFld, KS, 3 Aug 1943–12 Mar 1944; Charra, India, c. 13 Apr 1944; Dudhkundi, India, 1 July–12 Oct 1944.

Aircraft
B-26, 1943; B-17, 1943–1944; YB-29, 1943–1944; B-29, 1943–1944.

Operations
Combat in CBI, 5 June –26 Sept 1944.

Service Streamers
None

Campaigns
India-Burma; Air Offensive, Japan; China Defensive.

Decorations
Distinguished Unit Citations: Yawata, Japan, 20 Aug 1944.

680th BOMB SQUADRON
Lineage
Constituted 680th Bomb Sq (Very Heavy) on 25 Nov 1944. Activated on 4 Dec 1944. Inactivated on 15 June 1946.

Assignments
Second Air Force, 4 Dec 1944; 504th Bomb Grp; attached, 15 June 1945; assigned 14 Nov 1945–15 June 1946.

Stations
Alamogordo AAFld, NM, 4 Dec 1944–10 May 1945; North Field, Tinian, 15 June 1945; Clark Field Luzon, 13 Mar–15 June 1946.

Aircraft
B-29, 1945–1946.

Operations
Combat in Western Pacific, 22 June–14 Aug 1945.

Service Streamers
None

Campaigns
Air Offensive, Japan; Western Pacific.

Decorations
Distinguished Unit Citations: Yokohama, Japan, 28 May 1945; Japan and Korea, 27 July–14 Aug 1945.

712th BOMB SQUADRON
Lineage
Constituted 712th Bomb Sq (Heavy) on 6 Apr 1943. Activated on 1 May 1943. Redesignated 712th Bomb Sq (Very Heavy) on 5 Aug 1945. Inactivated on 4 Aug 1946. Activated in the reserve on 19 Apr 1947. Redesignated 712th Bomb Sq (Light) on 27 June 1949. Ordered to active service on 17 Mar 1951. Inactivated on 21 Mar 1951.

Assignments
448th Bomb Grp, 1 May 1943–4 Aug 1946. 448th Bomb Grp, 19 Apr 1947–21 Mar 1951.

Stations
Gowen Field, ID, 1 May 1943; Wendover Field, UT, 4 July 1943; Sioux City AAB, IA, 11 Sept–7 Nov 1943; Seething, England, 25 Nov 1943–5 July 1945; Sioux Falls AAFld, SD, 15 July 1945; McCook AAFld, NE, 25 July 1945; Biggs Field, TX, 23 Aug 1945; McCook AAFld, NE, 8 Sept 1945; Fort Worth AAFld, TX, 15 Dec 1945–4 Aug 1946. Long Beach AAFld, CA, 19 Apr 1947–21 Mar 1951.

Aircraft
B-24, 1943–1945; B-29, 1945–1946.

Operations
Combat in ETO, 22 Dec 1943–25 Apr 1945.

Service Streamers
American Theater.

Campaigns
Air Offensive, Europe; Normandy; Northern France; Rhineland; Ardennes-Alsace; Central Europe.

Decorations
None.

713th BOMB SQUADRON
Lineage
Constituted 713th Bomb Sq (Heavy) on 6 Apr 1943. Activated on 1 May 1943. Redesignated 713th Bomb Sq (Very Heavy) on 5 Aug 1945. Inactivated on 4 Aug 1946. Activated in the reserve on 12 July 1947. Redesignated 713th Bomb Sq (Light) on 27 June 1949. Ordered to active service on 17 Mar 1951. Inactivated on 21 Mar 1951. Redesignated 713th Fighter-Bomber Sq on 6 Oct 1955. Activated in the reserve on 8 Nov 1955. Inactivated on 16 Nov 1957.

Assignments
448th Bomb Grp, 1 May 1943–4 Aug 1946. 448th Bomb Grp, 12 July 1947–21 Mar 1951. 448th Fighter-Bomber Grp, 8 Nov 1955–16 Nov 1957.

Stations
Gowen Field, ID, 1 May 1943; Wendover Field, UT, 4 July 1943; Sioux City AAB, IA, 11 Sept–7 Nov 1943; Seething, England, 25 Nov 1943–5 July 1945; Sioux Falls AAFld, SD, 15 July 1945; McCook AAFld, NE, 25 July 1945; Biggs Field, TX, 23 Aug 1945; McCook AAFld, NE, 8 Sept 1945; Fort Worth AAFld, TX, 15 Dec 1945–4 Aug 1946. Long Beach AAFld, CA, 12 July 1947–21 Mar 1951. Davis Field, OK, 8 Nov 1955–16 Nov 1957.

Aircraft
B-24, 1943–1945; B-29, 1945–1946.

Operations
Combat in ETO, 22 Dec 1943–25 Apr 1945.

Service Streamers
American Theater

Campaigns
Air Offensive, Europe; Normandy; Northern France; Rhineland; Ardennes-Alsace; Central Europe.

Decorations
None.

714th BOMB SQUADRON
Lineage
Constituted 714th Bomb Sq (Heavy) on 6 Apr 1943. Activated on 1 May 1943. Redesignated 714th Bomb Sq (Very Heavy) on 5 Aug 1945. Inactivated on 4 Aug 1946. Activated in the reserve on 12 July 1947. Redesignated 714th Bomb Sq (Light) on 27 June 1949. Ordered to active service on 17 Mar 1951. Inactivated on 21 Mar 1951.

Assignments
448th Bomb Grp, 1 May 1943–4 Aug 1946. 448th Bomb Grp, 12 July 1947–21 Mar 1951.

Stations
Gowen Field, ID, 1 May 1943; Wendover Field, UT, 4 July 1943; Sioux City AAB, IA, 11 Sept–7 Nov 1943; Seething, England, 29 Nov 1943–5 July 1945; Sioux Falls AAFld, SD, 15 July 1945; McCook AAFld, NE, 25 July 1945; Biggs Field, TX, 23 Aug 1945; McCook AAFld, NE, 8 Sept 1945; Fort Worth AAFld, TX, 15 Dec 1945–4 Aug 1946. Long Beach AAFld, CA, 12 July 1947–21 Mar 1951.

Aircraft
B-24, 1943–1945; B-29, 1945–1946.

Operations
Combat in ETO, 22 Dec 1943–25 Apr 1945.

Service Streamers
American Theater.

Campaigns
Air Offensive, Europe; Normandy; Northern France; Rhineland; Ardennes-Alsace; Central Europe.

Decorations
None.

715th BOMB SQUADRON

Lineage
Constituted 715th Bomb Sq (Heavy) on 6 Apr 1943. Activated on 1 May 1943. Redesignated 715th Bomb Sq (Very Heavy) on 5 Aug 1945. 715th Bomb Sq (Medium) on 2 July 1948.

Assignments
448th Bomb Grp, 1 May 1943; 509th Composite (later Bomb) Grp, 6 May 1946; 509th Bomb Wing, 16 June 1952–.

Stations
Gowen Field, ID, 1 May 1943; Wendover Field, UT, 4 July 1943; Sioux City AAB, IA, 16 Sept–9 Nov 1943; Seething, England, 29 Nov 1943–5 July 1945; Sioux Falls AAFld, SD, 15 July 1945; McCook AAFld, NE, 25 July 1945; Biggs Field, TX, 23 Aug 1945; McCook AAFld, NE, 8 Sept 1945; Fort Worth AAFld, TX, 15 Dec 1945; Roswell AAFld, NM, 23 June 1946; Pease AFB, NH, 1 July 1958–.

Aircraft
B-24, 1943–1945; B-29, 1945–1951; B-50, 1951–1955; B-47, 1955–.

Operations
Combat in ETO, 22 Dec 1943–25 Apr 1945.

Service Streamers
American Theater.

Campaigns
Air Offensive, Europe; Normandy; Northern France; Rhineland; Ardennes-Alsace; Central Europe.

Decorations
None.

716th BOMB SQUADRON

Lineage
Constituted 716th Bomb Sq (Heavy) on 6 Apr 1943. Activated on 1 May 1943. Redesignated 716th Bomb Sq (Very Heavy) on 23 May 1945. Inactivated on 4 Aug 1946. Redesignated 716th Bomb Sq (Heavy), and activated, on 15 Nov 1962. Organized on 1 Feb 1963.

Assignments
449th Bomb Grp, 1 May 1943–4 Aug 1946. Strategic Air Command, 15 Nov 1962; 449th Bomb Wing, 1 Feb 1963–.

Stations
Davis-Monthan Field, AZ, 1 May 1943; Alamogordo AAFld, NM, 4 July 1943; Bruning AAFld, NE, 12 Sept–27 Nov 1943; Grottaglie, Italy, c. 4 Jan 1943–15 May 1945; Sioux Falls AAFld, SD, 29 May 1945; Dalhart AAFld, TX, 24 July 1945; Grand Island AAFld, NE, 8 Sept 1945–4 Aug 1946. Kincheloe AFB, MI, 1 Feb 1963.

Aircraft
B-24, 1943–1945; B-17, 1945; B-29, 1945–1946. B-52, 1963–.

Operations
Combat in MTO and ETO, 8 Jan 1944–26 Apr 1945.

Service Streamers
American Theater.

Campaigns
Air Offensive, Europe; Naples-Foggia; Anzio; Rome-Arno; Normandy; Northern France; Southern France; North Apennines; Rhineland; Central Europe; Po Valley; Air Combat, EAME Theater.

Decorations
Distinguished Unit Citations: Bucharest, Rumania, 4 Apr 1944; Ploesti, Rumania, 9 July 1944.

717th BOMB SQUADRON

Lineage
Constituted 717th Bomb Sq (Heavy) on 6 Apr 1943. Activated on 1 May 1943. Redesignated 717th Bomb Sq (Very Heavy) on 23 May 1945; 717th Bomb Sq (Medium) on 28 May 1948; 717th Bomb Sq (Heavy) on 16 May 1949; 717th Strategic Recon Sq (Photographic) on 1 Apr 1950; 717th Strategic Recon Sq (Heavy) on 16 July 1950; 717th Bomb Sq (Heavy) on 1 Oct 1955. Discontinued, and inactivated, on 1 Feb 1963.

Assignments
449th Bomb Grp, 1 May 1943; 28th Bomb (later Strategic Recon) Grp, 4 Aug 1946; 28th Strategic Recon (later Bomb) Wing, 16 June 1952; 4245th Strategic Wing, 1 Feb 1960–1 Feb 1963.

Stations
Davis-Monthan Field, AZ, 1 May 1943; Alamogordo AAFld, NM, 5 July 1943; Bruning AAFld, NE, 12 Sept–26 Nov 1943; Grottaglie, Italy, 5 Jan 1944–13 May 1945; Sioux Falls AAFld, SD, 15 June 1945; Dalhart AAFld, TX, 24 July 1945; Grand Island AAFld, NE, 8 Sept 1945–6 Oct 1946; Elmendorf Field, AK, 20 Oct 1946–24 Apr 1947; Rapid City AAFld, SD, 3 May 1947; Sheppard AFB, TX, 1 Feb 1960–1 Feb 1963.

Aircraft
B-24, 1943–1945; B-17, 1945; B-29, 1946–1950; B-36, 1949–1950; RB-29, 1950; RB-36, 1950–1957; B-52, 1957–1963.

Operations
Combat in MTO and ETO, 8 Jan 1944–26 Apr 1945.

Service Streamers
American Theater.

Campaigns
Air Offensive, Europe; Naples-Foggia; Anzio; Rome-Arno; Normandy; Northern France; Southern France; North Apennines; Rhineland; Central Europe; Po Valley; Air Combat, EAME Theater.

Decorations
Distinguished Unit Citations: Bucharest, Rumania, 4 Apr 1944; Ploesti, Rumania, 9 July 1944. Air Force Outstanding Unit Award: 1 Sept 1957–30 June 1958.

718th BOMB SQUADRON

Lineage
Constituted 718th Bomb Sq (Heavy) on 6 Apr 1943. Activated on 1 May 1943. Redesignated: 718th Bomb Sq (Very Heavy) on 23 May 1945; 718th Bomb Sq (Medium) on 28 May 1948; 718th Bomb Sq (Heavy) on 16 May 1949; 718th Strategic Recon Sq (Photographic) on 1 Apr 1950; 718th Strategic Recon Sq (Heavy) on 16 July 1950; 718th Bomb Sq (Heavy) on 1 Oct 1955. Discontinued, and inactivated, on 1 Feb 1963.

Assignments
449th Bomb Grp, 1 May 1943; 28th Bomb (later Strategic Recon) Grp, 4 Aug 1946; 28th Strategic Recon (later Bomb) Wing, 16 June 1952; 4128th Strategic Wing, 20 Feb 1960–1 Feb 1963.

Stations
Davis-Monthan Field, AZ, 1 May 1943; Alamogordo AAFld, NM, 5 July 1943; Bruning AAFld, NE, 12 Sept–26 Nov 1943; Grottaglie, Italy, c. 6 Jan 1944–15 May 1945; Sioux Falls AAFld, SD, 29 May 1945; Dalhart AAFld, TX, 24 July 1945; Grand Island AAFld, NE, 8 Sept 1945–6 Oct 1946; Elmendorf Field, AK, 20 Oct 1946–24 Apr 1947; Rapid City AAFld, SD, 3 May 1947; Amarillo AFB, TX, 20 Feb 1960–1 Feb 1963.

Aircraft
B-24, 1943–1945; B-17, 1945; B-29, 1946–1950; B-36, 1949–1950; RB-29, 1950; RB-36, 1950–1957; B-52, 1957–1963.

Operations
Combat in MTO and ETO, 8 Jan 1944–26 Apr 1945.

Service Streamers
American Theater.

Campaigns
Air Offensive, Europe; Naples-Foggia; Anzio; Rome-Arno; Normandy; Northern France; Southern France; North Apennines; Rhineland; Central Europe; Po Valley; Air Combat, EAME Theater.

Decorations
Distinguished Unit Citations: Bucharest, Rumania, 4 Apr 1944; Ploesti, Rumania, 9 July 1944. Air Force Outstanding Unit Awards: 1 Sept 1957–30 June 1958; 1 Mar 1960–30 June 1961.

719th BOMB SQUADRON

Lineage
Constituted 719th Bomb Sq (Heavy) on 6 Apr 1943. Activated on 1 May 1943. Inactivated on 11 June 1945. Redesignated 719th Bomb Sq (Very Heavy) on 7 Sept 1945; Activated on 17 Sept 1945. Redesignated: 46th Recon Sq (Very Long Range, Photographic-Weather) on 15 Nov 1945: 46th Recon Sq (Very Long Range, Photographic) on 23 Oct 1946. Inactivated on 13 Oct 1947.

Assignments
449th Bomb Grp, 1 May 1943–11 June 1945. 449th Bomb Grp, 17 Sept 1945. Fifteenth Air

Force, 4 Aug 1946; Alaskan Air Command, 19 Aug 1946; Yukon Sector, Alaskan Air Command, 1 Oct 1946–13 Oct 1947.

Stations
Davis-Monthan Field, AZ, 1 May 1943; Alamogordo AAFld, NM, 5 July 1943; Bruning AAFld, NE, 12 Sept 1943–26 Nov 1943; Grottaglie, Italy, 3 Jan 1944–15 May 1945; Sioux Falls AAFld, SD, 29 May–11 June 1945. Grand Island AAFld, NE, 17 Sept 1945–10 Aug 1946; Ladd Field, AK, 23 Aug 1946–13 Oct 1947.

Aircraft
B-24, 1943–1945; B-17, 1945–1946; B-29, 1945–1947; F-13, 1945–1947.

Operations
Combat in MTO and ETO, 8 Jan 1944–26 Apr 1945.

Service Streamers
American Theater.

Campaigns
Air Offensive, Europe; Naples-Foggia; Anzio; Rome-Arno; Normandy; Northern France; Southern France; North Apennines; Rhineland; Central Europe; Po Valley; Air Combat, EAME Theater.

Decorations
Distinguished Unit Citations: Bucharest, Rumania, 4 Apr 1944; Ploesti, Rumania, 9 July 1944.

720th BOMB SQUADRON
Lineage
Constituted 720th Bomb Sq (Heavy) on 6 Apr 1943. Activated on 1 May 1943. Redesignated 720th Bomb Sq (Very Heavy) on 23 May 1945. Inactivated on 15 Oct 1945. Redesignated 720th Fighter-Bomber Sq on 29 Oct 1953. Activated on 25 Dec 1953. Inactivated on 8 Aug 1955. Redesignated 720th Fighter-Day Sq on 13 Nov 1957. Activated on 11 Dec 1957. Redesignated 720th Tactical Fighter Sq on 1 July 1958. Inactivated on 18 Dec 1958. Redesignated 720th Bomb Sq (Heavy), and activated, on 15 Nov 1962. Organized on 1 Feb 1963.

Assignments
450th Bomb Grp, 1 May 1943–15 Oct 1945. 11th Air Division, 25 Dec 1953–8 Aug 1955. 450th Fighter-Day (later Tactical Fighter) Wing, 11 Dec 1957–18 Dec 1958. Strategic Air Command, 15 Nov 1962; 450th Bomb Wing, 1 Feb 1963–.

Stations
Gowen Field, ID, 1 May 1943; Clovis AAB, NM, 21 May 1943; Alamogordo AAFld, NM, c. 8 July–26 Nov 1943; Manduria, Italy, 2 Jan 1944–13 May 1945; Sioux Falls AAFld, SD, c. 31 May 1945; Harvard AAFld, NE, 24 July–15 Oct 1945. Ladd AFB, AK, 25 Dec 1953; Eielson AFB, AK 17 May 1954–8 Aug 1955. Foster AFB, TX, 11 Dec 1957–18 Dec 1958. Minot AFB, ND, 1 Feb 1963–.

Aircraft
B-24, 1943–1945; B-29, 1945. F-86, 1954–1955. F-100, 1958. B-52, 1963–.

Operations
Combat in MTO and ETO, 9 Jan 1944–26 Apr 1945.

Service Streamers
None

Campaigns
Air Offensive, Europe; Naples-Foggia; Rome-Arno; Normandy; Northern France; Southern France; North Apennines; Rhineland; Central Europe; Po Valley; Air Combat, EAME Theater.

Decorations
Distinguished Unit Citations: Regensburg, Germany, 25 Feb 1944; Ploesti, Rumania, 5 Apr 1944.

721st BOMB SQUADRON
Lineage
Constituted 721st Bomb Sq (Heavy) on 6 Apr 1943. Activated on 1 May 1943. Redesignated 721st Bomb Sq (Very Heavy) on 23 May 1945. Inactivated on 15 Oct 1945. Redesignated 721st Fighter-Bomber Sq on 31 Mar 1954. Activated on 1 July 1954. Redesignated: 721st Fighter-Day Sq on 8 Mar 1955; 721st Tactical Fighter Sq on 1 July 1958. Inactivated on 18 Dec 1958.

Assignments
450th Bomb Grp, 1 May 1943–15 Oct 1945. 450th Fighter-Bomber (later Fighter-Day) Grp, 1 July 1954; 450th Fighter-Day (later Tactical Fighter) Wing, 11 Dec 1957–18 Dec 1958.

Stations
Gowen Field, ID, 1 May 1943; Clovis AAB, NM, 21 May 1943; Alamogordo AAFld, NM, c. 8 July–26 Nov 1943; Manduria, Italy, 3 Jan 1944–16 May 1945; Sioux Falls AAFld, SD, c. 31 May 1945; Harvard AAFld, NE, 24 July–15 Oct 1945. Foster AFB, TX, 1 July 1954–18 Dec 1958.

Aircraft
B-24, 1943–1945; B-29, 1945. F-86, 1954–1955. F-100, 1955–1958.

Operations
Combat in MTO and ETO, 8 Jan 1944–26 Apr 1945.

Service Streamers
None

Campaigns
Air Offensive, Europe; Naples-Foggia; Rome-Arno; Normandy; Northern France; Southern France; North Apennines; Rhineland; Central Europe; Po Valley; Air Combat, EAME Theater.

Decorations
Distinguished Unit Citations: Regensburg, Germany, 25 Feb 1944; Ploesti, Rumania, 5 Apr 1944.

722d BOMB SQUADRON
Lineage
Constituted 722d Bomb Sq (Heavy) on 6 Apr 1943. Activated on 1 May 1943. Redesignated 722d Bomb Sq (Very Heavy) on 23 May 1945. Inactivated on 15 Oct 1945. Redesignated 722d Fighter-Bomber Sq on 31 Mar 1954. Activated on 1 July 1954. Redesignated: 722d Fighter-Day Sq on 8 Mar 1955; 722d Tactical Fighter Sq on 1 July 1958. Inactivated on 18 Dec 1958.

Assignments
450th Bomb Grp, 1 May 1943–15 Oct 1945. 450th Fighter-Bomber (later Fighter-Day) Grp, 1 July 1954; 450th Fighter-Day (later Tactical Fighter) Wing, 11 Dec 1957–18 Dec 1958.

Stations
Gowen Field, ID, 1 May 1943; Clovis AAB, NM, 21 May 1943; Alamogordo AAFld, NM, c. 8 July–26 Nov 1943; Manduria, Italy, 2 Jan 1944–16 May 1945; Sioux Falls AAFld, SD, c. 31 May 1945; Harvard AAFld, NE, 24 July–15 Oct 1945. Foster AFB, TX, 1 July 1954–18 Dec 1958.

Aircraft
B-24, 1943–1945; B-29, 1945. F-86, 1954–1955. F-100, 1955–1958.

Operations
Combat in MTO and ETO, 9 Jan 1944–26 Apr 1945.

Service Streamers
None

Campaigns
Air Offensive, Europe; Naples-Foggia; Rome-Arno; Normandy; Northern France; Southern France; North Apennines; Rhineland; Central Europe; Po Valley; Air Combat, EAME Theater.

Decorations
Distinguished Unit Citations: Regensburg, Germany, 25 Feb 1944; Ploesti, Rumania, 5 Apr 1944.

752d BOMB SQUADRON
Lineage
Constituted 752d Bomb Sq (Heavy) on 19 May 1943. Activated on 1 Jul 1943. Redesignated 752d Bomb Sq (Very Heavy) on 5 Aug 1945. Inactivated on 17 Oct 1945.

Assignments
458th Bomb Grp, 1 Jul 1943–17 Oct 1945.

Stations
Wendover Field, UT, 1 July 1943; Gowen Field, ID, 28 July 1943; Kearns, UT, 10 Sept 1943; Wendover Field, UT, 15 Sept 1943; Tonopah AAFld, NV, 4 Nov 1943–1 Jan 1944; Horsham St Faith, England, 1 Feb 1944–3 July 1945; Sioux Falls AAFld, SD, 15 July 1945; Walker AAFld, KS, 25 July 1945; March Field, CA, 22 Aug–17 Oct 1945.

Aircraft
B-24, 1943–1945; B-29, 1945.

Operations
Combat in ETO, 24 Feb 1944–25 Apr 1945.

Service Streamers
None.

Campaigns
Air Offensive, Europe; Normandy; Northern France; Rhineland; Ardennes-Alsace; Central Europe; Air Combat, EAME Theater.

Decorations
None.

753d BOMB SQUADRON

Lineage
Constituted 753d Bomb Sq (Heavy) on 19 May 1943. Activated on 1 Jul 1943. Redesignated 753d Bomb Sq (Very Heavy) on 5 Aug 1945. Inactivated on 17 Oct 1945.

Assignments
458th Bomb Grp, 1 Jul 1943–17 Oct 1945.

Stations
Wendover Field, UT, 1 July 1943; Gowen Field, ID, 28 July 1943; Kearns, UT, 10 Sept 1943; Wendover Field, UT, 15 Sept 1943; Tonopah AAFld, NV, 4 Nov 1943–1 Jan 1944; Horsham St Faith, England, 1 Feb 1944–3 July 1945; Sioux Falls AAFld, SD, 15 July 1945; Walker AAFld, KS, 25 July 1945; March Field, CA, 22 Aug–17 Oct 1945.

Aircraft
B-24, 1943–1945; B-29, 1945.

Operations
Combat in ETO, 24 Feb 1944–25 Apr 1945.

Service Streamers
None.

Campaigns
Air Offensive, Europe; Normandy; Northern France; Rhineland; Ardennes-Alsace; Central Europe; Air Combat, EAME Theater.

Decorations
None.

754th BOMB SQUADRON

Lineage
Constituted 754th Bomb Sq (Heavy) on 19 May 1943. Activated on 1 Jul 1943. Redesignated 754th Bomb Sq (Very Heavy) on 5 Aug 1945. Inactivated on 17 Oct 1945.

Assignments
458th Bomb Grp, 1 Jul 1943–17 Oct 1945.

Stations
Wendover Field, UT, 1 July 1943; Gowen Field, ID, 28 July 1943; Kearns, UT, 10 Sept 1943; Wendover Field, UT, 15 Sept 1943; Tonopah AAFld, NV, 4 Nov 1943–1 Jan 1944; Horsham

St Faith, England, 1 Feb 1944–3 July 1945; Sioux Falls AAFld, SD, 15 July 1945; Walker AAFld, KS, 25 July 1945; March Field, CA, 22 Aug–17 Oct 1945.

Aircraft
B-24, 1943–1945; B-29, 1945.

Operations
Combat in ETO, 24 Feb 1944–25 Apr 1945.

Service Streamers
None.

Campaigns
Air Offensive, Europe; Normandy; Northern France; Rhineland; Ardennes-Alsace; Central Europe; Air Combat, EAME Theater.

Decorations
None.

755th BOMB SQUADRON

Lineage
Constituted 755th Bomb Sq (Heavy) on 19 May 1943. Activated on 1 Jul 1943. Redesignated 755th Bomb Sq (Very Heavy) on 5 Aug 1945. Inactivated on 17 Oct 1945.

Assignments
458th Bomb Grp, 1 Jul 1943–17 Oct 1945.

Stations
Wendover Field, UT, 1 July 1943; Gowen Field, ID, 28 July 1943; Kearns, UT, 10 Sept 1943; Wendover Field, UT, 15 Sept 1943; Tonopah AAFld, NV, 4 Nov 1943–1 Jan 1944; Horsham St Faith, England, 1 Feb 1944–3 July 1945; Sioux Falls AAFld, SD, 15 July 1945; Walker AAFld, KS, 25 July 1945; March Field, CA, 22 Aug–17 Oct 1945.

Aircraft
B-24, 1943–1945; B-29, 1945.

Operations
Combat in ETO, 24 Feb 1944–25 Apr 1945.

Service Streamers
None.

Campaigns
Air Offensive, Europe; Normandy; Northern France; Rhineland; Ardennes-Alsace; Central Europe; Air Combat, EAME Theater.

Decorations
None.

768th BOMB SQUADRON

Lineage
Constituted 768th Bomb Sq (Heavy) on 19 May 1943. Activated on 1 July 1943. Redesignated 768th Bomb Sq (Very Heavy) on 20 Nov 1943. Inactivated on 31 Mar 1946. Redesignated 768th Bomb Sq (Heavy), and activated, on 15 Nov 1962. Organized on 1 Feb 1963.

Assignments
462d Bomb Grp, 1 July 1943–31 Mar 1946. Strategic Air Command, 15 Nov 1962; 462d Strategic Aerospace Wing, 1 Feb 1963–.

Stations
Smoky Hill AAFld, KS, 1 July 1943; Walker AAFld, KS, 28 July 1943–c. 12 Mar 1944; Piardoba, India, c. 16 Apr 1944–Apr 1945; West Field, Tinian, Apr–5 Nov 1945; MacDill Field, FL, Nov 1945–31 Mar 1946. Larson AFB, WA, 1 Feb 1963–.

Aircraft
B-26, 1943; B-17, 1943–1944; B-29, 1944–1946. B-52, 1963.

Operations
Combat in CBI, 5 June 1944–29 Mar 1945, and Western Pacific, 5 May–14 Aug 1945.

Service Streamers
American Theater

Campaigns
India-Burma; Air Offensive, Japan; China Defensive; Western Pacific; Central Burma.

Decorations
Distinguished Unit Citations: Yawata, Japan, 20 Aug 1944; Tokyo and Yokohama, Japan, 23, 25, and 29 May 1945; Takarazuka, Japan, 24 July 1945.

769th BOMB SQUADRON

Lineage
Constituted 769th Bomb Sq (Heavy) on 19 May 1943. Activated on 1 July 1943. Redesignated 769th Bomb Sq (Very Heavy) on 20 Nov 1943. Inactivated on 31 Mar 1946.

Assignments
462d Bomb Grp, 1 July 1943–31 Mar 1946.

Stations
Smoky Hill AAFld, KS, 1 July 1943; Walker AAFld, KS, 28 July 1943–c. 12 Mar 1944; Piardoba, India, c. 19 Apr 1944–Apr 1945; West Field, Tinian, Apr–5 Nov 1945; MacDill Field, FL, Nov 1945–31 Mar 1946.

Aircraft
B-26, 1943; YB-29, 1943; B-17, 1943–1944; B-29, 1943–1946.

Operations
Combat in CBI, 5 June 1944–30 Mar 1945, and Western Pacific, 5 May–14 Aug 1945.

Service Streamers
American Theater

Campaigns
India-Burma; Air Offensive, Japan; China Defensive; Western Pacific; Central Burma.

Decorations
Distinguished Unit Citations: Yawata, Japan, 20 Aug 1944; Tokyo and Yokohama, Japan, 23, 25 and 29 May 1945; Takarazuka, Japan, 24 July 1945.

770th BOMB SQUADRON

Lineage
Constituted 770th Bomb Sq (Heavy) on 19 May 1943. Activated on 1 July 1943. Redesignated 770th Bomb Sq (Very Heavy) on 20 Nov 1943. Inactivated on 31 Mar 1946.

Assignments
462d Bomb Grp, 1 July 1943–31 Mar 1946.

Stations
Smoky Hill AAFld, KS, 1 July 1943; Walker AAFld, KS, 28 July 1943–c. 12 Mar 1944; Piardoba, India, c. 19 Apr 1944–Apr 1945; West Field, Tinian, Apr–5 Nov 1945; MacDill Field, FL, Nov 1945–31 Mar 1946.

Aircraft
B-26, 1943; B-17, 1943–1944; B-29, 1943–1946.

Operations
Combat in CBI, 5 June 1944–29 Mar 1945, and Western Pacific, 5 May–14 Aug 1945.

Service Streamers
American Theater

Campaigns
India-Burma; Air Offensive, Japan; China Defensive; Western Pacific; Central Burma.

Decorations
Distinguished Unit Citations: Yawata, Japan, 20 Aug 1944; Tokyo and Yokohama, Japan, 23, 25, and 29 May 1945; Takarazuka, Japan, 24 July 1945.

771st BOMB SQUADRON

Lineage
Constituted 771st Bomb Sq (Heavy) on 19 May 1943. Activated on 1 July 1943. Redesignated 771st Bomb Sq (Very Heavy) on 20 Nov 1943. Disbanded on 12 Oct 1944.

Assignments
462d Bomb Grp, 1 July 1943–12 Oct 1944.

Stations
Smoky Hill AAFld, KS, 1 July 1943; Walker AAFld, KS, 28 July 1943–c. 12 Mar 1944; Piardoba, India, c. 13 May–12 Oct 1944.

Aircraft
B-26, 1943; B-17, 1943–1944; B-29, 1943–1944.

Operations
Combat in CBI, 5 June –10 Oct 1944.

Service Streamers
None

Campaigns
India-Burma; Air Offensive, Japan; China Defensive; Western Pacific.

Decorations
Distinguished Unit Citations: Yawata, Japan, 20 Aug 1944.

784th BOMB SQUADRON

Lineage
Constituted 784th Bomb Sq (Heavy) on 19 May 1943. Activated on 1 Aug 1943. Redesignated 784th Bomb Sq (Very Heavy) on 5 Aug 1945. Inactivated on 17 Oct 1945.

Assignments
466th Bomb Grp, 1 Aug 1943–17 Oct 1945.

Stations
Alamogordo AAFld, NM, 1 Aug 1943; Kearns, UT, 31 Aug 1943; Alamogordo AAFld, NM, 27 Nov 1943–10 Feb 1944; Attlebridge, England, 9 Mar 1944–Jul 1945; Sioux Falls AAFld, SD, 15 July 1945; Pueblo AAB, CO, 25 July 1945; Davis-Monthan Field, AZ, 26 Aug–17 Oct 1945.

Aircraft
B-24, 1943–1945; B-29, 1945.

Operations
Combat in ETO, 22 Mar 1944–25 Apr 1945, including pathfinder missions from July 1944.

Service Streamers
None.

Campaigns
Air Offensive, Europe; Normandy; Northern France; Rhineland; Ardennes-Alsace; Central Europe.

Decorations
None.

785th BOMB SQUADRON

Lineage
Constituted 785th Bomb Sq (Heavy) on 19 May 1943. Activated on 1 Aug 1943. Redesignated 785th Bomb Sq (Very Heavy) on 5 Aug 1945. Inactivated on 17 Oct 1945.

Assignments
466th Bomb Grp, 1 Aug 1943–17 Oct 1945.

Stations
Alamogordo AAFld, NM, 1 Aug 1943; Kearns, UT, 31 Aug 1943; Alamogordo AAFld, NM, 25 Nov 1943–9 Feb 1944; Attlebridge, England, 9 Mar 1944–Jul 1945; Sioux Falls AAFld, SD, 15 July 1945; Pueblo AAB, CO, 25 July 1945; Davis-Monthan Field, AZ, 26 Aug–17 Oct 1945.

Aircraft
B-24, 1943–1945; B-29, 1945.

Operations
Combat in ETO, 22 Mar 1944–Apr 1945.

Service Streamers
None.

Campaigns
Air Offensive, Europe; Normandy; Northern France; Rhineland; Ardennes-Alsace; Central Europe.

Decorations
None.

786th BOMB SQUADRON

Lineage
Constituted 786th Bomb Sq (Heavy) on 19 May 1943. Activated on 1 Aug 1943. Redesignated 786th Bomb Sq (Very Heavy) on 5 Aug 1945. Inactivated on 17 Oct 1945.

Assignments
466th Bomb Grp, 1 Aug 1943–17 Oct 1945.

Stations
Alamogordo AAFld, NM, 1 Aug 1943; Kearns, UT, 31 Aug 1943; Alamogordo AAFld, NM, 27 Nov 1943–10 Feb 1944; Attlebridge, England, 8 Mar 1944–Jul 1945; Sioux Falls AAFld, SD, 15 July 1945; Pueblo AAB, CO, 25 July 1945; Davis-Monthan Field, AZ, 26 Aug–17 Oct 1945.

Aircraft
B-24, 1943–1945; B-29, 1945.

Operations
Combat in ETO, 22 Mar 1944–25 Apr 1945.

Service Streamers
None.

Campaigns
Air Offensive, Europe; Normandy; Northern France; Rhineland; Ardennes-Alsace; Central Europe.

Decorations
None.

787th BOMB SQUADRON

Lineage
Constituted 787th Bomb Sq (Heavy) on 19 May 1943. Activated on 1 Aug 1943. Redesignated 787th Bomb Sq (Very Heavy) on 5 Aug 1945. Inactivated on 17 Oct 1945.

Assignments
466th Bomb Grp, 1 Aug 1943–17 Oct 1945.

Stations
Alamogordo AAFld, NM, 1 Aug 1943; Kearns, UT, 31 Aug 1943; Alamogordo AAFld, NM, 30 Nov 1943–10 Feb 1944; Attlebridge, England, 9 Mar 1944–Jul 1945; Sioux Falls AAFld, SD, 15 July 1945; Pueblo AAB, CO, 25 July 1945; Davis-Monthan Field, AZ, 26 Aug–17 Oct 1945.

Aircraft
B-24, 1943–1945; B-29, 1945.

Operations
Combat in ETO, 22 Mar 1944–25 Apr 1945.

Service Streamers
None.

Campaigns
Air Offensive, Europe; Normandy; Northern France; Rhineland; Ardennes-Alsace; Central Europe.

Decorations
None.

788th BOMB SQUADRON

Lineage
Constituted 788th Bomb Sq (Heavy) on 19 May 1943. Activated on 1 Aug 1943. Redesignated 788th Bomb Sq (Very Heavy) on 5 Aug 1945. Inactivated on 4 Aug 1946.

Assignments
467th Bomb Grp, 1 Aug 1943; VIII Air Force Composite Command, 11 May 1944 (attached to 801st Bomb Grp [Prov]); 467th Bomb Grp, 10 Aug 1944–4 Aug 1946.

Stations
Wendover Field, UT, 1 Aug 1943; Mountain Home AAFld, ID, 8 Sept 1943; Kearns, UT, 10 Oct 1943; Wendover Field, UT, 2 Nov 1943–12 Feb 1944; Rackheath, England, 12 Mar 1944; Harrington, England, 27 May 1944; Rackheath, England, 10 Aug 1944–12 June 1945; Sioux Falls AAFld, SD, 15 July 1945; Fairmont AAFld, NE, 25 July 1945; Alamogordo AAFld, NM, 22 Aug 1945; Harvard AAFld, NE, 8 Sept 1945; Clovis AAFld, NM, 7 Jan–4 Aug 1946.

Aircraft
B-24, 1943–1945; C-47, 1944 (for CARPET-BAGGER operations); B-17, 1945–1946; B-29, 1946.

Operations
Combat in ETO, 10 Apr–10 May 1944, 14 Aug 1944–25 Apr 1945. CARPETBAGGER operations, May–Aug 1944.

Service Streamers
American Theater.

Campaigns
Air Offensive, Europe; Normandy; Northern France; Rhineland; Ardennes-Alsace; Central Europe.

Decorations
French Croix de Guerre with Palm.

789th BOMB SQUADRON

Lineage
Constituted 789th Bomb Sq (Heavy) on 19 May 1943. Activated on 1 Aug 1943. Redesignated 789th Bomb Sq (Very Heavy) on 5 Aug 1945. Inactivated on 4 Aug 1946.

Assignments
467th Bomb Grp, 1 Aug 1943–4 Aug 1946.

Stations
Wendover Field, UT, 1 Aug 1943; Mountain Home AAFld, ID, 8 Sept 1943; Kearns, UT, 17 Oct 1943; Wendover Field, UT, 2 Nov 1943–12 Feb 1944; Rackheath, England, 11 Mar 1944–12 June 1945; Sioux Falls AAFld, SD, 15 July 1945; Fairmont AAFld, NE, 25 July 1945; Alamogordo AAFld, NM, 22 Aug 1945; Harvard AAFld, NE, 8 Sept 1945; Clovis AAFld, NM, 7 Jan–4 Aug 1946.

Aircraft
B-24, 1943–1945; B-17, 1945–1946; B-29, 1946.

Operations
Combat in ETO, 10 Apr 1944–25 Apr 1945.

Service Streamers
American Theater.

Campaigns
Air Offensive, Europe; Normandy; Northern France; Rhineland; Ardennes-Alsace; Central Europe.

Decorations
None.

790th BOMB SQUADRON

Lineage
Constituted 790th Bomb Sq (Heavy) on 19 May 1943. Activated on 1 Aug 1943. Redesignated 790th Bomb Sq (Very Heavy) on 5 Aug 1945. Inactivated on 4 Aug 1946.

Assignments
467th Bomb Grp, 1 Aug 1943–4 Aug 1946.

Stations
Wendover Field, UT, 1 Aug 1943; Mountain Home AAFld, ID, 8 Sept 1943; Kearns, UT, 17 Oct 1943; Wendover Field, UT, 2 Nov 1943–12 Feb 1944; Rackheath, England, 11 Mar 1944–12 June 1945; Sioux Falls AAFld, SD, 15 July 1945; Fairmont AAFld, NE, 25 July 1945; Alamogordo AAFld, NM, 22 Aug 1945; Harvard AAFld, NE, 8 Sept 1945; Clovis AAFld, NM, 7 Jan–4 Aug 1946.

Aircraft
B-24, 1943–1945; B-17, 1945–1946; B-29, 1946.

Operations
Combat in ETO, 10 Apr 1944–25 Apr 1945.

Service Streamers
American Theater.

Campaigns
Air Offensive, Europe; Normandy; Northern France; Rhineland; Ardennes-Alsace; Central Europe.

Decorations
None.

791st BOMB SQUADRON

Lineage
Constituted 791st Bomb Sq (Heavy) on 19 May 1943. Activated on 1 Aug 1943. Redesignated 791st Bomb Sq (Very Heavy) on 5 Aug 1945. Inactivated on 31 Mar 1946.

Assignments
467th Bomb Grp, 1 Aug 1943–7 Mar 1946; 468th Bomb Grp, 7–31 Mar 1946.

Stations
Wendover Field, UT, 1 Aug 1943; Mountain Home AAFld, ID, 8 Sept 1943; Kearns, UT, 17 Oct 1943; Wendover Field, UT, 2 Nov 1943–12 Feb 1944; Rackheath, England, 11 Mar 1944–12 June 1945; Sioux Falls AAFld, SD, 15 July 1945; Fairmont AAFld, NE, 25 July 1945; Alamogordo AAFld, NM, 22 Aug 1945; Harvard AAFld, NE, 8 Sept 1945; Clovis AAFld, NM, 7–31 Mar 1946.

Aircraft
B-24, 1943–1945; B-17, 1945–1946; B-29, 1946.

Operations
Combat in ETO, 10 Apr 1944–25 Apr 1945.

Service Streamers
American Theater.

Campaigns
Air Offensive, Europe; Normandy; Northern France; Rhineland; Ardennes-Alsace; Central Europe.

Decorations
None.

792d BOMB SQUADRON

Lineage
Constituted 792d Bomb Sq (Heavy) on 19 May 1943. Activated on 1 Aug 1943. Redesignated 792d Bomb Sq (Very Heavy) on 20 Nov 1943. Inactivated on 31 Mar 1946.

Assignments
468th Bomb Grp, 1 Aug 1943–31 Mar 1946.

Stations
Smoky Hill AAFld, KS, 1 Aug 1943–12 Mar 1944; Kharagpur, India, c. 13 Apr 1944–4 May 1945; West Field, Tinian, 7 May–15 Nov 1945; Fort Worth AAFld, TX, 1 Dec 1945; Roswell AAFld, NM, 9 Jan–31 Mar 1946.

Aircraft
B-17, 1943; B-29, 1943–1946.

Operations
Combat in CBI and Western Pacific, 5 June 1944–14 Aug 1945.

Service Streamers
None

Campaigns
India-Burma; Air Offensive, Japan; China Defensive; Western Pacific; Central Burma.

Decorations
Distinguished Unit Citations: Yawata, Japan, 20 Aug 1944; Tokyo and Yokohama, Japan, 23–29 May 1945; Takarazuka, Japan, 24 July 1945.

793d BOMB SQUADRON

Lineage
Constituted 793d Bomb Sq (Heavy) on 19 May 1943. Activated on 1 Aug 1943. Redesignated 793d Bomb Sq (Very Heavy) on 20 Nov 1943. Inactivated on 31 Mar 1946.

Assignments
468th Bomb Grp, 1 Aug 1943–31 Mar 1946.

Stations
Smoky Hill AAFld, KS, 1 Aug 1943–12 Mar 1944; Kharagpur, India, c. 13 Apr 1944–4 May 1945; West Field, Tinian, 7 May–15 Nov 1945; Fort Worth AAFld, TX, 1 Dec 1945; Roswell AAFld, NM, 9 Jan–31 Mar 1946.

Aircraft
B-17, 1943; B-29, 1943–1946.

Operations
Combat in CBI and Western Pacific, 5 June 1944–14 Aug 1945.

Service Streamers
None

Campaigns
India-Burma; Air Offensive, Japan; China Defensive; Western Pacific; Central Burma.

Decorations
Distinguished Unit Citations: Yawata, Japan, 20 Aug 1944; Tokyo and Yokohama, Japan, 23–29 May 1945; Takarazuka, Japan, 24 July 1945.

794th BOMB SQUADRON
Lineage
Constituted 794th Bomb Sq (Heavy) on 19 May 1943. Activated on 1 Aug 1943. Redesignated 794th Bomb Sq (Very Heavy) on 20 Nov 1943; 6th Recon Sq (Very Long Range, Photographic-RCM) on 17 Dec 1945. Inactivated on 31 Mar 1946. Redesignated 6th Strategic Recon Sq (Medium) on 14 Jan 1955. Activated on 24 Jan 1955. Redesignated 6th Bomb Sq (Medium) on 25 Oct 1961. Discontinued, and inactivated, on 25 June 1962. Redesignated 6th Bomb Sq (Heavy), and activated, on 15 Nov 1962. Organized on 1 Feb 1963.

Assignments
468th Bomb Grp, 1 Aug 1943; 311th Recon Wing, 7–31 Mar 1946. 70th Strategic Recon (later Bomb) Wing, 24 Jan 1955–25 June 1962. Strategic Air Command, 15 Nov 1962; 70th Bomb Wing, 1 Feb 1963–.

Stations
Smoky Hill AAFld, KS, 1 Aug 1943–12 Mar 1944; Kharagpur, India, c. 13 Apr 1944–4 May 1945; West Field, Tinian, 7 May–15 Nov 1945; Fort Worth AAFld, TX, 1 Dec 1945; Roswell AAFld, NM, 9 Jan–31 Mar 1946. Little Rock AFB, AR, 24 Jan 1955–25 June 1962. Clinton-Sherman AFB, OK, 1 Feb 1963–.

Aircraft
B-17, 1943; B-29, 1943–1946. RB-47, 1955–1962. B-52, 1963.

Operations
Combat in CBI and Western Pacific, 5 June 1944–14 Aug 1945.

Service Streamers
None

Campaigns
India-Burma; Air Offensive, Japan; China Defensive; Western Pacific; Central Burma.

Decorations
Distinguished Unit Citations: Yawata, Japan, 20 Aug 1944; Tokyo and Yokohama, Japan, 23–29 May 1945; Takarazuka, Japan, 24 July 1945. Air Force Outstanding Unit Award: 15 Feb–30 Dec 1957.

795th BOMB SQUADRON
Lineage
Constituted 795th Bomb Sq (Heavy) on 19 May 1943. Activated on 1 Aug 1943. Redesignated 795th Bomb Sq (Very Heavy) on 20 Nov 1943. Disbanded on 12 Oct 1944.

Assignments
468th Bomb Grp, 1 Aug 1943–12 Oct 1944.

Stations
Smoky Hill AAFld, KS, 1 Aug 1943–12 Mar 1944; Kharagpur, India, c. 13 Apr–12 Oct 1944.

Aircraft
B-17, 1943; B-29, 1943–1944.

Operations
Combat in CBI, 5 June –26 Sept 1944.

Service Streamers
None

Campaigns
India-Burma; Air Offensive, Japan; China Defensive.

Decorations
Distinguished Unit Citation: Yawata, Japan, 20 Aug 1944.

808th BOMB SQUADRON
Lineage
Constituted 808th Bomb Sq (Heavy) on 19 May 1943. Activated on 1 Sept 1943. Redesignated 808th Bomb Sq (Very Heavy) on 1 Dec 1943. Disbanded on 1 Apr 1944.

Assignments
472d Bomb Grp, 1 Sept 1943–1 Apr 1944.

Stations
Smoky Hill AAFld, KS, 1 Sept 1943; Clovis AAFld, NM, c. 8 Dec 1943–1 Apr 1944.

Aircraft
B-17, 1943–1944; B-29, 1943–1944.

Operations
Replacement training, Nov 1943–Apr 1944.

Service Streamers
None.

Campaigns
None.

Decorations
None.

809th BOMB SQUADRON
Lineage
Constituted 809th Bomb Sq (Heavy) on 19 May 1943. Activated on 1 Sept 1943. Redesignated 809th Bomb Sq (Very Heavy) on 1 Dec 1943. Disbanded on 1 Apr 1944.

Assignments
472d Bomb Grp, 1 Sept 1943–1 Apr 1944.

Stations
Smoky Hill AAFld, KS, 1 Sept 1943; Clovis AAFld, NM, c. 8 Dec 1943–1 Apr 1944.

Aircraft
B-17, 1943–1944; B-29, 1943–1944.

Operations
Replacement training, Nov 1943–Apr 1944.

Service Streamers
None.

Campaigns
None.

Decorations
None.

828th BOMB SQUADRON
Lineage
Constituted 828th Bomb Sq (Heavy) on 14 Sept 1943. Activated on 20 Sept 1943. Redesignated 828th Bomb Sq (Very Heavy) on 5 Aug 1945. Inactivated on 4 Aug 1946.

Assignments
485th Bomb Grp, 20 Sept 1943–4 Aug 1946.

Stations
Fairmont AAFld, NE, 20 Sept 1943–11 Mar 1944; Venosa, Italy, c. 30 Apr 1944–c. 9 May 1945; Sioux City AAB, IA, 24 July 1945; Smoky Hill AAFld, KS, 8 Sept 1945–4 Aug 1946.

Aircraft
B-24, 1943–1945; B-29, 1945–1946.

Operations
Combat in MTO and ETO, 10 May 1944–25 Apr 1945.

Service Streamers
American Theater.

Campaigns
Air Offensive, Europe; Rome-Arno; Normandy; Northern France; Southern France; North Apennines; Rhineland; Central Europe; Po Valley; Air Combat, EAME Theater.

Decorations
Distinguished Unit Citation: Vienna, Austria, 26 June 1944.

829th BOMB SQUADRON
Lineage
Constituted 829th Bomb Sq (Heavy) on 14 Sept 1943. Activated on 20 Sept 1943. Redesignated 829th Bomb Sq (Very Heavy) on 5 Aug 1945. Inactivated on 4 Aug 1946.

Assignments
485th Bomb Grp, 20 Sept 1943–4 Aug 1946.

Stations

Fairmont AAFld, NE, 20 Sept 1943–11 Mar 1944; Venosa, Italy, c. 30 Apr 1944–c. 9 May 1945; Sioux Falls AAFld, SD, 30 May 1945; Sioux City AAB, IA, 24 July 1945; Smoky Hill AAFld, KS, 8 Sept 1945–4 Aug 1946.

Aircraft

B-24, 1943–1945; B-29, 1945–1946.

Operations

Combat in MTO and ETO, 10 May 1944–25 Apr 1945.

Service Streamers

American Theater.

Campaigns

Air Offensive, Europe; Rome-Arno; Normandy; Northern France; Southern France; North Apennines; Rhineland; Central Europe; Po Valley; Air Combat, EAME Theater.

Decorations

Distinguished Unit Citation: Vienna, Austria, 26 June 1944.

830th BOMB SQUADRON

Lineage

Constituted 830th Bomb Sq (Heavy) on 14 Sept 1943. Activated on 20 Sept 1943. Redesignated 830th Bomb Sq (Very Heavy) on 5 Aug 1945. Redesignated 830th Bomb Sq (Medium) on 2 July 1948.

Assignments

485th Bomb Grp, 20 Sept 1943; 509th Composite (later Bomb) Grp, 6 May 1946; 509th Bomb Wing, 16 June 1952–.

Stations

Fairmont AAFld, NE, 20 Nov 1943–11 Mar 1944; Venosa, Italy, c. 30 Apr 1944–c. 9 May 1945; Sioux Falls AAFld, SD, 30 May 1945; Sioux City AAB, IA, 24 July 1945; Smoky Hill AAFld, KS, 8 Sept 1945; Roswell AAFld, NM, 23 June 1946; Pease AFB, NH, 1 July 1958–.

Aircraft

B-24, 1943–1945; B-29, 1945–1952; B-50, 1951–1955; B-47, 1955–.

Operations

Combat in MTO and ETO, 10 May 1944–25 Apr 1945.

Service Streamers

American Theater.

Campaigns

Air Offensive, Europe; Rome-Arno; Normandy; Northern France; Southern France; North Apennines; Rhineland; Central Europe; Po Valley; Air Combat, EAME Theater.

Decorations

Distinguished Unit Citation: Vienna, Austria, 26 June 1944.

844th BOMB SQUADRON

Lineage

Constituted 844th Bomb Sq (Heavy) on 14 Sept 1943. Activated on 1 Oct 1943. Redesignated 844th Bomb Sq (Very Heavy) on 17 Mar 1945. Inactivated on 17 Oct 1945.

Assignments

489th Bomb Grp, 1 Oct 1943–17 Oct 1945.

Stations

Wendover Field, UT, 1 Oct 1943–3 Apr 1944; Halesworth, England, c. 22 Apr–29 Nov 1944; Bradley Field, CT, 13 Dec 1944; Lincoln AAFld, NE, 17 Dec 1944; Great Bend AAFld, KS, 23 Feb 1945; Davis-Monthan Field, AZ, 3 Apr 1945; Fairmont AAFld, NE, 25 July 1945; Ft Lawton, WA, 23 Aug 1945; March Field, CA, 2 Sept–17 Oct 1945.

Aircraft

B-24, 1943–1944; B-29, 1945.

Operations

Combat in ETO, 30 May–10 Nov 1944.

Service Streamers

American Theater.

Campaigns

Air Offensive, Europe; Normandy; Northern France; Rhineland.

Decorations

None

845th BOMB SQUADRON

Lineage

Constituted 845th Bomb Sq (Heavy) on 14 Sept 1943. Activated on 1 Oct 1943. Redesignated 845th Bomb Sq (Very Heavy) on 17 Mar 1945. Inactivated on 17 Oct 1945.

Assignments

489th Bomb Grp, 1 Oct 1943–17 Oct 1945.

Stations

Wendover Field, UT, 1 Oct 1943–3 Apr 1944; Halesworth, England, c. 22 Apr–28 Nov 1944; Bradley Field, CT, 13 Dec 1944; Lincoln AAFld, NE, 17 Dec 1944; Great Bend AAFld, KS, 23 Feb 1945; Davis-Monthan Field, AZ, 3 Apr 1945; Fairmont AAFld, NE, 25 July 1945; Ft Lawton, WA, 23 Aug 1945; March Field, CA, 2 Sept–17 Oct 1945.

Aircraft

B-24, 1943–1944; B-29, 1945.

Operations

Combat in ETO, 30 May–10 Nov 1944.

Service Streamers

American Theater.

Campaigns

Air Offensive, Europe; Normandy; Northern France; Rhineland.

Decorations

None

846th BOMB SQUADRON

Lineage

Constituted 846th Bomb Sq (Heavy) on 14 Sept 1943. Activated on 1 Oct 1943. Redesignated 846th Bomb Sq (Very Heavy) on 17 Mar 1945. Inactivated on 17 Oct 1945.

Assignments

489th Bomb Grp, 1 Oct 1943–17 Oct 1945.

Stations

Wendover Field, UT, 1 Oct 1943–3 Apr 1944; Halesworth, England, c. 22 Apr–29 Nov 1944; Bradley Field, CT, 13 Dec 1944; Lincoln AAFld, NE, 17 Dec 1944; Great Bend AAFld, KS, 23 Feb 1945; Davis-Monthan Field, AZ, 3 Apr 1945; Fairmont AAFld, NE, 25 July 1945; Ft Lawton, WA, 23 Aug 1945; March Field, CA, 2 Sept–17 Oct 1945.

Aircraft

B-24, 1943–1944; B-29, 1945.

Operations

Combat in ETO, 30 May–10 Nov 1944.

Service Streamers

American Theater.

Campaigns

Air Offensive, Europe; Normandy; Northern France; Rhineland.

Decorations

None

847th BOMB SQUADRON

Lineage

Constituted 32d Recon Sq (Heavy) on 28 Jan 1942. Redesignated 421st Bomb Sq (Heavy) on 22 Apr 1942. Activated on 15 July 1942. Redesignated: 20th Antisubmarine Sq (Heavy) on 8 Feb 1943; 847th Bomb Sq (Heavy) on 5 Oct 1943. Inactivated on 28 Mar 1945.

Assignments

304th Bomb Grp, 15 July 1942; Newfoundland Base Command, 6 Nov 1942; AAF Antisubmarine Command, 8 Feb 1943; 489th Bomb Grp, 13 Oct 1943–28 Mar 1945.

Stations

Salt Lake City AAB, UT, 15 July 1942; Geiger Field, WA, 15 Sept 1942; Ephrata AAB, WA, 1 Oct 1942; St Johns, Newfoundland, 29 Oct 1942; Mitchel Field, NY, 25 June 1943; Casper AAFld, WY, 13 Oct 1943; Wendover Field, UT, 16 Dec 1943–3 Apr 1944; Halesworth, England, c. 22 Apr–29 Nov 1944; Bradley Field, CT, 13 Dec 1944; Lincoln AAFld, NE, 17 Dec 1944; Great Bend AAFld, KS, 23 Feb–28 Mar 1945.

Aircraft

DB-7, 1942–1943; A-20, 1942–1943; OA-12, 1942–1943; B-17, 1942–1943; B-24, 1943–1944; B-29, 1945.

Operations

Antisubmarine patrols, 1942–1943. Combat in ETO, 30 May–10 Nov 1944.

Service Streamers
None

Campaigns
Antisubmarine, American Theater; Air Offensive, Europe; Normandy; Northern France; Rhineland.

Decorations
None

869th BOMB SQUADRON

Lineage
Constituted 869th Bomb Sq (Very Heavy) on 19 Nov 1943. Activated on 20 Nov 1943. Inactivated on 31 Mar 1946.

Assignments
497th Bomb Grp, 20 Nov 1943–31 Mar 1946.

Stations
El Paso Mun Aprt, TX, 20 Nov 1943; Clovis AAFld, NM, 1 Dec 1943; Pratt AAFld, KS, 13 Apr–17 July 1944; Isley Field, Saipan, 17 Sept 1944–1 Nov 1945; Camp Stoneman, CA, 14 Nov 1945; March Field, CA, c. 26 Nov 1945; MacDill Field, FL, c. 5 Jan–31 Mar 1946.

Aircraft
B-17, 1944; B-29, 1944–1946.

Operations
Combat in Western Pacific, 28 Oct 1944–14 Aug 1945.

Service Streamers
None

Campaigns
Air Offensive, Japan; Eastern Mandates; Western Pacific.

Decorations
Distinguished Unit Citations: Japan, 27 Jan 1945; Japan, 26 July–2 Aug 1945.

870th BOMB SQUADRON

Lineage
Constituted 870th Bomb Sq (Very Heavy) on 19 Nov 1943. Activated on 20 Nov 1943. Inactivated on 31 Mar 1946.

Assignments
497th Bomb Grp, 20 Nov 1943–31 Mar 1946.

Stations
El Paso Mun Aprt, TX, 20 Nov 1943; Clovis AAFld, NM, 1 Dec 1943; Pratt AAFld, KS, 13 Apr–18 July 1944; Isley Field, Saipan, 17 Sept 1944–1 Nov 1945; Camp Stoneman, CA, 14 Nov 1945; March Field, CA, c. 26 Nov 1945; MacDill Field, FL, c. 5 Jan–31 Mar 1946.

Aircraft
B-17, 1944; B-29, 1944–1946.

Operations
Combat in Western Pacific, 1 Nov 1944–14 Aug 1945.

Service Streamers
None

Campaigns
Air Offensive, Japan; Eastern Mandates; Western Pacific.

Decorations
Distinguished Unit Citations: Japan, 27 Jan 1945; Japan, 26 July–2 Aug 1945.

871st BOMB SQUADRON

Lineage
Constituted 871st Bomb Sq (Very Heavy) on 19 Nov 1943. Activated on 20 Nov 1943. Inactivated on 7 Mar 1946.

Assignments
497th Bomb Grp, 20 Nov 1943–7 Mar 1946.

Stations
El Paso Mun Aprt, TX, 20 Nov 1943; Clovis AAFld, NM, 1 Dec 1943; Pratt AAFld, KS, 13 Apr–18 July 1944; Isley Field, Saipan, 17 Sept 1944–1 Nov 1945; Camp Stoneman, CA, 14 Nov 1945; March Field, CA, c. 26 Nov 1945; MacDill Field, FL, c. 5 Jan–7 Mar 1946.

Aircraft
B-17, 1944; B-29, 1944–1946.

Operations
Combat in Western Pacific, 2 Nov 1944–14 Aug 1945.

Service Streamers
None

Campaigns
Air Offensive, Japan; Eastern Mandates; Western Pacific.

Decorations
Distinguished Unit Citations: Japan, 27 Jan 1945; Japan, 26 July–2 Aug 1945.

872d BOMB SQUADRON

Lineage
Constituted 872d Bomb Sq (Very Heavy) on 19 Nov 1943. Activated on 20 Nov 1943. Inactivated on 10 May 1944. Activated on 19 Sept 1944. Inactivated on 4 Jan 1946.

Assignments
497th Bomb Grp, 20 Nov 1943–10 May 1944. 382d Bomb Grp, 19 Sept 1944–4 Jan 1946.

Stations
El Paso Mun Aprt, TX, 20 Nov 1943; Clovis AAFld, NM, 1 Dec 1943; Pratt AAFld, KS, 13 Apr–10 May 1944. Dalhart AAFld, TX, 19 Sept 1944; Smoky Hill AAFld, KS, 11 Dec 1944–1 Aug 1945; Guam, 8 Sept 1945 (ground echelon only; air echelon remained in US until inactivation); Tinian, c. Oct–15 Dec 1945; Camp Anza, CA, 28 Dec 1945–4 Jan 1946.

Aircraft
B-17, B-24, and B-25, 1944; B-29, 1945–1946.

Operations
No Combat

Service Streamers
American Theater; Asiatic-Pacific Theater.

Campaigns
None

Decorations
None

873d BOMB SQUADRON

Lineage
Constituted 873d Bomb Sq (Very Heavy) on 19 Nov 1943. Activated on 20 Nov 1943. Inactivated on 4 Aug 1946. Redesignated 873d Tactical Missile Sq, and activated, on 16 Sept 1960. Organized on 8 Feb 1961.

Assignments
498th Bomb Grp, 20 Nov 1943–4 Aug 1946. Pacific Air Forces, 16 Sept 1960; 498th Tactical Missile Grp, 8 Feb 1961–.

Stations
Clovis AAFld, NM, 20 Nov 1943; Great Bend AAFld, KS, 13 Apr–16 July 1944; Isley Field, Saipan, 7 Sept 1944–2 Nov 1945; March Field, CA, c. 7 Dec 1945: MacDill Field, FL, 5 Jan–4 Aug 1946. Kadena, Okinawa, 8 Feb 1961–.

Aircraft and Missiles
B-17, 1944; B-29, 1944–1946. Mace, 1961–.

Operations
Combat in Western Pacific, 28 Oct 1944–13 Aug 1945.

Service Streamers
American Theater

Campaigns
Air Offensive, Japan; Eastern Mandates; Western Pacific.

Decorations
Distinguished Unit Citations: Japan, 13 Dec 1944; Japan, 1–7 June 1945. Air Force Outstanding Unit Award: 8 Feb 1961–29 May 1963.

874TH BOMB SQUADRON

Lineage
Constituted 874th Bomb Sq on 19 Nov 1943. Activated on 20 Nov 1943. Inactivated on 4 Aug 1946. Redesignated 874th Tactical Missile Sq, and activated, on 25 April 1961. Organized on 8 Sept 1961.

Assignments
498th Bomb Grp, 20 Nov 1943–4 Aug 1946. Pacific Air Forces, 25 Apr 1961; 498th Tactical Missile Grp, 8 Sept 1961–.

Stations
Clovis AAFld, NM, 20 Nov 1943; Great Bend AAFld, KS, 13 Apr–16 July 1944; Isley Field, Saipan, 7 Sept 1944–1 Nov 1945; March Field, CA, c. 7 Dec 1945: MacDill Field, FL, 5 Jan–4 Aug 1946. Kadena, Okinawa, 8 Sept 1961–.

Aircraft and Missiles
B-17, 1944; B-29, 1944–1946. Mace, 1961–.

Operations
Combat in Western Pacific, 28 Oct 1944–13 Aug 1945.

Service Streamers
American Theater

Campaigns
Air Offensive, Japan; Eastern Mandates; Western Pacific.

Decorations
Distinguished Unit Citations: Japan, 13 Dec 1944; Japan, 1–7 June 1945. Air Force Outstanding Unit Award: 8 Feb 1961–29 May 1963.

875th BOMB SQUADRON
Lineage
Constituted 875th Bomb Sq (Very Heavy) on 19 Nov 1943. Activated on 20 Nov 1943. Inactivated on 4 Aug 1946.

Assignments
498th Bomb Grp, 20 Nov 1943–4 Aug 1946.

Stations
Clovis AAFld, NM, 20 Nov 1943; Great Bend AAFld, KS, 13 Apr–16 July 1944; Isley Field, Saipan, 7 Sept 1944–2 Nov 1945; March Field, CA, c. 7 Dec 1945: MacDill Field, FL, 5 Jan–4 Aug 1946.

Aircraft
B-17, 1944; RB-24, 1944; B-29, 1944–1946.

Operations
Combat in Western Pacific, 28 Oct 1944–13 Aug 1945.

Service Streamers
American Theater

Campaigns
Air Offensive, Japan; Eastern Mandates; Western Pacific.

Decorations
Distinguished Unit Citations: Japan, 13 Dec 1944; Japan, 1–7 June 1945.

876th BOMB SQUADRON
Lineage
Constituted 876th Bomb Sq (Very Heavy) on 19 Nov 1943. Activated on 20 Nov 1943. Inactivated on 10 May 1944. Activated on 28 Aug 1944. Inactivated on 29 Dec 1945.

Assignments
498th Bomb Grp, 20 Nov 1943–10 May 1944. 383d Bomb Grp, 28 Aug 1944–29 Dec 1945.

Stations
Clovis AAFld, NM, 20 Nov 1943; Great Bend AAFld, KS, 13 Apr–10 May 1944. Dalhart AAFld, TX 28 Aug 1944; Walker AAFld, KS, 14 Jan–11 Aug 1945; Tinian, 12 Sept–c. 14 Dec 1945; Camp Anza, CA, 29 Dec 1945.

Aircraft
B-17, 1944; B-29, 1944. B-29, 1945.

Operations
No Combat

Service Streamers
American Theater; Asiatic-Pacific Theater

Campaigns
None

Decorations
None.

877th BOMB SQUADRON
Lineage
Constituted 877th Bomb Sq (Very Heavy) on 19 Nov 1943. Activated on 20 Nov 1943. Inactivated on 16 Feb 1946.

Assignments
499th Bomb Grp, 20 Nov 1943–16 Feb 1946.

Stations
Davis-Monthan Field, AZ, 20 Nov 1943; Smoky Hill AAFld, KS, 1 Dec 1943; Clovis AAFld, NM, 11 Feb 1944; Smoky Hill AAFld, KS, 8 Apr–22 July 1944; Isley Field, Saipan, 22 Sept 1944–c. Nov 1945; March Field, CA, c. Nov 1945–16 Feb 1946.

Aircraft
B-17, 1944; B-29, 1944–1946.

Operations
Combat in Western Pacific, 24 Nov 1944–14 Aug 1945.

Service Streamers
None

Campaigns
Air Offensive, Japan; Western Pacific.

Decorations
Distinguished Unit Citations: Nagoya, Japan, 23 Jan 1945; Japan, 22–28 Apr 1945.

878th BOMB SQUADRON
Lineage
Constituted 878th Bomb Sq (Very Heavy) on 19 Nov 1943. Activated on 20 Nov 1943. Inactivated on 16 Feb 1946.

Assignments
499th Bomb Grp, 20 Nov 1943–16 Feb 1946.

Stations
Davis-Monthan Field, AZ, 20 Nov 1943; Smoky Hill AAFld, KS, 1 Dec 1943; Clovis AAFld, NM, 11 Feb 1944; Smoky Hill AAFld, KS, 8 Apr–22 July 1944; Isley Field, Saipan, 22 Sept 1944–c. Nov 1945; March Field, CA, c. Nov 1945–16 Feb 1946.

Aircraft
B-17, 1944; B-29, 1944–1946.

Operations
Combat in Western Pacific, 24 Nov 1944–14 Aug 1945.

Service Streamers
None

Campaigns
Air Offensive, Japan; Western Pacific.

Decorations
Distinguished Unit Citations: Nagoya, Japan, 23 Jan 1945; Japan, 22–28 Apr 1945.

879th BOMB SQUADRON
Lineage
Constituted 879th Bomb Sq (Very Heavy) on 19 Nov 1943. Activated on 20 Nov 1943. Inactivated on 16 Feb 1946.

Assignments
499th Bomb Grp, 20 Nov 1943–16 Feb 1946.

Stations
Davis-Monthan Field, AZ, 20 Nov 1943; Smoky Hill AAFld, KS, 1 Dec 1943; Clovis AAFld, NM, 11 Feb 1944; Smoky Hill AAFld, KS, 8 Apr–22 July 1944; Isley Field, Saipan, 22 Sept 1944–c. Nov 1945; March Field, CA, c. Nov 1945–16 Feb 1946.

Aircraft
B-17, 1944; B-29, 1944–1946.

Operations
Combat in Western Pacific, 24 Nov 1944–14 Aug 1945.

Service Streamers
None

Campaigns
Air Offensive, Japan; Western Pacific.

Decorations
Distinguished Unit Citations: Nagoya, Japan, 23 Jan 1945; Japan, 22–28 Apr 1945.

880th BOMB SQUADRON
Lineage
Constituted 880th Bomb Sq (Very Heavy) on 19 Nov 1943. Activated on 20 Nov 1943. Inactivated on 10 May 1944. Activated on 28 Aug 1944. Inactivated on 3 Jan 1946.

Assignments
499th Bomb Grp, 20 Nov 1943–10 May 1944. 383d Bomb Grp, 28 Aug 1944–3 Jan 1946.

Stations
Davis-Monthan Field, AZ, 20 Nov 1943; Smoky Hill AAFld, KS, 1 Dec 1943; Clovis AAFld, NM, 11 Feb 1944; Smoky Hill AAFld, KS, 8 Apr–10 May 1944. Dalhart AAFld, TX, 28 Aug 1944; Walker AAFld, KS, 14 Jan–11 Aug 1945; Tinian, 12 Sept–19 Dec 1945; Camp Anza, CA, 2–3 Jan 1946.

Aircraft
B-17, 1944; B-29, 1944. B-29, 1945.

Operations
No Combat.

Service Streamers
American Theater; Asiatic-Pacific Theater.

Campaigns
None.

Decorations
None.

881st BOMB SQUADRON
Lineage
Constituted 881st Bomb Sq (Very Heavy) on 19 Nov 1943. Activated on 20 Nov 1943. Inactivated on 17 Jan 1946.

Assignments
500th Bomb Grp, 20 Nov 1943–17 Jan 1946.

Stations
Gowen Field, ID, 20 Nov 1943; Clovis AAFld, NM, c. 16 Dec 1943; Walker AAFld, KS, 16 Apr–23 July 1944; Isley Field, Saipan, 19 Sept 1944–15 Nov 1945; March Field, CA, 29 Nov 1945–17 Jan 1946.

Aircraft
B-17, 1944; B-29, 1944–1945.

Operations
Combat in Western Pacific, 11 Nov 1944–14 Aug 1945; subsequently flew supplies to POW camps in Japan, Korea, and Formosa.

Service Streamers
None

Campaigns
Air Offensive, Japan; Eastern Mandates; Western Pacific; China Offensive.

Decorations
Distinguished Unit Citations: Nagoya, Japan, 23 Jan 1945; Japan, 15–20 June 1945.

882d BOMB SQUADRON
Lineage
Constituted 882d Bomb Sq (Very Heavy) on 19 Nov 1943. Activated on 20 Nov 1943. Inactivated on 17 Jan 1946.

Assignments
500th Bomb Grp, 20 Nov 1943–17 Jan 1946.

Stations
Gowen Field, ID, 20 Nov 1943; Clovis AAFld, NM, c. 16 Dec 1943; Walker AAFld, KS, 16 Apr–23 July 1944; Isley Field, Saipan, 19 Sept 1944–15 Nov 1945; March Field, CA, 29 Nov 1945–17 Jan 1946.

Aircraft
B-17, 1944; B-29, 1944–1945.

Operations
Combat in Western Pacific, 11 Nov 1944–14 Aug 1945; subsequently flew supplies to POW camps in Japan, Korea, and Formosa.

Service Streamers
None

Campaigns
Air Offensive, Japan; Eastern Mandates; Western Pacific; China Offensive.

Decorations
Distinguished Unit Citations: Nagoya, Japan, 23 Jan 1945; Japan, 15–20 June 1945.

883d BOMB SQUADRON
Lineage
Constituted 883d Bomb Sq (Very Heavy) on 19 Nov 1943. Activated on 20 Nov 1943. Inactivated on 17 Jan 1946.

Assignments
500th Bomb Grp, 20 Nov 1943–17 Jan 1946.

Stations
Gowen Field, ID, 20 Nov 1943; Clovis AAFld, NM, c. 16 Dec 1943; Walker AAFld, KS, 16 Apr–23 July 1944; Isley Field, Saipan, 19 Sept 1944–15 Nov 1945; March Field, CA, 29 Nov 1945–17 Jan 1946.

Aircraft
B-17, 1944; B-29, 1944–1945.

Operations
Combat in Western Pacific, 11 Nov 1944–14 Aug 1945; subsequently flew supplies to POW camps in Japan, Korea, and Formosa.

Service Streamers
None

Campaigns
Air Offensive, Japan; Eastern Mandates; Western Pacific; China Offensive.

Decorations
Distinguished Unit Citations: Nagoya, Japan, 23 Jan 1945; Japan, 15–20 June 1945.

884th BOMB SQUADRON
Lineage
Constituted 884th Bomb Sq (Very Heavy) on 19 Nov 1943. Activated on 20 Nov 1943. Inactivated on 10 May 1944. Activated on 28 Aug 1944. Inactivated on 29 Dec 1945.

Assignments
500th Bomb Grp, 20 Nov 1943–10 May 1944. 383d Bomb Grp, 28 Aug 1944–29 Dec 1945.

Stations
Gowen Field, ID, 20 Nov 1943; Clovis AAFld, NM, 1 Dec 1943; Walker AAFld, KS, 16 Apr–10 May 1944; Dalhart AAFld, TX, 28 Aug 1944; Walker AAFld, KS, 14 Jan–11 Aug 1945; Tinian, 12 Sept–c. 14 Dec 1945; Camp Anza, CA, 29 Dec 1945.

Aircraft
B-17, 1944; B-29, 1944. B-29, 1945.

Operations
No Combat

Service Streamers
American Theater; Asiatic-Pacific Theater.

Campaigns
None.

Decorations
None.

*Histories of the Squadrons who flew the B-29 are from the publication **World War II Combat Squadrons of the United States**. Smithmark Publishers, Inc., New York. 1992.*

A formation of B-29s from the 19th Bomb Group over the North Field in Guam. (Courtesy of James McFalls)

Crew of "Big Boots" in Fairmont, Nebraska in 1944. (l. to r.) Standing: Finn, James, Bailey, Tomes, Goldstein, and Doherty. Kneeling: Vondenbenken, Simons, Sahl, and Callahan. (Courtesy of Tom Doherty)

Time for a little good food, drink and relaxation. (Courtesy of Aubrey Traweek)

VETERANS OF THE B-29
"SUPERFORTRESS"

The crew of the B-29 "Queenie". (Courtesy of Bob Boles)

*This chapter represents B-29 veterans that were given an invitation to participate in this 50th anniversary book.
Unfortunately it was impossible to contact every B-29 veteran.*

THOMAS D. ADAMS JR., was born March 16, 1921 in Radford, VA; raised in Roanoke, VA and graduated high school in 1939. Employed at Naval Air Station, Norfolk, VA until 1941. During school years he worked part-time for pilots at Roanoke Airport and later Woodrum Field to pay for flight training. Had solo flight in 1938.

Entered the service and enlisted in Army Air Corps in August 1941 at Norfolk, VA. Units served through 1966: Air Corps Technical Training Command; B-29 Flight Engineer Ground and Flight Training; 19th BG, 28th Sqdn., Crew #14, Aircraft #M-2 *The City of Trenton*; 509th BG; AF Tech. Training Schools; 18th Fighter BG; Korean Conflict; Clark AFB, P.I.; Air Defense Command (438th and 323rd Fighter Interceptor Sqdns.); Tactical Air Command 401st TFW.

Crew #14 was assembled October 1945, Lincoln AB, NE; trained Pyote AB, TX and Clovis Field, NM. Received new B-29 at Kearney AB, NE and flew to Guam A/A in April 1945. He flew 24 missions.

Training locations: Keesler Field, Biloxi; Chanute Field, Rantoul; Lowry Field, Denver; Pyote Army Air Base, TX; Clovis Army Air Base, NM; and Kearney Army Air Base, NE.

Participated in air war over Japan (24 sorties); Korean War's Pusan Perimeter; and the Chinese Offensives and Counter Offensives. Was discharged May 1945 as master sergeant to accept direct appointment Flight Off., mustered out in 1946. Re-enlisted and retired April 1966 with the rank CWO4.

Employed by service contractors at NASA's John Stennis Space Center, MS. Married to Esther since June 1943 and has two daughters and one son.

BEN R. ALFORD, was born in Morehead City, NC on Jan. 14, 1919; drafted in the U.S. Army June 1941 and immediately re-enlisted three years in USAAC. Attended Officers Candidate School, specializing in supply. Served two and a half years with 417th Bombardment Sqdn. in Caribbean. In 1944 was assigned to the 93rd Bomb Sqdn., 19th BG as Group Supply Officer for impending move overseas to Guam. Was responsible for marking and moving all group supplies and equipment from Great Bend, KS to POE Seattle, WA.

Arriving overseas, Lt. Alford was promoted to captain, assigned to HQ 19th BG as technical supply officer. During this period of time every effort was being made to keep all aircraft flying. Capt. Alford set up a supply chain that greatly helped in this effort, and by negotiating with the Navy procured many parts that were on the Air Force critical list.

Separated from the service, December 1945 and remained in AF Reserve until serving in U.S. Army Field Artillery during Korean War. Always self-employed, owned and operated printing and office supply business for 25 years, then being a manufacturer's representative for 22 years representing 25 different companies.

Has lived in Morehead City, NC since December 1945 where he is still very active. He is married with five children and eight grandchildren.

LELAND E. ASHBY JR., was born Eldorado, IL on Feb. 17, 1924. Began aviation cadet pilot training Dec. 8, 1942, graduated Aug. 4, 1944. Completed B-17 transition training Nov. 1, 1944. Began B-29 training with newly formed crew Dec. 18, 1944 at Alamogordo Army Air Field, NM.

On April 20, 1945 he and crew proceeded to unit of assignment on Guam. Was assigned to 459th Sqdn., 330th BG, 314th BW, 20th AF. The crew flew 21 combat missions over the Japanese mainland. First raid was on the oil refineries and tank farms of Otake. The target was completely destroyed and the fire generated was unbelievable.

Released from active duty March 21, 1946 and assigned to [ ] Forces. Recalled to active duty for the Korean War and flew B-29 and B-50 aircraft. Returned to active reserve status until retirement Aug. 27, 1976 with the rank of colonel.

Retired from agriculture education career June 1982. Presently keeps busy watching his trees grow at Pine Meadows Tree Farm near Golconda, IL. He produces Christmas trees and other forest products. In 1988 his tree farm was judged the outstanding tree farm in the North Central Regional U.S.

Married Joyce and has a son, Douglas, and grandson, Chad.

ROBERT E. AXTHELM, was born Menlo, IA on Sept. 27, 1924. He enlisted at Perry, IA on Aug. 19, 1943. Commissioned navigator Hondo, TX June 1944. Radar at Boca Raton, FL. Joined 314th Wing, 29th BG, 6th Sqdn. at Pratt, KS and on to 20th AF on Guam February 1945. Completed 35 missions over Japan with Roach's crew #11 on *The Natural*.

Was awarded Air Medal with three clusters, Distinguished Flying Cross with cluster. Was on way home when A-bomb was dropped. Discharged as first lieutenant in November 1945 and returned to Iowa State College the same day. Received BS in engineering in 1948. Married Jean and raised family of three: Christine, Joan and David.

Embarked on sales career in electronic components. Received MBA from University of Dayton. Retired in San Diego in 1992. Sang in quartette and played in band on Guam. He still sings in choirs today.

CHARLES D. BACON, was born April 21, 1920 in Sharon, PA.

He enlisted in the AAF on Jan. 14, 1942 in Pittsburgh, PA. Basic training was at Biloxi, MS; Mechanics School at Glenn L. Martin, Baltimore, MD; then shipped to David Field, Panama where he joined the 45th Bomb Sqdn. Went on to Galapagos, Guatemala and back to Howard Field, Panama.

In July 1943, he arrived at Pratt, KS for combat training; February 1944, was deployed by ship to Casablanca and ATC to Chakulia. Flew many trips over the Hump and on to bombing raids over Japan, with one particularly memorable bombing raid over Tokyo at 9,000 feet. He flew as right gunner on Jack Ledford's crew.

Left the 40th Group at Tinian in July 1945 as staff sergeant. Was mustered out at Santa Ana, CA on Oct. 15, 1945.

He returned to Pennsylvania to resume his life as a machinist. In July 1955, he went to Cleveland, OH and worked as a die sinker for Alcoa until October 1968 when he took a job managing a mobile home park in Ft. Lauderdale, FL. He is semi-retired in the same park and doing repair work on the mobile homes.

Married June Aubel in November 1943 at Pratt, KS. They have two married daughters and four grandchildren.

ROBERT E. BATES, was born in St. Louis, MO on Aug. 29, 1921. He entered the Aviation Cadet Maintenance Engineering course June 1943 at Boca Raton, FL; graduated and commissioned February 1944 at Yale University. Was assigned B-29 ground/flying training at Seattle and Lowry Field, rated aerial observer (aerial engineer). Assigned to 9th BG, McCook, NE from August 1944-December 1944.

Group was stationed at Tinian, Marianas Islands from January 1945-September 1945. Made first lieutenant May 1945 and squadron flight engineer June 1945. On lead B-29 on first Japan-U.S. non-stop flight on Sept. 19, 1945. Flew 33 missions.

Received two Distinguished Flying Crosses, four Air Medals, two Distinguished Unit Citations and four Battle Stars. Was released to inactive duty Nov. 10, 1945. Recalled to active duty December 1950 at Rapid City AFB. Transferred to HQ AM at Wright-Patterson AFB as chief, guided missiles section. Discharged in May 1952.

Married Ann Liggett in July 1946, has three children. Employed 30 years with Ford Motor Co., including 11 years in Europe. He retired January 1978.

CHARLES FRANK BEARD, was born in St. Louis, MO on May 17, 1925. He enlisted in the Navy September 1943; served 30 months in construction battalion in Pacific Theater.

Enlisted in Air Force September 1949 and trained as aircraft instrument mechanic at Chanute AFB.

Was assigned to 19th BW, 28th Sqdn. on Guam, April 1950. Wing transferred to Okinawa at start of Korean War. Subsequent assignments as NCOIC in charge of squadron instrument shops were: B-29 Crew Training Wing, Randolph AFB, 6th Troop Carrier Sqdn. (C-124) Tachikawa, Japan, 2nd Field Maintenance Sqdn. (B-47) Hunter AFB, Georgia, 7272nd Air Base Wing (F-100) Wheelus AFB, Tripoli, Libya. He cross trained to Maintenance Data Analysis at Wheelus and subsequently retired at Holloman AFB, Alamogordo, NM in grade E-6 in October 1967.

Final employment with Hamilton Aircraft Co., Hughes Aircraft Co., Duval Copper Mine on industrial instrumentation, Tucson, AZ. Beard and his wife retired to lake front home near Titus, AL in August 1987. He owns three boats and has many relatives living near.

CAMERON ROBERT BENEDICT (BOB), was born May 15, 1920 in Buffalo, NY. He enlisted in April 1942 and served in Aviation Cadets and later in 45th Sqdn., 40th Group in Kansas, then Chakulia, India.

Trained at Maxwell Field, Childress, TX and Monroe, LA. Went down over Rangoon, Burma on Dec. 14, 1944 and captured by Japanese. Was in Jap prison until April 28, 1945.

Separated from the service in 1945 and discharged in 1950 with rank of second lieutenant.

Lived in Elmira, NY and had his own business until 1960 when he moved to Orlando, FL. Sold advertising for the local newspaper there for nearly 20 years, then retired. He and his wife enjoy spending time with family and traveling.

ROBERT V. BERRY, was born Aug. 11, 1920 on a farm near Iowa City, IA. He joined the Air Force in August 1942. In April 1944 he volunteered to become a B-29 flight engineer and received nine months training on bases in Colorado and New Mexico.

He joined Joe Dunn's crew at Clovis, NM in November 1944. The crew picked up a new B-29 at Harrington, KS in February 1945. They arrived at North Field, Tinian Island on March 9. They were the second replacement crew to arrive at the 39th Sqdn., 6th BG, 313th Wing.

Their new plane was given to a lead crew and a war-weary was assigned to the replacement crew. Bonnie Lewis, an excellent crew chief came with old B-34. John Disosway was assigned as AC. The crew flew three mining missions to Shimonoseki Straits and one to Fusan, Korea. Their plane was trapped eight minutes in the searchlights on the May 25th Tokyo raid, had two fighter attacks and shrapnel damage. On June 5 Kobe mission a flak burst wounded the bombardier and damaged the plane.

The crew was awarded the Distinguished Flying Cross for completing the mission. Altogether, the crew completed 31 missions, the gunners shot down two fighters, had one probable and two damaged.

Berry was discharged Nov. 11, 1945. He married and has two daughters and three grandchildren. He farmed for 35 years until retiring on Dec. 1, 1984.

JOSEPH M. BESEDA, was born in Port Lavaca, TX in 1914. He received his BBA from Texas Tech in 1941 and became Aviation Cadet in August 1941. Was commissioned with Bombardier rating at Midland AAF, April 1942. Served as instructor and then had short tour with 5th AF to New Guinea in B-24s.

Assigned to 40th BG (B-29) at Pratt, KS and went to India as Group Bombardier. Then assigned to 58th BW Staff Bombardier on Tinian Island.

Separated after WWII and was recalled in 1952 for Korean conflict. Flew B-29 missions out of Kadena, Okinawa. Went to James Connaly AFB, TX and upgraded to Navigator. Served there as squadron commander, group commander and provost marshal. Fin-

ished tour at HQ Pacific Air Force, HI with Air Inspector General.

Was awarded the Bronze Star, Air Medal with five Oak Leaf Clusters and two Air Force Commendation Medals. He retired in 1966 and moved to Austin, TX with wife, son and daughter. Worked several years as tax auditor with the Internal Revenue Service.

ROBERT S. BOLES, was born Aug. 17, 1916 in Richmond, IN. He enlisted in the Regular Army Air Corps on May 24, 1941 and served four and a half years with 20 months overseas. Was an airplane mechanic with a sheetmetal speciality. Served with the 39th Material Sqdn., 28th Service Group, 58th BW of the 20th AF.

Was stationed in Panama twice, one year in Chakulia, India, Tinian and returned from Saipan. Worked on P-40, P-47, A-20, B-17 and B-29. Rebuilt front landing gear section, bomb bay, underneath rear on B-29 named *Queenie*.

Discharged from Camp Atterbury on Oct. 11, 1945. He received the WWII Victory Medal, American Theater, American Defense, Asiatic-Pacific, Good Conduct and the Meritorious Service Award.

Was married 48 years to Pauline who passed away from cancer in 1990. They had four sons: Bill, Jim, Dave and John. Boles retired after 12 years with International Harvester and 25 years as metallurgist and melting foreman with Swayne Robinson Company, a local Grey Iron Foundry.

HENRY L. BORUM, was born Oct. 9, 1918 in Marion, IL. Was drafted Dec. 27, 1942 and went to basic training at Miami Beach, FL. Was selected to assist in setting test standards for Air Force inductees at Miami Beach, was tested for OCS, but lacked college math. Chose electronics for military career. Schooled at Congress Hotel, Chicago and Scott Air Base, Belleville, IL. Had special schooling for radio operator on B-29 at Truax Field, Madison, WI.

From there to Salina and Pratt, KS. Then to Chakulia, India. Was a member of 40th BG, 58th Wing at Chakulia. Received Presidential Unit Citation, four Battle Stars, Expert Medal for 45 caliber automatic and the Good Conduct Medal.

Returned to the States Dec. 25, 1944. Assigned to 2nd AF HQ in Colorado Springs, CO as communications tech. Was discharged Nov. 27, 1945 and attended Deforests and RCA Electronics Schools. Employed by Sangamd Electric Co. as lab tech for 28 years. Final three years prior to retiring was employed by Illinois State Police in communications lab.

He married Marjorie Moore on Dec. 17, 1942. They have two daughters and two sons. Oldest daughter was named Tanya after one of their B-29 bombers at Chakulia.

WILLIAM T. BRANTLEY JR., was born in Nash County, NC on May 4, 1930. He joined the USAF

on Dec. 15, 1950 and trained as a gunner on B-29 aircraft at Lowry AFB, Denver, CO. In August 1951, he was assigned to a B-29 crew at Randolph AFB, TX. In February 1952 this crew went to Kadena AB, Okinawa and was assigned to the 28th Bomb Sqdn., 19th BG.

He flew 24 combat missions over North Korea as a B-29 gunner on Command Decision, Cat Girl, and other B-29 aircraft. In October 1952 his crew was assigned to Lake Charles AFB, LA. In 1953 he was assigned to the 44th Air Refueling Sqdn. and trained as a boom operator on KC-97 tankers and was refueling B-47 and B-52 aircraft. He was discharged from the USAF as a staff sergeant on Dec. 21, 1953.

On Nov. 30, 1990 he retired with 29 years U.S. Government service as a compliance officer, Food Safety and Inspection Service, U.S. Dept. of Agriculture. He is currently involved in farming and lives with his family in Raleigh, NC.

CHARLES G. BROUGH, was born in 1918 in Methuen, MA. He graduated from Phillips Andover Academy in 1939 and enlisted in the USAF on Oct. 13, 1942. Basic at Ft. Devens, MA and Walnut Ridge, AR. Assigned to B-24 School, Keesler Field, MI; Electrical at Chanute Field, IL; B-29 Mechanical and Electrical, Boeing, Renton, WA.

Assigned Pratt Field and Great Bend, KS with 20th AF, 45th Sqdn. March 1944 entrained to Newport News, boarded liberty ship, *Newton D. Baker,* and debarked at Casablanca. Flew out late April in C-54 to Tripoli, Cairo, Abadan, Karachi and Agra, landed on a rainy night, April 23, at Chakulia, India.

Assigned to 45th Sqdn. Electrical, 40th BG at Chakulia and Hsinching, China. On May 6, 1945 shipped out of Calcutta on USS *Callan* to Tinian, MI via Fremantle, Australia. Maintained Flux Gate Compasses until end of war. Offered OCS, Australia and AO but declined. Flew Guam, Kwajalein, Oahu to Mather's Field, CA, then home to Westover Field, MA.

Discharged Nov. 12, 1945 with the rank staff sergeant. He received the Good Conduct Medal, Presidential Unit Citation, Asiatic-Pacific Ribbon with five Battle Stars, American Theater Ribbon, Victory Medal and later the China Medal.

Received SB in engineering from Harvard in 1949, a registered professional engineer in Massachusetts and New Hampshire. Was plant engineering supervisor at Front Royal, VA; chief industrial engineer, Oxford Paper Co., Lawrence, MA; plant engineer, Western Electric Co., N. Andover, MA; manager plant engineering and facilities, Kollsman Instrument Co., Merrimack, NH.

Married Rosamond H. Redpath (deceased Oct. 4, 1960) of North Andover, MA on Dec. 8, 1945. They lived in Front Royal, VA and N. Andover, MA and had two sons, Richard and George. Married Elaine L. Dalrymple of Methuen, MA on Aug. 25, 1962, has two stepsons, Robert and Carl. Robert served with distinction in Vietnam, an Army captain, and Carl was a Navy lieutenant.

Brough lived in Hampstead, NH for 25 years. Retired to Venice, FL in 1987. Now is writing war memoirs, one short story and five genealogies published in New England Historical Genealogical Society of Boston. He enjoys singing, golfing, Shriners, summers in New Hampshire with wife, family and old friends.

JOHN H. CANNON, was born Milwaukee, WI on April 4, 1918. He moved to Denver, CO in 1920 and enlisted in the flying cadet program at Ft. Logan, CO in 1940. Hemet, Randolph, Barksdale. Graduated April 1941, Class 41-C, commissioned second lieutenant, Selma, AL 1941-1942 Cadre Napier Field, AL 1942-1943. Smyrna, TN, 1943-1944, B-24 Trans., pilot, IP. Alamogordo, NM 1944. Hays, KS 330th BG 1944-1945 (Caterpillar Club Jan. 11, 1945 B-29 bail out). Guam 1945 330th BG (VH). Smyrna, TN 1945.

Separated 1946. From 1946-1947 was pilot for Continental Airlines. Regular commission USAF October 1947. Hensley Field, TX 1947-1949, Base DO, Senior Advisor Air Reserve Program. Great Falls, MT 1949, Berlin Airlift School. Rhein-Main, Germany 1949 Berlin Airlift. 1950-1951 Commander 25th Comm. Sqdn., USAFE. 1952 Carswell AFB, TX B-36 pilot, Sqdn. Ops., Ivy Project Kwajalein. 1953, Altus, OK Base DO, Base Vice Commander. 1959 Thule Greenland, Deputy, Operations. 1960 Vandenberg AFB, CA Base DO, 1st STRATAD, Deputy Dir. Safety. 1963 Ellsworth AFB, SD, Commander 68th SMS. August 1967. Retired.

Married to Elsie Hawkins for 49 years. Their children are Susan and twins, Donald and Deborah.

LEONARD W. CARPI, O.D., was born in Alhambra, CA on May 29, 1924. Attended Whitter College on a football scholarship and enlisted in the Army Air Corps Air Cadet Program. He received his pilot's wings at Marfa Army Air Base in Texas, B-17 training in Roswell, NM and B-29 training in McCook, NE where combat crews were formed.

Was pilot on a lead crew and went to Tinian Island in the Pacific with the 9th BG of the 20th AF in January 1945. Completed tour of 35 missions over the Japanese Empire including the March 9-10 Tokyo firebombing raid as a pathfinder crew. Flew his last few missions as one of the youngest airplane commanders in the Army Air Corps, barely 21 years old.

After discharge as a first lieutenant in 1945, he attended the University of Southern California and the Los Angeles College of Optometry, receiving his doctorate in 1954. Moved to Las Vagas, NV with his wife, Betty, and three children. He is currently still in practice. Dr. Carpi was one of the founders of the 9th BG Association, serving as its first president. He currently serves on the 20th AF Association Board of Directors.

ROBERT CASPER SR., was born July 22, 1930 in Milwaukee, WI and joined the service Sept. 3, 1947. Trained at Ft. Sheridan, IL and Kessler AFB.

Served with the 509th Bomb Wing, 14 years at Walker AFB and Pease AFB, 3920 CAMS Brizenorton England, 410th BWG K.I. Sawyer, MI.

Discharged with the rank master sergeant. Retired October 1974. Deceased January 1992. Wife, Betty, daughters, Bonnie Henderson, Carol McClendon, Sandra Kay, and son, Robert Jr.

JOHN L. CELLA, was born in Chicago May 2, 1915. Was inducted June 2, 1941 and served 17 months as enlisted man at Scott Field, IL and Sioux Falls, SD. Completed OCS in October 1942 and was assigned to Aerial Gunnery School at Kingman, AZ as squadron

adjutant. Graduated Aerial Gunnery School and AAF Intelligence School at Harrisburg, PA. Appointed instructor, Enlisted Mens Intelligence School, Kearns, UT.

Transferred to HQ, XX Bomber Command at Salina, KS as assistant A-2 in January 1944. Attended POW Escape and Evasion School, Washington, DC. Served as combat intelligence officer, A-2 Section, XXBC in Kharaghpur, India and Chengtu, China from February 1944 to August 1945, in charge of Search and Rescue for downed aircraft and securing and disseminating escape and evasion and survival information to command units.

Graduate, Jungle Survival School at Trincomalee, Ceylon. Wrote the XX Bomber Command Bulletin of Escape and Evasion and interrogated and composed reports on returning crew members who had bailed out during missions. Discharged Nov. 3, 1945 with rank of captain.

Civilian life included 35 years with downtown Chicago real estate office, including 15 with own firm. Retired in 1975. He is married with four children and six grandchildren.

WILSON M. CHAPMAN, was born Newton, MS on Aug. 28, 1918. Was raised in New Mexico and West Texas with degree in chemical engineering from Texas Tech, 1940. Accepted USSAAF for cadet training in California August 1941. Commissioned second lieutenant as pilot, Mather Field, March 1942.

Assigned 3rd AF, Heavy Bombardment Barksdale and McDill, May 1942 to new 98th B-24 Group at Ft. Myers, FL. Arrived Middle East July 1942 with 98th Assigned 9th AF supporting British 8th Army and later Allied North African invasion. May 1943 reassigned 2nd AF, U.S. training command. April 1944 assigned B-29 9th VHBG for staging, which was moved to Tinian January 1945 to join the 20th AF.

Completed the war as squadron operations officer, major, and had 55 combat missions in both theaters. Was awarded Distinguished Flying Crosses, Air Medals, and theater ribbons.

Married Dottie in 1943 and has two children. He resumed engineering and construction career in 1946, primarily oil refining and chemical plant related. Semi-retired in 1987 but doing consulting and writing some B-24 combat memoirs.

CHARLES G. CHAUNCEY, was born in Chanute, KS on April 16, 1923. Enlisted in the Army Air Corps, January 1943; boot camp at Jefferson Barracks, St. Louis, MO; College Training Detachment, St. John, MN; cadet preflight training, Class 44-D, Santa Ana, CA; primary flight training, Tex Rankin Aeronautical Academy, Tulare, CA; basic flight training, Taft, CA; advanced flight training (twin engine), Marfa, TX, and received Wings and was commissioned second lieutenant April 15, 1944; and B-17 training, Roswell, NM.

Entered B-29 training and formation of the 9th

BG of the 313th Wing, 20th AF, assigned to 5th Sqdn., McCook, NE. The 9th BG flying crews moved in mass to Tinian Island (Marianas) January 1945.

Flew as pilot (copilot) along with Capt. John Fleming, Airplane Commander (pilot), for 35 missions, 32 of those missions were aboard *Goin Jessie* brought from the States. Their crew was selected and dropped the 2,000,000th ton of bombs for the Air Forces on July 9, 1945 at Wakayama, Japan.

Going Jessie was a unique aircraft that flew 52 consecutive missions with no aborts. Upon completion of the planes' 50th mission, M/SGT C. Klabow received the Distinguished Service Medal. Earlier their crew had each received the Distinguished Flying Cross and the Air Medal with five Oak Leaf Clusters. Was discharged as a first lieutenant in October 1945.

Married Jayne Elliott and has three children: Paul, Charles II and Janie. Entered the family oil field supply business after leaving the service. Was the owner and operator of the stores, with machine shop facilities for 25 years before selling in 1989. Currently serving as a board director on the 9th BG Association Inc.

JOHN P. CONSTANDY, was born June 11, 1924 in New York City; joined the U.S. Army in March 1943; assigned to the 49th Armd. Inf. Regt., 8th Armd. Div. Transferred to USAAF and completed navigator training at Hondo AAF Base 44-11-4B. Assigned 25th Sqdn., 40th BG on Tinian and was proud to fly with A/C Thomas Turner and crew on *Genie*, #42-63455, (Sqdn. #10), in the air offensive against Japan. Separated December 1945 as second lieutenant and remained in the USAFR.

Volunteered for USAF active duty April 1951 for Korean Conflict. Separated November 1952 as first lieutenant, authored USAF manual *U.S. Code of Military Justice*.

Attended Oklahoma A&M (Aviation Cadet) School; University, Bridgeport; University, Miami; and Northeastern University of Law (LLB).

Was trial attorney; assistant district attorney, New York County; 14 years counsel various U.S. Senate and House of Representatives Congressional committees, last as chief counsel, U.S. Senate Permanent Subcommittee on Investigations; Foreign Service Officer (FSR-1); assistant secretary of state; officer and director of shipping company, trading company, petroleum exploration company and helicopter dealership (both in Peoples' Republic of China); and insurance agency. At present is attorney (New York and DC) corporate director.

Married to Arlette Louise Nicole Constandy (nee Schmitt) of Nice, France, residing in Washington, DC. Additional references: Who's Who in America.

JAMES R. CORLISS, was born Paulsboro, NJ on Sept. 2, 1919. He enlisted in the Army Air Corps Sept. 10, 1941. After completing Aircraft and Engine Maintenance School, flew as engineer and performed main-

tenance on B-17s. Graduated June 12, 1944 Flight Engineer School for B-29s, Lowry Field, CO. Assigned 504th BG, Fairmont, NE, July 15, 1944.

On Sept. 14, 1944 the squadron transferred to Wendover Field, UT to start the 509th Composite Group. Transferred June 16, 1945 to Tinian Island, 20th AF. On Aug. 6, 1945 flew as engineer on one of the three B-29s on the Atomic Bomb Mission to Hiroshima, Japan.

He received the Air Medal and was discharged November 1945 with the rank master sergeant. Married Ethel Doerrmann and has two daughters, Jane and Debbie.

Was recalled in Air Force in March 1950 for Korean War; shipped to Hawaii in Air Rescue Service. June 1956 cross-trained into Munitions Field; Dec. 25, 1965 arrived Bien Hoa AB, Vietnam, for one-year tour as munitions supervisor. Retired September 1967 from Air Force.

He operated power plant until final retirement August 1980.

THOMAS F. COSTA (TOM), from North Bronx, NY and enlisted in the Air Corps in November 1942 at the age of 20. Received basic training; attended 60 college training detachment at University of Pittsburg. He entered pre-flight at Maxwell Field in June 1943. Was unsuccessful at flight training and reclassified as bombardier.

Received his Gunners Wings and graduated bombardier/navigator training Class 44-8 DR June 9, 1944 at San Angelo and commissioned second lieutenant. Received combat crew training (B-17s and B-29s) with 393rd Sqdn., 504th BG (VH). Was one of 15 bombardiers trained in Cuba for atomic work in preparation for atomic bomb strike. Was promoted to first lieutenant Sept. 20, 1945.

Shipped out to Tinian June 10, 1945. Flew 200 B-20 combat hours, hitting Japanese targets with a six ton version of non atomic bomb. From July 4 to Aug. 14, 1945, missions to Marcus Island, Truk, and targets in Japan were performed as "lone wolf" strikes, (no guns or armament), part of tactics. WWII ended with dropping of atomic bombs on Aug. 6 and Aug. 9, 1945 by Col. Paul Tibbetts and Maj. Chuck Sweeney of 504th.

Discharged January 1946, decorated with Air Medal with two Bronze Stars, Asiatic-Pacific Theater Ribbon, Air Offensive Eastern Mandates and Japan. Recalled for Korean Conflict Sept. 26, 1951 and relieved from active duty December 1951, physical disqualification.

Married since July 1947 and has two daughters. He was a partner in a printing business until retirement in March 1990.

JAMES M. DEVINE, was born Newark, NJ on Aug. 17, 1931. He enlisted in Newark on Feb. 13, 1952; basic training was at Sampson AFB, NY; Gunnery School, April 1952, Lowery AFB, CO; crew training at Randolph AFB, TX and Forbes AFB, KS where he was assigned to A.C. Capt. Jablonski's crew as CFC gunner.

Departed for Kadena AFB, Okinawa, July 1953 and was assigned to 19th BW, 28th Bomb Sqdn., crew #N-26-AO and Superfortress #2253. The Korean truce was signed, but he remained to partake in reconnaissance and practice missions. Entire wing departed May 1954 for Davis-Monthan AFB, AZ where all B-29s were deactivated and placed into storage.

Was reassigned, as most gunners at that time were, to 26th ARS Lockbourne AFB, OH for training as in-flight refueling specialist on KC-97 aircraft. Was discharged as staff sergeant February 1956 and resides in South Plainfield, NJ.

Was employed as shipping supervisor. Devine has wife, Velma, daughter, Valerie, and son, James. He is a member of VFW, 19th Bomb Association and AFGA.

THOMAS P. DOHERTY, was born in Providence, RI on Feb. 26, 1924. He was drafted April 1943; basic training at Miami Beach; Radio School, Sioux Falls, SD; served with 404th BG 421st Sqdn. Fairmont, NE. Was radio operator on B-17s/B-29s January 1945 Tinian Island South Pacific, completed 35 combat missions on *Big Boots* Pilot Art Tomes.

Was awarded Air Medal, Distinguished Flying Cross, Oak Leaf Clusters, two Presidential Unit Citations. During nighttime mission over Japan, his job was to drop tinfoil to confuse enemy searchlights and A/A guns. Inadvertently his "throat mike" was pushed out. The joke was a rice farmer picked up the "mike" looked at it, said "We can do better" thus Sony was born.

Discharged as staff sergeant October 1945. He married Shirley Whittet and has one daughter, three sons, and seven grandchildren. Employed from 1946-1974 with Providence Police Dept., retiring as lieutenant, director, Radio Control Center 1974-1985 ITT Grinnell Security Director USA/Canada.

DONALD G. DUBBINS, was born Putney, London, England, July 23, 1918. Moved to Cleveland, OH in April 1920. Drafted into the Army in June 1941. Inducted at Ft. Hays, Columbus, OH, June 1941 and placed in the Army Air Corps. Assigned to Tucson Army Air Base (now Davis-Monthan) Army Air Corps 31st Service Group as a photographer, aerial and ground. Second station: Muroc Army Air Base (now Edwards) with rank of staff sergeant.

Entered Aviation Cadet CTD, Arizona State Teachers College (now Arizona State University). Preflight: Santa Ana, CA. Primary, Tex Rankin Air Academy, Tulare, CA. Basic at Tulare, CA. Advance, Pecos, TX, second lieutenant. B-17 transition: Hobbs, NM. B-29 OTU Walker, KS. Overseas: North Field, Guam; 21 missions over Japan; 314th Wing; 330th BG; 458th Sqdn. Aircraft: K-38, Ernie Pyle. Pilot - first lieutenant.

After peace came, they took a B-29, the *Waltzing Matilda,* with a crew of 12 to Australia for their Vic-

tory Bond Tour. In 42 days, they visited 19 Australian cities including Hobart, Tasmania. Was discharged Dec. 7, 1945.

Married Barbara and had two daughters, Barbara and Donna, and one son, Donald Timothy. Dubbins retired in 1988 from Goodyear Aerospace, Litchfield Park, Arizona as a senior designer.

DONALD F. DWYER, was born Jan. 3, 1923 in New York City. Was inducted Feb. 23, 1943 in Newark, NJ and graduated Bombardier School, at Midland, TX June 10, 1944. Was assigned to the 9th BG, 1st Sqdn., McCook, NE. Flew 28 missions on lead crew off Tinian Island. Received the Distinguished Flying Cross, Air Medal and Purple Heart.

As a pathfinder plane for the March 9, 1945 fire raid on Tokyo, their plane, *God's Will,* experienced radar trouble and IP of Chosi Point was not picked up. He noted that there were bright lights of a city off to the left. It was assumed that they were Yokohama and they turned in at another prominence to the north. He noted through the nose that at 6,400 feet they were flying close to land below them and inquired as to land heights between Chosi and Tokyo. Navigator said that they shouldn't be over two to three thousand feet. The A/C captain, Dean Fling, and pilot, Lt. H.L. Peterson, immediately climbed and took a 180 degree out to sea. They eventually bombed Tokyo but probably would have done so with the cities lights still on if the radar hadn't malfunctioned.

Married in 1956 to Marion Kern in New Providence, NJ. They have three children: Alison, Glenn and Douglas and five grandchildren. He is presently retired after 35 years in sales.

JAMES M. ELLIS, was born Aug. 20, 1924 in Louisville, MS. He entered basic training in April 1943 at Keesler Air Base, Gulfport, MS. Cadet training began in July 1943 at Ouachita College in Arkadelphia, AR. Received his Bombardier Wings at Midland, TX June 1944. Ellis joined B-29 crew, training at McCook, NE August 1944. Attached to the 9th BG, 313th Wing. Flew 35 missions from Tinian on Capt. Howard Thimlar's crew onboard the USS *Indiana*.

He was honorably discharged in October 1945 with the rank of first lieutenant.

He worked for Taylor Machine Works (manufacturers of heavy equipment) from November 1945 until his death in March 1983. At the time of his death, he was serving as director of production planning and control at Taylor Machine Works and also as administrative assistant to the president.

Survived by wife, Margaret, and two sons, Stephen and Paul, and five grandchildren.

RICHARD J. ELMORE, was born at Vallejo, CA May 13, 1923. He moved to Hawthorne, NV in 1930 and attended school in Hawthorne and the University of Nevada at Reno, NV.

He joined the Air Force in February 1943 and

was a member of the 19th BG, 93rd Bomb Sqdn. He received his training and was stationed at Lowry Air Base in Denver, CO; Clovis Air Base, Clovis, NM; Amarillo, TX·and Oklahoma A&M. Some of his most memorable events included landing on Iwo Jima before the landing strip was finished because the plane had been hit while on a bombing mission over Japan. His plane and crew were in the air over Japan flying a decoy mission the day the A-bomb was dropped. He was stationed at North Field on Guam.

Received an honorable discharge in February 1946 with the rank of staff sergeant.

He entered the wholesale electrical supply business in 1950 and is still working today. He is the owner and president of WEDCO, Inc. in Reno, NV.

BURTON A. ELSNER, was born Nov. 6, 1917 in Elbert, CO and was drafted March 25, 1941. He was part of the 63rd Coast Artillery in El Paso, TX. Transferred to USAAF Pilot Training Class 43G. Co-pilot B-29, 40th BG, 395th Sqdn., Pratt, KS.

Most memorable experience was crashing on take-off June 5, 1944 in Chakulia, India, only survivor, mission was Bangkok crew of 11, first bomb mission of B-29. Retired for disability with rank of first lieutenant.

Elsner and wife, Nellie Maye, have two daughters. He ran farm equipment business, was a rancher and was Elbert County Treasurer for 12 years.

AL ESCALANTE, was born in Brownsville, TX Aug. 19, 1917. He volunteered Jan. 28, 1942, Kelly Field, San Antonio, TX in Class 42-J. Received Bombardier Wings at Midland, TX, Nov. 24, 1942, sent to Class 42-16 Big Spring, TX as an instructor and then sent to Chanute Field to Transition School to train new pilots on bomb sight and automatic pilot.

Shipped for overseas training October 1944. Went to Guam with 458th Bomb Sqdn., crew 813, flew 23 missions over Japan, one of two lead bombardiers in squadron. Promoted to captain after mission over Nagoyo and given Distinguished Flying Cross along with Airplane Cmdr. Ray Smisek.

Honorably discharged in San Antonio, TX, Nov. 23, 1945.

Married Ozelle Owen in Big Spring, TX June 5, 1943 and they have three children. He has been a golf professional since 1946. Has been 30 years at present position.

JOHN C. FARR (JACK), was born in Philadelphia, PA Jan. 26, 1920. He was drafted Oct. 16, 1943. Qualified for flying officer Army Air Corps.

Attended CTD at Davidson College, NC. Program was disbanded by Army; sent to Gunnery School Ft. Myers, FL, graduated highest score in class; served in flight line at Shaw Field, SC; sent to Alamogordo, NM for flight training in B-29 as gunner (left side blister); assigned to Walker Army Air Base, Victoria, KS for crew training; Havana, Cuba for tropical flight train-

ing; Walker AFB and then to Mather Field, Sacramento, CA; Island of Guam where crew flew 28 missions over Japan. Crew received Distinguished Flying Cross and Air Medal plus two clusters among other citations.

Spent bulk of career in insurance. Retired in 1984. Has attended all reunions of 330th BG, plus Plaque Dedication Ceremony at Air Force Academy, Colorado Springs, CO.

BUD FARRELL, was born Jan. 3, 1933 in Philadelphia, PA and enlisted March 17, 1951. Flew 25 combat missions as left gunner in 93rd Bomb Sqdn. of 19th BG, Korean War June 21, 1952 to Dec. 21, 1952 out of Kadena AFB, Okinawa.

Refueling operator in K B-29s in 43rd Air Refueling Sq. of 43rd Bomb Wing, Davis-Monthan AFB Tucson, AZ January 1953 to October 1953.

Most memorable missions were Oriental Light Metalworks Sinuiju on Yalu River July 30, 1952; Suiho Dam on Yalu Sept. 12, 1952; Namsan-Ni Chemical Plant on Yalu Sept. 30, 1952; and several raids on Pyongyang, capital of North Korea.

He and his wife, Carole, have three sons. They recently moved from Richardson, TX to long time dream of log home in mountains near Durango, CO.

Retired in 1990 from Armstrong World Ind. (32 years, western sales manager). Continues contact with crew members and friends as member of board of directors of 19th BG. He says, "Friends lost or since gone will never be unknown nor ever forgotten."

WILLIAM R. FLAHERTY, entered cadet program in December 1942. Basic training, 22nd College Training Detachment; Classification: Pre-flight, Gunnery and finally Bombardier School; Deming, NM, Class 44-9.

B-29 crew training, McCook, NE, August 1944 through February 1945; Tinian Island, Marianas, February 1945 through July 1945, 1st Sqdn., 9th Group, 313th Wing. Flew 35 missions, then home and separated in Boston, MA in August 1945.

Was recalled in September 1951, B-26 training at Mather Field, CA and Langley Field, VA. Arrived K-9 Pusan, Korea, March 1952, 730th Sqdn., 452nd Wing. Flew 55 missions, highlight was destroying train near Wonson Harbor.

Home in July 1952, married and assigned to Forbes AFB, Topeka, KS as bombardier/navigator instructor. Transferred to Travis AFB, CA, B-36 Wing. Separated June 1953 and retired as a major in November 1968. Was awarded the Distinguished Flying Cross with cluster, Air Medal with seven clusters, Unit Citation with cluster and Korean Unit Citation.

SAMPSON LESTER FRIEDMAN, was born in Brooklyn, NY Nov. 5, 1923. Enlisted in the Air Corps December 1942 and inducted February 1943. Graduated Bombardier School in Deming, NM and was assigned to B-29 training 20th Air Force, 9th BG, 5th Bomb Sqdn. in McCook, NE. In January 1945 he

went overseas to Tinian Island in the Pacific. He flew 24 missions over Japan, some with Bill Dolan, captain of *Tokyo K-O,* and then with Capt. Carl Donica on #40.

It was on the Uji-Yamada mission, July 28, 1945, that the #40 was frontally attacked by a Japanese kamikaze. Lt. Friedman fired his six remote-controlled 50-caliber machine guns into the kamikaze cockpit, while the Japanese fired into the #40. Capt. Donica's control cables were cut but co-pilot, Lt. Conroy banked the B-29 to the right in time to avoid a head-on collision. The kamikaze passed under the left wing, went down and exploded. The damaged B-29 went to Iwo Jima for repairs and went on to finish the war on Sept. 2, 1945. He dropped POW supplies to Japan for several missions.

He was honorably discharged in February 1946 with the rank of second lieutenant. He was awarded the Air Medal, two Oak Leaf Clusters, Distinguished Flying Cross, Presidential Unit Citation, South Pacific War Ribbon and plus others.

He married his childhood sweetheart, Lila Ritter, in January 1946. They have three children and two grandchildren. He received a BS degree from New York University. He worked in the family jewelry business, DFS Manufacturing Company, and is now retired.

AUGUST F. FUTSCHIK, was born in Shiner, TX. He joined the service Feb. 23, 1933 at Dodd Field, TX. Trained with the 23rd Inf. Ft. Sam Houston, TX. He served with the 23rd Inf. 62nd School Sqdn. 5th Air Base, 11, 22 Bomb Sqdn. and 435th. Maintenance crew line chief.

His most memorable experience was when Pearl Harbor was bombed. They were five days out of Pearl Harbor on the USS *Republic* on the way to the Philippine Islands. There were 16 ships in the convoy without any protection or escorts.

He retired Oct. 1, 1965 as a S/MSGT with a total of 32 years, six months and two days of service. He was awarded the Bronze Star with Oak Leaf Clusters, Presidential Unit Citation with four Oak Leaf Clusters, Air Offensive Japan and the Eastern Mandates.

He and his wife, Edna, have two daughters, Janet (a nurse) and Mary (a cattle rancher). He is now a real estate agent.

RUSSELL E. GACKENBACH, was born in Allentown, PA on March 23, 1923. Graduated high

school in 1941; worked as machine-shop inspector for Bethlehem Steel, Bethlehem, PA. Enlisted in the Air Corps as aviation cadet October 1942. Received navigation training by Pan American Airways at Coral Gables, FL. Awarded navigator's wings and commissioned second lieutenant on Feb. 12, 1942. Assigned to the 1st AF, 1st Sea Search Attack Group at Langley Field, VA. Late March 1944, transferred to AAF Technical School, Boca Raton AAF, FL for radar bombardier training. In July 1944 was assigned to 393rd Bomb Sqdn., 504th BG at Fairmont AAF, NE as a B-17 crew member.

On Sept. 10, 1944 the 393rd Bomb Sqdn. transferred to Wendover AAF, UT; made transition to B-29s; became attached to the 509th Composite Group Dec. 17, 1944. Received special training in Cuba January 1945. Group transferred to Tinian June 12, 1945. As navigator was on photo plane during drop of atom bomb on Hiroshima on Aug. 6, 1945 and on weather observation plane over Kokura on Aug. 9, 1945.

Received Air Medal Sept. 14, 1945 for participation in Hiroshima mission. Returned to U.S. on Nov. 8, 1945. He received an honorable discharge March 13, 1946 with the rank of first lieutenant. He married Evelyn and they have two daughters, Carol and Janis.

Graduate 1950 with a BS degree in metallurgical engineering from Lehigh University. Joined American Cyanamid Company as a materials/corrosion engineer. He is author of many technical articles and a book *Materials Selection for Process Plants*. Active in National Association of Corrosion Engineers; held many section and regional offices; served on board of directors and retired from Cyanamid in 1985. Still consults on a limited basis.

EDGAR B. GAINES,

EDGAR B. GAINES, was born in Huntsville, AL Aug. 30, 1931 and enlisted in the Air Force at age 18. After basic training at Lackland AFB, TX, he attended Radio Training School at Keesler AFB, MS. Attended B-29 Combat Crew Training at Randolph AFB, TX in June 1950.

Was then assigned to the 376th Bomb Wing at Barksdale AFB, LA in January 1951. While assigned to the 372nd Bomb Sqdn., 307th Bomb Wing, Kadena AFB, Okinawa, was shot down in 1972 by a MIG-15 over North Korea near Sariwon. Was captured after bailing out and spent 14 months in captivity. Most of the POW time was in Camp II Annex in the Obul Valley.

Was repatriated Sept. 2, 1953 during operation Big Switch. After returning to duty, was assigned to the 301st Air Refueling Sqdn. at Barksdale AFB, LA as a boom operator on KC-97s. Then transferred to Harmond AFB, NFLD with the 376th Air Refueling Sqdn. for 18 months. February 1961 assigned to the 9th Air Refueling Sqdn. Mountain Home, ID. After the KC-97s were phased out in 1965; attended KC-135 Boom Operator School at Castle AFB, CA and assigned to the 372nd Air Refueling Sqdn., 19th Bomb Wing at Robins AFB, GA. Retired in September 1971 as a master sergeant after 22 years in the Air Force.

Retired from the National Life and Accident Insurance Co. after 12 years as an agent. Has had four heart attacks, open heart surgery twice, now retired and lives in Byron, GA.

CHARLES E. GIBBS, was born in Knoxville, TN Jan. 10, 1927 and enlisted in the USN January 1945. Served on battleship USS *New Jersey*. Honorably discharged 1946. Attended University of Tennessee 1946-

1949. Entered USAF Aviation Cadet Program 1949 at Randolph AFB, TX. Commissioned August 1950 at Vance AFB, OK. Assigned to 62nd Troop Carrier Wing (C-54s) 1950-1952, McChord AFB, WA. In June 1952 assigned to B-29 Bombers. Flew 28 combat missions during Korean War with 19th Bomb Wing, Kadena AB, Okinawa. Then assigned to SAC KB-29 tankers 1953-1957 at Dow AFB, ME and Bergstrom AFB, TX.

Then to KC-135 tankers Fairchild AFB, WA 1957-1960. In 1958 set seven closed course World Class Speed Records for jet transport aircraft with payloads. Assigned to SAC's Combat Evaluation Group, 1960, Barksdale AFB, LA. Graduated Air Command and Staff College, 1964. Assigned to SAC HQ, Offutt AFB, NE 1964-1968. Served in B-52/KC135 Operations at Kadena and U-Tapao, Thailand during Vietnam War, 1968-1971. Promoted to colonel in 1971. Wing Deputy Commander Maintenance 306th and 379th BW, Wurtsmith AFB, MI. Also Director Logistics 42nd Air Division Wurtsmith AFB, MI.

Retired as colonel 1975 and moved to Irving, TX. Received Air Medal with Oak Leaf Clusters, Meritorious Service Medal and many others.

Married to Dorothy Claiborne and has four sons. Spent business career with Cooper Airmotive, Dallas, TX as well as other corporate management positions in Dallas. Currently residing in Irving, TX.

JOHN D. GOLDHAHN, was born Fort Benton, MT March 31, 1914; grew up and received education in Geraldine, MT; inducted at Ft. Benton March 1942 and received basic training at Sheppard Field, TX. Was assigned to 305th BG B-17 Fortress at Salt Lake City, UT April 1942. Trained there and at Geiger Field, then went to Boeing Aircraft School at Seattle, WA until July 1942. Rejoined the Group at Muroc, CA, went to Ft. Dix, NJ then to England and the 8th Air Force Sept. 1, 1942. Was crew chief on planes *Yankee Gal*, *Boom Town* and *Yo-Yo*. Came back to the States April 1, 1944 and was assigned to 330th BG B-29 Walker Field, KS. Went to Guam 20th Air Force March 1945. Was crew chief on K-53.

After the war went back to the States and was honorably discharged at East Base, Gt. Falls, MT Nov. 15, 1945 with the rank of master sergeant

Married Margaret in 1944 and raised two sons and two daughters. Was active in aviation, farmed and ranched. He retired in 1980 and moved to Sapphire Village. They keep busy hand digging for sapphires and weaving baskets and rugs.

ROBERT J. GREGORY (JACK), was born Sept. 5, 1924 and drafted June 7, 1943. Basic training in Wichita Falls, TX until August 1943. Went to B-17 Mechanics School, September to December 1943, Amarillo, TX. Advanced Mechanic School on B-29 first part of 1944 at Boeing Aircraft in Seattle, WA, then McCook Air Base until departure for Tinian in November 1944. Assigned to 9th BG, 1st Sqdn.

He was honorably discharged January 1946 as a

sergeant at Fort Sam Houston, TX. Recalled during Korean War and served one year in HQ Finance at McDill AFB, FL.

Married Ruby Miller in August 1946. They have two children, Jack Jr. and Beth. Education in business, BBA and MBA, Southern Methodist University and Texas A&I. Retired from EXXON Company as senior financial analyst in 1986. His hobbies are tennis and jogging. Currently taking advance tax courses at H&R Block.

WILBURNE C. GROMATZKY, was born Pottsville, TX June 19, 1924. Enrolled in engineering and ROTC at John Tarleton Agricultural College, Stephenville, TX in September 1941.

Enlisted in Army Air Corps and Aviation Cadet Program in 1942. Began active duty April 1943 with usual schools, including Aerial Gunnery Laredo, TX through Advanced Navigation School at San Marcos, TX. Commissioned second lieutenant in June 1944.

Completed Radar School, Boca Raton, FL and B-29 Combat Crew Training, Clovis, NM. Assigned to 99th Sqdn., 9th Group, 313th Wing, 20th Air Force on Tinian Island in March 1945.

Completed 26 missions over Japan (B-29), and three missions (B-24) with 55th Long Range Weather Reconnaissance Sqdn. (Guam). Returned Stateside and was honorably discharged December 1945 with the rank of major.

His most memorable experience was flying Polar Region out of Thule, Greenland and parachuting materials for weather station construction by Denmark.

Enrolled at Southern Methodist University in March 1946. He married Flo and they have three sons: Charles, Steve and Carl. Graduated with BS in civil engineering, June 1947. Entire civilian career spanning 40 years with Texas Highway Department, Dallas District (less 21 months leave for active duty in USAF 1951-1953). Graduated from 1037 Aircraft Observer (Bombardment) School at Mather AFB in April 1952. Remainder of tour with 18th Air Force (troop carrier). Present occupation is constructing experimental aircraft.

WILLIAM J. GROSSMILLER III, was born May 26, 1925 at Philadelphia, PA and enlisted as Aviation Cadet in 1943. Flew 17 missions with the 330th BG as bombardier, including the longest 20th AF bombardment mission of 18 and a half hours against the Koriyama Chemical Plant in Northern Honshu.

Integrated as regular officer in 1947; pilot in 1949, then flew B-29s, B-50s, B-47s C-47s and T-29s. Attended Army War College, 1966. Pentagon 1966-1971, supporting senior USAF officials before congressional budget committees. Then as wing commander of 150 Minuteman missiles at Whiteman AFB. Grossmiller retired as colonel in 1973.

Married Loretta D. Cronin of Chicago, IL in 1948. They have four children: Karen, Gwen, William IV and Cynthia. Has BS, business administration; MS, international affairs; MA, public administration. Civilian retirement in 1981 as vice president, Finance of Public Service Satellite Consortium. Service organizations and Flight 13 Captain of Order of Daedalians, 1991.

EMICK P. GUIDRY, was born Feb. 24, 1921 in Carencro, LA and graduated from Carencro High School in 1940. Enlisted Aug. 26, 1942 and attended schools at Keesler Field, MS; Chanute Field, IL; Lowry Field, CO and Boeing Aircraft Factory, Seattle, WA.

Went to Pratt, KS where he rejoined with the guys from the 25th Sqdn. Was picked by Maj. Benton O'Neal as his left gunner and electrical specialist. They flew many hours Stateside checking new crews on B-29s from Pratt, KS to Gandor Bay, North Africa and Cairo, Egypt where they crash landed. The plane burnt along with all records of 25th Sqdn.

Sometime after arriving in Chakulia, India, Maj. O'Neal was grounded for health reasons. Guidry was then lucky to be able to fly with two of the Air Forces' best, Lt. Delmar D. Stevens and Maj. Woodrow P. Swancutt.

He was honorably discharged Oct. 24, 1945 with the rank of staff sergeant. He was awarded the Good Conduct, two Oak Leaf Clusters, three Distinguished Unit Badges, five Battle Stars and the Air Medal.

He met and married the sweetest gal in the world, Dorothy Domingue, in 1947. They have two lovely daughters, Katherine and Rebecca. Guidry retired in February 1986 after 38 years with a private utility company.

FREDERICK ERNST HAERTIG, was born Woodsboro, TX Nov. 15, 1913 and moved to Houston, TX in 1935. Entered the Army June 10, 1942; basic infantry training at Camp Robinson, AR; Adjutant General School Ft. Washington, MD. Assigned to Kelly AAF, San Antonio, TX in November 1942. Attended OCS April 1, 1944. Assigned 2nd Air Force via Smoky Hill AAF to Walker AAF, personnel officer. Assigned adjutant, 458th Sqdn, 330th BG, 314th Wing in March 1945. Transferred HQ 20th AF, duty with air inspector, September 1945.

Released from active duty March 1946 with the rank of captain. Recalled to active duty in March 1951, Ellington AFB, personnel officer, squadron adjutant, squadron commander. Released from active duty June 1953. Remained in the Active Reserve to June 1964. Retired with the rank of major.

Married Lola Hearn March 15, 1941. Employed with the U.S. Postal Service 1936 to 1971, retiring as postal service officer May 31, 1971 from the Dallas Regional Office, Post Office Department. Participates in church, Rotary, Tax Aide Program, cultural and other community affairs.

BROOKE SEYMOUR HARPER, was born Dec. 2, 1903 in Davis, WV. Received early flight training from his oldest brother Lt. Carl Brown Harper, a U.S. Naval Engineering test pilot. A designer of the Catapult System, Lt. Harper gave Amelia Earhart instrument instruction, during which time Col. Harper, then a civilian, was responsible for maintaining security for her aircraft at Curtis Wright Airport in Baltimore.

Prior to World War II, Col. Harper was Chief of Training for British and American Flying Cadets at Embrey-Riddle Aeronautical Institute in Florida. Requesting active duty after Pearl Harbor, he was assigned to advanced multi-engine training at Harlingen Field, TX.

Subsequently selected for duty in the Pacific with the 20th Air Force's 19th BG, known as the Famed 19th, the highest decorated group in the Air Force. He served as operations officer on Guam, flew over 25 combat missions in B-29s including the first pathfinder/bombing runs over mainland Japan.

After V-J day, he retired from the Air Force with the rank of lieutenant colonel. Military decorations include the Bronze Star and Air Medal with Oak Leaf Clusters. Joined Boeing Airplane Company in Renton, WA in capacity of engineering/experimental test pilot. Became director of Military Operations and liaison between Boeing and SAC. Retired from Boeing, moved to Columbia, SC and later to Baltimore-Towson, MD where he resides with his wife, Kitty, of 50 plus years.

JOE B. HEATON JR., was born Jan. 11, 1934 in Easley, SC; graduated from Easley Senior High School; USAF College with associate's degree in electronics and BS degree in business management from Limestone College. Had commercial over two engine rating and ATP rating.

He enlisted April 1, 1951 and was assigned to the 19th BG. He flew 32 combat missions as tail gunner on B-29 plane *No Sweat*. Helped in the rescue of European missionaries in the Belgian Congo (Angola); the Bay of Pigs (Cuba); polar mapping expeditions (Antarctica) and the Berlin Airlift. Served in Vietnam and Thailand, flying combat missions in AC-130 gunships.

Retired June 30, 1971 after 20 years with the rank of master sergeant. He received the Air Medal with one Oak Leaf Cluster, Air Force Commendation with two Oak Leaf Clusters, Korean Service Medal with two Bronze Stars, three Vietnam Service Medals, Good Conduct Army Medal with Silver Rope and two knots, Good Conduct Air Force with Silver Rope and two knots, Army of Occupation, National Defense Service Medal, Antarctic Service Medal with clasp, Air Force Expeditionary Medal, Vietnamese Service Medal with three Bronze Stars, United Nations Medal, Air Force Overseas Ribbon, Expert Marksmanship Ribbon, Republic of Vietnam Campaign Medal with Silver Clasp,

Republic of Korea Unit Citation and the Republic of Vietnam Presidential Unit Citation.

Work for the U.S. Postal Service before getting a job as Director of Avionics for Pinehurst Airlines. At the time of his death, July 9, 1991, he was working in avionics for Lockheed Aircraft Corporation in Greenville, SC.

He received full military rites at Greenlawn Memorial Park, Easley, SC.

CLEMENT HEDDLESON (CLEM), was born Wellsville, OH on Oct. 1, 1924. Joined the AAF in 1943 as an Aviation Cadet. Basic training at Miami Beach, FL; CTD, University of Tennessee, Knoxville, TN; pre-flight, Maxwell AAFB. Montgomery, AL; advanced navigation training, Ellington AAFB, Houston, TX and combat crew training, McDill AAFB, Tampa, FL.

Transitioned through Kearney AAFB Kearney, NB and assigned as a replacement combat crew navigator with 6th Sqdn., 29th BG, 314th Bomb Wing, 20th Air Force at North Field, Guam. Returned to civilian life in October 1946.

Returned to Ohio State University Columbus, OH, receiving a BSME in 1948 and a MSME in 1951. Joined General Electric Company in Oak Ridge, TN and held various management positions in the aerospace field in Cincinnati, OH; Valley Forge, PA and Washington, DC. Retired after 37 and a half years in February 1989.

Married Mary Ann Beatty in December 1948, they have one son and three daughters.

PAUL W. HILL, was born in Sidon, MS on March 31, 1922. He moved with his family to Jackson, MS and then to San Diego, CA. He returned to Jackson where he graduated from Herbert Hover High School in 1941 and then Hinds Jr College. He worked in Vicksburg, MS for R.G. Letourneau Company.

Enlisted Oct. 26, 1942 and reported as an aircraft mechanic at Maxwell Field, AL. Was sent to the 1804th Ord. Co. in Stockton, CA; then to Santa Ana where he trained as an aviation cadet; College Training Detachment in Missoula, MT; Gunnery School in Las Vegas, NV and graduated in December 1944 as a second lieutenant from the Navigation School in San Marcos, TX.

In Pratt, KS he was in the 8th Air Force in B-29s. Then attached to the 20th AAF on Guam from July 4 to September 1945. He flew 10 missions and rejoined the 8th AAF on Okinawa. He was honorably discharged May 1946 at Ft. Lewis, WA with the rank of first lieutenant. He received the Air Medal with Oak Leaf Cluster.

Returned to John Day, OR and worked in the lumber business until 1950. Then he moved to Chico, CA with his wife, Janice McKrola where he owned a Foster Freeze Store. In 1960 his son Fred was born and he sold the business and entered the Mutual Life Insurance company until 1966. After a divorce, he moved to Denver, CO and worked for Horizon Land Corporation and was transferred to Las Vegas, NV as a public relations manager for the Western Territory.

In 1974 he resigned and moved to Chico where he married Evelyn Weimer in 1979. He lost Evelyn in 1988. He met Thelma Snowden and began work for Coulter's Transfer Company. He likes to build model airplanes, refinish furniture and travel.

JOHN T. HINES, was born in Omaha, NE in 1925. Called to active duty from enlisted Reserve Corps Jan. 26, 1944.

Basic training at Jefferson Barracks (Pneumonia Gultch), MO. Gunnery School completed at Panama City, (Skunk Hollow), FL and B-29 Gunnery at Alamagordo (Oh My God, no), NM. Crew training with Crew 51, (The best of the best) 30th Bomb Sqdn., 19th BG at Great Bend, KS. Flew to Guam and got in on much of the "urban renewal" work in Japan, completing 32 missions as tail gunner shooting down one Tojo fighter and scaring lots of others.

Most memorable mission was Kolbe. Lost two engines on bomb run, eerie feeling watching engine parts and oil fly past windows. Crew shot down three "meat balls" and all guns were out of ammo, even with the extra 500 rounds he boot-legged for CYA. Aircraft commander made spectacular landing at Iwo Jima on third attempt with two engines out in a heavy rainstorm. Their B-29, *The City of Santa Monica*, went to the boneyard and they received a brand new B-29, built in Omaha and painted with the 3rd Marine Div. insignia in honor of the Marines. Flew the rest of the tour without a scratch.

Graduated from University of Nebraska at Omaha in 1950 with an engineering degree and received a direct commission. Spent the next 30 years back in uniform in the Korean call up, the Vietnam call up and with the Iowa Air National Guard as an engineer.

Retired as colonel in 1980 and as an Air Force Civil Engineer civilian in Washington, DC 1983. He received the Distinguished Flying Cross, four Air Medals, three Battle Stars, three Unit Citations and 15 other decorations.

Married Janice Saisslin in 1946, has four children, six grandchildren and two great-grandchildren. Currently engaged in civic work and real estate in Sioux City, IA.

HERBERT W. HOBLER, was born in St. Louis, MO Sept. 25, 1922. Entered Air Corps from Princeton University Class of 1944 on Feb. 28, 1943 at Atlantic City. He trained at Michigan State College, Santa Ana; Las Vegas Gunnery School; Hondo, TX, navigation; Boca Raton, FL, radar; McCook, NE, B-29 training; 9th BG, Tinian, arrived Jan. 28, 1945.

Navigator on Lloyd Welken crew 1st Sqdn. Missions included four of five March fire raids.

He is married and has four children. Radio, TV and cable TV for a 44 year career while living in Princeton, NJ. President of 9th Bomb Group Association 1987 to present.

RUDOLPH W. HOGG, was born in Bronte, TX on July 7, 1924 and moved to Big Spring, TX in 1929. Volunteered at Big Spring, TX Oct. 26, 1942 and was assigned to 8th Air Force, Big Spring, TX from October 1942 to January 1943. Then to Childress, TX AAFB January 1943; Salt Lake City, UT 1945; assigned to 509th 1st Ord. Sqdn., at Wendover Field, Wendover, UT; Seattle, WA 1945; Tinian Islands April 1945.

With the 509th Composite 1st Ord., 20th Air Force B-29 Bombers, Gen. Paul Tibbets as commanding officer. Aug. 6, 1945, his squadron dropped the

first atomic bomb on Hiroshima. Returned to the USA October 1945 to Roswell, NM AFB then to San Antonio, TX SAC AFB. Received honorable discharge Jan. 26, 1946 with the rank of corporal.

Married Velma, has two sons, James and Lee, and two daughters, Larna and Joni. Entered into farming and oil field work. Moved to Arizona in 1952 and worked in the copper mines. Retired in January 1990 from San Manuel Arizona Railroad Company as railroad engineer.

WALTER C. HOUSTON, was born in Caldwell, ID on Oct. 16, 1918. He enlisted in the Army Air Corp Oct. 28, 1940 and was assigned to 43rd AB Sqdn., McChord Air Field, WA. Reassigned to 7th BG. Was headed for the Philippine Island when Pearl Harbor was bombed. They were then sent to Java Dutch East Indies. After end of WWII was discharged from the service.

He re-entered the service in November 1949 and was sent to Castle AFB, Mercod, CA on B-29s as crew chief. Has been crew chief on B-17s, B-29, KB-29, B-50 and B-52s. Retired from service in 1965 at McChord Field, WA as SMSGT.

FOSTER B. HUFF, was born Oct. 21, 1919 in Monarch, UT. He joined the Utah National Guard in 1937. Drafted into Army in February 1942 and selected for Aviation Cadet Training.

Assigned to Class 43-F; primary, Sweetwater, TX; basic, Enid, OK; advanced, Pampa, TX. Was commissioned in June 1943. Assigned to Liberal Army Air Base, KS for B-24 training. Selected to be a B-24 instructor pilot. Applied for B-29 training and transferred to Walker AFB, KS. Flew B-29 to Guam in April 1945. Assigned to 20th Air Force, 314th Wing, 330th BG,

458th Bomb Sqdn. Flew 20 missions as B-29 airplane commander (1st pilot) of the *City of Spanish Fork, Utah.*

Requested release from active duty in November 1946. Opened a photographic business in 1948. Recalled to active duty in 1951. Business, which had been leased to an employee, burned to the ground. Assigned to Intelligence Functions in Korea for one year. After several years in States, spent a three year tour in Germany. Assigned to 8th AF, Westover AFB, MA. Assigned to Vietnam 1965-1966.

Retired February 1967 as lieutenant colonel. Received two Air Medals.

Married Geraldine Chittenden on March 6, 1945. They have two children, Ronald and Janelle; son-in-law, David Gebhardt; and two grandsons, Stuart and John.

JOHN H. HUG, received Pilot Wings February 1943. Flew Bombadiers at Roswell, NM then trained in B-29s at Clovis, NM in 1944. Assigned to 45th Sqdn., 40th BG at Chakulia, India. First combat mission was to Singapore, 18 hours, 25 minutes flying time with over 9.5 hours on three engines. Completed 17 combat missions.

On V-J day his crew was over Tokyo for four hours dodging airplanes most of the time. That day was max effort with nearly 800 B-29s in the air. Instructed B-29 combat crews at Randolph AFB two years during the Korean Conflict. Assigned to Air Weather Service in 1952.

Flew hurricanes and typhoons in WB-29s, WB-50s, WB-47s and WC-130s for 16 years. After flying C-130s for two years in Vietnam, he retired as lieutenant colonel with 30 years.

Idaho is home since retirement, flying charter, back country and instructing single and multi-engine. Member of QB and Air Forces Flyers Club (ham radio). Accumulated over 13,000 hours in 50 years of accident-free flying.

JOHN JARZABEK, was born in Shamokin, PA on Jan. 13, 1910. He enlisted in the U.S. Army at Ft. Hoyle, MD on Aug. 22, 1926. He served six years in Field Artillery, re-enlisted in the Army Air Corps at Rockwell Field, Coronado, CA in 1934. Served with 19th BG, transferred to March Field in 1935 to 30th BG, transferred to Hawaii in May 1941, was at Hickam Field when WWII began.

Was sent to South Pacific, Guadalcanal, North Solomons and New Guinea Campaigns. Returned to the States in July 1944 and was stationed at Hamilton, Salinas, March, Davis Monthan, McChord, Portland, Anderson (Guam) and Travis AFB.

Retired April 30, 1954 at Travis AFB with the rank master sergeant. He received the Asiatic-Pacific Campaign, American Defense, Good Conduct and Battle Stars for Hawaii, (Dec. 7, 1941), Guadalcanal, North Solomons and New Guinea.

Returned to Riverside, CA and worked at Northrup Aircraft, Southern California Aircraft, Pacific Airmotor Corp. and for the U.S. Post Office for 14 years. He retired from the post office in June 1973.

Married Floy Elrod in June 1940. They had three children: James G., Nyoni L. and David C. On July 27, 1983, John Jarzabek passed away from lung cancer.

EINO E. JENSTROM, was born May 15, 1921 in Waukegan, IL; private pilot, Govt. CPT, June 1941 - Ruth Harmon Inst., Kenosha, WI; Aviation Cadet Nov. 6, 1941, Grad. Kelly AFB, May 20, 1942; married Jean Huttleston of Waukegan same day. Flt. instructor, Goodfellow AFB, TX; flt. inst. advanced, Kelly AFB, TX; instructor at Flt. Inst. School, Randolph AFB; Bombers B-24; B-29, 40th BG, Tinian Island, May 1, 1945, flew Eddie Allen, dedicated B-29, May 23, 1945, target: Tokyo, airplane scrapped, mission article Air Force Mag., August 1990. Discharged colonel, July 1971. Attorney, VA State Bar July 1973. Daughters, Linda and Kathleen.

Sq. CO, B-29 from Yokota, Japan on Korean and Sq. CO, B-36 at Spokane, WA; Air Tac. School, Maxwell AFB, 1948; Special Weapons, Sandia, NM 1948; Staff and Command School, Maxwell AFB, AL 1954; Plans, Hq. 15AF, 1954-58; B-52, 1957; Plans, Hq. USAF, 1958; National War College, 1964; Research Assoc. Johns Hopkins U., DC, 1964-65; Plans, SACEUR 1965-68; Arms Control, JCS, 1968-71; BA, Commerce, Univ. of Maryland 1963; MA, Intl. Aff., George Washington Univ. 1964; LLB, Georgetown Univ. 1973; Vestry of St. Andrews Episcopal Church, Arlington, VA; Virginia State Bar, American Bar Ass'n and attorney, Arlington, VA since 1973; Golden Wedding May 20, 1992. Have had a lot of fun living.

JOHN R. JEWETT (JACK), was born in Niagara Falls, NY March 14, 1921. He enlisted in the Reserve Air Force in 1942 and continued college education at Ohio University following two years at Purdue. Called to active duty May 1943 to OCS at Boca Raton, FL. In August 1943 was assigned to engineering training Yale University. Volunteered in B-29 flight engineering and commissioned second lieutenant February 1944. Trained at Boeing Factory School, Lowry Field, McCook NE, Harrington, KS.

Assigned to 9th BG, 99th Sqdn., Tinian Island January 1945. Flew seven missions, one to Japan. Mission to Tokyo March 10, 1945 was first low altitude incendiary bombing. Ran into problems, ditching near Pajoris, volcanic island, on return flight. Plane broke in two in rough seas. Nine of crew struggled into three rafts, three others died (one a trainee). Rescued from island by Navy after one and a half days. Awarded Purple Heart.

He was on a crew flying airmen to U.S. in late November 1945. Was discharged December 1945.

After marriage at Yale in 1944, one child was born before overseas duty and three more in subsequent years. Joined Kimberly Clark Corp. in 1946; employed 34 years as industrial engineer and accountant at Niagara Falls Mill and New Milford (Ct.) Mill. Retired from Ct. Mill and enjoying retirement there since 1981 with frequent travels around the country.

ARTHUR J. JOHNSON, was born July 30, 1917 in Outlook, MT. Entered the service in Missoula, MT on June 16, 1942. Discharged Roswell AFB, Roswell,

NM on Nov. 16, 1945. Was recalled to active duty for the Korean War at McChord AFB, WA on Sept. 1, 1950 to Aug. 31, 1951. Served in 509th Composite Group, 1st Atomic Bombardment, 20th AF during WWII.

Duty assignments include base sergeant major, Wendover Field, UT prior to transfer 509th Composite Group as group sergeant major. Medals awarded include the Bronze Star and Asiatic-Pacific Theater with two Battle Stars. Highlight of service was seeing the B-29 *Enola Gay* return from successful mission over Hiroshima Aug. 6, 1945 and *Bock's Car* from Nagasaki Aug. 8, 1945.

Upon discharge he attended Stanford University for post-graduate degrees. Retired from career in business education at high school and college level in teaching and administration.

LOUIS M. JONES, was born July 21, 1918 in Dallas, TX. Newman High School, 1935. Bachelor of business administration and juris doctorate degrees from Tulane University, 1941.

Drafted Feb. 4, 1941. Discharged as a sergeant in October 1942 upon graduation as a second lieutenant from Army Air Force Administrative School, Miami, FL the same month. Graduated from Army Air Force Combat Intelligence School, Harrisburg, PA in January 1943.

Joined 45th Bombardment Sqdn. of the 40th Group stationed in Galapagos Islands in January 1943. Graduated from Evasion and Escape School in Washington, DC in February, 1944.

Remained with the 40th Group during the India and China operations. Invented a survival vest that was used on the first B-29 bombardment mission over Bankok, Thailand, June 5, 1944. Awarded the Bronze Star.

Assigned as Army Air Force representative to the American Military Mission to Yenan, Communist China in June 1944 to assist in rescue operations of Army Air Force personnel down in communist controlled territory in China.

Discharged as a captain from the Army Air Force in November 1945. Returned to New Orleans, LA where he has been engaged in the private practice of law as well as serving on the staff of the Attorney General of Louisiana.

ORVAL H. KAISER, was born in New Athens, IL on June 9, 1925. He was drafted in Belleville, IL in October 1943.

Military locations/stations: Fort Sheridan, IL; Jefferson Barracks, MO; Perrin, TX; Clovis, NM; University of Alabama; Panama City, FL; McCook, NE; Herington, KS; Mather, CA; Tinian in January 1945 with the 9th BG; Mojave, CA; back to Tinian, then San Pedro, CA.

Kaiser received the Distinguished Flying Cross with one Oak Leaf Cluster. He served as a radar operator. He was discharged in December 1945 with the rank of staff sergeant. He was recalled in May 1951 until August 1952.

He married Ruth and they have two daughters and five grandchildren. He received a BSBA at Washington University. Kaiser was a certified internal auditor and retired in 1986 from the Lockheed Aircraft Corporation.

HARVEY H. KEMP, was born in Taft, FL on May 11, 1922. He entered NYA School of Aviation, in Ocala, FL. Resigned to join the Army Aviation Cadet Train-

ing beginning of WWII. He entered basic training on Nov. 7, 1942 at Miami Beach, FL. Transferred CDT at Memphis State College, Memphis, TN.

He entered classification and Preflight School in Santa Ana, CA. He completed pilot training in Tucson, AZ. Had basic at Ontario, CA; twin engine advancement at Pecos, TX and graduated as a flight officer. He completed B-17 transition in Hobbs, NM. He was then assigned to B-29 Combat Crew, completing transition in Alamagordo, NM.

He was stationed with the 20th AF, 313th Wing, 504th VH BG, 680th Sqdn., in Tinian, Marianas Islands in the Pacific. He completed 23 bombing and mining missions against Japan. His assignments for active duty included Panama, Puerto Rico, North Africa, Minnesota and Florida.

His memorable experiences include a close miss by kamikaze over Tokyo, "no flap" fast landing at Iwo Jima, near miss with B-29 in bad weather near Nagoya, Japan, "Hung bomb" in rack after Tokyo run, mining mission in the sea of Japan along the China Coast and the flak "like hail on tin roof," customary on most missions.

He returned to States and was discharged from active duty. Entered Reserves, Jan. 19, 1946. Re-entered active duty in Air Force and served 22 years, retiring as master sergeant. Retired Oct. 3, 1974, W0-1, USAF, 30 years. He received the Distinguished Flying Cross, Air Medal with four Oak Leaf Clusters, Commendation Medal and the Good Conduct Medal with five Bronze Loops.

He is married to Helen, they have a son, Stephen, and two daughters, Donna and Kathleen. They reside in Umatilla, FL.

JOHN KERR, was born on June 26, 1917 and graduated from Harrod High School in 1935. He was drafted in 1943; trained in Gunnery School in Texas and was selected as a gunner on B-29 crew in McCook, NE.

He flew 35 combat missions in B-29s with the 9th BG as an airplane electrical mechanic left gunner while on Tinian.

His crew flew 35 combat missions and bombed Japan proper, Manchuria, Iwo Jima and Truk. He cared for and repaired defects on guns and turrets. He fired 50 caliber guns while in combat.

Received the Distinguished Flying Cross and the Air Medal with three Oak Leaf Clusters. Returned to the States and was discharged in November 1945 with the rank of staff sergeant.

Received a BA degree while attending the universities of Alabama, Pittsburgh and Ohio Northern an MBA from Bowling Green, KY.

Worked 29 years as a manufacturing engineer with Aerospace Division, Lima Westinghouse. Worked on electrical system for the Apollo Space Ship. He retired from Lima Electric.

Kerr and his wife have been married for 52 years, they have two children and two grandchildren.

OTTO KERSTNER, was born in Lorain, OH in 1916. After high school graduation, he joined the CCC camp and later worked for U.S. Steel. In January 1941 he was drafted into President Roosevelt's one year draft (166th Inf.) After Pearl Harbor, he joined cadets, Class 42-X (Hap Arnolds' Guinea Pigs), then he became a basic flying instructor at Randolph Field and Garden City, KS.

In 1944 he attended B-29 School in Clovis, NM. As pilot of B-29 flew to Chakulia, India in the latter part of 1944. Was assigned to the 25th Bomb Sqdn. 40th BG. Flew a number of missions in CBI, made several trips to China, then to Tinian. After several missions over Japan, he bailed out into the Pacific. The crew was split up, he became co-pilot for Maj. John Childs' lead crew. He flew a total of 29 missions.

Was awarded the Distinguished Flying Cross, Air Medal with two Oak Leaf Clusters and the Asiatic Medal with three Battle Stars.

After his discharge he attended Indiana Tech, he received a BSME degree. He worked for Hughes, Northrup and Rockwell International. Retired in 1982, married in 1963 and has two stepsons.

CECIL NEUHAUSER KING, was born in Birmingham, AL on April 26, 1919. With a BS in economics he entered the USAF in June 1942. Aircraft mechanics-Keesler; commissioned at Chanute in December 1942; OTS Miami; maintenance officer 411 HB Training Squadron, Gowen Field; B-29 School, Seattle; 393rd VHB Sqdn. in Fairmont, then the 509th Composite (Atomic Bombardment).

He was discharged in March 1946 with the rank of captain. Married Jappie in 1942, had a son in 1944 and a daughter in 1952. Received a BSME in 1949; a MS auto engineer in 1951.

Had a career in automotive manufacturing as a foundry, engineer, manager, designer and consultant. Was also a college instructor/professor, management and accounting. Published in Foundry and Modern Castings.

Military accomplishments: Bronze Star; being responsible for maintenance crews with enviable record of zero lost aircraft/air crews in training or combat; primary solution of one cause of in-flight fires B-24.

Civilian accomplishments: redesign front suspension bearing T-43 Tank; directed conversion of Argentine foundry to automotive work; began production in Mexican foundry of engine castings for diesel truck, tractor gasoline automotive, six-cylinder and V-8. Latter facility is today's largest independent Mexican foundry.

ROBERT T. KISER, was born on April 19, 1932 in Detroit, MI. He enlisted into the USAF on April 21, 1949 and assigned to San Antonio and Witchita Falls, TX for aircraft mechanic training.

Assigned to the 28th Bomb Sqdn. 19th BG for Korean War service from Guam. Okinawa and Japan. Returned to the States in 1952 for re-assignment to Morroco, North Africa and subsequent honorable discharge at Tucson, AZ on Nov. 25, 1952 with the rank of staff sergeant.

Recipient of the United Nations Service Medal and the Korean Service Medal with three Bronze Stars and the National Defense Medal.

After service, he had a career in credit/finance with the Goodyear Tire & Rubber Company. He married M. Frances Alexander, they have two sons and three daughters. Presently retired in Anderson, SC.

RUSSELL J. LA CROIX, was born on May 7, 1923 in Chicago, IL and was inducted into the USAF on Dec. 3, 1942. Was called to active duty on Jan. 31, 1943. Sent to Scott Field for Radio School and graduated as a ground station radio operator in May 1943.

Assigned for training to the 393rd Bomb Sqdn., 504th BG at Fairmont, NE. In October 1944 the 393rd was detached from the 504th and became part of the 509th Composite BG, 1st Atomic Bombardment at Wendover Field, UT. After training in Utah, the 509th moved overseas to Tinian Island in the Marianas in May 1945.

The bombs were dropped in August and he returned to the States in October 1945. Discharged with the rank of sergeant in February 1946.

Married Catherine and has a daughter, Nicolette. Worked as a carpenter until 1988 when he retired. He grows Dahlias for a hobby, exhibits them at shows and belongs to four Dahlia societies.

SEYMOUR LANDAU, was born on Oct. 25, 1921 in Brooklyn, NY and had two years of college. He joined the USAAF in October 1942. Aircraft and Engine Mechanics School in Amarillo, TX; Flight Engineers School, Pratt, KS; B-29 School in Seattle, WA.

Military locations/stations: Fort Dix, NJ; Miami Beach, FL; Amarillo, TX; Pratt, KS; Seattle, WA; Salina, KS; Edwards AFB, CA; Chaculia, India; China; Tinian and Marianas Islands.

Memorable experiences include: flying over the Himalayas (the Hump); caving in the gates of the Singapore dry docks; receiving the Distinguished Flying Cross from Gen. Curtis LeMay.

As a flight engineer, he flew on his first B-29 mission over Bangkok, plus missions over Manchuria, Formosa, Singapore and Japan. Served with 20th AF, 40th BG (VH), 44th Bomb Sqdn. (VH).

He was discharged in October 1945 with the rank of flight officer. He also received three Air Medals, the Presidential Unit Citation with eight Battle Stars and the New York State Conspicuous Service Cross.

Married and has five children and five grandchildren. He worked 38 years with one firm, from shipping clerk to president and chief operating officer last eight years. He retired in 1981 and bought a country inn to manage and live in from June 1981 to October 1984.

GLENN H. LEECH, was born on Sept. 23, 1913 in Albany, TX to a pioneer ranching family. Volunteered for the USAF on Feb. 14, 1942. Received training in Lubbock, TX, Denver, CO and McCook, NE.

Was sent to Tinian in 1944. He completed 35 missions over Japan as a flight engineer on B-29 *Daring Donna*. From one mission, the crew returned in

the badly damaged plane with half tail and only one engine operating. All missions were made with the original crew flying *Daring Donna*.

He received the Distinguished Flying Cross and was discharged in October 1945 with the rank of flight officer.

Returned to Albany, TX and continued in the ranching operation. He is active in community affairs, the 9th Bomb Group Association and attends all re-unions.

Married Grace Gillean, they have two daughters and one son.

GEORGE J. LEMMON (JIM), was born on Nov. 27, 1919 in Denver, CO and moved to Long Beach, CA in 1928. He enlisted as an aviation cadet May 12, 1942 and was commissioned second lieutenant on Nov. 13, 1943.

He was assigned to Combat Training B-17s in Rapid City, SD in January 1943, then to the 95th BG to England on May 29, 1944. Flew 33 missions as a bombardier (1031-Pathfinder Radar Norden). Led group, combat wing, division, Air Force leads, including two shuttle missions to Russia. Returned to the States on Nov. 7, 1944, assigned to the 21st Bomb Command, Guam on May 30, 1945. With the 330th BG (B-29), he flew 19 missions. Received the Silver Star, Distinguished Flying Cross (recommended two clusters) and the Air Medal with five clusters.

Re-assigned to Hamilton AFB (released active duty) on Sept. 15, 1945, assigned to AF Reserve. Transferred to California Air National Guard Aug. 12, 1949. Recalled to active duty in the USAF on Nov. 16, 1951 with the 144th AC&W Sqdn. (Intelligence Officer-2051). Assigned to 87th Air Base Sqdn., Geiger AFB in Spokane, WA on Jan. 19, 1952. He assumed command of the 530th Air Base Sqdn. on Feb. 27, 1953. Transferred to Air Force Reserve on June 29, 1953. He retired from the USAF on Nov. 27, 1979 with the rank of lieutenant colonel.

Freshman crew coach (Rowing) University of California, Berkeley 1954-1959, Varsity crew coach 1960-1966, Varsity Crew National Champions in 1960, 1961 and 1964. He was dean of men at the University of California in 1966. Retired as director of Student Activities & Services (Dean of Men, Emeritus) June 1982. Published book in 1989 *Log of Rowing, University of California 1870-1987.*

Married Jean Rogers in 1950. They have two daughters and four grandchildren.

ROBERT E. LE MON (BOB) LT/COL., USAF RES, RET, was born Feb. 6, 1920 in Poseyville, IN. Enlisted in the Army Air Corps Oct. 28, 1942 at LaFayette, IN, Private S/N 15109579. Inducted into Air Cadet training April 28, 1943 at Fort Thomas, KY.

Underwent basic training at Keesler Field, Biloxi, MS. Following this he was sent to the College Training Detachment, CTD at Syracuse University, Syracuse, NY. Next was classification at the Nashville, TN Aviation Cadet Classification Center (NACCC), classified as a Bombardier, and sent to Bombardier Preflight School at Santa Ana, CA. Following this, he was sent to Aerial Machine Gunnery School at Kingman, AZ and then to Army Air Force Bombardier School, Kirtland Field, Albuquerque, NM.

Comissioned a 2nd Lt. Bombardier, Kirtland

Class 44-9 July 1, 1944, and assigned to 2nd Air Force. Sent to Lincoln Army Air Field, Lincoln, NE for leave of absence and re-assignment. Joined 29th Bomb Group (VH) B-29s Pratt Army Air Field, Pratt, KS. Assigned to 6th Sqdn. for overseas Bombardier training at Puerto Rico and Pratt, KS.

Staged at Herington, KS, assigned new B-29 airplane and allied overseas equipment. Arrived in Guam Feb. 26, 1945, assigned to 20th Air Force, XXI Bomber Command 314th Bomb Wing, 29th Bomb Gp. (VH), 6th Bomb Sqdn., Crew No. 11, name of plane: "The Natural." He flew 35 missions to Japan. Total bombs dropped 195 tons, 263,500 lbs. incendiaries; 105,500 lbs. high explosives; 21,000 lbs. fragmentations. Flew alternate lead or deputy lead bombardier on last 23 missions.

Memorable missions; Osaka, Tokyo fire raids and Omura Aircraft Naval Station. (Shot down one Japanese fighter plane.)

Decorations: Distinguished Flying Cross with Oak Leaf Cluster, Air Medal with two Oak Leaf Clusters, Asiatic-Pacific Theater Ribbon with Bronze Service Star, World War II Victory Medal, American Campaign Medal and the Armed Forces Reserve Medal.

Discharged on Dec. 5, 1945, San Antonio, TX.

Bob returned to his former employer, U.S. Rubber Company, Mishawaka, IN as middle management of military aircraft fuel cell testing while serving 18 years in the USAF Ready Reserves. Fully retired since 1984.

JOHN J. LESNIEWSKI, was born Nov. 2, 1920 in Rutland, VT and moved to Philadelphia, PA in 1925. Drafted into the USAF on March 28, 1944 in New Cumberland, PA.

Basic training at Sheppard Field, TX; Wendover, UT as a flight line airplane and engine mechanic on P-47, C-46, C-54 and B-29. Assigned to the 393rd Bomb Sqdn., 509th Composite Group on May 6, 1945, Marianas (Tinian Island) with the ground crew (#82 Enola Gay); Nov. 4, 1945 Roswell, NM. Discharged with rank PFC on April 8, 1946 at Fort Meade, MD.

Married Josephine Lyszczasz on Jan. 16, 1943 and had son Robert on Dec. 7, 1944. Received FAA certificate A&P Mechanic in December 1940. Spent his career in aviation at the Philadelphia Airport in Pennsylvania. He was associated with the Kelley Auto Gyro, Piasecki Helicopters, Vertol, Boeing Helicopters, HRP-1, H-21, CH-47, XYH-16, CH-46, XCH-62, YUH-61A, HUP-25, Model 234, Model 347 and B-0105. He retired from the Boeing Helicopters in Pennsylvania in August 1982 after 35 years and has moved to Sun City West, AZ.

RUSSELL J. LOCANDRO, was born on Nov. 5, 1922 in New Brunswick, NJ. Drafted into the USAF in February 1943. Basic training in Miami Beach, FL; Radio Operator School at Scott Field AFB, IL. Was radio operator and mechanic at Traux Field, Madison, WI in 1943; Radar Mechanic Sea Search Observer Tech. School, Boca Raton Field, FL where he graduated in April 1944.

Participated in China, Burma, India, Tinian Island campaigns. Had 500 hours of flying time, 275 hours combat time and 16 bombing missions in Japan.

Being a professional musician, clarinet under arm, organized music groups wherever he was stationed. On Tinian Island, 1944 to 1945 he organized a band, "Stateside 7." In between flying bombing missions they played at hospitals, Officer's Clubs, Non-Com Clubs, etc. 40th BG, 44th Sqdn. officially named its original Kagu Tsuchi Group Band and was known as the best little "Big" band on Tinian Island. Members were: Russ Locandro, Eddie Seymour, Eddie Bishop (deceased), James Houseman (deceased), Vito Mancino, Art Hall, William Wolfson and Max Corzilius.

After 46 years the Stateside 7 volunteered and played music at the 40th BG re-union in Orlando, FL in Oct. 2-6, 1991. Only the five living remaining members played. Max Corzilius was unable to be there and was replaced by Rocky Ray, friend of Russ who lives in Florida. The band received many letters of appreciation for furnishing music as it brought back many memories of life on Tinian, it was very well planned successful re-union enjoyed by all.

He was honorably discharged on Oct. 24, 1945 at Mather Air Force Field in Sacramento, CA. He completed his education at Rutgers University, New York Institute of Finance. He has had several business careers and after 30 years as a portfolio manager with a major New York stock exchange firm he retired in June 1990.

In retirement he wrote a technical computer program to trade the stock market and daily supervises and manages his own financial portfolio. He is actively playing music again and making musical computer arrangements by adding a slight rock rhythm to the big band music in order to make it more compatible and acceptable to both the older and younger generation. He has been president of the Community Crime Watch for 30 years. He is happy and enjoying to be able to do all these things in his retirement years.

DOUGLAS H. LOGAN, was born on Feb. 2, 1918 in Bokchito, OK; received a BS degree at Florida State University and master's degree from University of Southern California. Enlisted in Army Air Corps at Oklahoma City, OK, September 1939; arrived March Field, Riverside, CA; Aircraft Armament School, Lowry Field, Denver, CO; assigned to 30th Sqdn., 19th BG.

Military locations/stations were many, some of them were: Clark Field, Pampanga, Luzon Philippines; flew B-17 missions from Del Monte, Mindanao, Batchelor Field, Australia; Singosari Airbase, Malang Java, flew missions to straits of Makassar; Camp Royal Park, Melbourne, Australia; Cloncurry, Australia flew missions to Port Moresby and Lae, New Guinea, Rabaul, New Britain etc.

In August 1942, he was wounded in a B-17 crash near Horn Island and convalesced in Brisbane, Sydney and Melbourne. Came back to the States and after preflight, primary, basic and advanced flight training, graduated from pilot school in December 1944. Attended Command and Staff College, Flight Safety Officer School. Stayed in service and worked in various positions until retiring on May 31, 1966 with the rank lieutenant colonel.

He was married to Mary and had three daughters, then divorced. He married Betty and had two stepsons. He was employed by the McDonald Douglas Corp. in California as an engineer for 10 years.

In 1984 he had major surgery. Unfortunately, he was given a blood transfusion and the blood was contaminated. Consequently, he suffered and died from AIDS on May 5, 1987.

He was a very virtuous, courageous and wonderful man!

RAYMOND C. MAGUIRE, was born Feb. 2, 1922 in Providence, RI and was drafted into the service on Jan. 13, 1943. He received radio operator training at Scott Field, IL and was assigned to the 19th BG, 314th Bomb Wing at Great Bend, KS.

He arrived in Guam February 1945. His first mission was the now famous first low level Tokyo raid on March 9, 1945. The 93rd Sqdn. lost three aircraft including the squadron commander. On May 25, 1945 after the attack on Tokyo, their CFC gunner was killed and two scanners wounded. This was several miles off the coast by a B-29, which immediately turned back towards Japan. An investigation of navigator logs found no other B-29 in the area at that time. Their plane was named the *City of Clifton* where Capt. Charles Neil, aircraft commander, lived. He was awarded the Distinguished Flying Cross and the Air Medal with five Oak Leaf Clusters after flying 32 missions.

Was discharged on Nov. 2, 1945. Later spent five years as instructor in the Navy and subsequently 17 years in the USAF as Russian linguist.

Retired since 1972, he is married and has three children.

ELMER W. MARTIN, was born on Oct. 15, 1912 in Williamsport, MD. He joined the USAF on Nov. 7, 1930 at Langley AFB in Virginia.

Participated in the battles of WWII and Korea. Discharged on Oct. 31, 1953 with the rank of master sergeant. Received Certificate of Appreciation, Korean Service Medal, United Nations Service Medal and the Bronze Star Medal.

After retiring from the USAF, he worked at Rohr, Riverside from 1958 to 1976 as a supervisor. From 1953 to 1958 he was in the construction of the Navy hospital at San Diego, CA.

MARK P. MARTY, was born March 4, 1919 in Milwaukee, WI and grew up in Minneapolis, MN. Drafted into the Army Medics in 1942, basic training was in Grenada, MS with the 331st Med. Reg., in the

Tennessee Maneuvers in 1943. He was a surgical technician for one and a half years.

In 1943 he transferred into the AAF; basic training at Miami Beach, FL; Gunnery School, Harlingen, TX. He was a tail gunner on a B-24. Took advanced training in Alamagordo, NM. Was a RT-blister gunner on B-29. In 1944 was assigned to Harry Hayes' crew, 43rd Sqdn., 29th BG, 314th Bomb Wing.

From Guam in February 1945, he completed 35 combat missions over Japan (five times over Tokyo) and shot down four Jap-fighters. He received the Distinguished Flying Cross and other medals.

Was discharged in October 1945 in Santa Ana, CA with the rank of sergeant.

He and Millie were married for 47 years and have three sons, three daughters and 11 grandchildren. Graduated from the NW Chiropractic College and Western State College. He had a chiropractic practice for 43 years. In 1970 he was president of the Mn. Chiropractic Association. Was awarded the Distinguished Service Award in 1975, in 1988 the Chiropractic Family of the Year Award (13 Dr. Marty's all D.C.s)

He retired in 1992 and lives in Minneapolis, MN. His wife Millie passed away Sept. 24, 1993.

WILLIAM T. MATTINGLY SR.,

was born on July 1, 1921 in Blackford, KY and was drafted on July 25, 1942. He had eight months in Army training at Camp Swift in Austin, TX and at Fort Sam Houston in San Antonio, TX. He was then transferred to the Air Corps where he spent several months in training to be a pilot. This was at San Antonio and at Chickasha, OK.

After a few weeks at Wichita Falls, TX, he was transferred to Amarillo, TX for training in airplane mechanics. From there he was sent to Boeing Factory School in Seattle, WA to train to be a B-29 crew chief. While waiting for his plane to come off the assembly line, he served as crew chief of a B-17 at McCook, NE. After completing this training, he was sent to Tinian where he was responsible for maintenance of the plane *Sweet Sue.*

He was discharged on Nov. 26, 1945 with the rank of staff sergeant.

Married Geneva Morrow in 1946 and they have three children: William Taylor Jr., Edward Allen and Ruth Ellen. He spent 31 years as a rural letter carrier in Clay, KY. He retired in February 1980 and is currently farming in Crittenden County, Kentucky.

HOWARD W. McCLELLAN,

was born on June 18, 1918 in Buchanan, MI. He joined the USAF on Dec. 30, 1940 as an aviation cadet, Class 41-F. Primary training was at Ontario, CA; basic at San Angelo, TX; and advance training at Barksdale AFB, LA.

He served on a ferrying command, 330th BG, 10th Depot Group, 2nd BG, AFLC, chief log plans, 7th Air Force. He flew 32 missions (B-29s from Guam) and 24 missions (support Ops. Saigon Vietnam).

His memorable experience was when the first Atom bomb was dropped on Hiroshima, Aug. 6, 1945, the B-29 *City of Omaha* crew had a ring side seat. They were flying a radar reconnaissance mission and arrived over Japan at 10,000 feet about 11 hours after the bomb had been dropped. The total destruction was awesome; a once very large city no longer existed.

Discharged with the rank of lieutenant colonel, he received the Distinguished Flying Cross with four clusters; Air Medal with nine clusters; Pacific, Europe,

Korea, Vietnam Theater; Occupation Germany, Berlin Air Lift, Bronze Star and the Air Force Commendation Medal.

Worked for Boeing Aerospace Co. KSC for 14 and a half years and Lockheed Aerospace Co. for one and a half years. Now retired, he supports the AFA, TROA, American Legion, Dadelions and church. Has six children, 16 grandchildren and one great-grandson.

FREDERICK A. McDOWELL (FRED),

was born on Dec. 11, 1919 in Franklin, PA and enlisted in the USAF on Feb. 6, 1942. Instructor, aircraft maintenance, Keesler Field in Biloxi, MS to November 1943; sergeant B-24, maintenance and flight engineer, Kirkland AFB in Albuquerque, NM to April 1944.

Then to B-29 Boeing School, Renton, WA; Flight Engineering School, Lowry Field, CO; Combat School, Clovis, NM. He was staff sergeant on B-29, flight engineer, 44th BG, 40th Bomb Sqdn. His plane was *Miss You* and pilots were McLarten and Burchett.

Was in China, Central Burma and Japan campaigns. Stationed at Chiculia, India and Tinian Island. Received the Air Medal with three Oak Leaf Clusters. He was discharged on Nov. 6, 1945 with the rank of flight officer.

He was married Nov. 22, 1941 in Pittsburgh, PA.

JAMES W. McFALLS,

was born on Jan. 21, 1921 in Youngstown, OH and moved to Girard, OH in 1940. He was drafted in Girard, OH in Oct. 23, 1942. Finished Mechanics School at Keesler Field, MS in April 1943. Was assigned to 444th Fighter Sqdn. as a mechanic on P-51s and P-47s at Bartow Air Base in Bartow, FL.

Went on to complete Aircraft Electrical School at the end of May 1943 at Chanute Field, IL. He was assigned to the 20th Air Force, 19th BG, 93rd Sqdn. in June 1943 as a mechanic and electrician on B-17s at Great Bend Air Base, Great Bend, KS. He was made crew chief of a B-29, 19th BG 93rd Sqdn. Was sent to North Field, Guam on Feb. 2, 1945.

Participated in Air Offensive Japan. Received the American Theater Ribbon, Asiatic-Pacific Theater Ribbon with one Bronze Star, Good Conduct Ribbon and the Bronze Star Victory Medal. Was discharged on Jan. 7, 1946 with the rank of technical sergeant.

Married the former Ida Isoldi and has four children: Florence, James, William and Margaret. He worked as an electrician for U. S. Steel, McDonald, OH. He retired in 1981 as a conductor after 31 years on the Youngstown and Northern Railroad.

FRANK W. McKINNEY,

was born Dec. 14, 1920 in El Paso, TX. He joined the USAAC as an aviation cadet at Ft. Bliss, TX in May 1942. He graduated from Advanced Bombardier and Celestial Navigation Schools and was then assigned to the 44th Sqdn., 40th BG at Pratt, KS.

He flew combat missions as lead crew bombardier and as navigator from Chakulia, India and Hsing Ching, China. He also served as assistant squadron bombardier. Returned to the States and was assigned to Muroc (Edwards) AFB, CA as an instructor. When the war ended he was relieved from active duty at Ft. Bliss, TX in December 1945.

His most memorable experience was being the bombardier on the first B-29 bombing Japan on the Yawata mission on June 15, 1944 and witnessing the great "fireworks" display put up by the Japs in trying to knock them down.

He continued a part-time career in the active Air Force Reserve and retired on Jan. 1, 1974 as a colonel commanding a Security Police Detachment. His awards include the Distinguished Flying Cross with one Oak Leaf Cluster, Air Medal with one Oak Leaf Cluster, Air Force Commendation Medal, Asiatic-Pacific Theater Ribbon with six Battle Stars, plus all other awards awarded to WWII veterans.

He was a licensed public accountant in Texas and practiced accounting, tax and management services as sole practitioner from 1947 to date. Now semi-retired, but maintains an office with a limited practice to keep busy. Was active in helping to organize the 40th Bomb Group Association and served as first treasurer of the association.

He married Mary Jane Marion of Pennsylvania in 1945. They have six daughters and one son: Pamela, Patricia, Priscilla, Paula, Penny, Mary Lou and Frank John.

CARLIS J. McLEOD,

was born on Dec. 20, 1924 in Walton County, FL. He enlisted as an aviation cadet at Elgin Field; was inducted into Camp Blanding on June 24, 1943 and had basic at Miami Beach, FL.

LaGrande, OR, Santa Ana, CA (pre-flight-washed December 1943); Scott Field, IL; Lowry Field, CO; Buckingham Field, FL (January-June 1944-technical training, aerial gunnery); Laredo, TX; Lincoln, Grand Island, NE; Pyote, TX (B-29 crew training July 1944-May 1945); Herington, KS.

Mather Field, CA to Guam with 330th BG. Flew 21 missions as a CFC gunner with the Lt. Walter L. Ormand AC (May-November 1945). 19th BG, Guam (November-December 1945). Returned stateside on the USS *Clearmont* via Saipan, Camp Stoneman, CA. He was discharged on Jan. 16, 1946 at Fort Logan, CO with the rank of tech sergeant. Air Corps Reserve. Retired USAR in 1963 with the rank first lieutenant.

Employed with U.S. Public Health Service from 1946-1947. University of Georgia (ROTC, commissioned 1949 with a BS in forestry in 1951). Employed by Georgia Forestry Commission/International Paper Company Bainbridge, GA (1951-1960); Hudson Pulp & Paper Corp./Georgia-Pacific Corp. Palatka, FL (1960-1990), retiring in 1990.

He married Edna Taylor-Thomasville from Georgia on Aug. 8, 1948. They have three children and four grandchildren.

GEORGE F. MELLORS, was born May 18, 1921 in Latrobe, PA. He attended Indiana State Teachers College in Pennsylvania. Inducted Greensburg, PA (VOC) Dec. 28, 1942. Assigned to Fort Knox, KY, then transferred to the Army Air Corps on July 27, 1943. Basic Training Center #10 in Greensboro, NC. Then to the 60th College Training Detachment at the University of Pittsburgh.

Attended service schools at Buckley and Lowry Fields, Denver, CO. Received aircrew training at McCook, NE, assigned to the 5th Sqdn., 9th BG, 313th Wing as a B-29 crew CFC gunner. Arrived in Tinian on Feb. 8, 1945. He completed 35 missions by Aug. 6, 1945. Returned to the States on Aug. 26, 1945. Discharged on Oct. 22, 1945 with the rank of tech sergeant.

He married Mildred Carroll and they have three daughters and two sons: George, Jacqueline, Theodore, Betsy and Susan. He enlisted in the Pennsylvania National Guard on Jan. 18, 1948. He was discharged July 7, 1952 as a first lieutenant, artillery, battery commander, Btry. C, 724th AAA Gun Battalion.

Business career in civil engineering. Retired in 1983. He is a member of the Iron and Steel Engineers, American Concrete Institute and the Society of American Military Engineers.

PAUL METRO, was born on July 6, 1923 in Linden, NJ. He was drafted into service on Jan. 31, 1943.

He was with the 393rd Bomb Sqdn., 509th Composite Group as a radar mechanic, sergeant, Tinian Islands, Marianas.

Married and has one daughter, Felicia. Was a loss control consultant in property and casualty insurance and is a member of ASSE (American Soc. of Safety Engineers) & Certified Safety Professionals.

GERALD C. MICHAEL, was born on Jan. 19, 1931 in Fairmont, WV. He enlisted in the USAF in 1948; served with the 19th BG, 30th Bomb Sqdn. from 1949 to 1950 on Guam and Okinawa (North Field, later Anderson AFB on Guam; Airborne Radar School in Japan; Kadena Air Base, Okinawa).

He flew 35 missions as a VO/radar mechanic during the Korean action. He received the Air Medal and the Commendation Medal. Was discharged in August 1952 as a staff sergeant.

Married Patricia A. Utt in September 1955 and has four children: Kimberlea, Tracy, William and Jay. Received his BS and MS in physics (1955-1956) from West Virginia University, PhD in solid state technology (1969) from Penn State. He taught physics at West Virginia University (1956-1960). He was a staff physicist at HRB Singer in State College (1960-1970). Moved to Indianapolis in a business partnership (1970-1976). Was a vice president of engineering with Hurco Manufacturing Co. (1976-1987).

Presently serving as president of the Indiana Microelectronics Center. He joined the 19th Bomb Group Association in 1988 and has attended three re-unions.

ALVIN L. MILLER, was born on Nov. 11, 1919 in Jersey City, NJ and entered the USAAC in 1942 and remained in the Air Force thru the Korean War. He retired from the Reserves as a major.

Had B-17 training at Lockbourne, OH; B-29 training at McCook, NE. He fought in battles and campaigns in Western Pacific, A/O Japan; Eastern Mandates, air combat in Iwo Jima. He was assigned to the 313th Bomb Wing, 9th BG, 20th Air Force. His bomber

(nicknamed *NIP NEMESIS*) flew on 33 missions over Japan. He earned the Distinguished Flying Cross, five Air Medals, four Bronze Battle Stars and two Presidential Unit Citations.

His last mission was to fly over Hiroshima at a low altitude so that the Signal Corps cameramen could take pictures of the aftermath of the bomb drop just days after it happened. He was with the World Air Rescue Headquarters setting up B-29 Hurricane Hunters after the war. He was also involved on Gulf Stream patrols on crash boats (converted PT boats). The mission assisted disabled boats and downed planes.

He received a master's degree in business administration at the State University of New York, Buffalo and his CLU from the American College of Life Underwriters, Bryn Mawr, PA. Before retiring to Florida in 1983, he spent his business career as an insurance executive.

He was a member of the United States Power Squadron for 32 years and attained full certificate in 1989, successfully completing all boating courses. His hobbies were game fishing and boating. Al died on Aug. 23, 1991 in Stuart, FL. He is survived by his wife, Dorothy. He had two sons, two daughters and two grandchildren.

ROBERT B. MILLER, was born in 1909 in Rumsey, KY and graduated from IULA High School in 1927 and junior college in 1929. With the Coast Artillery 1931 to 1933 in Hawaii. Drafted into the USAAF, Armament School for student/instructor at Lowry AFB; aviation cadet (ground), Yale University.

Commissioned on Feb. 11, 1944, assigned to Walker AAF (383rd BG) ARMO. Overseas, 9th BG ARMO, Tinian and Philippines. Returned to States, released from active duty, assigned to Reserves.

Civil service employment, Spokane, Grieger Field as Instr. Supply, AVN Eng. School; moved with Tech School to F.E. Warren AAFB; training materials specialist, AVN Eng. Transferred Sheridan VA Hospital for vocational rehabilitation therapy, chief mat. sect. Assisting disabled veterans was very rewarding. Helped organize Sheridan flight, AFR, later commander.

Four of AD tours were w/colleges, aerospace education. Retired at age 60 with rank lieutenant colonel, speciality, communications.

Registered rehabilitation therapist, active in local and national rehabilitation organizations; national president of the American Association for rehabilitation therapists. Retired since 1973, he operates a health program for Senior Citizens Center. HEALTH IS WEALTH.

GORDON K. NELSON, was born in Windom, MN on Aug. 9, 1920. He was inducted into active duty with the Minnesota National Guard on Jan. 6, 1941, called into flying cadet training in September 1941, graduating as pilot, second lieutenant at Stockton Field, CA in September 1942.

Was basic flying instructor at Lemore Army Air

Field, CA until 1944, then trained in four engine at Hobbs, NM; B-29 crew training at Pyote, TX, 1944; flew a new replacement B-29 as aircraft commander February 1945. Arrived in March 1945 and assigned to 5th Bomb Sqdn., 9th BG, North Field, Tinian. Flew over 25 missions including last two missions over peace signing Tokyo Bay. Returned to States and inactive duty.

Recalled for Berlin airlift in 1948. Flew B-29s and B-36s with 23rd Strat. Recon Sqdn., Travis AFB. Went overseas to Japan and Korea, 1951-1953. Retired as major, USAFR in October 1963. He received the Distinguished Flying Cross and Air Medal with two Oak Leaf Clusters. Graduated in 1967 from University of Houston, TX. Was mental health worker, director of counseling and psychiatrist assistant 1963-1978. Fully retired in 1980. He is a member of the 9th Bomb Group Association 1988 to date, presently second vice president and reunion chairman for 1993.

FRED L. NIBLING, was born in Belton, TX on Sept. 12, 1917. He enlisted in the U.S. Army Air Corps, Dodd Field, San Antonio, TX on July 7, 1942. Completed Radio Operator Mechanic School, Sioux Falls, SD in December 1942. Entered Air Corps Cadet Training Course February 1943 in Communications. Completed course and received commission at Yale University, New Haven, CT in August 1943.

Completed Radar Operator School, Boca Raton, FL and Radar Countermeasures School at Eglin Field, FL in May 1944. Was assigned to 330th BG, Walker Air Base, KS in June 1944. In January 1945 was sent to Guam. Flew on nine missions to Japan as RCM officer operating airborne radar jamming equipment. Received Air Medal for jamming mission over Shimonoseki, Japan for 90 minutes at high altitude, jamming enemy radar during bombing raid. Was discharged in December 1945 with the rank of captain.

Married Gladys Cale, his college sweetheart at SW Texas State University, while at Yale. They have two children, Fred Jr. and Susan, and two grandsons. Spent five years teaching, part-time rancher and with the Veterans Administration in personnel management until retirement in 1976.

GILLON NICELY, was born June 5, 1923 in Bellevue, KY and lived in Elizabethtown, KY and Hardin County most of his life. During WWII he volunteered and was assigned to the infantry. Later he took an Air Force exam for cadets, passed and was transferred to the Air Force.

Washed out of cadets and after attending several schools, he was selected for crew of 29 to participate in dropping the atomic bomb. Trained at Wendover Field, UT, flew overseas and based on Tinian in the Marianas Islands for duration of war. As tail gunner he participated in dropping of bomb on Hiroshima.

Discharged with the rank of staff sergeant. He received the Distinguished Flying Cross, two Air Medals with clusters, Pacific Theater and the Good Conduct Medal. His outfit was the 509th BG, 393rd Bomb Sqdn. commanded by Col. Paul Tibbits. He was proud to serve his country and flew on a great plane with a super crew.

He opened an appliance and furniture business and is still in retail with Sleep Shop in Elizabethtown, KY.

FRED J. OLIVI, was born in (Pullman) Chicago, IL on Jan. 16, 1922. He volunteered for cadet training, Air Corps, 1942 and was called to active duty in February 1943. Attended East Central Teachers College, Aviation student, March-September 1943, College Training Detachment, Ada, OK. Passed qualifying physical, mental and coordination tests for pilot training, November 1943 at San Antonio, TX. Completed pre-flight, primary, basic, twin-enigine, advanced flight training and graduated as second lieutenant (pilot) on Aug. 4, 1944.

Was assigned to B-24 Pilot Transition School, Fort Worth, TX in August 1944. Graduated November 1944, Lubbock, TX. Assigned to the 509th Composite (Atomic) Group, 393rd Bomb Sqdn., January 1945 posted to South Pacific, Tinian Island, Marianas, June 1945. Dropped the second atomic bomb, Nagasaki, Japan on Aug. 9, 1945 as co-pilot on B-29 *Bockscar*.

Returned to the States November 1945 and was discharged from active duty February 1947 at Roswell, NM. Joined Air Corps Reserve Troop Carrier Sqdn. O'Hare Field, Chicago, until 1958. Was assigned as Air Force Academy liaison officer 1958-1972. Retired as lieutenant colonel in 1972 after 30 years of military service.

Employed by city of Chicago in 1950. Retired as manager Bridge Maintenance and Operations in 1986 after 36 years of civil service.

HOWARD J. OTIS, was born in Barron, WI on July 9, 1918. Received BS at River Falls Teachers' College in 1940 and was drafted July 1941. Went to Las Vegas Gunnery School; OCS 1942-D, Miami Beach, FL; HQ 2nd AF, WA and Colorado Springs, CO; Combat Intelligence School, Harrisburg, PA, November 1943. 40th BG, Pratt, KS; Chakulia and Kharagpur, India; Tinian. Separated as captain, Army Reserve, January 1946.

Graduated Law School, Madison, WI, 1948; law practice, Ladysmith, WI. Air Force recall as judge advocate, March 1952. Served Keflavic, Iceland; McChord, WA; Bunker Hill, IN; Vietnam; and Lowry AFB, CO.

Retired as lieutenant colonel in 1968. Was awarded the Bronze Star Medal and two Air Force Commendation Medals.

He resides in Aurora, CO and was Colorado assistant attorney general, deputy district attorney and county judge. Partial retirement as senior judge, 1985. Served as senior judge until full retirement October 1991. Served as principal, Hope Lutheran School, Aurora, 1985-1986.

Married Frieda Herrmann and has three sons.

JAMES L. PARADIS, was born Feb. 16, 1920 in Norridgewock, ME. He enlisted in the U.S. Army in September 1939 and was assigned to the 24th Medical Battalion, Schofield Barracks, Hawaii. Entered pilot training in July 1942. Was a B-17 instructor pilot for one and a half years; B-29 aircraft commander in the

25th Bomb Sqdn., 40th BG on Tinian, Marianas Islands. Had six combat missions over Japan.

Post war assignments included B-29 and B-36 aircraft commander at Carswell AFB, Fort Worth, TX and additional duties as a gunnery officer and 7th Bomb Wing armament officer. Attended the Air University in 1949 and the Armament Officers School.

Highest enlisted rank, senior master sergeant. Highest commissioned rank, major. Retired from the USAF in 1960 and joined the Federal Aviation Agency as an enroute air traffic controller at Cleveland and Boston Air Traffic Control Centers attaining journeyman radar controller status prior to retiring in 1976.

Was at Schofield Barracks in Hawaii when the Japanese attacked Pearl Harbor and on the last bombing mission over Japan in August 1945

VIVIAN A. PARKS JR., was born Tillery, NC, Dec. 9, 1924. Drafted Halifax, NC July, 1943. Inducted at Fort Bragg. Assigned to Army Air Corps, Biloxi, MS, Chattanooga, TN, Santa Anna, CA, Sioux Falls, SD (Radio School), Walker Air Field, KS.

Overseas to Guam with 330th BG, 457th Sqdn. as radio operator on B-29. Flew 13 missions over Japan April through August 1945. Was awarded the Air Medal with Oak Leaf Cluster. Discharged as staff sergeant at Fort Bragg on Nov. 26, 1945.

Graduated from University of North Carolina, Chapel, NC in August 1948. Worked over 41 years in accounting and finance with the American Tobacco Company in Durham, NC, Richmond, VA, New York City, and Stamford, CT. Retired December 1989.

Married Kathryn Coppedge in September 1947. They have four children and four grandchildren. Currently resides in Midlothian, VA.

MARVIN W. PAULE, was born in Toledo, OH on July 30, 1920. Went to the University of Detroit, Aeronautical engineering. Drafted in Toledo, OH, October 1943. Joined 1st Sqdn., 9th Group, 313th Wing at McCook, NE in August 1944. Sent to Tinian in January 1945 as radar operator on *Queen Bee* crew with Bertagnoli/Merrow, then Brown/Merrow. Bailed out on April 28, 1945 after Kyushu raid.

Rotated stateside with 58th Group during deactivation. Discharged at Fort Benjamin Harrison, IN on Oct. 29, 1945.

Returned to civilian job for Air Force as an aeronautical engineer, logistician, weapon system manager. Served at Wright Patterson AFB, Norton AFB, Hill AFB. Retired from Wright Patterson in December 1979.

Married Dora Matlock in September 1942. They have five children: Cheryl, Cathryn, Richard, Patricia and David. They spend summers in Dayton, OH and winters in Palmetto, FL.

EDWARD P. PIATEK, was born Meriden, CT on Sept. 19, 1923. He enlisted Dec. 15, 1942 and served with the 20th Air Force, 313th Wing, 9th BG, 99th Sqdn. Had B-17 training at Lockbourne AAB, Columbus, OH; B-29 training at Clovis AAF, Clovis, NM. Based at Tinian, Mariana Island. Completed 31 combat missions, eastern mandates and Air Offensive Japan.

Memorable experiences: being caught in the enemy searchlights for at least 15 minutes while dropping mines into the Shimonoseki Straits; as superdumbo, saw the atomic bomb explode over Nagasaki; being part of the display of power force at the signing of the peace treaties in Tokyo Bay.

Discharged Dec. 10, 1945 with the rank first lieutenant, pilot 1093.

Received BA from University of Connecticut in 1949. Spent career in printing, city government and currently a real estate broker. Married to Dorothy and has two children.

ROBERT J. PIELSTICKER, was born in North Platte, NE and joined the service in 1943. Trained at Yale and McCook, NE, he served with the 5th BG, 9th Sqdn. and participated in action at Tinian. Memorable experiences closely related to first Atomic bombing.

Received honorable discharge in October 1946 with the rank of captain.

Retired in October 1982 as vice president. Pielsticker passed away Jan. 19, 1990.

MICHAEL POPRIK, was born in Ford City, PA on June 20, 1925. He enlisted in the Army Air Corps in August 1943. Took basic training in Greensboro, NC; cadet training at Elon College, NC and gunnery training at Buckingham Army Air Field. Joined a B-29 crew at Pyote, TX and transferred to the 9th BG, 5th Sqdn. based on Tinian in April 1945.

He flew 20 missions, received his Distinguished Flying Cross for the Yawata mission on Aug. 8, 1945. Returned to the U.S. in December 1945 and was discharged as a sergeant.

Poprik graduated with a BS degree in 1952 and received a DDS degree from the University of Pittsburgh Dental School in 1956. Joined the Army Dental Corps in 1956 and had a year's internship at Walter Reed Army Medical Center. Retired as a colonel in September 1984.

He is married and has four children.

J. IVAN POTTS JR., received his commission at University of Kentucky in 1942. First assignment was squadron adjutant, 152nd Observations Sqdn., 26th Observation Group, Ft. Devens Army Field, MA.

Activated 11th Airdrome Sqdn. at Hunter AAF, Savannah, GA. Applied for pilot training and received wings in Class 43-K. Attended Advanced Twin Engine Instructors School, Randolph Field, TX. Became twin engine instructor at Moody AAF, GA in 1944. Completed B-17 Instructors School, Lockbourne AAF, OH. Volunteered for B-29 program and assigned to 25th Bomb Sqdn., 40th BG (VH), Chakulia, India in 1944.

Completed eight Hump trips and 34 combat missions, CBI and Tinian. Awarded the Distinguished Flying Cross with Oak Leaf Cluster, Air Medal with three Oak Leaf Clusters, Army Commendation Medal, Presidential Unit Citation with Oak Leaf Cluster, Asiatic-Pacific Campaign Medal with four Battle Stars, American Campaign Medal with one Battle Star and Personal Citation from Gen. H.H. Arnold.

On Sept. 18-19, 1945 was crew member on Gen. LeMays crew which set four Air Force records. Flight was from Hokkaido, Japan to Washington, DC in 27 hours and 30 minutes.

Separated from active duty with the rank of captain. Retired TN-ANG as colonel. Married Katherine Dale of Nashville, TN in 1949. They have one son. Was Ford-Mercury dealer in Shelbyville, TN from 1955-1980. Presently assistant director, Business Development Center, Middle Tennessee State University.

He says it was a great honor to be a member of the 40th Bombardment Group, the finest group of men he ever knew.

CHARLES L. PULSFORT, was born Bellevue, KY on April 14, 1924. He celebrated his 21st birthday over Tokyo as co-pilot of the *Big Time Operator.* Tokyo was 10th of 35 missions out of Tinian with 1st Sqdn., 9th BG. Was awarded Air Medals and Distinguished Flying Cross. Became airplane commander and reached rank of first lieutenant. Trained in Southeast, then in B-17, at Columbus, OH and in B-29 at McCook, NE.

After service he obtained chemical engineer degree from University of Cincinnati, married Ann Baueries of Covington, KY and joined the American Cyanamid Company. Stayed with Cyanamid for 35 years. Pulsfort and Ann were blessed with seven children, all of who obtained professional degrees.

At Cyanamid, work centered in chemical, pharmaceutical and formica manufacturing ending with eight years as director of manufacturing for international operations in 22 countries.

Retired to northern Kentucky, he enjoys golfing, traveling and visiting his children throughout the country. Found the BTO is also retired at Beale AFB in California.

STANLEY G. PUTNAM, was born in Drumright, OK on June 26, 1925. Moved to Springfield, OH in 1929. Drafted Sept. 3, 1943; attended Aviation Cadet College, Albion, MI; Aerial Gunnery School, Tindale, FL. Was assigned to 20th Air Force, 314th Bomb Wing out of Guam.

Flew 35 missions over Japan in a B-29. They had to land on Iwo Jima as a result of losing all but one engine on a mission to Tokushima, Japan July 3, 1945.

Received Air Medal and Distinguished Flying Cross during combat. Discharged as a sergeant Dec. 4, 1945.

Married Esther and has a son Rennie. Spent 41 years as a shop employee and retired in 1988.

GLEN D. RALSTON, was born June 26, 1921 in rural Augusta, KS. Enlisted in the Army Air Corp Aviation Cadet School for pilots and was accepted into the service in January 1943. Graduated from Advanced Flight School with the Class of 44-C. Attended B-17 transition training at Hobbs, NM and B-29 transition at Clovis, NM with Phillip Wells' crew as co-pilot.

The crew joined the 58th Wing, 444th Group, 677th Sqdn. in India. Flew with Lt. Wells in C109 tankers from India to China, completing 16 round trips over the "hump" before flying their first combat mission out of India and China. Moved with the 58th Wing to Tinian and continued flying combat missions as co-pilot for Lt. Wells and Capt. Hugo Provano, completing 31 missions when the war was over. Returned to the States in October 1945 and was discharged as first lieutenant, December 1945.

Graduated with a BS degree from Kansas State University in June 1948. Retired in 1982 after working 34 years as a professional engineer.

GLYNN N. REESE, was born Izoro, TX on June 28, 1923. Drafted at Fort Sam Houston, San Antonio, TX, Nov. 26, 1943. Received basic training at Shepperd Field, Wichita Falls, TX. After training at various locations, he joined the 9th BG, 1st Sqdn., McCook, NE. Received training as sheet metal mechanic to repair battle damage on B-29s.

Was shipped overseas from Seattle, WA on Nov. 29, 1944, destination Tinian, Marianas Islands. He helped load atomic bomb that was dropped on Hiroshima. Discharged with the rank of sergeant on March 2, 1946.

Married Evelyn and had daughter, Glynda, and son, Kent. Spent business career in building and car sales in Dallas, TX. Retired in mid-70s to ranch in Lampasas, TX. Enjoyed career change until his death on Jan. 4, 1992. *Submitted by wife, Mrs. Glynn N. Reese.*

VERNARD A. REESE, was born in Izoro, TX on July 3, 1920. He was drafted into the Army Air Force at Fort Sam Houston, San Antonio, TX in November 1943. He received basic training at Sheppard Field, Wichita Falls, TX. Joined the 9th BG, 1st Sqdn. at McCook, NE. There he was trained as a sheet metal mechanic to repair battle damage on B-29s.

Embarked from Seattle, WA for overseas duty and stationed at several bases in the South Pacific before he reached Tinian Island where he remained until the war ended. The first atomic bomb was flown from his unit on Tinian. He left the island in January 1946 and was discharged March 1, 1946.

He went into business as a building contractor and then moved into the automobile business. He married before entering the service and afterwards had two daughters.

ARTHUR F. REIBE JR., was born Adams, WI in 1921, attended elementary school there, high school and one semester junior college at El Dorado, AR and Arkansas National Guard.

Late 1939 he joined Army Air Corps at Barksdale Field, LA; Air Mechanics School at Delgado Jr. College, New Orleans, LA. In 1940 was assigned NO Army Air Base 122nd Observations Sqdn. Air National Guard as mechanic/observer/gunner in O-47 aircraft flying anti-sub patrols in the gulf.

Attended Lowry Field, CO Bombsight School, returned to the 30th BG at New Orleans early 1942 as sergeant bombardier, B-17s. Appointed warrant officer in bombsights and aircraft engineering October 1942 at Baer Field, IN. Reassigned to 11th Anti-sub Sqdn., Ft. Dix, NJ with B-34 aircraft.

At Olmstead Field, PA early 1943, was assistant armament officer and made chief warrant. Joined 28th Air Service Group in New Jersey as assistant engineering officer. Assigned B-29 School at Wichita, KS in late 1943. Joined the 40th BG after initially being in the 444th BG at Great Bend, KS in early 1944. Served as assistant engineering officer with his squadron in the CBI as well as in the Marianas (Tinian Island).

Discharged at Randolph Field, TX in late 1945 from Marianas Islands. Joined the 40th BG while in Chakulia, India. Retired from a large chemical refinery in 1983 after 33 years.

Married his New Orleans sweetheart and has two sons. Rejoined the 40th Bomb Group Association in 1981.

RICHARD N. RICE, was born Cashtown, PA on Jan. 27, 1925. Graduated from Hershey High School, Hershey, PA in 1942 and volunteered for the Aviation Cadet Program in 1943. Graduated from Navigation School, Selman AFB, LA in October 1944. Assigned to B-29 crew January 1944 and to 330th BG, 314th Bomb Wing, 20th AF, Guam in April 1945.

Flew 23 missions over Japan from May to August 1945. Considerable flak damage Tokyo mission in July 1945, with one wounded gunner and emergency landing on Iwo Jima. B-29 was named *City of Hershey.* Crew and aircraft returned to Hershey, PA for a post war bond tour.

Discharged 1946 as first lieutenant. Graduated from Gettysburg College in 1949. Recalled to active duty in March 1952 for Korean Conflict. Assigned RB-29 reconnaissance crew, 91st Strategic Recon Sqdn., Yokota AFB, Japan.

Returned to the States and became nuclear weapons officer, Westover AFB, MA. Assigned to B-47 jet bomber crew, Whiteman AFB, MO, 340th Bomb Wing. Later assigned to 340th Bomb/Nav Staff. Assigned 341st Strategic Missile Wing (Minuteman) at Whiteman AFB, assistant quality control and evaluation officer. Last AF assignment at Vandenberg AFB, 3901st Strategic Missile Evaluation Squadron, chief missile maintenance evaluation.

Retired 1968 with senior missile and master navigator rating. His awards and decorations include the Distinguished Flying Cross, Air Medal with two Oak Leaf Clusters, Army Commendation Medal, Air Force Commendation Medal with one Oak Leaf Cluster, three Bronze Battle Stars to Asiatic-Pacific Theater Ribbon, Distinguished Unit Badge with one Oak Leaf Cluster and the Outstanding Air Force Unit Award.

Attended University of California, Santa Barbara, CA for one year, post graduate studies. Returned to Hershey and taught school seven years. Was head tennis professional for 16 years at Hershey Country Club, retiring in 1989. Rice resides in Hershey with his wife Marian. They have four married sons and seven grandchildren.

THOMAS F. RICHMOND,

THOMAS F. RICHMOND, was born May 18, 1919 in Walnut Grove, MS. He enlisted in Jackson, MS on Jan. 30, 1941. Basic training at Maxwell Field, AL; Aircraft and Engine Mechanics School, Chanute Field; Chevrolet Pratt and Whitney R-1830-43 Aircraft Engine School, Detroit; Aircraft Engineering Technician's School, San Bernardino; B-47 Aircraft Maintenance School, Amarillo; NCO Academy, Bergstrom AFB.

Served Tyndall Field, FL, 1941-1946; 509th BW, 830th BS Walker AFB NM, 1946-58 (participated in Crossroads, Kwajalein Island); 509th BW, Pease AFB NH, 1958-60; 48th TFW Lakenheath England, 1960-63; 416th BW Griffiss AFB, NY, 1963-66; QC AF Special Weapons Center Kirtland AFB NM, 1967-72.

Retired with over 30 years service on May 4, 1972 with the rank chief master sergeant. He received the Meritorious Service Medal, Soldiers' Medal, AF Commendation Medal with Oak Leaf Cluster.

After retirement, he volunteered most of his time to working with veterans' organizations. Married Eleanor Woodward Richmond on Feb. 14, 1959. Has five grandchildren, two great-grandchildren and stepdaughter (deceased). In May 1991 Richmond suffered massive strokes and is now wheelchair bound. He enjoys seeing old friends.

ROBERT M. ROBBINS,

ROBERT M. ROBBINS, was born in Wilkes-Barre, PA on May 15, 1916. He received his pilot's license in 1934 and aeronautical engineering degree from MIT in 1938.

Was Pan Am flight engineer 1938-1941 on the first Boeing B-314 trans-Atlantic flying boats. Boeing civilian experimental test pilot and aircraft commander on B-17s, the XPBB-1, the #1 XB-29, the #1 XB-47 from 1942 to 1948. Boeing project engineer, assistant director of engineering and program manager for B-47, B-52 and KC-135 programs from 1948 to 1979. Retired in 1979 in Ormond Beach, FL.

He was the second Boeing experimental test pilot to command the #1 XB-29 after Eddie Allen was killed in the crash of the #2 XB-29 on Feb. 18, 1943 and was on every one of the 337 engineering/experimental test flights on the #1 XB-29 from Aug. 28, 1943 until the end of WWII. He flew 482 hours as project test pilot and aircraft commander on that airplane which was dubbed *The Flying Guinea Pig.*

In August 1943 he flew the first and in 1991 he flew the last flyable B-29, *Fifi.* His pilot's license is still valid.

JAMES W. ROBINSON,

JAMES W. ROBINSON, was born Feb. 24, 1921, Mansfield, OH. Organizations: Citizens Military Training Camp, Fort Benjamin Harrison, IN 1937 basic infantry; 1939 Btry. D, 134th FA, cannoneer, discharged October 1940, no serial number, private; graduate Milwaukee School Engineering 1940-1941; Royal Canadian Air Force 1941, pilot training, discharged November 1941 (honorable).

Returned to USA; USAAF, February 1942-1945, enlisted 1946, retired, July 1, 1962, no basic training or draft number; first phase B-29 training 1944, Clovis, NM; B-17 eng. instructor, assigned B-29 tail gunner November 1944. Sent to CBI India, 58th Bomb Wing 444th BG, 676th Sqdn., Dudkhundi, India. First replacement crews flew Hump and bombed out of China, Tinian, May 1945; 31 missions, a/c was *Snuffie,* rank staff sergeant. Son born while he was over Kure. Was on last mission of WWII, Hikari, Japan. Electronics mechanic, 10 years with Navy, 1965-1975.

Currently retired, attends WWII reunions, enjoys children and grandchildren.

DAVE L. ROGAN,

DAVE L. ROGAN, was born in Middlesboro, KY on Oct. 7 1914. He joined Royal Canadian Air Force in April 1941. Trained as pilot at Brandon, Manitoba. Departed for England on Nov. 14, 1941. Flew Bristol Blenheim MK-4 on bombing missions with RAF and laid smoke screen for commando landing at Dieppe, France, on Aug. 19, 1942.

Transferred to 8th Air Force, Sept. 29, 1942, assigned to 358th Sqdn., 303rd BG "Hell's Angels." Flew 25 combat missions as B-17 pilot. Returned to USA on Aug. 24, 1943. Was stationed at Alamogorda, NM, Ardmore, OK and B-29 pilot training at McCook, NE.

Departed Jan. 13, 1945 for Tinian. Served as flight commander for 1st Sqdn., 9th BG. Flew 14 combat missions in *Man O War* and 19 combat missions in *The Spearhead* without an abort. Returned to USA Oct.

18, 1945. Assigned to Flight Test Division at Wright-Patterson Field, Dayton, OH.

Discharged with the rank of major on Dec. 24, 1946. He received Distinguished Flying Cross with three Oak Leaf Clusters, Air Medal with seven Oak Leaf Clusters, Purple Heart, Asiatic-Pacific with four Bronze Stars, European-African-Eastern Theater, American Defense Ribbon, Pre-Pearl Harbor, Victory Ribbon, British General Service and Foreign Allied Service Ribbon.

Married Elizabeth and has four daughters and seven grandchildren. Retired in 1986 from family owned wholesale mine supply business.

FRANK J. ROSE,

FRANK J. ROSE, was born in DeWitt, MI on Feb. 9, 1917 and was drafted June 3, 1941 at Ft. Wayne, Detroit, MI. Fort Custer, Battle Creek, MI to Camp Wolters, Mineral Wells, TX for basic training. Joined Co. I, 134th Inf., 35th Div., Camp Robinson, Little Rock, AR (three years), rank corporal.

Joined the Air Force, Keesler Field, Biloxi, MS on June 3, 1944. Pre-flight at Beloit, WI; advanced at Santa Ana, CA; Navigation, San Marcos, TX (graduated F/O). Joined B-24 Crew, Biggs Field, El Paso, TX. Transferred to Langley Field, VA; Radar, Boca Raton, FL (graduated Aug. 24, 1944). Transferred to B-29 Crew, 458th Sqdn., 330th BG, 20th AF, Dec. 8, 1944, Walker Air Base, KS. Sea Search and Rescue, Guantanamo Bay, Cuba (April-September) Guam (flew 27 combat missions over Japan).

Discharged at Ft. Sheridan, IL on Nov. 4, 1945 with the rank second lieutenant. He received the American Defense Medal, American Theater Ribbon, Asiatic-Pacific Ribbon with star, Air Medal with cluster, Distinguished Flying Cross and the Presidential Unit Citation with star.

Married with two sons. He retired from the Michigan State Police after 25 years. Lives at Walloon Lake, MI.

WALTER RAYMOND ROSS,

WALTER RAYMOND ROSS, was born in Philadelphia, PA on Feb. 20, 1920 and enlisted June 13, 1942 in camouflage unit, assigned to 79th Inf. Div. Graduated OCS, Ft. Benning, GA on Aug. 10, 1943 as second lieutenant (infantry).

Transferred in-grade Air Force October 1943. Pre-flight Santa Ana, CA, December 1943. Awarded Bombardier Wings, Kirtland AFB, Albuquerque, NM Class 44-13 in May 1944. Assigned to Keller Crew, November 1944 for flight training in B-29s at Almagordo, NM.

Sent to Tinian April 1945 as a replacement crew, assigned to 5th Sqdn., 9th BG, 313th Wing, 20th AF. Crew flew B-29 named the *Sad Tomatoe.* Made five emergency landings on Iwo Jima. Shot down on Aug. 8, 1945 while flying to bomb Yawata (city in Japan). Returned to the States from POW camp September 1945.

Released from active duty with rank of captain on March 12, 1946 at Greensboro, NC.

Awarded the Asiatic-Pacific Ribbon with three Battle Stars, Purple Heart, ATO Ribbon, WWII Victory Ribbon, POW Medal, Air Force Sharpshooter, Air Medal and Presidential Unit Citation, each with one Oak Leaf Cluster.

Returned to Philadelphia. Spent business career in life insurance. Retired on March 1, 1985. Active in Boy Scouts, is charter scout master for three troops, cubmaster and explorer leader. Was awarded Silver Beaver Award. Avid birder with over 500 species identified in lower 48 states.

Married Lucille E. Waring of Philadelphia on Dec. 20, 1942. Son, Ray, is a medical doctor and son, Paul, is a degree registered nurse. They have four grandchildren.

Visited Japan in 1983 to participate in the making of a documentary film for TV named *Genbaku Shi,* a story about the Keller crew.

JAMES LES ROWE,

was born on April 25, 1908 in Mohawk, MI. He lived there until 1925 when he moved to Detroit. Enlisted on Feb. 9, 1942. Went to Fort Custer in Yipsilante, MI for his induction and tests. First station was Hammer Field, Fresno, CA; became an armorer and instructor on weapons and bombs. OCS at Aberdeen, MD; assigned to the West Coast Training Command, Santa Ana, CA. In January 1944 was transferred to the HQ, 4th AAB and became Armament Officer of the 4th AF.

Sent to Bomb Disposal School, Aberdeen, MD and became Bomb Disposal Officer; sent to the War College and in December 1944 was assigned to Lemoor AFB as Base Ordnance Officer. April 1945, reported to Wendover Field, UT as project officer. By innovation, hard work, long hours, gallons of sweat and unbelievable pressure, they brought the Little Boy Bomb (Hiroshima) to ready state on July 18 and the Fat Man (Nagasaki) on July 28, thus ending WWII.

On Dec. 7, 1945 his group was placed on detached service to the Manhattan District Engineers at Los Alamos; on Sept. 15, 1945, along with 60 men, traveled by air to Albuquerque and activated Oxnard Base. He soon found himself to be the recipient of the U.S. Nuclear Arsenal as it existed at that time. In addition, he had the only bomb assembly building, adjacent to the only bomb loading pit in the country; and the only organized assembly crew that could become active instantly and the bomb material that could be assembled. By October 1946, the U.S. Congress voted to assign our nation's nuclear energy to civilian control. As the Army had no further use for the training facility, he chose to separate in the grade of major.

He accepted a position with the University of California. He remained with the Atomic Bombs Programs for a number of years; joined a research team at the West Lab; assigned to the explosives area and engaged in the disassembly of the Mark III and Mark IV and the production of the Mark V. He returned to plant maintenance, assumed the position of head of plant engineering, plant maintenance and speciality shops and finally department manager.

Retired in 1970 from the Sandia National Laboratory in Livermore, CA. In 1978 went to work at Intel Corporation, retiring from there in 1986.

Rowe is a widower and says all his life has been a great adventure.

RICHARD H. SABEY,

was born on Nov. 20, 1923 in Chicago, IL. He graduated from the Chicago Academy of Fine Arts in 1943 and was drafted in March.

Graduated from Radio School at Sioux Falls, Truax Field, WI; CNS School at Tomah, WI; was assigned to the 9th BG at Dalhart, TX in 1944. His overseas training was at McCook, NE, then sent to Tinian.

Sabey was discharged in January 1945 with the rank of sergeant. His awards and medals include the Distinguished Unit Citation with Oak Leaf Cluster, Good Conduct Medal, Asiatic Pacific Campaign Medal with three stars, American Campaign Medal and the World War II Victory Medal.

He was a commercial artist, art director, art salesman and vice president. He is married with nine children and 16 grandchildren. He is a member of American Legion, VFW, Air Force Association, 9th BG Association, 20th AF Association, McCook Air Base Society and the Danish Brotherhood.

Sabey is retired and active in Legion and Danish Brotherhood. He is extremely proud of having served with the men of the 9th BG, 20th AF in WWII. "God Bless America."

SAM SAN FRATELLO,

was born Aug. 20, 1923 in Batavia, NY to Mr. and Mrs. Angelo San Fratello. He was inducted in the USAF on Feb. 26, 1943 at Fort Niagara, NY; basic training at Keesler Field, MS, Fort Warren, Cheyenne, WY; and schooling at Salt Lake City Air Base. He was a quartermaster when he transferred to 509th Composite Group. He was also with the 1027th Air Matl. Sqdn. Departed from Seattle, WA and arrived Tinian Island, Marianas.

Memorable experience was sitting at the outdoor movie house on Tinian facing Saipan, waiting for the movie to start and listening to the song of *Sentimental Journey.* They could hear a loud roar coming across the channel knew the war was ending. This event took place after they dropped the second bomb. "Thank the Lord, It was finished."

Discharged at Santa Ana Air Base on Jan. 30, 1946 with rank of sergeant.

Married Loretta on June 29, 1946, they have one daughter, Francine Grazzianto; two sons, Raymond and Jeffrey; daughter-in-law, Carole; son in-law, Richard Grazzianto; and four grandchildren: Kara Marie, Gina, Michael and Jason.

He is retired and works part-time to keep busy and active.

HARRY G. SHEPHERD JR.,

was born on July 13, 1924 in Los Angeles, CA and was inducted April 3, 1943 at Ft. McArthur, CA. He attended AAF Technical School, Squadron Engineer and Operation Clerks, Ft. Logan, CO. He was assigned to 1027th Air Matl. Sqdn., 509th Composite Group as a supply clerk at Wendover, UT.

Sent to Tinian Island in May 1945. Participated in air offensive of Japan and Eastern Mandates Campaign. He was promoted to sergeant in June 1945.

Discharged in February 1946 with the rank of staff sergeant. His awards and medals include the Asiatic-Pacific Campaign Medal, American Theater Ribbon, WWII Victory Medal and the Good Conduct Medal. Was in the reserves February 1946 to February 1949.

Married Mary and has four sons: Jim, Bob, Jeff and Jon. He graduated from the University of Southern California in 1950. Worked for Hughes Aircraft Company as an accountant and manager for 37 years. Retired in 1988. He was a participant in semi-annual reunions of the 509th Composite Group. He compiled records of umpires in major league games of 1890's for Society of American Baseball Research.

Shepherd passed away Aug. 2, 1992.

LEASOM D. SHOEMAKER,

was born Aug. 24, 1920 in Pennsylvania and moved to Long Island, NY

in 1926. He volunteered for induction at Camp Upton, NY in August 1942.

Completed basic training at Miami Beach, FL and was shipped to North Carolina State College as an aviation cadet. He went to Gunnery School in Ft. Myers, FL and then to McCook, NE for training on B-29s.

Was assigned to the crew of the *Queen Bee* and arrived in Tinian in January 1945 as part of the 9th Group, 1st Sqdn. and flew a total of 18 combat missions to Japan.

On the 13th sortie over Japan they were attacked by Jap fighters and, as a result of the damage, they were ordered to bail out. They spent 28 hours on a one man raft until rescued by the USS *Pogy,* a submarine doing air sea rescue. Ten of the 11 man crew were saved. The *Queen Bee* was last seen plunging into the ocean.

Shoemaker received an honorable discharge at Fort Dix, NJ on Nov. 25, 1945 with the rank of staff sergeant. He has worked as an auto insurance adjuster, owned a couple of auto body shops and retired in 1988. He now lives in Satellite Beach, FL with his wife Ruth.

WESLEY E. SMITH SR.,

was born March 15, 1922 in Coraopolis, PA. He moved to Sewickley, PA in 1946. He enlisted Sept. 8, 1942 in Pittsburgh, PA in the Aviation Cadet Program.

Was stationed in Nashville, TN; Maxwell, AL; Newport, AR. He graduated as 2nd Lt. Stuttgart, AR (Advanced Twin Engine). He was sent to Sebring, FL for B-17 transition then Tyndall Field, Panama City, FL for Gunnery School. Went to Alamogordo, NM for B-29 training as aircraft commander. Combat in the South Pacific on Guam with 20th AF, 314th Wing, 330th BG, 459th Sqdn. He completed 22 combat missions over Japan.

He returned to the States and was discharged on Nov. 26, 1945 with the rank of first lieutenant. He was awarded the Air Medal with two Oak Leaf Clusters, Distinguished Flying Cross, the WWII Victory Medal, American Campaign Medal and the Asiatic-Pacific Campaign Medal with one Battle Star.

Entered Korean Duty in November 1951 and served as assisstant operations officer with the 98th BG, Yokota, Japan after training at Randolph Field, TX and Air Force Survival School from Topeka, KS. Was discharged on Jan. 11, 1953 with the Korean Service Ribbon.

Married Myrtle on Dec. 8, 1943 and they have a son, Wesley Jr., and a daughter, Pamela.

He was employed at Shenango, Inc. in Pittsburgh, PA for over 41 years in various positions as a general control analyst, production and inventory accountant. He retired in 1982 as treasurer/traffic manager of Company P&OV Railway.

Smith is active in Masonic Fraternity in Pennsylvania.

A.D. SNYDER (JIM),

was born on Oct. 6, 1928 in Cincinnati, OH. He graduated from Loveland High School (Ohio) in June 1947 and worked at the Pennsylvania Railroad as a block operator. He enlisted in the USAF in September 1950.

Attended Gunnery School at Lowry AFB in May 1951. Was assigned to the Harry L. Shryock crew as

CFC gunner and crew trained Randolph Field, TX and Forbes Field, KS. Was assigned to the 93rd Sqdn., 19th BG, Okinawa in June 1952. He flew 28 missions over North Korea and while there made lead crew.

On Dec. 30, 1952 he was on a mission that lost three B-29s from MIG15 gunfire. He returned to the States in January 1953 and was assigned instructor gunner at Randolph Field, TX.

Was discharged in October 1953 with the rank of sergeant. He returned to the Pennsylvania Railroad, worked various positions in transportation and retired in November of 1990.

Snyder is a member of various fraternal organizations such as the American Legion and Veterans of Foreign Wars. He is also a member of the 19th Bombardment Group Association. His hobbies include playing drums in dance bands and reading.

He is married with three children and nine grandchildren.

DANIEL E. SNYDER, was born on Aug. 14, 1920 in Valley Forge, PA. Moved to Collegeville, PA area in 1935. Married high school classmate, Arline Walt, in 1942. He left Critical Military Industry to enter service in October 1943. Arline enlisted as second lieutenant in the Army Nurse Corps.

Entered the Air Cadet Program in November 1943. Due to a major reduction in the cadet program, he was re-assigned to flexible gunnery in the summer of 1944. He attended Flexible Gunnery School in Fort Meyers, FL. Was assigned as a Scanner B-29 replacement crew, Peyote, TX. The crew joined the 330th BG on Guam in April 1945. He was on the primary plane K-65 and flew 15 missions over Japanese homeland during the height of the air campaign. The crew set the record for the heaviest bomb load of incendiaries of the campaign, Tokyo, night of June 26, 1945. Was discharged in January 1946 with the rank of staff sergeant.

He has three children: Pamela, Daniel and Lawrence. He spent his business career in manufacturing, retired as manager of manufacturing engineering from a unit of ITT and became a manufacturing consultant.

MILTON C. SPROUSE JR., was born April 14, 1922 in Corinth, MS and inducted into the USAAC on April 20, 1943. Basic training was in Miami Beach, FL. Attended several different schools at Chanute AFB,

IL; Wright Patterson Factory, NJ; Amarillo AFB, TX; Castle AFB, CA; Bergstrom and Lackland AFB, TX and Roswell AFB, NM.

Served with 509th Composite Gp., 393rd Bomb Sqdn.; 830th Bomb Sqdn.; 509th Organization Maintenance Sqdn.; 3918th AB Gp.; 4126th Strategic BW, HQ Sqdn.; 2064th Communications Sqdn.; 4661st AB Gp. and 216th AB Gp. He was crew chief on the B-29, B-50, B-47 and the B-52.

Memorable experiences: first arrival at the Salt Lake Desert Base of Wendover, UT, isolated & barren; first time to fly in a new B-29; participating in 1945 in the historical mission of 509th Composite Group, 393rd Bomb Sqdn. at Tinian Island; first atomic bombardment of Hiroshima and Nagasaki, Operations Cross Roads; atomic test A&B, Kwajalein Islands in 1946.

Retired from the USAAC with the rank of SMSGTH. He received the AF Commendation Medal, Presidential Unit Citation with Bronze Oak Leaf Cluster, AF Outstanding Unit Award, AF Good Conduct Medal with Silver Oak Leaf Cluster, Good Conduct Medal with three Bronze Loops, the American Campaign Medal, the Asiatic-Pacific Campaign Medal with two Bronze Stars, WWII Victory Medal, National Defense Service Medal with one Bronze Star, Armed Forces Expeditionary Medal, Air Force Longevity Service Award Ribbon, USAF NCO PME Graduate Ribbon and the Small Arms Expert Marksmanship Ribbon.

Was a Park Ranger at the Golden Gate National Park in San Francisco, CA; superintendent of single family home construction; and manager at the Escondido Swap Meet, Escondido, CA for 13 years.

He married Margaret L. (Peggy) in 1958 and they have three sons, Tommy, Bobby and Glenn Sprouse. His wife retired from Social Security Administration and Air National Guard (USAF) as a lieutenant colonel.

DONALD G. STARKEY, was born on May 1, 1918 near Pine Grove, WV and enlisted into the USAAC on Nov. 7, 1941 as a cadet. Commissioned as second lieutenant, navigator at Lackland AFB in July 1942. Was assigned to the 6th Bomber Command, 40th BG in Guatemala City in September 1942. He served as the 44th Sqdn. Navigator February 1943 to December 1944.

Joined the B-29s in Pratt, KS, May 1943 and transferred to Chakulia, India in April 1944. Flew Hump to Hsinching, China and combat missions in Nippon Nipper including Yawata, Anshan, Nagasaki, Formosa, Rangoon, Bangkok and Nanking. He was re-assigned to Continental Training Command in December 1944. He reverted to reserve status in December 1945 as captain.

His decorations and medals include: the Air Medal with three clusters, the Asiatic-Pacific Campaign with four Battle Stars, American Defense, American Campaign and the WWII Victory Medal. He was recalled to active duty during the Korean Conflict and retired May 1, 1978 with the rank of lieutenant colonel.

Starkey received a BA and MA degree from SMU in 1949. He spent 25 years in Aerospace. He is married and has two sons. He is presently a free-lance writer.

MORTIMER E. STEVENSON, was born Oct. 3, 1916 in Rochester, NY. He completed cadet pilot training and received wings and commission at Williams AFB on July 28, 1943.

He earned instructors rating at Randolph Air Base in twin engine aircraft. After 1,000 hours of first pilot time, he became a B-29 superfortress airplane commander training with the crew at Walker Air Base. On

April 13, 1945 he was ordered to combat with the 20th Bomber Command on Guam.

Completed 33 combat missions over Japan returning to the States in October 1956.

He was awarded the Distinguished Flying Cross and Air Medal with three Oak Leaf Clusters. He remained active in the reserves, retiring as a lieutenant colonel in 1976.

Stevenson was employed as an executive with the Rochester Midland Corp., a distributor of sanitary supplies. He retired in 1981 after 34 years of service. He served on several boards and committees within the community. His hobbies are golf, tennis, gardening and candlemaking.

ALBERT R. SULLIVAN, was born June 26, 1921 in Wellington, KS and was drafted into service on Feb. 9, 1943, National City, CA. Basic training at Fresno, CA; Air Corps Technical School in Glendale, CA where he became an aircraft mechanic; then Marona, AZ and worked on AT-6s and BT-13s. In April 1944 he was transferred to McCook, NE and the 9th BG. Left there on Jan. 28, 1945 and went to Tinian.

Returned to the States in December 1945 and was discharged on Jan. 4, 1946 with the rank of staff sergeant. His awards/medals include the American Campaign Medal, Asiatic-Pacific Campaign Medal, Good Conduct Medal and the WWII Victory Medal.

He is a widower, has one daughter, one son and five grandsons. He retired from the Cessna Aircraft Company in 1984.

JAMES B. SULLIVAN, was born on Feb. 23, 1923 in Minneapolis, MN and moved to Pasadena, CA in 1934. He enlisted in the USAAF on Dec. 9, 1942 in Los Angeles, CA. Was trained as a clerk/typist, engineering at Clerical School in April 1943. His unit trained with the 393rd Bomb Sqdn. (VH), 509th Composite Group at Fairmont AFB, Nebraska and at Wendover Field, UT. Their B-29 Unit flew to Tinian Island June 1945 and dropped two atomic bombs.

Memorable experience was in January 1945 while training at the Batista Field, Cuba, and he played an exhibition tennis match with S/Sgt. Andrew Demo against Pauline Betz and Dorothy Bundy.

Sullivan was discharged in November 1945 with the rank of corporal.

He returned to California and married Barbara, they have four children: Kathy, John, Debra and Melissa and seven grandchildren. After 22 years with Globe Ticket Company and 10 years with Prudential Insurance, he retired to Sun City, AZ in 1985. Now enjoys golf, leisure and memories.

JOHN TOPOLSKI, was inducted in the USAAF in 1942 and sent to Shepherd Field, TX. From there it was on to Steven's Hotel in Chicago, IL for training in

radio mechanics and code. Next he took a gunnery course in Harlingan, TX, then went to March Field in Riverside, CA where he was assigned to a B-24 crew. He went into Shemya in the Aleutians where he took part in the campaign to take Kiska, which was held by the Japanese.

He next stopped in Pratt, KS where he was trained on B-29s. After that he went to Boca Raton, FL for a course about the PP1 Radar Scope. He was sent to India where he joined the 20th AAF, 58th Wing, 40th Group, 44th Sqdn. It was there that the radar was really pioneered for use in preparation for a bombing raid on Japan from their home base in Chengtu, China.

Was shot down over the Indian Ocean while returning from a mission in Singapore. He was rescued by a British submarine after spending 29 hours in a Mae West. Their remaining nine crewmen joined their squad in the South Pacific where they were assigned to Iwo Jima to fly escort missions for P-51 fighter planes. After the completion of this tour he was sent to Tinian where he was stationed when the A-bomb was dropped on Japan.

The war was over and he was discharged on Oct. 12, 1945 at Camp McCoy, WI. His tour in the AAF was like flying the Hump because you never knew where you would end up. He received the Distinguished Flying Cross, Air Medal with two Oak Leaf Clusters and the Unit Citation.

AUBREY C. TRAWEEK, was born on April 16, 1912 in Snyder, TX. He worked in the Experimental Dept. at Northrup Aircraft prior to enlisting in the USAF. He reported to Fort Bliss, TX on Jan. 6, 1943 for basic training at Jefferson Barracks, MO. Was shipped to Salt Lake City Air Base, then to Spokane, WA for training at the 2nd Air Force Ord. Armament School. From there he went to B-17 Base at
Windover, UT and then to Sioux City Air Base, Scribner Air Base, Carnie Air Base, NE, back to Sioux City, then to Dalhart Air Base, TX in June 1943, attached to the 330th BG HQ, very heavy as Ordinance Armament Sergeant, then sent to Walker Air Base in Kansas and Camp Forest, in Seattle, WA.

He was shipped out of Seattle with a stopover in Hawaii, stopover on Eniwetok, Atoll and then to North Field, Guam Island. Was assigned to Group Ordinance Armament servicing B-29s. Was shipped out on the USS *Lander* back to the States. He was discharged in January 1946 with the rank of tech sergeant in Fort Bliss, TX.

His awards include: the American Campaign Medal, Asiatic-Pacific Campaign Medal, Good Conduct Medal and the WWII Victory Medal.

In memory of his youngest brother, Emmett A. Traweek, 1st. Marine Brigade and all other brave servicemen who gave their lives securing the island of Guam. Their supreme sacrifice made it possible for B-29s and those who serviced the planes to deliver the bombs which ultimately destroyed the Japanese empire.

EDGAR B. VANE, was born March 8, 1933, raised in Encampment, WY and Berkeley, CA and enlisted in the USAF on Aug. 7, 1950. On Feb. 24, 1951 he completed B-29 Aerial Gunnery School at the Strategic Air Command Gunnery School, Biggs AFB, El Paso, TX.

From May 1951 through December 1951, he was assigned to the 19th BG, 93rd Sqdn. on Okinawa. As a lead crew tail gunner he flew 27 missions over Korea including the historic flights of October 22nd and 27th near the Yalu River and Red China.

It was on one of these missions that nine B-29s of the 19th and their 24 F-84s cover was attacked by an estimated 350 North Korean Mig-15s. Post mission briefing revealed most of the Migs were flown by student pilots. The students did not engage the B-29s until after the instructors had made several "how to do it" firing passes through the formation.

The missions, including a show of force mission near Vladivostok, Russia, were flown in the reliable Max Effort under the command of George Gibson. Max Effort's crew (L69AO) consisted of George Gibson, Marvin Hagemier, Julius Taylor, George Martin, Alexander Leslie, John Gilmore, Kenneth Dunbar, Charles Baisden, Kenneth Peat, Newell Branison and Vane.

On returning from overseas, the crew (R67AO) was appointed Wing Standardization Crew for the then forming 308th Bomb Wing in Topeka, KS. The 308th was later assigned to Hunter AFB in Savannah, GA. The overseas assignments for the 308th included Bermuda, the Azores and North Africa.

Sergeant Vane was honorably discharged on Sept. 13, 1953 at Hunter AFB in Savannah, GA. He was awarded the Air Medal, Korean Service Medal, United Nations Service Medal, National Defense Service Medal, Good Conduct Medal and the Korean Presidential Unit Citation.

EUGENE J. VOSS, was born Oct. 8, 1920 in Peoria, IL. He enlisted in the USAAF on Oct. 12, 1942. He graduated from Bradley University with a BS in 1942.

He was an aviation cadet in Boca Raton, FL from May until September 1943. He entered AAF Technical Training School at Yale University in September 1943, graduated and was commissioned on Dec. 9, 1943 as an aerial photographic officer 8502.

His assignments included the 19th BG Photo Officer, Commanding Officer 24th Photo Lab. BG VH, 314th Wing Photo Officer. He served 19 months overseas.

Awards and medals include: the Asiatic-Pacific Theater Medal with three Bronze Stars, Philippine Liberation Medal, Victory Medal, American Theater Medal and the Presidential Unit Citation with one Oak Leaf Cluster.

He is a retired chemical engineer from Caterpillar, Inc. Married and has five children and 19 grandchildren.

DAVID WADE, was born June 15, 1911 in Claiborne Parish, LA; was educated at Homer College and Louisiana Tech University; joined the Louisiana National Guard in 1928 and entered the USAAC as a cadet in February 1935.

In addition to other assignments during his 32 years of service, he held the following commands: Bruning Army Air Field; Blythe Army Air Field; Walla Walla Army Air Field; 9th BG North Field, Tinian Island and Clark Field; 19th BG North Field, Guam; 98th BW Yokota AFB Tokyo; 303rd BW Davis Monthan AFB; 92nd BW Fairchild AFB; 57th Air Div. Spokane; 21st Air Div. Forbes AFB; Inspector General Offutt AFB; Chief of Staff SAC; First Commander of 1st Missile Div. Vanderberg AFB; 16th Air Force Torrejon AFB; 2nd Air Force Barksdale AFB; 8th Air Force Westover AFB.

He recieved the following decorations and service awards: the Distinguished Service Medal, Legion of Merit with one Oak Leaf Cluster, Distinguished Flying Cross, Soldier's Medal, Air Medal with one Oak Leaf Cluster, Air Force Commendation Medal, American Defense Service Medal, Asiatic-Pacific Campaign Medal, WWII Victory Medal, National Defense Service Medal, Korean Service Medal, Air Force Longevity Service Award Ribbon with one Silver and Bronze Oak Leak Cluster, Philippine Liberation Ribbon, Republic of Korea Presidential Unit Citation; Philippine Independence Ribbon and the United Nations Service Medal.

From March 1, 1967 until May 1972, General Wade held positions of Director of Corrections, Adjutant General, Director of Safety and Superintendent of Police in his home state of Louisiana. Upon retirement, he was awarded the Louisiana Distinguishhed Service Medal. Lt. Gen. Wade passed away May 11, 1990.

WILLIAM C. WEAVER SR. was born July 21, 1919 in Harriman, TN. He was drafted into the USAF on Feb. 4, 1942 in Fort Oglethorpe, GA. Basic training was at Keesler Field, MS. He was assigned to technical training commission in Sioux Falls, SD from June 1942 to June 1944 in supply. He graduated Radio School at Scott Field, IL in January 1945

He married Catherine Marie Baker on Feb. 10, 1945 on route to Lincoln, NE for his crew assignment. He had flight crew training at Alamagordo, NM. He ferried a new B-29 from Kearney, NE to West Field, Tinian. He was assigned to the 25th Sqdn., 40th Group of 58th Wing. He flew night raids, day raids, P.W. supplies to Korea and coverage over the USS *Missouri* Sept. 2, 1945. He helped ferry planes back to Sacramento, CA one month before his son Bill was born.

Was discharged on Nov. 28, 1945 with the rank of staff sergeant, then returned to his old job with Burlington Ind. in Harriman, TN. He retired in December 1981.

CHARLES L. WEEDEN, was born in 1924 in Sycamore, IL. He enlisted in the Aviation Cadet Program on Dec. 7, 1942, graduated in the class of 44E at Stockton Field, CA; Pilot School in May 1944; Instructor School at Randolph Field in San Antonio, TX. Instructed instrument flying basic twin engine at Stockton Field, CA.

With the closing of Stockton Field, he was assigned transition to B-17 Rosewell, NM AFB. As hostilities lessened in Europe, no more B-17 crews were needed, so in early 1945 he was transferred to B-29s at Rattlesnake AFB, Pyote, TX.

Joined the 58th BW, 40th BG, 44th Bomb Sqdn., Island of Tinian in May 1945. He flew 13 bombing missions over home islands of Japan. Was discharged in March 1946.

He farmed for 44 years retiring in 1990. Served 12 years on Sycamore School Board, elected Director of Kishwaukee Division of Illinois Association of School Boards and served various other local elected government bodies. He is now operating a self-storage business in Sycamore, IL.

RALPH H. WEINBERG,
was born in Philadelphia, PA on Oct. 11, 1918. Enlisted in Aviation Cadet Program on Nov. 1, 1941. Boarded train to Tulsa, OK for primary pilot training. Forced out December 6. Sent to Navigation School at Kelly Field, TX and trained as an instructor. Upon graduation in June 1942, moved with the Navigation School to Hondo, TX. In August 1943 all field instructors at Hondo Navigation School were sent to Roswell, NM for bombardier training for the B-29 program.

Sent to India in 1944. The route assigned the B-29 to fly supplies to China had not been mapped. He was part of the crew of the 45th Sqdn. and took part in mapping the Hump. After one flight over the Hump, he refused to fly with them again. The movies he had taken during the flight kept him from being court-martialed.

Returned home via Hawaii and returned to civilian status Nov. 1, 1945. Remained in Air Force Reserves and retired in August 1966 with the rank of lieutenant colonel. Received the Distinguished Flying Cross with one Oak Leaf Cluster, Air Medal with three clusters, Purple Heart, Presidential Unit Citation and others.

Starting with the burial of the men killed in an accident on a flight line, he participated in an ecumenical service along with the chaplain of their service group and has continued to do so at their reunion memorial services.

Retired in December 1988 from business and lives quietly with his wive, Eleanor, in Central City, PA.

GLENN D. WHALEN,
was born Aug. 2, 1925 in Dora, AL and entered the service on Nov. 11, 1943. He became an Aerial Gunner in the AAF Air Crew, 5th Bomb Sqdn., 9th BG, 313th BW of the 20th Air Force and at the age of 19, he flew 35 missions on the "Goin' Jessie" and the "Early Bird" over occupied territory of Japan, Iwo Jima and Truk

Discharged Jan. 11, 1945, he received the Distinguished Flying Cross, Victory Medal, American Theater Ribbon, Asiatic Pacific-Theater Ribbon with three Bronze Stars, Air Medal with four Bronze Clusters and the Good Conduct Medal.

His fondest and most humorous wartime story was, upon returning to base from his last flight mission, when the loss of an engine over the ocean caused him to panic so that in his efforts to lighten the load of the plane he threw out his (Mae West) life jacket!

After returning from the service he met and married Miriam C. Coble. They had five daughters: Lynn, Susan, Beverly, Salena and Glenda and four grandchildren.

An established and renowned homebuilder and developer in the Birmingham area for 30 years, Glenn D. Whalen passed away July 21, 1990.

FRANK WHITEHOUSE JR.,
was born Nov. 20, 1924 in Ann Arbor, MI. He moved to Ypsilanti, MI in 1929 and took his Aviation Cadet examinations at Selfridge Field, MI in November 1942. Went into active duty from the Reserves to Scott Field, IL in March 1943.

Took his Aviation Cadet Pilot training at St. Petersburg and Miami Beach, FL; CTD Elkins, WV; classification, Nashville, TN; basic, Maxwell Field, Montgomery, AL; flight training-primary, Camden; basic, Walnut Ridge; and advanced, Blythville, AK; Class 44-H, second lieutenant B-24 transition, Maxwell Field, Montgomery, AL; B-29 training, Alamagordo, NM. Pacific Theater: Saipan 73rd BW, 500th Gp, 881st Sqdn., Pilot Z-11, seven combat (including Toyama) and three POW missions, first lieutenant and Air Medal, July to October 1945; Guam 501-2 Gp. until March 1946. Inactive Reserve Camp Atterbury April 1946.

He was discharged in 1953. His memorable experiences include three Z-11 aircraft. The first was destroyed in a crash landing, the second was lost over Nagoya and the third finished the war with more than 40 missions. It is the center upper aircraft in the widely circulated "Bombs Away" photograph of May 29, 1945, Yokahoma mission. This photo was used on the 600,000 warning leaflets dropped on 11 Japanese cities on July 27, 1945.

Attended the University of Michigan College of LSA 1942-1943 and 1946-1949. He received a Hopwood Literary Award 1947 and lettered in Big Ten lighweight football 1947-1948; Medical School 1949-1953. Did internship Blodgett Memorial Hospital, Grand Rapids, MI 1953-1954. A member of the University of Michigan Department of Microbiology and Immunology Medical School Faculty 1954 to present with 60 plus medical science, education, and history articles and abstracts; and various musical compositions.

He is active in teaching and counseling health science students. He was co-founder and first executive director of the Regional and National Associations of Advisors for the Health Professions. Fulbright-Hayes Senior Lectureship in Microbiology 1979-1980.

CLEMETH R. WILLOCKS,
was born Nov. 11, 1925 in Maryville, TN. He joined the USAAF 0n Dec. 8, 1943. Took his basic training in Miami Beach, FL and took B-29 training at McCook, NE.

He joined the 9th Group, 5th Sqdn. in Northfield, Tinian as a radio mechanic (754).

Was discharged on Nov. 22, 1945 with the rank of sergeant. He retired from the University of Tennessee in June 1990.

CLARK OLIVER WILSON,
Jan. 15, 1917-Lockport, IL Air Force; Feb. 18, 1942-Sheppard Field,

TX; Feb. 28, 1942-shipped out New Orleans; March 11, 1942-arrived Puerto Rica San Juan; March 18, 1942-train to Borinquin Field.

To the best of his knowledge this was the birth of 40th BG. Only a few planes B-18 Scoop Martin was crew chief and Wilson was an apex chief.

Carl Weese, from Petersburg, WV, and Wilson left Texas as special vehicle operator 932. They were in charge of an old Red Cross ambulance. At the approach of planes they were to start vehicle ready to roll. Six start ups was a busy day.

He received 21 bucks per month. Shipped to Panama France Field. Four months later they convoyed outfit north to David Field (used to be the capital of Panama). Shipped to Galapagos Islands 500 miles from Ecuador, owned by Ecuador. Four months on Rock shipped to Panama. To California on way to Pratt, KS. To start using B-29s coming off line at Wichita.

He escaped a month's service on the Rock as Captain Miller needed a driver in Guatemala in 44 B. SQ. Thanks to Capt. Miller he enjoyed the service. He knew many in the Motor Pool.

Their CO Col. Oscar Schaff flew the first B-29 into Pratt Field, he was a top notch pilot. Col. Schaff let him fly over India with his crew while checking out replaced engines.

While waiting for more B-29s, he was driving a command car used to take Louis Jones in to Pratt where his wife had a room with a fine Kansas couple. This is where she turned a vest into a survival kit for crews down in water. *Reader's Digest* in 1945 had an article on this.

He used to pick up Col. Walter Lucas at O.Q. and take to Operation. He was in Pacific with a B-17 before coming to B-29. He was always smiling except once in Chakulia first raid on Japan. His plane had a problem. Col. Lucas stayed at the plane for hours and had to miss that mission.

Gustave Vanderlooven of Essexville, MI was a close buddy for four years. He was best man at Wilson's wedding in Wichita. The night before the wedding Bessie was at her girl friend's family. Their pastor, Rev. Life, performed the ceremony. Gus and Wilson slept in the Red Cross Hotel, very clean and for one dollar each.

Col. Lucas gave them a three day pass. Col. Lucas checked out Col. Morgan on B-29 former pilot of *Memphis Belle* which is now on pedestal at Memphis, TN.

He left Pratt for Riverside, CA on Feb. 7, 1944. On Feb. 14, 1944 he boarded the *U.S. Mount Vernon* for Bombay, India for 40 days. The only stop was at Melbourne, Australia for three days. "Toyko-Rose" came on radio claiming Japan Navy sunk them. They departed India by Calcutta.

After a year in India and nine months on Tinian and Saipan, they were shipped back to California to be discharged. He went back to Greensburg, KS for his wife, Bessie Allison, and daughter, Carolyn, who had been living with Bessie's parents on a large wheat farm. He had left his 1940 Willy with them. Bessie had two sisters at home. She often said Carolyn had four mothers plus grandpa Allison. They have another daughter, Marti. Both daughters have two sons. One lives two miles north of them and one lives two miles south.

He returned to Johnson & Johnson for 35 years. A super Apex place for employment. After 40 years they retired.

For 10 years, their winter months have been in

Florida doing volunteer service with Florida Bible College at Hollywood & Kissimmee.

Their desire is that all of their friends and loved ones would place their trust and faith in Christ. May our Lord bless you with joy and good health. Plus happy days ahead in the 90s.

HAL G. WORLEY, was born Dec. 31, 1921 in Kinston, NC. He attended the University of North Carolina and Virginia Polytechnic Institute where he received an engineering degree. He went into the service in August 1943.

His assignments for training were at the University of Tennessee; BTC No. 10 Greensboro, NC; Panama City, FL; Lincoln, NE and McCook, NE. He was assigned to a B-29 crew of the 99th Sqdn., 9th BG, 20th AF based on Tinian Island. He flew 25 bombing missions against the mainland of Japan. He was assigned to Muroco Air Base for lead crew training and returned to Tinian for the duration.

Was discharged in December 1945 with the rank of staff sergeant.

His career began with Western Electric, a manufacturer of electronic equipment for AT&T and the military, in Winston-Salem, NC. He transferred to various locations around the country as a manager of manufacturing and engineering support for field installations.

He married Rosemary Thorpe of Winston-Salem, where he retired in 1984. He engages mostly in volunteer efforts and working with bankruptcy courts.

HERBERT WILLIAM WRIGHT, was born Sept. 28, 1915 in Bay City, MI. He joined the USAAC on June 20, 1942 in Saginaw, MI. Was screened in Nashville, TN; preflight in Montgomery, AL; primary flight in Lafayette, LA in PT-19s; basic training in Greenville, MS in BT-13s; and advanced training in Laurenceville, IL in AT-10s. He also received his wings and commisssion there.

Proceeded to Lockborne, OH for four engine transition in B-17s. Then to Pratt, KS for B-29 introduction training. On to Clovis, NM for combat training and assignment of his crew. On to Harrington, KS to pick up his plane.Then he was off to India via British Gayana, Napal, Brazil, Accra, Gold Coast Africa, Cano, Belgian Congo, Karachi, Bombay and finally to Chakulia in September 1943.

He was assigned to the 40th BG, 25th Bomb Sqdn. In December 1943 he was sent to Tzgon, India to the Provintal Squadron as a check pilot, but he got stuck flying gas over the Hump for the next three months or so. Was involved in the battles of India, China, Coral Sea and Japan. He and his crew always hit their primary targets, never had to abort a mission, or salvage any of their bomb loads.

He received the Purple Heart, WWII Victory Medal, American Defense Service Medal, National Defense Service Medal, Good Conduct Medal, Bronze Star, Air Medal with Silver Oak Leaf, Distinguished Flying Cross with Gold Oak Leaf Cluster,

Asiatic-Pacific Campaign Medal with four Battle Stars and Honorary Wings from the Republic of China.

Returned to the States on Jan. 15, 1946 to be discharged with the rank of captain. He immediately joined the Reserves and was discharged on Sept. 28, 1975 with the rank of lieutenant colonel.

Retired from the Michigan Bell Telephone Co. after 42 years of service on all levels in 1978. Now he just takes life easy!

MARTIN L. ZAPF, was born on Nov. 20, 1925 in Princeton, NJ. He was drafted in February 1944 at Fort Dix, NJ; trained at Greensboro, NC and Scott

Field, IL. He joined a B-29 crew at Alamagordo, NM in October 1944 and transferred to 9th BG, 313th Wing based on Tinian in March 1945

Flew 16 combat missions and was shot down over Yawata and bailed out over the Sea of Japan on Aug. 8, 1945. He spent one week in a life raft before being captured by the Japanese. He interned in Hiroshima and Mukaishima.

Returned to the States in September 1945 and was discharged with the rank of staff sergeant in March 1946.

Graduated with a BS degree from Rider College in June 1949. He spent 35 years in sales and marketing with Unisys Corporation. He retired in 1986. He is married and has four children.

Strike photo by Crew K-5, 457th Bomb Sqdn. was taken on longest bombardment mission dropping of heavy explosives. The 18 hr. and 30 minute mission was flown by the 330th Bomb group against the Koriyama Chemical plant on northern Honshu. (Courtesy of William J. Grossmiller)

Cpl. Brough and a snake charmer at Hotel Majestic in Calcutta, India in 1944. (Courtesy of Gordon Brough)

125